ABR-NAHRAIN

AN ANNUAL PUBLISHED BY THE DEPARTMENT OF SEMITIC STUDIES UNIVERSITY OF MELBOURNE IN ASSOCIATION WITH THE DEPARTMENT OF SEMITIC STUDIES UNIVERSITY OF SYDNEY

EDITED BY

J. BOWMAN

ASSOCIATE EDITOR

E. C. B. MacLAURIN

ASSISTANT EDITOR

WILLIAM CULICAN

VOLUME IV

1963-1964

LEIDEN
E. J. BRILL
1965

ABR-NAHRAIN

ABR-NAHRAIN

AN ANNUAL PUBLISHED BY THE DEPARTMENT OF SEMITIC STUDIES UNIVERSITY OF MELBOURNE IN ASSOCIATION WITH THE DEPARTMENT OF SEMITIC STUDIES UNIVERSITY OF SYDNEY

EDITED BY

J. BOWMAN

ASSOCIATE EDITOR

E. C. B. MacLAURIN

ASSISTANT EDITOR

WILLIAM CULICAN

VOLUME IV

1963-1964

LEIDEN
E. J. BRILL
1965

PRINTED IN THE NETHERLANDS

CONTENTS

EDITORIAL NOTE

The publication of this fourth volume of *Abr-Nahrain* has been possible by money made available by the bequest fund of the late Professor M. D. Goldman, first Professor of Semitic Studies at Melbourne University, and by the generous subsidy of the Australian Humanities Research Council. We acknowledge our great indebtedness for this aid.

In Australia there are two University Departments of Semitic Studies, that of the University of Sydney and our own in Melbourne. Because of the importance Asian Studies as a whole ought to have in Australia, a Conference for the Development in Australian Universities of Middle Eastern Studies, as part of the programme of Asian Studies, was jointly held in August 1963. The Conference was formally opened on August 12th in the University of Melbourne by Major General Sir Ivan Dougherty, C. B.E., D.S.O., E.D., B.Ec., Pro-Chancellor of the University of Sydney. A reception and dinner were held at the Royal Commonwealth Society, Melbourne, with Sir William Upjohn, O.B.E., M.D., M.S., F.R.C.S., F.R.A.C.S., Deputy Chancellor of the University of Melbourne, the Right Reverend Bishop Felix Arnott, M.A., and Sir Bernard Evans, D.S.O., E.D., F.R.A.I.A., President of the Royal Commonwealth Society, as guest speakers.

After an introductory address by myself on 'The Scope and Purpose of the Conference', Mr. E. C. B. MacLaurin, M.A. (Cantab.), B.D. (Syd.) spoke on 'Australia and the Islamic World' and later followed this by two papers entitled 'An analysis of existing non-language courses in the area of the Middle East' and 'An analysis of the present techniques and methods of teaching the languages of the Middle East and associated non-language courses'. Other papers were given by Dr. A. K. Kazi, B.A., Ph.D. (Lond.), Maulvi Fazil (Panj.), Ulamiya (Al Azhar, Cairo), lecturer in Islamic Studies, University of Melbourne, ('Analysis of existing degree courses in Arabic, Hebrew, Persian, Turkish and Urdu, both classical and modern, in Australian Universities'); Mr. A. D. Crown, M.A. (Leeds), lecturer in Semitic Studies, University of Sydney, ('Analysis of present teaching of Asian Studies in Australian Schools'); Mr. D. Broadribb, M.A. (Illin.), B.D. (Union), lecturer in Hebrew, University of Melbourne, ('Biblical

Studies and Biblical Languages as part of Asian Studies'); Mr. W. Culican, M.A. (Edin.), Senior lecturer in Semitic Studies, University of Melbourne, ('Archaeology in Biblical Studies'); Professor John Bowman, M.A., B.D. (Glas.), D.Phil. (Oxon), M.A. (Melb.), ('The Study of Syriac Christianity and its Spread through Asia from the first century to 1400 A.D.'); Mr. G. Bolster, M.A., B.D. (Edin.), lecturer in Comparative Religion, University of Melbourne, ('The Teaching of Comparative Religion as part of Semitic Studies').

A Report on the Conference was broadcast on Radio Australia's Asian service by Professor Bowman, Mr. MacLaurin and Dr. Kazi. Among recommendations formulated by the Conference, importance was given to: 1) the need for funds and additional staff and books etc., and pooling of resources; 2) coordination of courses in Middle Eastern Studies with those in Far Eastern (Oriental) Studies; 3) relations with other University Disciplines, e.g. History, Social Studies, Political Science and Commerce; 4) grants for overseas travel for Staff and post-graduate students; 5) special Undergraduate scholarships.

It is intended that such a conference will be called each second year and continue to further development of Asian Studies and Middle Eastern Studies in Australia.

Among the lectures given to the Melbourne University Afro-Asian Society this session we should like to note that of Dr. Donald Daniel Leslie of the Department of Oriental Studies, University of Canberra, and that of Dr. N. Mirza, lecturer in Arabic, University of Melbourne. Dr. Leslie's paper on 'The Rise and Fall of the Jewish Community of Kaifeng' appears in this volume of *Abr-Nahrain*. Dr. Mirza's paper will be published in a subsequent volume.

Abr-Nahrain has been able to bring out the first of its Supplementary Publications Series with Professor L. A. Meyer's *Bibliography of the Samaritans* edited by Mr. D. Broadribb. Our thanks are due to Mrs. Vera Bryce Salamons for her generous help in making this publication possible.

Dr. A. Murtonen has published *Broken Plurals* in the Australian Humanities Research Council Monograph Series. The editor's lectures to Biblical Literature and Antiquities Part III, University of Melbourne, are currently appearing as Volume VIII of Brill's *Studia Post-Biblica* as The Gospel of Mark: The New Christian Jewish Passover Haggadah.

It was my privilege to attend, as representative of the University of Melbourne, the XXVIth. International Congress of Orientalists at Delhi in January 1964. Thereafter I was able to visit Kerala in connection with my research on Indian Syrian Christianity. As a UNESCO Fellow in the East-West Major Project, I intend to continue research in Iran and Iraq on ancient and modern aspects of Nestorian Christianity from October 1964 to March 1965.

We would like to express our gratitude to all readers of *Abr-Nahrain* for their continued support and interest.

Editor,

JOHN BOWMAN
Professor of Semitic Studies,
University of Melbourne.

HEBREW AND ARABIC LEXICOGRAPHY

A COMPARATIVE STUDY

BY

ALFRED GUILLAUME

IV

Since my last study appeared Professor Izz al-Din has published the second volume of the *Kitāb al-Ibdāl* which completes the work, and thanks to that and to his scholarly notes I have been able to add slightly more than another hundred parallels to Hebrew roots and words. Some of these demand a translation different from that commonly accepted and they will enable readers to remove many of the irritating 'emendations' in the footnotes to Kittel's *Biblia Hebraica.*

It is fitting that in drawing this study to an end I should say something about what has been done and what remains to be done. Excluding words of non-Semitic origin which obviously have no place in this enterprise I have failed to find Arabic parallels to 88 Hebrew words. Of this number 21 at least are not found in pre-exilic authors and would appear to belong to an Aramaic sphere of influence. In other words approximately a quarter of the words which I have had to abandon, for the time being at least, seem to belong to a language which went its own way and departed from the older stream of Semitic etymology.

Doubtless some at least of the 67 Hebrew words which I have been unable to identify in Arabic will be brought to light by younger scholars. An idea of the magnitude of the task that awaits them will become apparent from the fact that the *Ibdāl* lists 21 mutations of ג; 32 of ח (ح and خ); and 26 of ז (ذ and ز). Some consonants have more, some less; and all these mutations could be subject to metathesis! Unless one of these is instantly recognized as an Arabic equivalent of a Hebrew word the labour of identifying it is enormous, because it is not enough to consult Lane's Arabic-English Dictionary, the Supplement of Dozy, and the invaluable Dictionary of Hava; but one must go on to look up the *Lisân al-'Arab* to see if there is a rare word (like أَزْعَكِّى 'short' for example), books on *Nawādir*, Ibnu 'l-Athîr's *al-Nihâya fî gharîb al-Ḥadîth*, and other lexical works, before one can be satisfied that no Arabic cognate is known to have existed.

No addition to our knowledge is to be regarded lightly, but one cannot escape the suspicion that time and research could be put to better use, except when the scholar is looking for a cognate word which could throw light on an important point of exegesis. In such a task the emendations recommended or proposed or hazarded in *BH* would serve a useful purpose by drawing attention to words that are not understood.

For the guidance of any who may be disposed to pursue these researches further I would add that I have frequently consulted the *Thesaurus Syriacus* to see whether it provides a suitable Arabic cognate for the Syriac word by which the Peshitta translates a particular Hebrew word. The yield, so far as I recall, has been very small and in one case definitely misleading; for it gives سَرَنٌ and صَرَنٌ as alternative Arabic equivalents of סרן axle. These are words unknown to the author of the *Lisân* and other authorities, and no Arab whom I have consulted has ever heard of them.

Perhaps a few remarks on *badal*, the mutation of consonants, will not be out of place here. (i) The most obvious are those which are phonetically akin like ב and ם. (ii) Another class is formed by those triliterals which appear to rest on a primitive biliteral root like the oft cited קץ phoneme with all its permutations. Its ramifications in Arabic are most extensive. (iii) Others are due to dialectic differences which prevail among different tribes in different areas. (iv) The remainder are worth consideration however dubious they may appear at first sight.

Among the possible *badals* which seem to me to be dubious are:

אמיר top of a tree — جامور top of a mast

This is an alleged *badal* which the editor of the *Ibdâl* has supplied from another source. He himself does not accept is as legitimate.

ארה plucked — ارم devoured, destroyed the whole crop, bit
ارم finger tips

'Finger tips' could be held to supply a denominative verb 'plucked' appropriate in Ct. 5,1 where myrrh and balsam are the objects plucked; and, too, the verb could apply to the devouring of all the grapes in

Ps. 80,13. But ארי and אריה 'lion' are strange forms even if they are to be associated with 'devouring'. *Ibdâl*, II, 451f.

בזא	divided, cut through	جَزَأ	*id.*

This, again, is an equation that the editor, in my opinion rightly, refuses to recognize. *ib.* II, 578

נקיק	cleft of a rock	أُنْبُوب	track or streak in a mountain, pipe
II צוק	poured out and cf. יצק *id.*	صَابَ	*id.*

Two examples of the mutation are found *ib.* 369 and the editor adds another.

תזז	struck away	تَبَّ	cut off

This *may* be the meaning of the verb (found only) in Is. 18, 5, but one cannot be sure.

These examples are sufficient to show that it would not be difficult to cite a number of words which could be explained from Arabic if one relied simply on the chance coincidence of one of the hundreds of permutations in Arabic books on *badal*; but to do so might well bring into disrepute a field of research which one hopes has been shown to be not only valuable for lexicographical studies but also for bringing to light the meaning of obscure words in the Hebrew of the Old Testament, and at the same time vindicating the Massoretic Text.

אביון	adj. in want, needy, poor.	أَبْيَانٌ	one who refuses food, hates what is base

In Heb. צם meant 'fasted voluntarily'; in old Arabic it meant 'went without food' because none was available. Here the roles are reversed. The אביון cannot get food because he is poor; the أبيان declines it. The parallel holds in the moral sphere. Cf. Am. 2,6 etc. where אביון is synonymous with צדיק.

אים	adj. dreadful	هَيُوبٌ	*id.*
אימה	n.f. terror	هَيْبَةٌ	*id.*
אפה	baked	*mūfā*	bread-oven (Aden) *Annual of Leeds Oriental Society*, II, 1961, p. 29

אפר	n. covering	عُفْرَة	*id.*

BDB queries this identification, but it is quite legitimate. See *Ibdāl*, II, 551.

ארג	wove	نَسَجَ	*id.*

أ = ن and ر = س *Ibdāl*, II, 566 and II, 38.

ארר	cursed	*ʿerer*	(Soq.) *id.*
אשׁ	n. fire	أَجَّ	burned, blazed (fire)

ج = س *Ibdāl*, I, 225.

[ביה]		بَاهَ	remembered, was mindful of.

In Ps. 68,5 and Is. 26,4 the form בְּיָהּ should be pointed בֵּיָהּ and rendered ‘be mindful of’. See my note in *JTS.*, 1962, p. 322.

בלם	curbed, held in	أَبْلَمُ	had swollen lips

The semantic connexion is obvious.

במה	n. high place	نَبْوَة بَنَاوَة and رَبْوَة	*id.*
ברקנים	n. briers	مَرْقَة	a swift piercing
גאל	redeemed acted as kinsman	أَجَلَهُ	he confined, restricted, barred it

See *Annual of Leeds Or. Soc.* 1964 for a note on Jb. iii, 5.

גבעה	n. hill	عَقَبَة	*id.*
גבעל	n. bud	قُبْعَة	calyx
גביע	n. cup	قُنْبَعَة	calyx
קבעת	n. cup	مُقَعَّب	cup-shaped

قُنْبَعَة would be a better parallel than قُبْعَة cited in *BDB* because the *daghesh* in קבעת is to be explained as the assimilation of the *nūn*.

In *Abr-Nahrain*, III, p. 2 قُمْعُولَة ‘bud’ was given as the equivalent of גבעל.

גג	n. roof top	سَجَّة	roof plastered with mud
דקר	pierced	ذَقِرَ	was surfeited

This is the meaning in La. 4,9. See a forthcoming note in *The Annual of Leeds Oriental Society*.

זוב flowed, gushed — سَابَ went quickly
La. 4,9. See last note.

זון fed — زُوَانٌ food
Al-Nawādir, p. 179, explains that this word is synonymous with نَقَاوَةٌ which means good or bad food. Obviously in Gn. 45,23 the former is intended.

[I חגג] copulated — خَجَّ *id.* (L)
A new entry in the Lexicon is called for. In I Sam. 30,16 David caught up with the Amaleqite raiders as they were "eating and drinking and fornicating with all the great spoil of women that they had taken" חגגים בכל השלל הגדול. Ju. 5, 30 shows that שלל, though a general term for 'booty', applies particularly to captured women: once it is followed by 'wench', and once it is said that the dyed embroidered shawls were for the "necks of the שׁלל.

Once the meaning of the verb is understood the preposition ב at once falls into place. Canon Driver in *NHTS*, p. 223, refused to accept the meaning 'dancing' here. It is strange that the great Orientalist Nöldeke failed to recognize the word. Recently it has been found in a 'Thamudic' inscription at Quraiya where a descendant of the old Amaleqites recorded his amours. See A. van den Branden, *Les Textes Thamoudéens de Philby*, Louvain, 1956, II, p. 115.

חול was firm, strong — حَوْلٌ strength

[IIIחלל] was emaciated — خَلَّ *id.* See on דקר

חלוף n. a passing away — خَلَفَ was stupid, unintelligent

The RV translates Pr. 31, 8 thus:

Open thy mouth for the dumb,
In the cause of all such as are left desolate.

The margin offers the alternative "are ready to pass away". Parallelism is lacking, and obviously the injunction is to plead the cause of those who can make no appeal for themselves. With the lead that Arabic gives us we may translate:

Speak up for those who cannot speak for themselves
For the cause of all that lack understanding.

חפף See under לחף
II חפץ bent down — حَصِيفٌ firm, strong, compact

The word is used in Jb. 40, 17 to describe the tail of the hippopotamus. See a forthcoming note on the word in *Annual of the Leeds Oriental Soc.*

חפש was free حَفَّشَ he stayed in his tent

In two texts at least it is very doubtful if the idea of freedom is present at all. Thus (i) 2 K 15, 5 = 2 Ch. 26, 21 says that King Azariah was a leper וישב בבית החפשית. The Versions all guessed at the meaning. The best of these guesses is that of the Peshitta which renders "in a house meṭašyāīth hidden away." Klostermann improved on this by transferring the *he* to *beyth* and so rendered "in his house at freedom". But freedom implies the right to go out, and it is extremely unlikely that the historian would say that the king had the right to walk about his house and garden, for he would have had to be fettered to prevent his doing so. Moreover Ex. 21, 2 and 5 expressly grant the slave who is *ḥofšî* the right to go his way. The slave could go his way, but plainly the king could not. From this it follows that he was not free in the full sense of the word, but rather, in modern parlance, under house arrest. Therefore it would be wiser to follow the path of comparative philology and commonsense and translate the clause 'he dwelt in his house without leaving it'.

(ii) Ps. 88, 6 במתים חפשי כמו חללים שכבי קבר is rendered by the RV:

Cast off among the dead
Like the slain that lie in the grave.

The LXX adds *errimenoi* = משלכים (a verb used "especially of casting dead bodies" as *BDB* 1021a points out) and ignores חפשי.

If this word is restored to the text there would be three beats in each hemistich, as the metre requires, and the verse would run:

Shut in among the castaway dead
Like the slain that lie in the grave.

The objection to the equation of Hebrew *shîn* with Arabic *sîn* has been shown to be antiquated and untenable, and it is ruled out of court by evidence for the existence of forms with *shîn* and *sîn* in this verb in Arabic. See *Ibdāl*, II, 343 where it is said that اَلْحِفْسُ (with *sîn*) means 'the man who does not leave his station in battle'. The learned editor points out that the form with *shîn* is more commonly used and is to be preferred.

חקק cut in, decreed. خقّ made a furrow, حقّ duty

Here two different roots should be indicated and kept distinct.

חקר searched حفر dug into, searched, = I חפר

Conversely in Jb. 3, 21. חפר is used in the sense of searching where one would expect חקר. At first sight it might be thought that in Arabic a simple mistake has occurred in writing ف for ق and vice versa; but al-Asmā'ī expressly states that the people of the uplands say *zuḥlûfa*, while the Banû Tamîm and their Hawāzin neighbours say *zuḥlûqa* (seesaw). See *Ibdāl*, II, 338 with Prof. Izz al-Din's notes thereon.

חרך unknown خرق made a hole in

n. lattice or other opening خرق hole in a wall

ق = ك *ib.*, II, 353

חתך divided, determined بتك cut

ب = ح *ib.*, II, 580. This is not a very convincing parallel, but in default of any other suggestion I let it stand. In Arabic one would expect محتوم 'decreed, ordained'; but the works on *ibdāl* in Arabic do not recognize an interchange of ك and م, nor can I recall one.

I יער n. wood, forest, thicket عروة thicket

عرين forest, thicket

BDB and *KB* offer وعر was rugged, and وعر rough place as parallels; but there is no obvious connexion between a rugged spot and a forest. Am. 3, 4 speaks of the lion roaring ביער where the Arabs would say بالعرين. However 'rough ground' may be the meaning in Is. 21, 13.

II יער n. honeycomb أرى honey

יצב took his stand وصب was firm (*BDB*); add وظب *id.*

יקש laid a bait, laid snares فقسه ٱلفخ the trap killed it

n. bait, lure مفقاس snare, trap.

The *Lisân* describes two different kinds of snares: one catches the bird in a net when the spring is set off; the other dislocates its neck and leaves it on the ground. Burney's note on Jd. 2, 3 "it is probable that *môqēsh* caused the striking (knocking down or piercing) of the victim" is much to the point, except that there is no evidence to indicate that the victim was pierced in any way. Doubtless a misunderstanding of Jb. 40, 24 has led to this statement.

ف = ى *Ibdāl*, II, 351.

[כדם] أُكْدِمَ held in bonds

In *JTS*, 1942, 324 I took this to mean that the ship was held fast as a sunken wreck, but Professor Driver has suggested that the meaning should be 'moored'. This interpretation is certainly preferable, and **כדומה** in Ezk. 27, 32 should be so translated.

כמריר darkness, gloominess? رَكَمٌ thick layer of clouds.

In Jb. 3, 5 the RV translates "all that make black the day", and the *ICC* simply "blacknesses". In view of the mention of clouds in the preceding clause it is natural to connect the word with رَكَمٌ (Lane, *Arabic-English Lexicon*, p. 1148b explains مَرْكُومٌ, an epithet of midnight, thus: "meaning ظُلُمَاتُهُ مَرْكُومٌ i.e. densely dark, as though its darknesses were heaped one upon another".)

תלאה n. weariness See **תלא** below

[לחף] لَاحَفَهُ He protected him

Gn. 49, 13: **זבולן לחוף ימים ישכן והוא לחוף אניות**

Zebulon shall dwell at the shore of the sea
And he shall be a haven of ships.

The translation is perfectly correct and ancient authorities agree that this is the meaning. Ibn Janāḥ in his *K. al-Uṣûl* expresses doubt about the derivation of the word which *BDB* connects with **חפף**.

The second **לחוף** is the equivalent of the verbal noun لِحَافٌ 'protection' and is a fine example of the writer's use of paronomasia.

מאס rejected مَاءِسٌ one who rejects advice

מבול n. flood وَبَلَ it rained violently

Gesenius suggested **יבל** (cf. **יבלי מים** streams) but *BDB* rejected the derivation. For the omission of the initial *yôd* and the doubling of the following consonant cf. מַדָּע and מַצָּע.

מגר cast, threw — وَجَنَ *id.*

م = و *Ibdāl*, II, p. 444f; ن = ر *ib.*, p. 339.

מין n. kind, species — فَنّ *id.*

م = ف *ib.* II, 345.

מן n. string — مُنَيْن a weak rope

מלק nipped off — مَلَخَهُ pulled it out stripped the meat from the bone

ق = خ *ib.* I, 340 and *Lisān* under مَلَخَ.

מצח n. brow, forehead — وَضَحَ was clear, conspicuous

BDB postulates a √מצח and *KB*, with a query, צחח rightly perceiving that the *mîm* is preformative; but צחח is perhaps too strong, and I prefer وَضَحَ because of its associations in Arabic. For the omission of the *yôdh* of the root compare משרים from ישר in Pr. 1, 3.

משי n. costly material, silk — وَشْيٌ silk brocade

There is thus support for the rabbinic tradition that silk is the meaning in Ezk. 16, 10, 13.

و = م *ib.* II, 444

ממשק n. place of possession — وَسَقَ it contained

Arabic explains ממשק חרול, Zp. 2, 9 'a place containing nettles'. If Hölscher, as cited in *KB Supplementum*, 170, is right in interpreting בן משק in Gn. 15, 2 as '*res familiaris*, *servus*' this too could be linked with the meaning in Arabic.

נאר abhorred, spurned — مَئَرَ hated

נגה shone — جَهَرَ dazzled

מַדּוּחַ n. a thing to draw aside — أَنْدَخُ fool

This word occurs only in La. 2, 14 where we should translate: 'They have seen for thee oracles of vanity and folly'.

I נחל divided for a possession — نَحَلَ allowed to share something

In Arabic the first, second, and fourth forms of the verb are used in this sense, and so there is no need to alter the pointing of the verb in Nu. 34, 17, 18, and Jos. 19, 49 from *Qal* to *Pi'el* as *BDB* and *KB* direct. For explanatory examples of the use of this verb in Accadian see H. W. F. Saggs, *The Greatness that was Babylon*, London, 1962, 294f.

II נחל n. torrent, wady — خَلَلٌ gap, interstice

خَلَّةٌ hole

The primary meaning of the word is retained in Jb. 28, 4 פרץ נחל 'he breaks open a shaft'.

נכד n. progeny — انْتَقَدَ he grew up

ق = ك *ib*. II, 353.

נשך bit — نَسَفَ *id.*

ف = ك *ib*. II, 339.

נתך pour forth, mel[t] — نَسَكَ poured = נסך

س = ت *ib*., II, 115.

סלד sprang — سَفَدَ leapt

This word is found only in Jb. 6, 10. The LXX understood its meaning. No 'emendation' is called for, and most of the philological note in *ICC* should be deleted as irrelevant and mistaken.

סלח forgave — سَامَحَ *id.*

ل = م *ib*. II, 379.

סלל lifted up, cast up — تَلَّ *id.* (Egyptian)

סללה n. mound — تَلٌّ *id.*

س = ت.

סנפיר n. fin — زِعْنِفَةٌ and زَعْنَفَةٌ *id.*

ع = ر as in the quadriliteral noun قُرْشُومٌ = قُعْشُومٌ *ib*. II, 45f.

עשק contended — عَسَقٌ injustice = עשק

The *Lisān al-'Arab* under عشق records that *sîn* and *shîn* are sometimes written indifferently. So, in effect, Prof. Beeston in *JSS*, 1962, p. 230.

Gn. 26, 20 is rendered correctly by LXX "he called the name of the well Injustice because they behaved unjustly towards him''. RV has missed the point.

עת n. time — إِنَى أَنَى إِنَاءٌ *id.*

עתה adv. now — الآنَ *id.*

BDB and *KB* quote the latter equation. Nöldeke *ZDMG*, 40, p. 725, favoured عَنَّ 'appeared'; but in view of the fairly frequent interchange of *alif* and *'ayin* in Arabic I favour the equation given above. The meaning in both languages exactly coincides.

פאר beautiful — بَهَرَهُ surpassed him in beauty (بَهْرٌ)

פארה bough — فَأْرٌ and فَارٌ kind of tree (Arafat)

פגע met, encountered

פגש *id.* — فَجَأَ *id.*

س = ع *ib.*, II, p. 199.

פחז n. wantonness, recklessness unbridled license — فَحَزَ was immoderate, was obscene. (L)

Gn. 49, 4 should therefore be translated 'incontinent as water', thus retaining the two meanings of the word in Arabic. Another root must be added to the Hebrew Lexicon.

פכה trickled — بَكَى = בכה wept

A poetical synonym. Cf. بَكَتِ السَّحَابَةُ 'the cloud shed a little rain'.

אֶפְרֹחַ n. young of birds — أَفْرُخٌ and أَفْرَاخٌ *id.*

The broken plurals of paucity in Arabic furnished with the Hebrew plural ending.

פרט n. the broken off — فَرَطَ shook off (nuts) from a tree (Syrian).

[III] פרץ broke over (limits), increased — فَرْطٌ excess (Gn. 30, 30)
فَرَطَ came first (Gn. 38, 29)

See a forthcoming note in *JSS*.

פשח	tore in pieces	فشح	strayed from the right path (Syrian)

Lam. 3, 11 דרכי סורר ויפשחני שמני שמם.

RV. "He hath turned aside my ways, and pulled me in pieces".

There is no cogent reason why the lion should be the subject, and the third verse of the acrostic cannot possibly refer to an animal.

If we render:

> He turned aside my ways and made me go astray
> He left me deserted

a good sense and parallelism are obtained. Ehrenkrantz's suggestion to interpret the word from Accadian *upashshakha* 'left me untilled' is adopted in *KB*.

פשׂע	stepped, marched	فشخ	took long strides (Syrian)

This equation has already been noted in *Thesaurus Syriacus*, II, p. 3191a. פשׂע = Syr. pesāʿā = فشخة step. خ = ع *Ibdāl*, II, 310.

פשׂע	transgressed	فسق	*id.* ع = ق *ib.* II, 310.
פתה	was wide, open	فتح	opened = פתח

ح = ى *Ib.* I, 328.

צמח	sprouted, sprang up	اضماكّ	was fertile (land); was green, fresh (plant)

خ = ك *Ibdāl*, I, p. 343.

צעקה	n. cry	صاعقة	*id.*

BDB gives only the meaning "thunderbolt"!

צפן	hid, treasured up	صان	preserved, laid up, reserved

The meaning 'reserved' comes out plainly in Jb. 21, 19. ف = و *ib.*, II, 351 note.

קוט	felt a loathing	قزّ	*id.*
קוץ	ز = ط *ib.*, II, 139		
קמט	seized	قمط	*id.* (L.)

קצף was wroth — غَضِبَ *id.*

غ = ق *ib.*, II, 328.

רכשׁ collected, gathered (property) — رَغَسَهُ and أَرْغَسَهُ he prospered him, made him increase

רכשׁ n. property, goods — رَغْسٌ *id.*

The verb is found only in Gn. 12, 5; 31, 18; 36, 6 and 46, 6. It is possible, though not imperative, that the meaning *increased* should be preferred in all these texts. Gn. 36, 6 says that Esau took all his family, cattle, and possessions which had multiplied in the land of Canaan and went to Seir (so the Versions) because the land could not provide grazing for the two families which had multiplied so formidably. The Versions prefer to render 'acquired'.

غ = ك *ib.* II, 330.

רץ n. piece, bar — رَضَاضٌ pebble

The word is found only in Ps. 68, 31 and it is generally emended to בצרי with one MS. But the whole verse is most obscure.

רשׁשׁ beat down, shattered — رَضَّ *id.* = רצץ

ش = ض *ib.* II, 196.

רתח boiled — نَتَحَ sweated

שׂבר waited, hoped — صَبَرَ was patient

ش = ص *ib.* II, 220.

שׂדד harrowed — شَتَّتَ broke up, dissolved

שׂחה swam — سَبَحَ *id.*

ح = ب *ib.* II, 580; final ح and final ى *ib.* II, 316 and 318.

שׂלק kindled, burnt — صَلَقَ roasted

In Is. 44, 15 ישׂיק roasts, is followed by אפה bakes, and 'roasted meat' is expressly mentioned in the sequel. The semantic connexion between roasting, burning, and making a fire is obvious.

ش = ص *ib.* II, 220.

שׂרה ruled — سَرُوَ was of high rank

שׂרר *id.*

שׂרף burnt — = רשׁף flame

שוה	was even	سَوَّى	he put it right
	Pi. resembled	أَسْوَى	he recovered his health

Lam. 2, 13 מה אשוה־לך ואנחמך is rendered in the RV:

"What shall I equal to thee that I may comfort thee?" which *BDB* quotes as parallel to דמה in the first line of the verse. But this yields a very poor sense. The LXX translated "Who will *save* and comfort thee?". This, though not strictly accurate, gives a better sense. השוה here, though it appears to be a synonym of דמה, as it is in Is. 46, 5, bears another meaning: How can I cure thee and comfort thee? This is another *tauriya*, or hidden play on words, similar to that which the author has used in 4, 9. As the third line shows, Jerusalem's hurt is incurable. No 'emendation' of the text is called for.

שנה	repeated	ثَنَى	*id.*

So *K. al-Nawādir*, 9. This rare meaning is not to be found in Lane's *Lexicon*.

שרץ	swarmed, teemed	فَرَطَ	exceeded due bounds = פרץ
שתה	drank	سَقَى	gave to drink = השקה

It is well known that Hebrew uses the *Hif'îl* of שקה for the doubly transitive meaning 'gave him drink', whereas the Arabs simply say سَقَى, and use a different verb altogether for 'drank'. In reality שקה and שתה are one and the same verb in origin. The shift from *Q* to *T* is illustrated in *Ibdāl*, I, 138. The meaning 'drank' without the doubly transitive sense is plain in the expression سَقَى بَطْنُهُ 'his belly was swollen with dropsy', which literally must mean 'had drunk (water)'.

[תלא]	n. weariness	تِلْوٌ	that which is behind
		تَوَالِى	hinder parts

La. 3, 5 בנה עלי ויקף ראש ותלאה is generally rendered.

"He hath built against me and compassed me with gall and weariness". Thus the Vulgate, but LXX has "my head". The meaning surely must be 'He has surrounded me before and behind'.

תקע	thrust, clapped, gave a blow	صَقَعَ	struck, slapped, raised the voice, attached a

n. blast of a horn	rope (صُقاع) to the tent
	صَعْقَة *id.* (metathesis).

In Ju. 4, 21 Jael knocks a tentpeg into Sisera's head. This verb among the Arabs was commonly used of inflicting head wounds. Therefore it would seem that in Gn. 31, 25 when Jacob pitched his tent the verb refers to knocking in tentpegs. On the other hand it might refer to fastening the ends of a rope to two pegs already fixed in the ground. This is what the Arabs mean by صقع البيت which, of course, in English would be translated 'pitched the tent'. The point is of some importance because in IS. 31, 10 where the same verb is used the Philistines fixed Saul's body to the wall. Either we must follow the Vulgate's *suspenderunt* and understand that the corpse was held to the wall by ropes; or adopt the interpretation 'fastened it to the wall' (by nails or pegs) as the LXX κατέπεξαν requires.

It would be better to render Ex. 10, 19 ,where a strong wind took up the locusts, *blew* them into the Yam Suf, rather than 'drove' them as *BDB* and *KB*.

For the equation ص = ت *Ibdāl*, I, 123f.

Some Arabisms in the Book of Job

All but one (צלם) of the following equations have been made, and their effect on the meaning of the Hebrew discussed, in *Promise and Fulfilment*, Edinburgh, 1963; or they will be published shortly either in *Islamic Studies*, Karachi, or in *The Annual of Leeds Oriental Society*. Nevertheless in order to make this study as comprehensive as possible I venture to append them here. They are:

אי	adv. not	أَيّ	whosoever, 22, 30
אפיק	adj. strong	أُفُقٌ	noble 12, 21
גב	bulwark	جابَة	answer 13, 12
גיל	n. rejoicing	جالٌ	side of a grave 3, 22
דכא	crushed	دُكَّ	was ill 19, 2
זהב	n. gold	ذَهْبَة	rain 37, 22
זעך	extinguished	أَزْعَكِيّ	short

A few of the Arabisms that occur in this book are derived from roots not to be found in Hebrew lexicons nor elsewhere in Hebrew They are:

השך		حَشِيكٌ	continuous 38, 23
כזר		كُرَّزٌ	impotent, contemptible 41, 2

to be distinguished from אכזר cruel = جَزَّارٌ.

ספר		سَفَرَ	dispersed, sent forth 38, 37
צלמות	n. death shadow	ظَلِمَ	was dark
		ظُلُمَات	wrong doing 24, 17
צנה	(מִצְּנִים !)	ضَنِيَ	was emaciated 5, 5
תקוה	n. hope	تَقْوَى	piety 17, 15
רעב	adj. hungry	رَعِيبٌ	weak, cowardly 18, 12
שיא	loftiness	شَوًى	crown of the head 20,6.

To my former colleague Dr. Arafat I owe the following:

גלם	wrapped up	جَنَّ	*id.*
גֹלם	n. embryo	جَنِينٌ	*id.*
יצת	kindled, burnt	ضَاءَ	was bright (fire)
נגח	thrust, gored	نَطَحَ	*id. Ibdāl*, I, 233
נץ	n. hawk	نَضَّ	moved its wings in flight
נצה	fell in ruins	أَنْضَى	exhausted (tr.), wore out
		نضوة	worn out garments
נשת	was dry, parched	سَنَتَ	suffered drought

In Jer. 18, 14 the text is altered wrongly to יִנָּשְׁתוּ in *BH*. It is yet another example of metathesis in this verb.

סות	incited, instigated	سَاطَ	stirred, stirred up.
ספן	covered in	سَفَنٌ	thick skin covering the hilt of a sword

ADDENDA

גומץ	n. pit	غَمْضٌ	very low ground concealing what is in it.
די	n. sufficiency, abundance	دَاوٍ	much, abundant
חול	whirl, writhe	حَلَّ على	light upon, befall

In I IS. 3, 29 David says "May the blood of Abner fall upon (על) the head of Joab". The form used is יָחֻלוּ. Jer. 23, 19 and 30, 23 have יחול in the same sense. In Hos. 11, 6 the form is וחלה. In these contexts either the pointing of the MT is responsible for the shortcomings of the Hebrew lexicon, or חול is a metaplastic form of חלל.

חץ	arrow	خُصًى	testicles

Balaam's words in Nu. 24, 8 were:

> He shall devour nations, his adversaries,
> Break their bones and shatter their testicles

Attempts have been made to extract a meaning 'smite them through with arrows'; but as מחץ means rather 'to shatter, smash' it is an unsuitable word to apply to a wound caused by an arrow, and the syntax is not above suspicion. It has been suggested that חלציו 'loins' should be read here; but as this word (and מתנים also) are synonyms for the procreative organs there seems to be no valid reason for tampering with the words of a barbarous gentile seer.

יעץ	advise, counsel	وَعَظَ	warned

Though the Arabic root with the meanings "exhort, admonish" is given in *BDB* the reader is not told that the meaning of Nu. 24, 14 is "I *warn* you of what this people will do to your people in time to come".

מזה	adj. sucked out, empty	رَذِيَ	was thin, and weak = רזה

BDB, followed by *KB*, connects the word which occurs only in Dt. 32, 24 with مَزَّ 'sucked out' which, as is pointed out in the *ICC* is a variation of the more usual مَصَّ. The commentator evidently doubted whether the Hebrew word had the meaning of 'sucked out'. None of the ancient versions provided a meaning with any philological support. Grätz (quoted in *ICC*) suggested that רזי 'emaciated' was intended. He was undoubtedly right, but there is no need to alter the text, for R and M are recognized *badals* in Arabic, see *Ibdāl*, II, pp. 82-87.

נאץ	contemned, spurned	أنْغض	he wagged his head in derison

أ = غ *Ibdāl*, II, 559. Arabic preserves the primitive meaning of the verb.

סבב	surrounded	ثَبَّ	sat down in comfort

All authorities, ancient and modern, adopt the rendering 'sit down' in I S. 16, 11. The RVm affirms that the Hebrew means 'sit around', but it does not. There is no need to emend the text to נשב as suggested in *BH*. Both Arabic and post-biblical Hebrew support the current interpretation. س and ث are recognized *badals* in Arabic. *Ibdāl*, I, 168-174.

סכן I	was of use, benefited	ثَكَمَ	was continually occupied in remained in a place

This Arabic verb well illustrates Hebrew usage in Nu. 22, 30 and Jb. 22, 21, and is not out of line with Ps. 139, 3; but it hardly seems to fit those contexts where profit or benefit are implied.

סרב	n.m. rebel	ثَرَبَ	he blamed, reviled, insulted

It can be seen from Ezk. 2, 6 "Fear neither them nor their words" that the people are not so much 'rebels' as bitter controversialists who reject the prophet's words. Syriac *serabh* and Ecclus. 41, 2 אל תסרב bear the meaning 'contradict'. In view of the presence of the word in Arabic it is unlikely that it is an Aramaic loan word as *BDB* suggests.

תוה made a mark

Since the ancient versions translate ויתו in I S. 21, 14 'he drummed on the doors of the gates', a reading ויתף from תפף has been recommended by commentators and adopted in *BH*. Quite apart from the question as to whether drumming or scratching on a door are actions more proper to a madman neither can claim the support of the text, for و and ف frequently interchange in Arabic, as can be seen in *Ibdāl*, II, 351 and Prof. Izz al-Din's notes thereon. In any case no alteration in the MT can be tolerated.

THE CHINESE-HEBREW MEMORIAL BOOK OF THE JEWISH COMMUNITY OF K'AIFENG

BY

DANIEL LESLIE

PART ONE

TABLE OF CONTENTS

---

[1] I owe a special debt to Professor L. C. Goodrich of Columbia University and Professor J. Bowman of Melbourne University without whose encouragement this research would never have been undertaken. My thanks go also to the many colleagues at the Australian National University who have helped me, in particular to Otto van der Sprenkel, Wang Ling, Liu Ts'un-yan, Igor de Rachewilz, and Jeremy Davidson. Dr. J. C. Caldwell has kindly discussed with me some of the demographic problems concerned. Though I correct him at every point, I owe a heavy debt to William C. White, whose *Chinese Jews*, 1942, Toronto, has been the mainstay of my work.

Introduction

This article is devoted to the Chinese-Hebrew Manuscript or Register from the K'aifeng synagogue. But before we attack the manuscript itself, we need to know something about the other sources on the Jewish community of K'aifeng which may be used as controls for our analysis.

a. *The Synagogue Inscriptions*

Our most reliable knowledge of the K'aifeng Jews comes from the synagogue inscriptions of 1489, 1512 and 1663, inscribed on stone tablets and written in Chinese [2]. To these should be added a further stone inscription of 1679 of less value [3]; and several shorter inscriptions of which the dated ones are mostly between 1656 and 1679 [4]. These are all reproduced, together with a translation, in Part II *Inscriptional* of William Charles White, *Chinese Jews*, 1942, Toronto (in 3 parts) [5].

---

[2] The stone tablet, with the inscription dated 1489 on one side and the inscription of (probably) 1512 on the other, still existed in K'aifeng in 1942 (White II, p. 5). The stone tablet containing an inscription dated 1663 on one side (a) and another of about the same date (b) was last seen in 1851. Ink rubbings and copies were made by the Jesuit missionaries in China in the first years of the 18th Century and sent to Rome.

[3] The stone tablet with the inscription dated 1679 on one side still existed in 1942 according to White (op. cit.). It was heavily scratched, and the text given by White after reconstruction by Chinese scholars must be used with caution.

[4] The shorter inscriptions are lost. The extant copies come from various visitors to the community in the 18th and 19th centuries. See, e.g., Tobar, pp. 8, 21; White II, pp. 121, 135.

[5] These inscriptions, apart from the 1679 one, are also found in Jerôme Tobar, S.J., *Inscriptions juives de K'ai-fong-fou*, Variétés Sinologiques No. 17, 1900, Shanghai. The text of White, following Ch'en Yüan 陳 垣 and Yeh Han 葉 瀚, *K'ai-feng Yi-tz'u-lo-yeh Chiao K'ao* 開 封 一 賜 樂 業 教 考 Shanghai, 1925, and that of Tobar, based on copies and ink-rubbings from Rome and from K'aifeng, hardly differ. Tobar's translations are often better than White's; but he has fewer annotations. He has not actually seen our manuscript.

b. *The Local Gazetteers*

Of the persons mentioned in these inscriptions, some are identifiable in the Chinese local gazetteers, in particular in those of Hsiang-fu 祥符, a *district* (*hsien* 縣) forming part of the *prefecture* (*fu* 府) of K'ai-feng 開封[6]. In such cases we have valuable confirmation of the inscriptions, and occasionally further information and family connections. The most striking case is that of Chao Ying-ch'eng 趙映乘, mentioned in the inscriptions as a believer and Hebrew scholar active in the synagogue, who was sufficiently successful in Chinese society to be mentioned in the gazetteers of Hsiang-fu (*district*), K'ai-feng (*prefecture*), Honan (*province*) and Fukien (*province*).

I hope to demonstrate later, following White, that this Chao Ying-ch'eng appears in the Register under the Hebrew name of Moses.

A. The Nature of the Manuscript

a. *The Inferior Interpretations of the Sinologists*

The Chinese-Hebrew manuscript, which is now in the Library of the Hebrew Union College at Cincinnati, came from the K'aifeng Jewish community to Shanghai as far back as 1851, together with copies of the Torah and of prayers[7]. It contains prayers in Hebrew (and Aramaic), followed by 'lists of names in the form of a genealogical register, written in a combination of Chinese and Hebrew script' (White III, p. 1). This 'genealogical register' (called a Tsu-p'u by Ch'en Yüan, and a *Chia-p'u* in the *Chinese Repository*)[8] gives lists of

[6] There are three distinct gazetteers for Hsiang-fu, all entitled *Hsiang-fu hsien chih* 祥符縣志: Of *Shun-chih* 18 (1661), in 6 volumes (not seen by White); of *Ch'ien-lung* 4 (1739), in 22 volumes; and of *Kuang-hsü* 24 (1898), in 24 volumes. Of less value for the Jewish community are the gazetteers for K'ai-feng fu: Of *Wan-li* 13 (1585), in 34 volumes; of *Shun-chih* 16 (1659), in 35 volumes; of *K'ang-hsi* 34 (1695), in 40 volumes (reprinted in 1863).

[7] According to Laufer (White III, p. 11), Tobar, p. 102, and White II, p. 156, it was first described (by the Reverend W. H. Medhurst?) in the *North China Herald* of Shanghai, August 16, 1851 (reproduced by S. Wells Williams in the *Chinese Repository* XX (1851), pp. 436-466, especially p. 465). White (III, p. 1) states that it was obtained from the K'aifeng synagogue by the two Chinese delegates sent to the community from Shanghai in 1851, whose reports are found translated in G. Smith (and W. H. Medhurst), *A Narrative of a Mission of Inquiry to the Jewish Synagogue of K'aifung fu, on behalf of the London Society for promoting Christianity among the Jews*, 1851, Shanghai; and largely reproduced by White II, pp. 97-133; and also by Wells Williams, pp. 436-62 (loc. cit.).

[8] White II, p. 159. We shall see later just why this term 'Family Register' *Chia-p'u* 家譜 (or 'Ancestral Register' *Tsung-p'u* 宗譜 or 'Clan Register'

men's names, together with their father's name, arranged by surname; the maiden names of women, together with their father's name, but arranged under the clan by marriage; and a few husbands and sons of these women; and a few other family connections. Some names are in Hebrew, some in Chinese.

According to White (III, p. 2), "The Hebrew script appears to have been written entirely by Hebrew stylus and not by Chinese brush pen, while the Chinese on the whole has been written with Chinese brush". According to Laufer [9], "the Chinese characters are very crudely written, apparently with a stylus and by several inexperienced scribes". The Hebrew calligraphy on the other hand is mostly of a high standard, though more than one hand is evident. There are misspellings and other mistakes. It seems probable that the Hebrew copyist had little knowledge of the language.

The first description of the manuscript in the *Chinese Repository*, XX (1851), p. 465 footnote, by S. Wells Williams, (quoting the Reverend W. H. Medhurst?) goes as follows:

> 'If so, this will sufficiently indicate the date of the little book to be sometime during the fifteenth century, as the names recorded are apparently individuals who were all living at the same time.

This is utterly wrong?

A more detailed study of the manuscript was given by Berthold Laufer in 1930. He gave an interesting description of the Jewish community, but unfortunately completely distorted the nature of the manuscript whenever he mentioned it. He writes (White III, p. 6):

> It turned out to contain a register of the Jewish congregation of K'ai-feng Fu drawn up between the years 1660 and 1670, giving first the names of male individuals, then those of women, both in Hebrew and Chinese,

and (White III, p. 13):

> The total number of individuals recorded is 712. Assuming that there were several hundred children and that there were a number of

---

Tsu-p'u 族譜) is unsuitable for our manuscript. For details of such genealogical registers see the 宗譜の研究 (*An Analytic Study of Chinese Genealogical Books*) by Taga Akigorō 多賀秋五郎, Toyo Bunko, 1960, Tokyo. There is little likelihood of finding any such registers for our Jewish families.

[9] B. Laufer, 'A Chinese-Hebrew Manuscript, a New Source for the History of the Chinese Jews', *The American Journal of Semitic Languages and Literature*, XLVI, No. 3, 1930, pp. 189-197; reprinted in *Folklore Studies*, IV, 1945, pp. 319-326; and also by White, Part III, pp. 6-15. Cf. review by A. C. Moule in *T'oung Pao* 28, 1931, pp. 125-128.

Jewish farmers scattered over the villages in the environment of the city and not officially registered by the synagogue of K'ai-feng, we may arrive at an estimate of about a thousand souls.

Laufer's views are repeated, almost unchanged, by Löwenthal, who, in 1947, wrote [10]: 'According to the Chinese-Hebrew MS . . . the Kaifeng community counted 712 persons between 1660/70, 453 men and 259 women.'

We shall see later just how primitive were Laufer's methods for arriving at these figures, 453 men and 259 women, blindly accepted by Löwenthal (1, p. 105). Here I wish to emphasise rather the total misreading of the manuscript by Laufer, who has ignored completely its genealogical nature. For example, in one clan in the men's Register, the names extend over 10 generations. We are clearly not dealing with the Register of the living members of a Congregation.

A further serious error of Laufer (also made by Ch'en Yüan in his otherwise excellent study of the Chinese Jews) is to take the Chinese names given as corresponding in some way to the Hebrew names. Laufer (White III, p. 12) writes:

> There is no relation between the Chinese and Hebrew names. Ben Israel, Ben Josef, Ben Aaron, Ben Mosheh, Ben Jehosha, and Abraham Ben Israel are among the most frequent names,

and (White III, p. 14):

> I am planning to publish this register *in extenso*, giving the Chinese names in one column with the corresponding Hebrew names in the next column.

In fact, as White has demonstrated, the men of the Register are given only one name, some a Hebrew one, others a Chinese one. White's own figures for the names of individuals contained in the Register are reasonably accurate. He gives (III, p. 102) a 'combined total of 902 men's names, that is, 465 in Hebrew and 437 in Chinese. Of the Hebrew names there would be repetitions, but the 437 Chinese names are all different individuals'.

Laufer's treatment of the manuscript was superficial, and he did not live to do a real job on it. The first to deal seriously with its contents was William C. White. In Part III *Genealogical* of his *Chinese*

---

[10] R. Löwenthal (1), 'The Nomenclature of Jews in China', *Monumenta Serica* 12, 1947, pp. 97-126, esp. 102, note 10. Cf. Löwenthal (2), 'The Jews in China: An Annotated Bibliography', *The Chinese Social and Political Science Review* XXIV, No. 2, 1940, pp. 113-234, esp. 160; and (3), 'The Early Jews in China: A Supplementary Bibliography', *Folklore Studies*, V, 1946, pp. 353-398, esp. p. 387.

Jews, 1942, Toronto, he includes a complete translation of this Register which he calls a Codex. White's translation and romanization of the names has been accurately done [11]. We will only rarely need to refer to (a microfilm of) the original manuscript. White has also commenced the identification of the names given with those found in the synagogue inscriptions in Chinese and also with the names of scholars and officials mentioned in the local gazetteers. Some of these identifications are sound, though some are wild. However, their real significance was missed.

For White too, though eliminating Laufer's mistakes, has misunderstood the real nature of the manuscript.

He writes (III, p. 112):

> None of these names is found in the Codex; the five sons were probably not mature men when the Codex was written, and so would not be enrolled on the list.

White has clearly taken the manuscript to be similar to a Chinese *Chia-p'u*. In particular he has assumed that the Register is concerned with men living at the time of its composition, together with their ancestors. This is confirmed by his attempts (see, e.g., II, p. 91, note 10) to identify Hebrew names in the Register with Chinese names in the inscriptions.

b. *The Correct Interpretation of the Judaic Scholars*

Laufer and White have used the identification of certain names found in both the Register and the synagogue inscriptions as a means of dating the manuscript. Laufer (White III, p. 12) writes:

> Half-a-dozen names listed in the most recent inscription of 1663 recur also in our register, so that the latter must be coeval with the date of this inscription or must have been prepared shortly afterward, say, roughly, during the decade of 1660-70.

White (III, p. 4) writes:

> As further proof ot this dating of 1642 as the centre of the period covered by the Codex, there is the fact that many names from the Codex list are to be found on the stone inscriptions of 1663 and 1679.

Though there are excellent reasons, as we shall see, for accepting Laufer's date of 1660/70 as the date of closure of the manuscript, it is

[11] However the 21 odd pages of Hebrew (and Aramaic) prayers still require serious study, especially in view of the large number of textual corruptions. The translation by White, in collaboration with Ronald James Williams, in his Part III, pp. 28-35, notes pp. 83-87, is full of mistakes and lacks adequate interpretation.

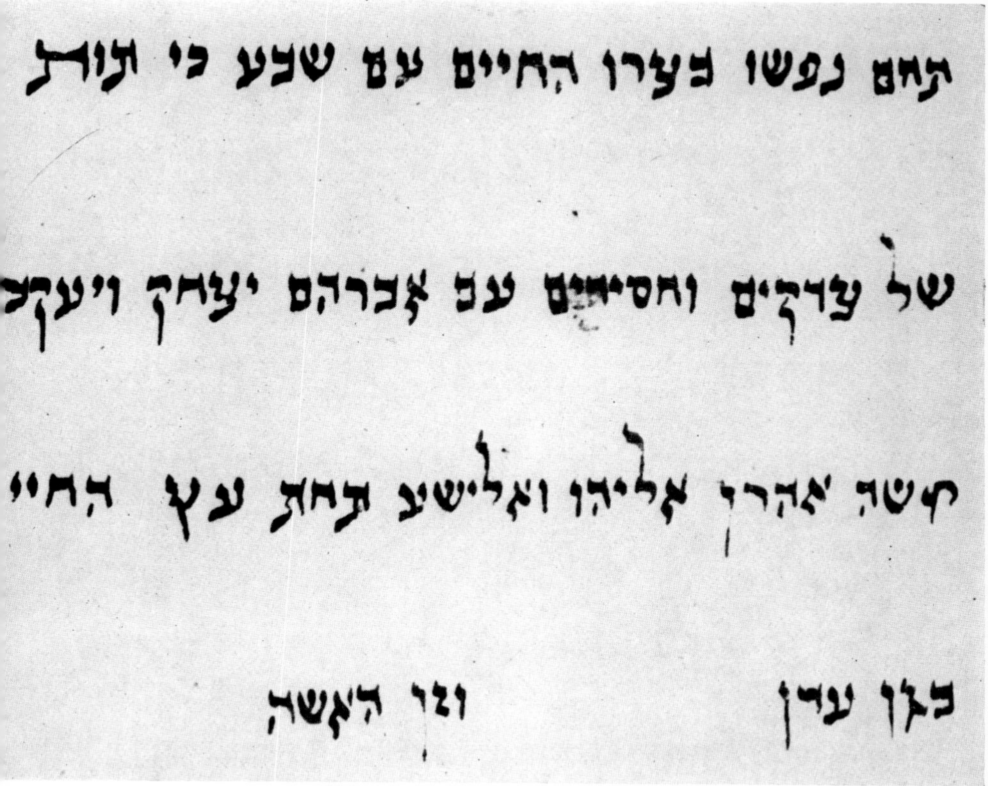
תחם נפשו בצרו החיים עם שבע כי תורת
של צדקים וחסידים עם אברהם יצחק ויעקב
משה אהרן אליהו ואלישע תחת עץ החיי
בגן עדן
וזו האשה

End of Register of Men; Introduction to Register of Women (p. 64, White p. 65 of the Chinese-Hebrew Manuscript).

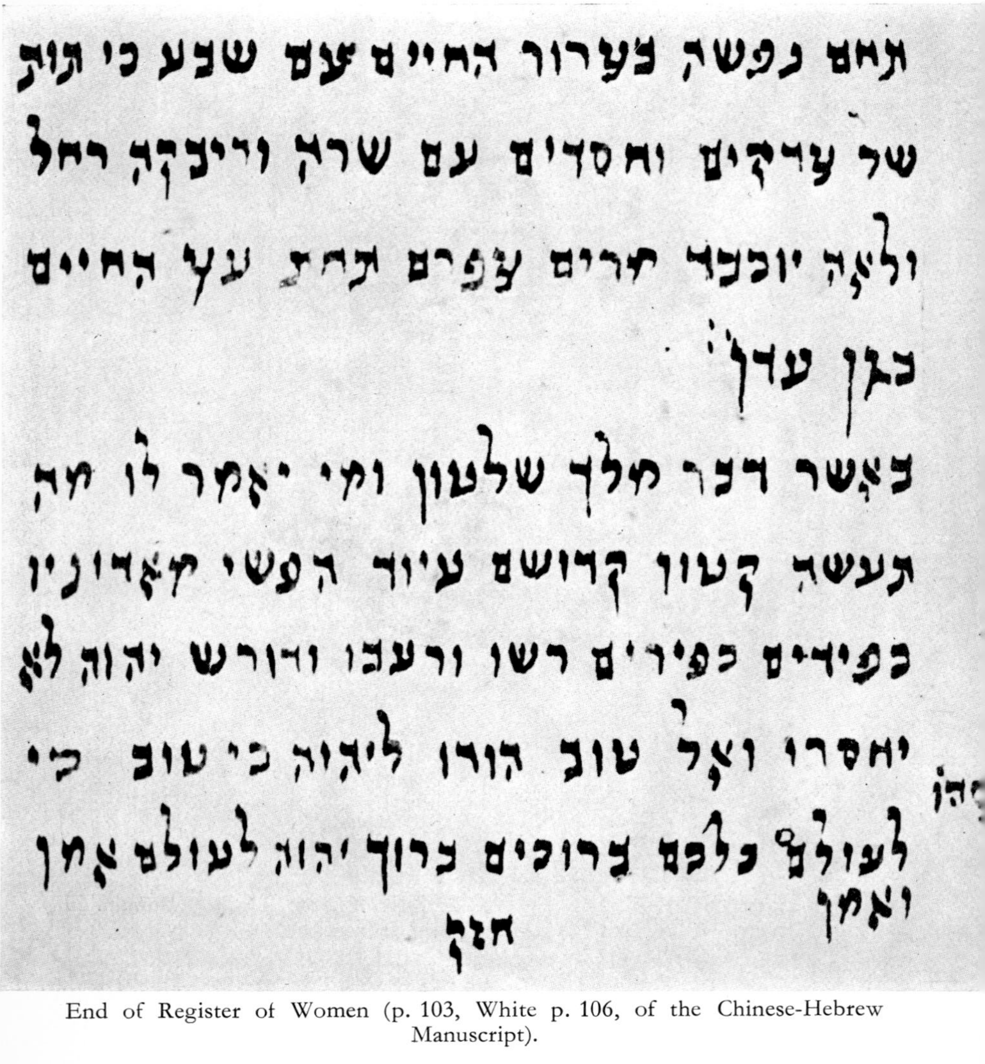

תהא נפשה בערור החיים עם שבע כי תות
של עדיקים וחסדים עם שרה ורבקה רחל
ולאה יוכבד מרים עפרם תרת עע החיים
בגן עדן
באשר דבר מלך שלטון ומי יאמר לו מה
תעשה קטון קדושם עיור הפשי קאדיניו
כפידים כפירים רשו ורעבו ודורש יהוה לא
יחסרו ואל טוב הודו ליהוה כי טוב כי
לעולם כלבם ברוכים ברוך יהוה לעולם אמן
ואמן
חזק

End of Register of Women (p. 103, White p. 106, of the Chinese-Hebrew Manuscript).

ויחנך: ישא יהוה/ פניו אליך וישם לך שלוד ·

יך שמי על בני ישראל ואני אברכב:

ב . . . עליכם ועל בניכם ליהוד

עתה שמים דוברן עג ועי ת נשא ויכתב

מעליםא ברסלת העדרים ומיעת וירי ל

דחסדים נפשתא דיתנדר חודין עלת :

דרכם הגדול התיקי ים שמים קרינו ורינו

יון הידן

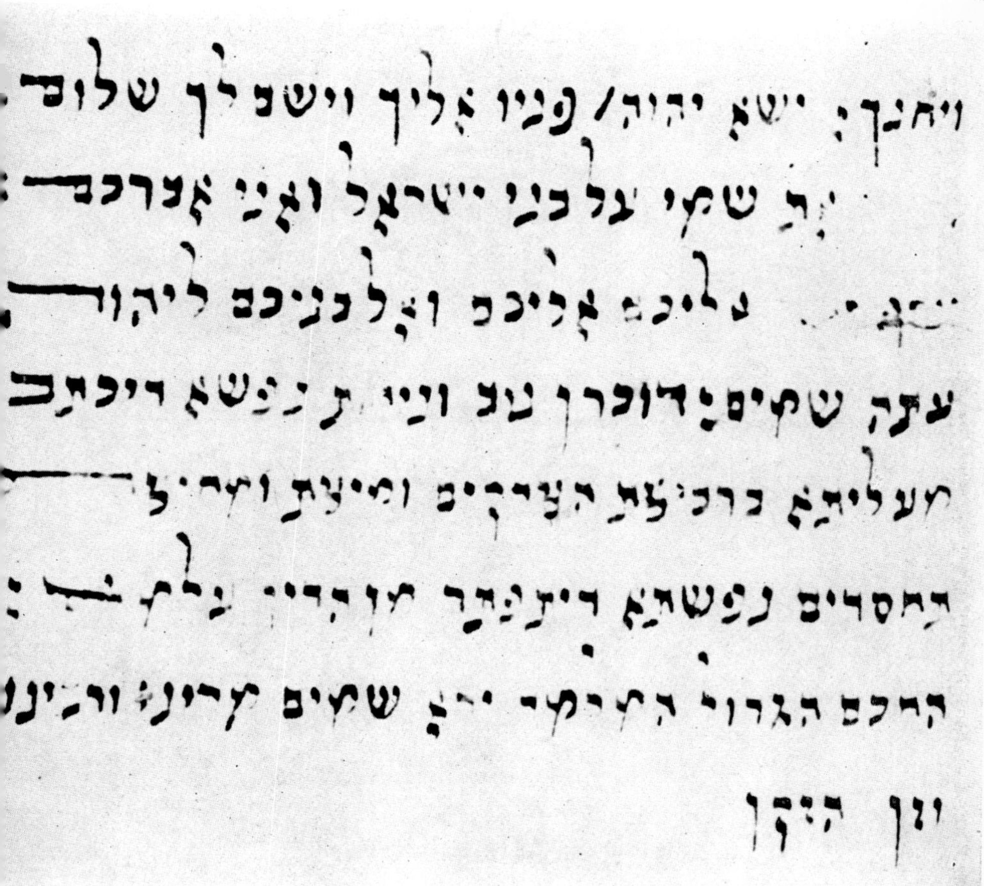

Introduction to the Register of Men (p. 21, White p. 22, of the Chinese-Hebrew
Manuscript).

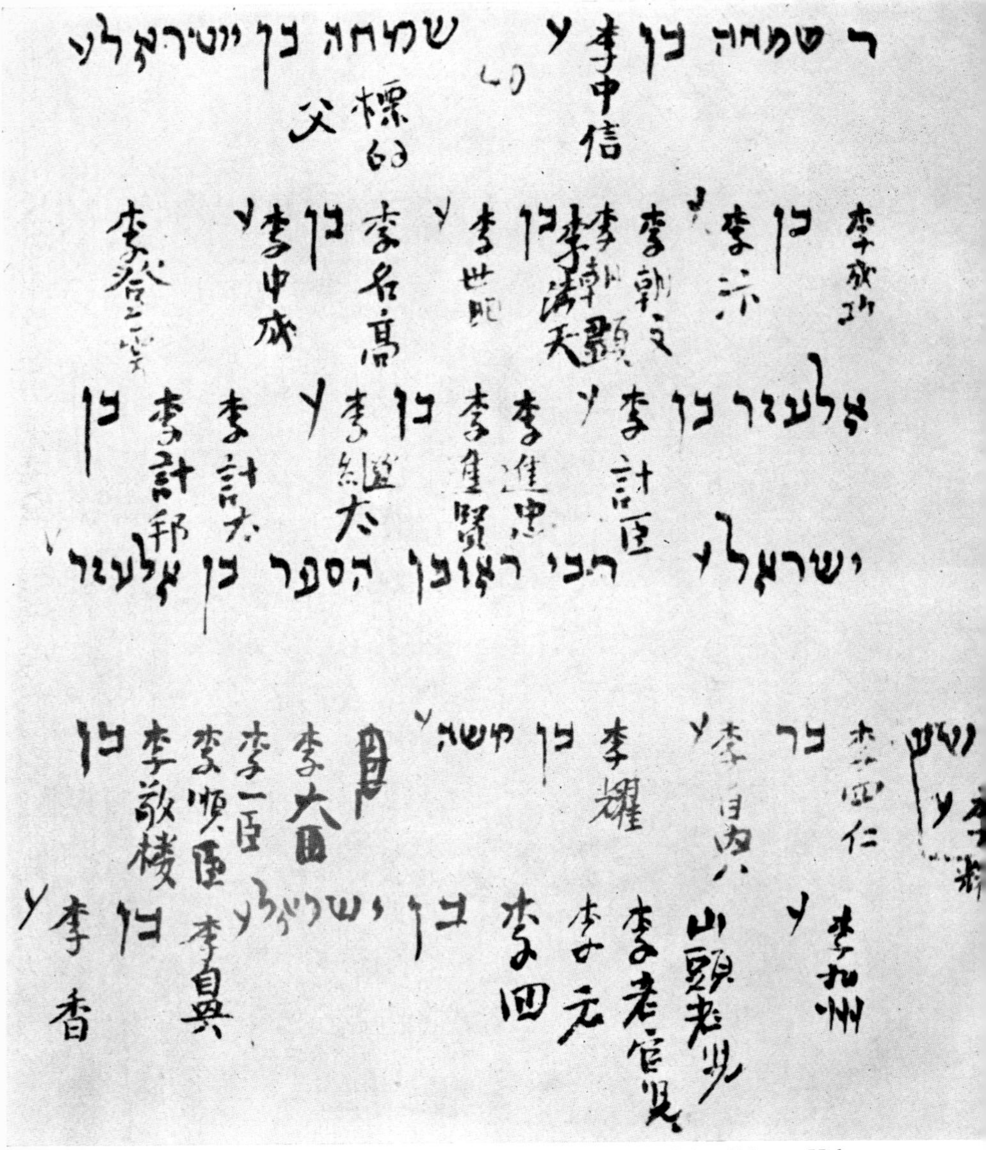

A Typical Page of the Register of Men (p. 40, White p. 41 of the Chinese-Hebrew Manuscript).

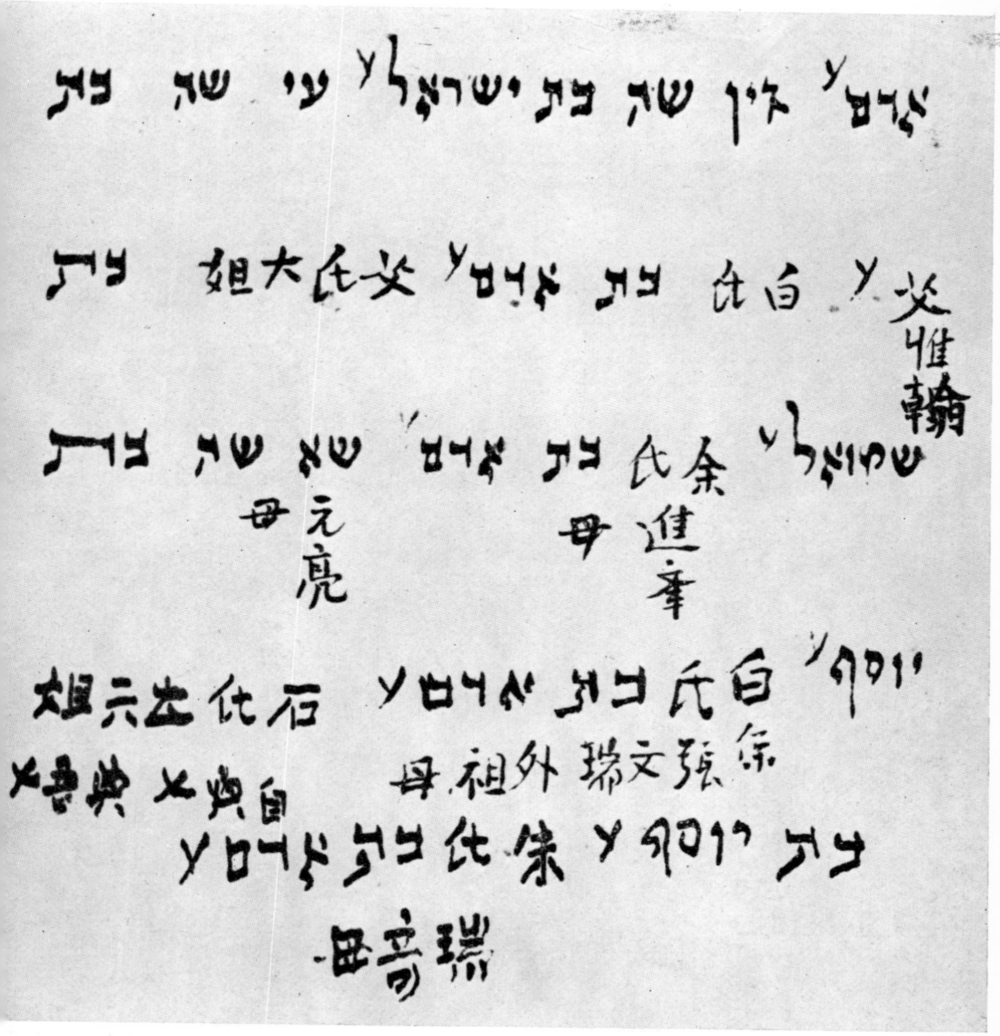

A Typical Page of the Register of Women (p. 69, White p. 70, of the Chinese-Hebrew Manuscript).

exceedingly puzzling that some prominent Jews in the inscriptions are included in the Register, but not others. Of the 14 Jews (out of a total 33) mentioned in the 1663 inscriptions who are identifiable in the Register, 6 appear only in the Register of women, 2 in both Registers, and 6 only in the Register of men. We may add that not one of the 15 names (of living men) mentioned in the inscriptions after 1663 (until 1679) is found in the Register, except Chao Ying-tou, found only in the Register of women.

The solution to this puzzle is simple. The manuscript is a REGISTER OF THE DEAD.

This fits very well the general arrangement of both Registers. It also gives a possible explanation of why several men mentioned in the Register of women do not appear in the Register of men, even though clearly of mature age. The fact that far more of the Chinese-named fathers are unaccounted for in the Register of men is also significant. For the Hebrew-named ones are more likely to have been dead. It also explains to some extent the large number of "sons of Israel".

All these points provide strong circumstantial evidence that our Register is not merely geneological, but confined to the dead members of the Community (of the seven clans only).

The key to an understanding of the nature of the manuscript lies in the prayer on page 64 of the manuscript (p. 65 of White III, p. 55), given as plate no. II. It follows immediately after the Register of men, and introduces the Register of Women.

This was translated by Medhurst (see Wells Williams, pp. 465-6 and Tobar, p. 102), and by Laufer (White III, p. 12); and again by White and Williams, (III, p. 55) as follows:

> The complete record (?) of their persons in the bundle of (BṢRW!) the living, together with seven, for among the righteous and pious (are they), with Abraham, Isaac and Jacob, Moses, Aaron, Elijah and Elisha, under the tree of life (HḤYY!) in the garden of Eden.
> The classification of the women:

(Then follows the Register of women).

A similar passage, with seven women replacing the seven men named here, concludes the Register of women (see plate no. 3).

There are several points in the Hebrew text which require discussion [12], and White and Williams have made several mistakes. A provisional translation is:

---

[12] These Hebrew prayers need to be examined in detail. I must thank Professor

> May his soul be bound up in the bundle of life together with the seven groups of righteous and pious men, with Abraham, Isaac and Jacob, Moses, Aaron, Elijah and Elisha, under the tree of life in the garden of Eden.
>
> The classification of the women:

Not one of the sinologues working on this manuscript has appreciated its nature. On the other hand, Kaufmann Kohler, the author of the article on the Chinese Jews in *The Jewish Encyclopedia*, (1904 and 1916 edition), Vol. IV, p. 38, though the translations (by Henri Cordier) from the Chinese inscriptions are poor, is completely aware of the significance of the manuscript, which he calls a *Hazkarat Neshamot* (Memorial of the Dead).

When we turn to the article on *Hazkarat Neshamot* in Vol. VI, pp. 283-4, by L. N. Dembitz, we have striking confirmation.

We read that in the German ritual, the following prayer is recited at certain dates of the year:

> May God remember the soul of my respected father,—son of—, who has gone to his eternal home; on whose behalf I vow as alms—; may his soul be bound up in the bundle of life [see I Sam. XXV. 29] with the souls of Abraham, Isaac, and Jacob, Sarah, Rebekah, Rachel, and Leah, and all other righteous men and women that are in the Garden of Eden, and let us say, Amen.

We read further that

> In many Sephardic synagogues a "Hashkabah" (laying to rest) for a long list of deceased members is read on Kol Nidre night: in others, vows for the dead are made in the daytime, between musaf and minḥah.

and

> Primarily, the "Hashkabah" is recited at the grave as a part of the burial service; when it is used at the synagogue a vow of alms, somewhat like that in the German ritual, is sometimes added.

As further evidence we may quote page 21 (p. 22 of White, p. 35), our plate no. 4, which comes just before the Register of men. It is translated by White and Williams as:

> .. and be gracious unto thee: the Lord lift up his countenance upon thee, and give thee peace. [And they shall put] my name upon the children of Israel; and I will bless them." (Num. 6: 24-27). "[The

Bowman, and also Mr. Gershon Weiler of the A.N.U. who first brought my attention to these prayers, for advice here. However they should not be held responsible for my superficial analysis of the Hebrew and Judaic aspects of the manuscript. Professor Bowman hopes to join me later in a proper analysis of the Hebrew part of the manuscript.

Lord shall inc]rease you more and more, you and your children." (Psalm 115: 14). The heavens now are the Lord's.

A good memorial and rest of the soul, that the excellence shall be written in the resting place of the righteous, and (in) the midst (MYṢT!) and compartment of the pious (TḤSDYM!), the souls who will depart from this world. The great and learned sage, fearing Heaven, our master and Rabbi.

The classification of the elders:

All the prayers require further study. But enough has been given to show beyond any doubt that our manuscript with its Register is used for the *Hazkarat Neshamot* (Memorial of the Dead). It is in other words a Memorial Book of the dead souls of the Jewish community of K'aifeng.

B. The Register of Men

a. *General Description*

The Register of Men (pp. 26-63 of the manuscript in White's enumeration) consists almost entirely of names in Hebrew and in Chinese, linked by the Hebrew word *ben* בן 'son (of)'. In place of *ben* for 'son (of)' we find (twice) *bar* בר 'son (of)', and (four times) '*fu* 父 "father (of)" . . ., *ben* בן "son (of)" . . .'The plural form of *ben* is never used, and commonly two or more names, all in Chinese, or all in Hebrew, or some in Hebrew and some in Chinese, are followed by *ben* בן. This singular form has been taken by White and Williams to be 'sons of', the singular form being used under the influence of the Chinese language which lacks a plural. The two or more names side by side thus refer to brothers, whether they are given in Chinese or Hebrew. There is no justification for the implication that there are Hebrew and Chinese names for the same man. Each set of names is separated by a letter or sign resembling the Hebrew *ayin* ע. No Chinese or Hebrew signification is known for this sign.

The men are listed under seven clan names:

Chart No. 1.
The Clan Pages of the Register of Men

Ai	艾 pp. 26, 27, 36, 37, and almost certainly 30-35 (in the enumeration of White, Nos. 1-21, 45-107).
Li	李 pp. 28, 29, 40, 41, and probably 44, 45 (nos. 22-44, 128-161, and 186-199).
Chang	張 pp. 38, 39, 42, 43, 46 (nos. 108-127, 162-185, 200-201).
Kao	高 pp. 47-52 (nos. 202-255).

Chao 趙 pp. 54-58
(nos. 256-301).
Chin 金 pp. 59-61
(nos. 302-325).
Shih 石 pp. 62-63.
(nos. 326-346).

Pp. 30-33 have Hebrew names only, but are clearly continued by p. 34, which includes two men surnamed Ai, and is in turn continued by p. 35, which includes one man surnamed Ai. P. 35 is then continued by p. 36 and p. 37, clearly of the Ai clan.

P. 44 is taken by White to be of the Chao clan, p. 45 of the Chao and Li clans. Some of his worst speculations are based on, or the cause of, this identification. The reasons in favour of including both these solely under the Li clan are as follows:

P. 44 has only Hebrew names but is clearly continued by p. 45 which includes 4 men surnamed Li. We may add that 2 pages (28 and 29) of the Li clan are sandwiched between pages of the Ai clan (26-27, 30-37), and another 2 pages (40 and 41) between pages of the Chang clan (38-39, 42-43). Pp. 44, 45, which I take to be of the Li clan, are similarly sandwiched between other pages of the Chang clan 42-43, 46, in fact with the Chang and Li clan pages running two by two. These pages are certainly not connected with the Chao clan (pages 54-58 only) [13]. We may add that the large number of rabbis on these pages 44-45 tallies better with the Li clan than the Chao clan, especially when we consider that several on these pages have special titles (see below). The Hebrew names given here also fit well with those for the Li clan from the Register of women.

b. *Statistics of the Register of Men*

Laufer (White III, p. 11), followed blindly by Löwenthal (I, p. 105), has added up the number of names appearing in Chinese by clan to arrive at his figures. He gives Li clan 109, Kao 76, Chao 74, Chang 73, Ai 56, Chin 42, Shih 23, total 453 men. He has ignored the fact that many of these names occur as sons and then again as fathers. He ignores too all clan members who have Hebrew names (presumably because he assumes wrongly that they are the same men but with a Hebrew instead of Chinese name). Löwenthal's statistics add the

[13] It is tempting to see in these divisions a reflection of the original duplications of the 3 surnames, Li, Chang and Chin (see below), mentioned in the 1489 inscription. However the 1663 inscription merely gives these seven clans with no subdivisions. Moreover the Ai clan is here split up, the Chin not; and both the Li and Chang lists are in three parts.

number of rabbis listed, but are inaccurate and misleading, not merely because he too includes duplications, but also because he follows White's inferior view of pp. 44-5 of the Register.

Assuming that we are correct in allocating pp. 44-5 to the Li clan, we have the following statistics for the men of the community listed in the Register of Men.

Table No. 1.
The Men Registered in the Register

Surname	Hebrew sons of Hebrew	Hebrew 'sons of Israel'	Hebrew sons of Chinese	Total Hebrew names	Chinese sons of Hebrew	Chinese 'sons of Israel'	Chinese sons of Chinese	'Sons of Adam'	Total Chinese names	Grand Total Registered
Ai	112	—	1	113	26	6	19	—	51	164
Li	43	2	4	49	26	11	43	—	80	129
Chang	9	6	2	17	15	16	25	—	56	73
Kao	38	2	2	42	24	6	22	1	53	95
Chao	14	2	4	20	10	21	21	1	53	73
Chin	6	—	2	8	17	2	12	—	31	39
Shih	14	—	—	14	12	8	2	—	22	36
Total	236	12	15	263	130	70	144	2	346	609

We may note, as contrast to the 82 'sons of Israel' בן ישראל, only 2 'sons of Adam' בן אדם (i.e. non-Jews or sons of non-Jews) [14]. Most of the 'sons of Israel' are named with Chinese surname and personal name. There are two possible explanations of this term 'son of Israel'. The first, which is that given by White, is that the man is the son of a Jew whose name has been forgotten. The second, a less likely explanation, is that these men have been adopted or converted into the religion.

It is common, in all the clans, to find Hebrew-named sons of Hebrew-named fathers, Chinese-named sons of Chinese-named fathers, and also Chinese-named sons of Hebrew-named fathers. But rare (approx. 15 out of 609) to find Hebrew-named sons of Chinese-named fathers. This clear sign of assimilation to the Chinese surround-

[14] No. 240, Kao Ch'i; and No. 259, GMLYN GYM גמלין גים of the Chao clan. This seems to be a Chinese name transliterated, of surname Chin or Chang (though in this case why he is included in the Chao Clan is not clear). Both have (Jewish) sons named in the Register.

ings is also supported by the fact that the sons of rabbis are more commonly found named in Hebrew. Similarly, when we construct family trees, we find generally that the earlier generations have Hebrew names, the later ones Chinese ones. Moreover, on the whole, Chinese personal names with one character are of earlier generations than those of two characters, a definite distinction between the Jews named in the 1489 and 1663 inscriptions.

The total number of men registered is 609. However, besides these, a small number of men occur who are only listed as fathers, and strictly speaking are not part of the Register. This is made clear by the following table, of which the last two columns can only be approximate, especially for the Hebrew names.

Table No. 2.

The Fathers of the Register of Men

Surname	Total Number of Sons	Total Number of Fathers	'Sons of Israel'	Sons, Father named	Fathers named	Fathers Hebrew named	Fathers Chinese named	Fathers, not in Register	
								Hebrew named	Chinese named
Ai	164	84	6	158	79	67	12	12	2
Li	129	71	13	116	62	35	27	21	6
Chang	73	46	22	51	28	10	18	3	3
Kao	95	54	8	87	47	29	18	11	7
Chao	73	46	23	50	27	9	18	3	5
Chin	39	24	2	37	22	11	11	9	3
Shih	36	21	8	28	14	13	1	4	0
Total	609	346	82	527	279	174	105	63	26

The fact that, in all clans, the ratio of sons to (named) fathers lies between 1.6: 1 and 2: 1 might suggest a steady increase in size of the community. On the other hand we have no way of telling from the Register how many men died young or remained unmarried or without progeny, for living offspring would not be recorded. Moreover those who died without offspring might by accident or neglect have been overlooked. We have no guarantee that all dead members of the community are recorded in the Memorial Book. Were children included? We do not know. On the whole, men with Hebrew names have more offspring recorded, which is simply explained on the grounds that more of the living sons and only recently dead fathers would have Chinese names.

The Ai clan has the largest number of men registered, in particular with Hebrew names. This is not necessarily due to its size in the community, in my opinion, but because one particular family (of around 150 men) has a tree extending over 10 generations, as opposed to 7 generations for one family of the Li clan, and 5 or 6 generations at most for the other clans. Moreover, in this connection we may note the large number of rabbis listed for the Ai clan, in spite of the fact that it seems, from the inscriptions, that the Li clan were predominant in the religious aspects of the community. Some clans, the Ai in particular, presumably kept better records than others.

We shall be analysing later the genealogies of the various clans, together with possible identification of individuals. We will also defer, for the moment, the discussion of the actual numerical size of the community.

C. The Register of Women

a. *General Description*

The Register of women (pp. 66-104) follows the phrase וזן האשה taken by Williams to be 'The Classification of the women'. The main formula is a Chinese surname (if a Jewish one, often written in Hebrew letters) [15], followed by the Chinese word *shih* 氏 (written, in the case of the names transliterated, with the Hebrew letters *ŠH* שה or as *ŠH DZ* שה דז) [16] meaning *née*, thus signifying the family

[15] See White III, p. 80. Apart from one single name *TN* תן (no. 507), all the Hebrew transliterations are for the Jewish surnames: עי for Ai (28 of 39); לי for Li (47 of 55); גן for Chang (13 of 22); שא for Shih (8 of 11); גין (4, apparently in the Li clan pages only), and גים (19, apparently for the other clans, apart from Ai) for Chin (total 30). Three women transcribed as לי Li (nos. 388, 618, 650) are however 'daughters of Adam'. These transcriptions are entirely reliable, for exact equations are found with the Chinese characters, several times for each of these surnames. Kao and Chao are never transcribed. One transcription שי (no. 550) is taken by White as Chao. But the father's name Issachar, though found in most clans (but not the Chao), is best taken to be of the Ai עי clan (see especially no. 665). Note that Hebrew names in the Register, on the other hand, are never written phonetically with Chinese characters, though this was done in the inscriptions for Abraham, Moses, etc.

[16] The word *dz* דז occurs 20 times, and *sz* סז five times. White (III, p. 95) takes דז as perhaps *tzu* 字 'word' or 'character', I suggest rather *tzu* 子 'child (of)'. There are also ·*Z*, ·*YZ*, ·*WZ* (עז, עיז, עוז) and other combinations, which are unexplained. These words are only used for Jewish women.

of origin; and then *bat* 'daughter (of)', followed by a man's name in Chinese or Hebrew. Apart from those of named Jewish father, there are 50 'daughters of Israel' בת ישראל, and 113 'daughters of Adam' בת אדם. These clearly refer to Jewesses and non-Jewesses by origin. We shall see the full significance of this when we discuss the clan surnames.

There is one peculiarity of the text which must be noted here. The Hebrew letter *chaf* כ often comes before the word *bat* בת 'daughter (of)'. White and Williams (III, p. 94) make the ingenious suggestion that this must stand for the Chinese word 契 *ch'i* or *k'i* ,which is one of the terms used for 'legal adoption'. We shall discuss this suggestion later.

We commonly find, usually beneath the woman's surname of origin, in addition to the name of the father, the Chinese words *mu* 母 'mother (of)' or '*ch'i*' 七 taken by White to stand for 妻 *ch'i* 'wife (of)', which also occurs occasionally; together with a man's name, in Chinese, usually given without a surname.

This suggests that the Register is one of wives (and mothers), and not of daughters. This view is supported by the fact that only 8 (or 9) [17] sets of sisters are mentioned, 5 pairs of known clan and father, and three other sets (of 2, 2, and 3 sisters respectively) of known father, but unknown clan. In one case only (No. 400) these sisters are given as married to different men (of one clan). We may note that 16 'eldest sisters', 6 'second sisters', 5 'third sisters', 4 'fourth sisters', 1 'fifth sister', 2 'sixth sisters' and 1 'seventh sister' are mentioned (in Chinese characters), all (except two only) being of Jewish fathers.

In addition to this, the women's surname of origin varies from page to page, and we can accept as almost certain White's view that the pages are arranged by the clans of the husbands (and sons). The following chart gives, modifying White, a list of which pages refer to which clans. It is based on the following (hardly contravertible) assumptions.

1. The women are actually arranged in some order based on husbands (and sons) and not fathers; this order must be based on the seven clans.

2. Pages continuing others are of the same clan.

[17] As against White, I take DW·MYN דו׳אמין (nos. 424, 434) to be a description, rather than a name.

3. Women of given surname are extremely unlikely to marry into this surname (though we have a problem with Jews and non-Jews of the same surname). Sometimes Hebrew-named fathers may be provisionally identified by clan, especially in the case of the rabbis. In which case intermarriage can again be checked.
4. Husbands or sons mentioned without surname can often be identified with certainty, an identification with a man of the same personal name in the Register of men of known clan being postulated. Sometimes the name given, though not found elsewhere, may resemble the names of members of a specific clan.

Chart No. 2.

The Clan Pages of the Register of Women

Page	*Notes*	*Clan*
66	No indication of clan given Intermarriage with Chang, Chin, Kao and non-Jewish Li	Unknown (Ai? or Li?) (White gave Ai?)
67-8	Li Hsiu; and 5 other men identifiable as of Li clan Intermarriage with all clans except Li	Li
69-70	Li Shu; and 3 other men identifiable as of Li clan Chang Wen-jui's maternal grandmother, mentioned here, married into the Li clan, for Wen-jui (see p. 83, no. 523, but cf. no. 524) had a mother of the Li clan Intermarriage with all clans except Chao and (Jewish) Li	Li
71	(Li) Ming-kao identifiable. (Li) Shao-t'ai found also on p. 69 (also of the Li clan) Intermarriage with Ai, Chang, Kao (and a non-Jewish Li)	Li
72	No indications Intermarriage with Hebrew-named women of Ai, Chao, Li	Unknown (White gave Ai?)
73-77	No indications Intermarriage with Chang, Chao, Kao, Li; and also (Hebrew-named) Ai, Shih	Ai?
78	No indications Intermarriage with Chin clan; and Ai and Kao (Hebrew-named)	Unknown (Chang?) (White gave Ai?)

Page	*Notes*	*Clan*
79	No indications Intermarriage with Chao, Li; and Hebrew-named Ai	Unknown (Chang?) (White gave Ai?)
80-81	Ai Chih; and 2 others of the Ai clan identifiable. But also perhaps (Chang) Ting, and (Chin) Ying-chi Intermarriage with Chao, Kao, Li, Shih	Ai? (White gave Ai and Chin? Ai and Chang?)
82	Possible identification of (Chao) Chin-hsiao Intermarriage with Li	Unknown (Chao? or Chang?) (White gave Chao)
83-84	12 members of Chang clan identifiable Intermarriage with Ai, Chin, Kao, Li, and non-Jewish Chao	Chang
85	6 members of Chang clan identifiable. Intermarriage with all but Chang and Chao	Chang
86	6 members of Chang clan identifiable Intermarriage with Ai, Kao, Li	Chang
87-91	No indications Intermarriage with all clans but Kao	Kao
92	Kao Wei-jung Intermarriage with Ai, Chin, Li, Shih and non-Jewish Chao	Kao
93	(Kao or Ai or Shih) Teng-k'uei also found elsewhere Intermarriage with Chao and Chin	Kao? (White gave Shih?)
94-96	Chao Ts'ui; and one other identifiable as of Chao clan Intermarriage with all but Chao and Shih	Chao
97-98	One man identifiable as of Chao clan The mother-in-law of Kao Wen-yü mentioned here presumably had a Chao daughter who married him Intermarriage with all clans except Chao and Chang	Chao (White gave Kao? for 98)
99-100	Blank	—
101-102	Chin Chih-jui Intermarriage with all clans except Chin and Shih	Chin (White gave Chao? for 101)
103	No indication Intermarriage with Ai, Chang, Chao, Li	Chin? (or Shih?) (White gave Shih?)
104	No indication Intermarriage with all except Shih and Ai	Shih.

We can feel certain of the clan pages for the Chang and also for the Li, for several husbands and sons are identifiable. There may of course be other unidentified pages belonging to these clans. These identifiable pages also confirm strongly our hypothesis that marriage within the clan does not occur. We are thus fairly confident in our ascription of the Chao, Kao and Chin pages, based on intermarriage and some identifications. Our real difficulty is with the Ai clan. It is perhaps the largest clan (expecially counting Hebrew names). We follow White's suggestion for pp. 73-77. But prefer to leave pp. 66, 72, 78 and 79 as "unknown", rather than White's Ai clan. If we take into account the clans of the Hebrew-named fathers, we find intermarriage for pp. 72-79 with all clans (especially the Ai clan) except the Chin clan. I have rejected this because of the following striking correlation of the pagination of the male and female clan pages.

Chart No. 3.

The Clan Pages

	Male	*Female*
Ai	26-27, 30-37	73-77? 80-81?
Li	28-29, 40-41, 44-5	67-71
Chang	38-39, 42-43, 46	78-79? 83-86; and 82?
Kao	47-52 (53 is blank)	87-92; and 93?
Chao	54-58	94-98
Chin	59-61	99-100 and 101? (renumbered from 101-103, for 99-100 are blank)
Shih	62-63	102 (renumbered from 104).

One interesting feature of the men's names is of importance here. A large number of cases occur of men having the same name, though usually of different clan. White has taken p. 93 as perhaps of the Shih clan, overlooking the fact that the name Teng-k'uei is found in the men's register under the Ai, Kao and Shih clans. This incidentally encourages us to postulate a few unregistered men of a given name even when such a man is found in the Register of Men under the 'wrong' clan. For example I do not accept as likely White's identifications of Chin Ying-chi with Ying-chi (p. 80, probably of the Ai clan); of Chang Ting with Ting (p. 81, probably of the Ai clan); of Chao Chin-hsiao with Chin-hsiao (p. 82, perhaps of the Chang clan).

We are now in a position to give the statistics of the women.

b. *The Statistics of the Women*

The women in the Register, 380 in all, may be subdivided as follows: —

Table No. 3.

The Women

	—	*Chaf* כ	Total
Daughters of Jewish fathers (Hebrew name, or Chinese name and surname), clan known	146	6	152
Hebrew-named daughters of Hebrew-named (Jewish) father; clan of origin not given	2	63	65
'Daughters of Israel', clan of origin known	50	—	50
'Daughters of Israel', clan of origin unknown	—	—	—
'Daughters of Adam', clan of origin known	81	9	90
Hebrew-named 'Daughters of Adam', clan of origin unknown	—	23	23
Total	279	101	380

We may subdivide those of known clan as in Table No 4

We have distributed women of named Jewish father but of unknown clan on the basis of probable identification of the father. These figures are given in brackets.

There are several points of interest which arise from these tables. We shall discuss later the full significance of the surnames of origin mentioned. But it is quite clear that the term 'daughter of Israel' refers to a woman of Jewish origin, and 'daughter of Adam' to a woman of non-Jewish origin.

The letter *chaf* כ occurs almost entirely (86 cases out of 101) for Hebrew-named women of unknown clan. I can see no completely satisfactory explanation of this. White's suggestion that these women were adopted into the clan is feasible, though it does not explain why

Table No. 4.

The Women by Clan of Origin

Surname of Origin	Of named Jewish father (Hebrew or Chinese)	'Daughter of Israel', father unnamed	*Chaf* כ daughter of known father	'Daughter of Adam'	Total
Ai	28 (+ 12)	12	1	—	41
Li	38 (+ 11)	17	—	6	55 (+ 6)
Chang	17 (+ 0)	6	—	2	23 (+ 2)
Kao	23 (+ 5)	1	3	1	27 (+ 1)
Chao	8 (+ 5)	4	—	4	12 (+ 4)
Chin	23 (+ 1)	5	2	—	30
Shih	9 (+ 2)	2	—	—	11
Unknown	— (+ 29)	—	—	—	—
Chou	—	2	—	—	2
Tso	—	1	—	—	1
Huang	—	—	—	1	0 + 1
Po	—	—	—	3	0 + 3
Others	—	—	—	73	0 + 73
Total	146 (+ 65)	50	6	90	292

some are named as daughters of Hebrew-named fathers, others 'daughters of Adam'. It seems unlikely that it can refer to conversion into the religion, for the 81 "daughters of Adam" of known non-Jewish clans were presumably converted at marriage. The possible explanation that these women are not given clan names because they were unmarried breaks down when we attempt to identify their fathers, for they are spread over the clans in the same manner as the others. Moreover who are the 23 (+ 9) *chaf* 'daughters of Adəm'? The total number of women of Jewish origin recorded is less than half that of the men. A likely explanation of this is that only those married are included. That is to say: all girls who died unmarried are not recorded. For the Register is one of wives and mothers only. We have no reason to suggest female infanticide.

The tabulation by clan of marriage is uncertain. We can suggest as probable: —

Table No. 5.

The Women by Clan of Marriage

Surname	Certain	Highly Probable	Probable	Distributed	Total
Ai	—	—	78	(13)	91
Li	56	—	—	(12)	68
Chang	43	—	—	(21)	64
Kao	11	55	5	—	71
Chao	—	44	—	(1)	45
Chin	—	20	11	—	31
Shih	—	10	—	—	10
Unknown	—	—	—	47	—
Total	110	129	94	47	380

The correlation of the women by clan of origin with that of the men of the Register is only fair. The figures for the women originating from the Chao and Chin clans perhaps correlate inversely with those for "Sons of Israel" of these clans. The correlation between the two tables, of women by clan of origin and by clan of marriage, is poor. That between the women by clan of marriage and the men is better. Any conclusions to be drawn are highly problematic.

The table of inter-marriage is also by necessity problematical. Only the Li and Chang clans can be considered as certainly known (at least in part).

Table No. 6.

Intermarriage

Surname	of mar-riage	Ai	Li	Chang	Kao	Chao	Chin	Shih
of origin		—	—	—	—	—	—	—
Ai	—	0 (+ 2)	10	4	9	11	2	—
Li	—	6 (+ 4)	[2]	9 (+ 1) + [1]	19	9 + [1]	7	3
Chang	—	1	9	—	4	1	2	3
Kao	—	4 (+ 1) + [1]	4	5	—	5	6	1
Chao	—	3 (+ 2) + [1]	3 (+ 1)	[1]	1 + [1]	—	1	1
Chin	—	—	6	7	5	7	—	1
Shih	—	1 (+ 1)	4	1	4	1	—	—
Others	—	10	14	11	20	9	2	1
Total		37	53	40	63	44	20	10

The figures in brackets ( ) refer to women of unnamed clan whose clan has been deduced from the Hebrew name of the father. Those in square brackets [ ] refer to 'daughters of Adam'. We see that the only exceptions to our rule forbidding marriage with the same surname are for the marriage of the Li clan with 2 women of the surname Li, but non-Jews; and the marriage within the Ai clan of two women of Hebrew-named fathers identifiable with fair probability as of the Ai clan.

It is because of this that we have been unable to guarantee the Ai clan pages in the Register of women. We have two possible explanations (if our pagination is correct). Firstly on the grounds that those with Hebrew names were probably less assimilated to the Chinese environment and such marriages might still have occurred. Secondly that only *chaf* daughters of the Ai clan are involved; and these might perhaps have been adopted into the clan, and thus marriage within the clan permissible.

Intermarriage was clearly common between the clans, except apparently between the Chang and Chao. Of the remaining surnames (mostly non-Jews), none are specially attached to any one clan. The Chin and Shih clans seem to have avoided marrying out of the religion more than the other clans. This may explain their survival (until the 19th century) equally with the other larger clans. It will also explain their relatively small numbers compared to the other clans.

D. The Men in the Register of Women

a. *The Fathers in the Register of Women*

The men mentioned in the Register of women may be divided up into fathers (of the clan of origin of the women), and husbands and sons (of the clan by marriage).

White (III, pp. 167-187), in his list of 437 Chinese-named men in the Register, includes fathers and husbands and sons of the Register of women. We have nothing to add to this list for the fathers with Chinese names. The fathers with Hebrew names may be listed as follows:

List No. 1.

The Fathers of known Clan with Hebrew Names in the Register of Women

Surname	Name	Page	Surname	Name	Page
Ai	Aaron	67, 69, 90	Kao	Asah (?)	69
	BTL·L	67		Benjamin	80
	Ezra	103		Bethuel	101
	Issachar	97, 85?		Isaiah	102
	Jeremiah	94		Joseph	66, 68
	R. Judah	84		Joshua	66, 96
	R. Mordecai	71, 95, 96		Judah	96
	Putiel	96		Zebulun	69
	Samuel	70			
	Shaphat	101	Chao	Aaron	68
	Zedaiah (?)	88		Heber	73
				Moses	104
Li	Eliezer	79		Phinehas	68
	Ithamar	84			
	Jacob	86, 91	Chin	Abram	67
	R. Jacob	88		Benjamin	66
	Jesse	101		Ephraim	95
	Joshua	84, 87, 91		Ezekiel	66, 87
	Judah	77		Jesse	94
	Moses	84, 91, 94		R. Joseph	83
	Simcha	81		Joshua	78
	R. Simcha	85		Mattithiah	85, 90
				Mordecai	93
Chang	Asher	87, 89			
	Cyrus	76	Shih	Berachah	88
	Gershon	66, 71		R. Eliezer	68
	Joseph	68		(Issachar)	85 ?
	Judah	88		Joseph	70
	Mordecai	71, 94		Solomon	85

For these fathers of named clan with Hebrew names, we can check against the Hebrew names in the Register of men. We find that all names in the Kao, Ai and Shih clans are mentioned in the Register of Men. But not: —

Asher	Chang clan
Cyrus	Chang clan
Eliezer	Li clan (though found in the Ai and Chin clans)
Heber	Chao clan
Joshua	Chin clan (but found commonly in the other clans)

Note that Zedaiah of the Ai clan is only found on pp. 32 and 34; and Judah and R. Jacob of the Li clan are not found in the pages of the Li clan except on pages 44 and 45, thus giving slight confirmation that these pages are truly of the Li clan.

Though we cannot guarantee our identifications, especially in the case of duplicates, the fit is excellent with only 5 names of 48 unaccounted for. The 6 rabbis are all found in the Register of men.

Several of the fathers with Hebrew names but of unnamed clan can also be identified with fair certainty, as may be seen in the following list.

List No. 2.

Fathers with Hebrew Names in the Register of Women, clan not given

Name	Page	Found in Men's Register in Clan
Aaron	79	Chao, Kao, Li
Abariah (?)	75	—
R. Abdiel	78	Ai, Li
R. Abraham	72	Chao
Adonijah	78	Ai
Amran	74	Ai, Li
Baruch	72	—
Bethuel	76	Ai, Kao
David	72	Ai
R. Eber	73	Li
Elijah	72, 74	Ai
Ephraim	67, 74	Chao, Chin, Li
Ezekiel	76	Chao, Chin, Kao, Li
GYRH	76	—
R. Halpon (?)	79	Ai
Hananiah	74	Ai
Hayyal (?)	77	Li
Hillel	73	—
Hosea	76	Li
Isaac	78	Kao
Isaiah	76	Kao
Issachar	76, 79	Ai, Chin, Kao, Li, Shih
Ithamar	83	Ai, Li
Jesse	89	Chin, Li
Job	73	Shih
Joseph	72, 75, 87	Ai, Chang, Chin, Kao, Li, Shih
Joshua	77, 78, 79	Ai, Kao, Li
Judah	75, 77	Ai, Chang, Chin, Kao, Li
R. Judah	68, 72, 103	Ai, Shih

Name	Page	Found in Men's Register in Clan
Mordecai	76	Ai, Chang, Chao, Chin, Shih
Moses	75, 76	all
R. Moses	72, 75	Li
MZYR	72	—
Naphtali	74	—
Nemuel	74	—
Phinehas	78	Chang, Chao, Li
RYHB	73	—
Salmuth (?)	77	—
Samuel	75, 76, 77	Ai, Kao, Li
Shemaiah	67, 75, 76	Chao
R. ŠLPWDYM	83	Li

We may note that several of these names, in particular those of most of the rabbis, are only found under one clan, giving quite a fair chance of identification.

Our statistics of the different names for the fathers are as follows:

Table No. 7.

The Fathers of the Register of Women

Surname	Chinese name	Hebrew name, clan given	Hebrew name, clan not given, probable distribution	Total
Ai	10	11	5 (+ 4)	30
Li	19	10	5 (+ 4)	38
Chang	7	6	— (+ —)	13
Kao	12	8	2 (+ 2)	24
Chao	3	4	2 (+ 1)	10
Chin	11	9	— (+ 1)	21
Shih	3	4 (or 5)	1 (+ 1)	9 (or 10)
Unknown	—	—	9 (+ 4)	13
Total	65	52 (or 53)	41	158 (or 159)

These figures naturally correlate extremely well with those for the women (table no. 4); but also quite well with those for the Register of Men.

b. *The Husbands and Sons in the Register of Women*

All the husbands and sons mentioned in the Register of Women, without exception, have Chinese names.

The following 8 men are named with surname:

Name	*Page*	*Relationship*
Ai Chih	81	Son
Chang Wen-jui	70	Grandson
Chao Ts'ui	94	Grandson (and son)
Chin Chih-jui	102	Husband
Kao Wei-jung	92	Husband
Kao Wen-yü	98	Son-in-law
Li Hsiu	67	Son
Li Shu	69	Husband

Of these, Li Shu is found in the Register of Men, nos. 145, 146; and as a father in the Register of Women, nos. 389, 506, 714. Chang Wen-jui is found in the 1663b Inscription. Of the 8 names, 3 are not the normal husband or son, but grandson or son-in-law, requiring perhaps a surname to guarantee identification. Alternatively these men (all but Li Shu) were still alive and not mentioned in the Register of men, hence the surname.

In addition 35 men without surnames are mentioned as husbands, and 33 as sons. The following list gives their identification by clan and the evidence for this identification. It is intimately connected with the chart of the page numbers in the Register of Women (given above); for each reinforces the identification of the other.

List No. 3.

The Husbands and Sons of the Register of Women

Page	Name	Clan	Relationship	Found elsewhere with Clan given	If not found, similar named men of the Clan.
67	Fa-t'ien	Li	Son, Grandson	1663a Inscription. Cf. P. 69 (also Li Clan).	
	Li Hsiu	Li	Son		
	Ying-yüan	Li	Son	no. 139; (also found in Chin)	
68	Ch'eng-hsien	Li	Son	1663a, 1663b Inscriptions	
	Shou-chiao	Li	Husband		Chin
	Yen-shou	Li	Son	No. 518 as father.	
	Yen-nien	Li	Husband	No. 140	

List No. 3 (*Continued*)

Page	Name	Clan	Relationship	Found elsewhere with Clan given	If not found, similar named men of the Clan.
69	Li Shu	Li	Husband	Nos. 145, 146, and also 389, 506, 714 as father.	
	Fa-t'ien	Li	Son	1663a Inscription. Cf. p. 67 above.	
	Shao-t'ai	Li	Husband	Cf. p. 71.	
70	Chin-chü	Li	Son		Li, Chao, Chang
	Yüan-liang	Li	Son		Kao, Chao
	Chang Wen-jui	Chang	Grandson	1663b Inscription	
	Tzu-hsing	Li	Husband	Nos. 157, 161	
	Hsing-wu	Li	Husband		
	Jui-ch'i	Li	Son		
71	Chien-huan	Li	Husband		Ai
	Ming-kao	Li	Son	No. 151	
	Shao-t'ai	Li	Husband	Cf. p. 69 (also of the Li Clan)	
80	Fa-chih	Ai?	Son, grandson		
	Wei-yi	Ai?	Son	1663b Inscription.	
	Tzu-cho	Ai?	Husband		Ai, Li, Shih
	Ying-chi	Ai? or Chin?	Husband	(No. 309, Chin Clan)	Ai, Chao, Kao, Li
81	Sheng-chih	Ai?	Husband	No. 104; 1663b Inscription	
	Ai Chih	Ai	Son		
	Tzu-ch'eng	Ai?	Son		Ai, Li, Shih
	Kuei-lin	Ai?	Son		Ai
	Shih-yün	Ai?	Son		Ai, Chang, Li
	Ting	Ai? or Chang?	Husband	(No. 124, 125, Chang Clan)	
82	Chin-hsiao	Chang? or Chao?	Husband	(No. 282, 284, Chao Clan)	Chang, Chao, Li

List No. 3 (*Continued*)

Page	Name	Clan	Relationship	Found elsewhere with Clan given	If not found, similar named men of the Clan.
83	Chü-jung	Chang	Son		Chang, Ai
	Wen-chün	Chang	Son	Nos. 127, 175, and also 695 as father	
	Wen-chi	Chang	Son, husband	No. 162	
	Wen-jui	Chang	Son	No. 399 as grandson, 1663b Inscription.	
	Mei	Chang	Son	No. 175. Cf. p. 84, 85, 86 (also of Chang clan)	
	Hsiu	Chang	Son	(No. 369, Li Clan)	
	Wen-hsiang	Chang	Husband	No. 163	
	Shih-yin	Chang	Son		Ai, Li
84	Ta-lun	Chang	Husband	No. 117	
	Ta-pen	Chang	Husband	No. 116, 165	
	Teng-ti	Chang	Husband		Ai, Kao, Li Shih.
	Chiu-te	Chang	Son	No. 173	
	San-chi	Chang	Son	Cf. p. 85 (also of Chang clan)	
	San-shan	Chang	Son		Chang
	San-te	Chang	Son	No. 183	
	T'ien	Chang	Husband	No. 175	
	Chih	Chang	Husband	No. 176. Cf. p. 85 (also of Chang clan)	
	Mei	Chang	Husband	No. 175. Cf. p. 83, 85, 86 (also of Chang clan)	
85	Mei	Chang	Husband	No. 175. Cf. p. 83, 84, 86 (also of Chang clan)	
	Chih	Chang	Husband	No. 176. Cf. p. 84, (also of Chang clan)	
	Fa	Chang	Husband	No. 176	
	Hsing	Chang	Husband	No. 175	
	Sheng	Chang	Husband	No. 176	
	San-chi	Chang	Husband	Cf. p. 84 (also of Chang clan)	
	Hsiang-yü	Chang	Foster-son		
	Li	Chang	Husband	No. 178	
	Hsin-yü	Chang	Husband		Ai, Chang

List No. 3 (Continued)

Page	Name	Clan	Relation-ship	Found elsewhere with Clan given	If not found, similar named men of the Clan.
86	San-kuei	Chang	Son		Chang
	Mei	Chang	Husband	No. 175. Cf. p. 83, 84, 85 (also of Chang clan)	
	Lung	Chang	Son	No. 184	
	Hsi-chao	Chang	Husband	No. 173	
	Hsi-k'ung	Chang	Husband	No. 173	
	Chin-te	Chang	Husband	No. 173	
	Hsi-li	Chang	Husband	No. 173	
	Hsiu-chi	Chang	Son		
92	Kao Wei-jung	Kao	Husband		
	Tung-cheng	Kao	Husband		Kao
93	Teng-k'uei	Kao?	Husband	No. 208; (also no. 19, Ai Clan; and 337, Shih clan) 1663a Inscription	Ai, Kao, Li Shih
	Yüan-liang	Kao?	Son		Chao, Kao, Li
	Yüan-pi	Kao?	Son		Chao, Kao, Li
94	Hsing	Chao	Husband		
	Chao Ts'ui	Chao	Son, grandson		
	Yün-chung	Chao	Son	1663a, b Inscriptions	
	Chien	Chao	Son		
96	Yüan-hsiang	Chao	Son		Chao, Kao, Li
97	Ying-tou	Chao	Husband	1663a, b, 1679 Inscriptions, and other inscriptions	
98	Kao Wen-yü	Kao	Son-in-law		
	Chiu-wu	Chao	Husband		Chang, Li
102	Kuang	Chin	Husband, Son		
	Chin Chih-jui	Chin	Husband.		

The statistics of the husbands and sons are as follows:

Table No. 8.

Husbands and Sons of the Register of Women

Surname	Husbands	Sons	Both as husbands and sons	Total
Ai	0 (+ 2?)	1 (+ 5?)	—	1 (+ 7?)
Li	7	9	—	16
Chang	15	11	3	29
Kao	2 (+ 1?)	0 (+ 2?)	—	2 (+ 3?)
Chao	3	4	—	7
Chin	1	—	1	2
Shih	—	—	—	—
Unknown	3	—	—	3
Total	34	32	4	70

Four of these men (sons) are also mentioned as grandsons. One other (Chang clan) is a foster-son, and another (Kao clan) a son-in-law.

Some are listed with more than one wife.

Chang Mei, husband of	Kao, Wang, Hou wives,	p. 84
	Jen, Li wives,	p. 85
	Wu wife,	p. 86
Chang Chih, husband of	Chin wife,	p. 84
	Su wife,	p. 85
Chao Ying-tou, husband of	Ch'i, Fang wives,	p. 97
Li Shao-t'ai, husband of	Ch'en wife,	p. 69
	Ch'en wife	p. 71

We may note that none of these are married to more than one wife of Jewish origin.

Two men are listed as sons of more than one mother:

Li Fa-t'ien,	with mother of Jen clan,	p. 67
	with mother of Chu clan,	p. 69
Chang Wen-jui,	with mother of Li clan,	p. 83
	with mother of Hsü clan,	p. 83

If we assume that only one man is involved in each case, we must accept that the father had married two wives, both of whom are considered to be mothers.

We must beware of reading too much into these statistics for it seems that only certain clans recorded the (Chinese) names of husbands and sons of the women recorded. It is perhaps significant that the Chang, Li and Chao clans seem to have done so more than the others. For the Chang and Chao clans, and to a certain extent the Li clan, seem also to have comparatively more Chinese-named members and more unknown "sons of Israel", though fewer women recorded.

c. *New Names in the Register of Women*

As we have seen, a large number of the names in the Register of Women, both Hebrew and Chinese, can be identified with fair certainty in the Register of Men. The following table gives the number of men mentioned not identifiable in the Register of Men (out of a total of 225 names).

Table No. 9.

Men in the Register of Women not found in the Register of Men

Surname	Hebrew-named father	Chinese-named father	Surnamed husbands and sons	Other husbands and sons not mentioned as fathers	Total
Ai	—	8	1	6 (+ 2)	15 (+ 2)
Li	1	8	1	9	19
Chang	2	2	1	10 (+ 1)	15 (+ 1)
Kao	—	5	2	1 (+ 2)	8 (+ 2)
Chao	1	—	1	6	8
Chin	1	3	1	1	6
Shih	—	1	—	—	1
Unknown	9	—	—	5 (→ 0)	14
Total	14	27	7	38	86

This figure of 38% (86 out of 225) not found in the Register of Men is not high, especially when we consider that c. 12% (c. 89 of 696) of the men mentioned in the Register of Men are fathers, otherwise unknown. A large number of the 86 must be assumed to have been still alive at the time of compilation of the Register. The fact that very few Hebrew names are unaccounted for also fits. For more

Chinese-named men would be alive at the time of compilation of the Memorial.

In the following parts of this article we will be dealing also with the living members of the community who were responsible for compiling this Memorial Book for the dead.

(*To be continued*)

Canberra 1964.

OPENING AND CLOSING NARRATIVES IN THE GOSPELS AND ACTS

BY

BARBARA THIERING

The question of the abrupt ending of St Mark's Gospel has recently been revived by Dr Austin Farrer [1]. He maintains in both his essays on the subject that the original final scene was, as the textual evidence indicates, that of the terrified women fleeing from the empty tomb, although in the later work he argues for an original final sentence describing the apostolic mission.

The mystery of the inconclusive ending of Acts remains unsolved. Dr R. Morgenthaler [2] gives a summary of conjectures that have been made to explain it, even including (with suitable comment) that '*das Papier sei Lukas ausgegangen*!' He himself agrees with Bengel that Luke leaves Paul in Rome because he has thereby reached the summit of the geographical-theological plan of Luke-Acts. Yet he does not deal with the objection that the reader naturally expects to be told the outcome of the trial, and not to be left in contemplation of St Paul in comfortable captivity.

Two inconclusive endings out of five books arouse one's curiosity. To these problems may be added that of the unique endings of Matthew (in which alone Jesus is found on a mountain in Galilee), of Luke (in which alone the disciples visit the Temple), and John (in which alone Peter receives forgiveness).

Thus the endings of all five books represent a minor problem of one kind or another. Furthermore, the opening section of each contains unique material, some of which attracts attention by its unexpectedness. Matthew alone begins with a genealogy, and most of his birth-stories, including that of the slaughter of the innocents, are unique. Mark begins with the phrase 'the beginning of the gospel . . .', which is a little strange in the light of the fact that he intends to narrate more than the beginning. Luke opens with the original tale of the birth of John the Baptist, and the arresting introduction to John's Gospel has no parallel elsewhere. Admittedly there is much original material within the body of these works also, but it is nevertheless striking that four books which tell the same story and are so dependent on each other should yet contrive to begin in such diverse ways.

The hypothesis is here put forward that one rule, a rule of literary composition, is responsible for this succession of small problems. It seems that each of the authors concerned included in his opening and closing narratives a parallel or allusion to the opening and closing narratives of a particular O.T. book. Thus, the opening and closing narratives of both Mark and John allude to the corresponding passages in Genesis, Matthew to those of Exodus-Deuteronomy, and Luke-Acts to those of I Samuel-II Kings.

This observation does not preclude the use of other O.T. books and sequences in both the extremes and the main body of these works, but it appears to be one at least of the systematic uses of the O.T. which the authors of the New Covenant observed [3].

It is axiomatic that the opening passage of John's Gospel alludes to Genesis 1. But it appears to have escaped notice that the story which almost concludes John's Gospel (21: 15-17), that of the forgiveness of Peter, with the command, 'Feed my sheep', contains echoes of the story that is second last in Genesis, in which Joseph's brothers come to him for forgiveness for having betrayed him. Joseph 'comforted them, and spake kindly unto them', and said: 'I will nourish you, and your little ones'. (Gen. 50: 21).

Mark also appears to have had Genesis in mind, as his opening phrase, 'the beginning' would indicate to any Jewish reader, for whom 'Bereshith' was the proper name as well as the opening word of Genesis. It is possible that Mark's opening succession of events may owe something to the order of events in Gen. 1-3, although this may be no more than coincidence. The parallels are as follows:

Genesis	*Mark*
'The beginning' (1: 1)	'The beginning' (1: 1)
(Creation of the world)	(John the Baptist's mission)
First appearance of Adam (1: 26-7)	First appearance of Jesus (1: 9-11)
Temptation of Adam (3: 1-21)	Temptation of Jesus (1: 12-13)
Adam begins his work (3: 23-4)	Jesus begins his work (14-15)
Adam begets two sons (4: 1-2)	Jesus calls two sets of brothers as disciples (1: 16-20)

In the last chapter of Genesis, after Jacob 'yielded up the ghost', Joseph sent to Pharaoh to ask for the body of his father, in order to bury it in a cave in his own land (50: 4-13). Mark parallels this in 15: 39 and 15: 43-46. Finally, Joseph himself died, and Genesis ends very abruptly with 'he was put in a coffin in Egypt'. The tradition of the removal of Joseph's bones from the coffin in Egypt to his own land is prominent within the Bible itself: the instruction to do so immediately precedes the verse in question (Gen. 50: 25). It is the only detail given of Joseph in the list of the heroes of faith in Heb. 11 (v. 22), and it is also referred to indirectly in the summary of O.T. history in Acts 7 (vv 15-16).

Is it therefore too much to conjecture, in view of the literary principle now emerging, that it is this final passage of Genesis, the story of Joseph's (subsequently) empty tomb, which is the chief controlling factor in the termination of Mark's Gospel at the empty tomb of Jesus?

Matthew, it would appear, is concerned with the remainder of the 'Christian Pentateuch'. His parallels to the opening of Exodus and the close of Deuteronomy are in accordance with his emphasis on Jesus as another Moses, who is the hero of Exodus-Deuteronomy.

Exodus opens with a very brief genealogy, a list of the names of the twelve sons of Israel. It is significant that its opening phrase 'these are the names of', 'We'elleh Shemoth', gave its title to the book, thus bringing the genealogy more prominently to the memory than its length would justify. Matthew begins in the same way, and includes among his birth-narratives a parallel to Exodus' account of the slaughter of the innocents and the hiding of the child in Egypt.

Matthew's Gospel closes with the scene of Jesus on a mountain, commanding the disciples to go forth and conquer the world in his name. Parallels with the classical scene at the end of Deuteronomy, in which Moses on a mountain surveys the lands that are to be entered, must again have been obvious to the Jewish reader.

Luke-Acts contains allusions in the appropriate places to the corresponding passages in the historical books of I Samuel-II Kings inclusive. Note that the division between I and II Samuel was not made until the fifteenth century A.D. in Hebrew Bibles, although it was made in the LXX [4]. The case with I and II Kings was the same [5], but Luke seems to have recognised some division, as will be shown. The Gospel thus corresponds to I-II Samuel, and Acts to I-II Kings.

I Samuel opens with the story of the birth of Samuel to barren parents of great piety. Allusions to this in Luke's birth-story of John the Baptist are clear and frequent. Hannah's prayer in I Sam. 2 is also well-known to be the model for the Magnificat. The textual evidence supporting the ascription of this song to Elisabeth rather than Mary [6] would make the parallel stronger. The allusions to the child Samuel in the story of Jesus' childhood visit to the Temple have been recognised by Daube and others [7].

At first sight there appears to be no clear allusion to the ending of II Samuel in the final narrative of Luke's Gospel. The last story in II Sam. is that of the purchase of the threshing-floor of Araunah the Jebusite. The link with Luke's closing verse: 'and were continually in the temple, blessing God', is seen when a fact of common knowledge to Jewish readers is pointed out: that the threshing-floor of Araunah the Jebusite became the site of the Temple (II Chron. 3: 1).

I Kings 1 is chiefly concerned with the story of the attempted usurpation of David's throne by Adonijah. Eventually the rightful heir, Solomon, is put in his place (I K. 1: 39), and Adonijah is put to death (I K. 2: 23-5). It may be no more than a coincidence that Acts, after the introduction (1: 1-11) opens with the story of the replacement of Judas in the number of the apostles, and of Judas' death, but the possibility of a deliberate allusion to the opening of I Kings cannot be overlooked in view of Luke's use of other parallels in the appropriate places.

In assessing the weight of the allusions at the end of Luke and the beginning of Acts, it should be kept in mind that Luke-Acts is essentially a unity, just as the four books of Kings were regarded as closely connected. (Note that the appearance of Jesus in Luke and the opening scene of Acts corresponds to the appearance of David in I-II Sam. and the opening scene of I Kings). The strongest parallels appear to have been reserved for the beginning of Luke and the ending of Acts.

It is generally conceded that Acts falls into two parts: chs. 1-12, and 13-end. It is at this point that Luke seems to have recognised the two divisions of the book of Kings, without, however, making a clear break.

An interesting series of parallels with the last chapter of I Kings and the first two chapters of II Kings occupies Acts 12: 20-20: 38, i.e. the whole account of Paul's missionary journeys. These, of course, are minor themes only in a great deal of narrative material which has no connection with the O.T. book, but the strength of the parallels, and the fact that they appear in the same order as in the O.T., would seem to indicate the deliberate adoption of a literary device, that of systematic O.T. allusions, in this section.

The parallels, in order, are as follows:

I Kings 22: 41-53	Acts 12: 20-24
Spectacular death of the wicked king Ahab	Spectacular death of the wicked king Herod.
I Kings 22: 41-53	Acts 13-20
Acts of Jehoshaphat parallel those of kings previously recorded (e.g., sending ships of Tarshish to Ophir, cf. Solomon I Kings 9: 26-8; removal of sodomites, cf. Asa I Kings 15: 12)	Acts of Paul parallel those of Peter etc. in early part of Acts (see *HDB*, art. 'Acts')
I Kings 22: 49	Acts 15: 36-40
Jehoshaphat refuses to let Ahaziah's servants go in his ships	Paul refuses to let Barnabas' protege (John Mark) go with him.
I Kings 22: 53	Acts 19: 23-41
Worship of Baal	Worship of Diana
II Kings 1: 1-17	Acts 20: 7-12
Ahaziah falls down from a window in an upper chamber, and dies (v. 17)	Eutychus falls down from a window in an upper chamber, and dies.
II Kings 2: 1-12	Acts 20: 17-38
Elijah bids farewell to Elisha, as he is to go to Jordan and die.	Paul bids farewell to the elders of Ephesus, as he is to go to Jerusalem, perhaps to die.

The opening section of Luke's Gospel has provided a strong series of parallels to the opening of I Samuel. One looks therefore to the end of II Kings for an explanation of the problematic ending of Acts, and this explanation is immediately manifest. The concluding passage of II Kings is as follows:

'Evil-merodach king of Babylon . . . did lift up the head of Jehoiachin king of Judah out of prison; and he spake kindly to him, and set his throne above the throne of the kings that were with him in Babylon. And he changed his prison garments, and did eat bread before him continually all the days of his life. And for his allowance, there was a continual allowance given him of the king, every day a portion, all the days of his life'. (II K. 25: 27b-30, R.V.)

As with the ending of Mark, it would appear that the corresponding passage in the O.T. model has been the chief controlling factor in causing Luke to cease his narrative at this point, where his prisoner is left in comfortable captivity under the protection of the king of the 'new Babylon'. As Luke-Acts opens with a strong parallel to the opening of I Samuel, it closes with a strong parallel to the closing of II Kings. Whether this literary device has been operative in the creation, or simply in the selection of material is a question which it is beyond the scope of this article to discuss, but the existence and placing of these parallels is a fact which must be taken into account in any study of these passages.

Several observations should be made about the use of the literary device here demonstrated:

1) It is the controlling factor in the presentation of a small portion of the material only in each of the N.T. passages concerned. Each contains much original material, as well as references to other parts of the O.T. To observe the use of this device is to pick out one thread only, albeit a significant one, from a number of interwoven threads.

2) The opening and closing sections of the Gospels and Acts may also contain independent narratives which have no parallel in the corresponding positions in the O.T. models. Eg., in Matthew several birth-stories without parallel in Exodus 1 intervene between the genealogy and the slaughter of the innocents.

3) Application of the device ranges from extended parallels, such as Luke's birth story of John the Baptist, to such a brief allusion as Luke's reference to the Temple in the final verse of his Gospel.

With these reservations, the use of the device of paralleling opening and closing narratives appears to be well enough established to add fresh evidence to current studies of the extent to which N.T. writers have made systematic use of the Old Testament. This evidence also seems conclusive enough to establish the fact that the present endings of Mark and Acts are, in fact, original.

NOTES

[1] *A Study in St. Mark*, 1951; *St. Matthew and St. Mark*, 1964.

[2] R. Morgenthaler, *Die lukanische Geschichtsschreibung als Zeugnis*, 1 Teil, pp. 188-194.

[3] See C. F. Evans, 'The Central Section of Luke's Gospel' in *Studies in the Gospels*, ed. D. E. Nineham, Oxford, 1955, pp. 37ff., where Luke's systematic use of Deuteronomy is maintained; also Jacob J. Enz, 'The Book of Exodus as a Literary Type for the Gospel of John', *JBL* LXXVI, 1957, p.p 208-16; also A. Guilding, *The Fourth Gospel and Jewish Worship*, Oxford, 1960.

[4] See art., I and II Samuel, Peake's Commentary (new version).

[5] See art., 'Kings', *HDB*.

[6] Some OL MSS, texts known to Origin, and Irenaeus (Adv. Haer. LI IV, vii, 1 in some MSS).

[7] D. Daube, *The N.T. and Rabbinic Judaism*, 1956, p. 13, and Creed, *The Gospel According to St. Luke*, 1930.

A HISTORICO-PHILOLOGICAL SURVEY OF THE MAIN DEAD SEA SCROLLS AND RELATED DOCUMENTS

BY

A. MURTONEN

The purpose of this article is to give a general outline of the linguistic development reflected by the Dead Sea Scrolls. The main sources upon which the investigation is based are the larger Isaiah scroll, the commentary on the Book of Habakkuk, the Book of Hymns (or Thanksgivings), the Manual of Discipline (in both the shorter and longer forms), and the scroll of the War of the Sons of Light against the Sons of Darkness. For purposes of comparison and supplementation, the smaller fragments thus far published are also used. For the reconstruction of the history of the sect, which serves as a background for the linguistic development, we also use the so-called Zadokite Document, the main manuscripts of which were discovered in the Cairo Geniza towards the end of the last century.

For the main documents a shorter terminology is used than that established by Barthelemy and Milik in *Qumran Cave I*; it is based on that used by Gaster in his translation, with such augmentation and modification as was necessary: *Is a* for the large Isaiah scroll; *H* for the Book of Hymns, *HC* for the Habakkuk Commentary, *M* for the Manual of Discipline, *MFC* for the Manual for the Future Congregation, *W* for the War scroll, *Z a* for the original form of the Zadokite Document, which is preserved in a more complete form (Ms. A), and *Z b* for the later revision of which only a fragment is preserved (Ms. B).

I

The historical sketch is also intended to keep within the limits defined in the rubric, and is therefore based mainly on linguistic arguments. Accordingly, it cannot raise the claim of conclusiveness; but if the presumably historical references in the scrolls can be explained on that basis, it can be said to have a high degree of probability. To put it on trial from the beginning, we choose the beginning of Z a as our starting point, under the assumption that it is not *only* a collection of Biblical and other pious quotations and allusions, but *also* contains reflections on the history of the sect, even if not in a strictly chronological sequence. It seems to me that the document is one coherent whole, although not completely preserved, and that its compiler, consciously or unconsciously, imitated the composition of the Book of Deuteronomy. It may be no accident that this book is rather prominently represented among the texts discovered. The sect was preparing its members for a war of conquest, just as the situation is pictured in Deuteronomy, where the outcome is also 'expected' to be a clear-cut victory.

On the first page, after a general introduction of two lines, the first probably historical allusion is the statement that God hid His face, i.e., withdrew His favour from Israel and from His own Temple, because of the sin they had committed in forsaking Him. Rabin thinks this is an allusion to Lev xxvi 40, but it has not one single word in common with that verse, apart from the relative particle, and even the similarity in contents is very vague and limited to the first half of the sentence. Since the idea of God's hiding His face normally means that He abandons people to their own fortunes, and this can hardly be said of the events connected with the Maccabaean revolt, the most plausible remaining alternative—because of the express mention of the Temple—is the first revolt against the Romans, the outcome of which can be regarded with good reason as such a punishment. The apostasy referred to is probably the usurpation of the office of the High Priest by non-Zadokite, illegitimate families, and the general failure of the people to join the sect.

On the fourth line, a more detailed account is begun by the word *wbzkrw*, to be translated: 'For as long as he remembered . . .'; 'the covenant of the first ones' probably refers to the High Priesthood of the Aaronides, suspended by the destruction of the Temple. 'The epoch of wrath' would refer to the Seleucid persecution; the fact that it did not commence *exactly* 390 years after the desctrution of Jerusalem by Nebuchadnezzar should not be given too much significance, since it anyway came closer to that figure than that calculated by the author of the Book of Daniel; and if we assume that the author —in retrospect—counted the 'period of wrath' from the beginning of the Seleucid domination, the correspondence is practically as exact as one can wish. It is quite possible that the author, a member of an extreme national-religious party, regarded not only the active persecution, but also the persuasive hellenization preceding it as a sign of Divine wrath; and the priestly members of the sect could have been capable of more exact calculation than the author of the Book of Daniel. The 'root of plantation' grown up from 'Aaron and Israel' naturally refers to the sect; the verb *pqd* is accordingly used in a positive sense, as in Gen. l. 25 etc. The consciousness of their sinfulness well fits the moral code and extreme apocalyptic character of the sect; but the practical organization did not take place until after about 20 years from the commencement of the movement, under the leadership of a man to whom is assigned the title, *More Ṣædæq* or 'The Right Teacher' [1]. With the last word of l. 11 a further elaboration of the events of the Seleucid persecution and its consequence begins; l. 12 first states that what God has done to 'the congregation of apostates' (apparently the Jews who did not join the sect) He has made known to 'the generations of the last ones' (i.e., the sect) as a warning example. The scoffer on l. 14 seems to stand for both Jason and Menelaos; maybe the memory of the former had faded by the time our author was writing; 'the pride of the world' in l. 15 may, as Rabin suggests, be a result of conflation between Hab. iii 6 and Isa. ii 17—i.e., God, and the statement may therefore refer to the consecration of the Temple to Zeus; it is not expressly stated to be the work of the scoffer, but a consequence of his activity. 'The removal of the landmark', l. 16, apparently again refers to the usurpation of the High Priesthood by non-legitimate families; the preceding word *ṣdq* may be an allusion to the rightful one. 'The seekers of smooth things', l. 18, can be understood easily as a further reference to the Hellenists and in ll. 19-20, 'the righteous one' has close resemblance to the last legitimate High Priest, Onias III, with a view to his death; those that 'pronounced the wicked one righteous' accordingly include the party of Hasmonaeans and their successors in High Priesthood. Those that did not approve of their claims were persecuted —l. 21—; as a consequence—according to the author—God's wrath was kindled against them, which culminated in the sweeping away of 'all their multitude'—when the revolt against the Romans was crushed; this showed that 'their deeds only contributed to make them unclean before Him' (p. ii, 1).

It is against this background that we have to examine certain terminological developments in non-Biblical texts. First of all, it is instructive to view the development of the priestly title. In W, the only attribute assigned to priests is 'the sons of Aaron' (vii 9). In MFC, this attribute still occurs twice (? once partly restored) in connection with the title of priests, but in no further documents published so far. On the other hand, in the same document priests are three times called also 'the sons of Zadoq', in one case in an identical context with the partly restored case of 'sons of Aaron' (i 24 and 15-16, respectively). Considering the fact that some documents appear to be revised later on, the variation at first seemed to be due to the same factor; however, there are no more objective clues suggesting such a revision in this small document, and therefore it may be safer to assume that there is some difference in meaning, comparable to the practical difference between high-priestly families and common priests in late post-exilic Judaism generally. Also the expression, '*from* the sons of Aaron' in W is suggestive of such a difference. We could thus conclude that these two documents still represent the general Judaistic position in this respect. On the other hand, in M only the attribute 'the sons of Zadoq' is used of the priests (v 2, 9); and conversely, it is not used of anybody else. True, in ix 14 the reference is not clear; but the article before *ṣdwq* seems to indicate that the word here has a different meaning (perhaps we should read *haṣṣidduq* and take the title as referring to the sect in general, as those that have been declared just by God). Accordingly M seems to represent a stage where the difference between Aaronite and Zadokite priesthood has been systematically worked out and only the latter recognized as legitimate. This is well comprehensible with a view to the high-priestly schism leading to the Maccabaean revolt, and the subsequent usurpation of the office by the Maccabaeans and Hasmonaeans. Since our sect adhered strictly to the legitimate Zadokite line, but the legitimate heir apparently did not join them, the distinction between the 'sons of Zadoq' and the other priests in the Book of Ezekiel was interpreted in this way (cf. Z a iii 21 sq.) to make a practical distinction between the sectarian priests and the other ones possible—the former might have belonged to Zadokite families altogether. Finally, in Z we find the terms 'priests' and 'sons of Zadoq' as designations for *different groups*, both interpreted metaphorically (iv 2 and 3-4, respectively): 'priests' are *those of* the 'returned ones' of Israel (i.e., of the members of the original sect) who left the land of Judah, while the sons of Zadoq are 'the chosen ones of Israel called by name which are going to stand up at the end of time'. On the ground of this terminology, it seems that W and MFC were written either before, or early in the Maccabaean period, when the non-legitimate men or families had not yet assumed the High Priesthood, or there was in any case hope of its not remaining permanently so; M would have been compiled during the subsequent period, when things were more settled and the headquarters of the sect probably in Qumran; while Z a would derive from the time after the destruction of the Temple and apparently the Qumran 'monastery' in connection with the so-called First Jewish Revolt, compiled by the part of the sect which left Judah and fled to the region of Damascus before the final catastrophe—those that joined the revolt with the other Jews were stamped as apostates; Z a iii 10-12 probably deals with them, cf. the subsequent lines and iv 11, which clearly presupposes that there were such persons: '. . . there will *no longer* be affiliation to the house of Judah . . .' The fact that only Z describes the sect as dwelling in the land of Damascus also strongly suggests that the reference is historical, not metaphorical; the reference to the return 'from the wilderness of the nations' in W i 3 apparently means the return from the war outlined on the following pages; and since it seems clear by now that the sect had to abandon their headquarters about 70 A.D. and yet it continued to exist after that time, there must be some place where they went; and 'the land of Damascus' is the only one possible mentioned in the literature of the sect. Therefore it should not be dismissed so lightly at this stage, when the relations of the different documents are far from worked out. The fact that fragments of Z a were found in the 'small' Qumran caves shows only that some members of the remaining sect at least revisited the place of their earlier headquarters—perhaps in order to participate in the Bar Cochba rebellion in defiance of the decree (iv 11, cf. above); the fragments found can very well have been left behind accidentally when the place was abandoned again. The passage xi 17-21 does not presuppose the existence of the temple either, except hypothetically (cf. Talmud and—theoretically—Deuteronomy). This conclusion is further corroborated by the revision reflected by Z b. The crucial passage is Z a vii 10 to viii 5, and the corresponding passage in Z b. In Z a, it runs as follows: '. . . when that word *came* true which is written in the words of the prophet Isaiah son of Amoz, who has said: "A time will come upon you, your people, and your family the like of which has (not) come since Ephraim turned away from Judah"; when the two houses of Israel separated, Ephraim became ruler over Judah and all the backsliders were delivered to sword; but those that remained steadfast escaped to the land of North—as it is said, "I shall exile the tabernacles of your King and the establishment (?) of your images from my tent to Damascus"—the books of the Law are the tabernacles of the King, as it is said, "I shall erect the fallen tabernacle(s?) of David". The King is God [2], and the establishment of the images are the books of the prophets the words of which Israel despised; and the star is the expounder of the Law who came to Damascus, as it is written: "A star has stepped forth from Jacob, and a sceptre stood up from Israel"; the sceptre is the prince of the whole congregation; when he stands up, he strikes shatteringly all the sons of Seth. These they let escape during the first epoch of visitation, but the backsliders they delivered to the sword; and so it will be with all that join His covenant, but do not hold fast to these, so that they will be doomed to extinction through Belial; it is the day when God will visit; the princes of Judah have become those on which the wrath is poured; they hope for healing, but all rebels will break their teeth because they did not withdraw from the way of traitors . . .' In Z b, this is replaced by the following section: '. . . When that word *will come* true which is written by the hand of the prophet Zechariah, "Sword, awake against my shepherd and against my confidant, is the saying of God, smite the shepherd that the flock will be dispersed; but I shall bring back my hand upon the shepherd boys"; but those that keep an eye on him are the poor of the flock; these will escape at the time of the visitation, while the rest will be delivered to the sword, when the Messiah of Aaron and Israel will come. As it was at the epoch of the first [3] visitation, as it is said through Ezekiel: " . to draw the cross on the foreheads of those that sigh and groan"; while the rest was delivered to the sword which executed the vengeance of the covenant. And so it will be with all those that join His covenant, but do not hold fast to these decrees, so that they will be doomed to extinction through Belial; it is the day when God will visit, as He has spoken, "The princes of Judah have become as those that remove the landmark; upon them I shall pour wrath like water"; for they entered the covenant of repentance, but did not withdraw from the way of traitors . . .'

Rabin believes that there is a gap in the text in Z b after the word *ktwb* 'is written', since *byd* is nowhere else attested following that term; but in DSS there are many other 'unorthodox' terms and combinations, and *in its present shape* the text contains this combination in any case; this shows that the latest copyist did *not* find anything strange in it—hence, is it impossible that the original compiler of Z b did not, either? That so wide a gap as Rabin supposes

—i.e., which could have contained the whole parallel section of Z a—would have been created by oversight does not seem possible, as the space over which the scribe should be supposed to have shifted his eyes would cover a considerable number of lines in any ms., and supposing he overlooked a whole column the odds against the probability of two subsequent columns starting with essentially similar expressions and one scribe omitting the first, the other one the second of them and only these two in that way defective texts surviving—are literally astronomical. Hence, we must conclude that the section in Z a was omitted consciously, and if the scribe had so free an attitude towards the text, he certainly would have adjusted the introductory formula too, if he felt it odd—and what is so odd about an expression 'written by the hand of So-and-so'? Certainly it was by hand that they did write. Moreover, if the section of Z a was omitted intentionally, we are again faced with the fact that the parallel section of Z b is lacking in it—and with the free attitude of the scribe of Z b towards the text established, it seems far more natural to suppose that the section in Z b replaces that in Z a rather than that the scribe of Z a would have, intentionally or unintentionally, omitted the former. True, there is one presupposition, viz., that a reason can be pointed out for the omission of the original passage; but we do believe there was such a reason—even the present shape of the Z a text hints it clearly enough. It is the reference to the 'star' which has been omitted from the quotation, Am. v 26 sq., although the subsequent interpretation presupposes it—the similarity of the name with the 'throne-name' of Bar Cochba appears to have been too much for the sectarians after the rebellion. It could be that a considerable part of the sect actually had seen in him the expected 'star' and for that reason joined him; this makes the antipathy of the remaining 'faithful ones' towards him well understandable. Moreover, after the new apostacy the quotation from Is. vii 17, Dan. xi 32; Zech. vi 8; did not hold good any longer, since all those that had escaped to 'the land of North' had *not* 'remained steadfast'.

The last sentence of the new quotation, Zech. xiii 7, is apparently understood in a positive sense; 'the poor of the flock' will be saved by God's hand, since they watch for it. In the light of the reference to 'the princes of Judah' who had 'entered the covenant of repentance etc.', 'the poor of the flock' may be meant literally, if the 'princes' refer to the leaders of the community who had participated in the First Revolt, then readmitted under the condition of permanent disaffiliation from the rest of the Jews; and again found 'unfaithful' in the Bar Cochba revolt [4].

The present writer does not see any gap after page viii in the historical part of Z a, either; if we remove the words of viii 20-21 lacking in the parallel text of Z b (they seem to have originated as a marginal note), the concluding words of that page run: 'And an analogous judgment will be meted out to every one who rejects God's commandments and abandons them, if they turn to the stubbornness of their heart; viz., (of) all the people who have entered the new covenant in the land of Damascus.' In the following section of Z b there is nothing that could not be interpreted from the situation after the Bar Cochba rebellion. The very first words, 'and *again* acted treacherously . . .' are illustrative enough. In ll. 13sqq. (of the second page), the interval between the death of 'the teacher of the community' (NB. *not* 'the right teacher') and the end of the 'men of war who went back with the Man of Lie' is stated to be *about* 40 years; if this were an apocalyptic prophecy, the preposition 'about' is out of style and blunts the edge of the whole pronouncement. On the other hand, it is quite understandable as an attempt to bring the magical number into a past history as the measure of a significant period: it would have been ideal for the interval between the death of the 'Teacher' and that of the 'Man of Lie', but this appears to have been too short; therefore this was extended to the death of the last of his followers, but even for that, it was probably slightly too much. 'The Man of Lie', again, without seeking recalls 'The Son of Lie' (= Liar), Bar Cochba's nickname among the other Jews after his failure. In l. 15, the spot before *ḥrh* at the end of the line does not seem to be Yod, but rather unintentional, like the other one ca. a quarter of an inch above it; accordingly, the reference is still to the past; and the language of the document being largely Biblical still, *'z ydbr* in l. 17 is parallel to it, and *wyqšb* at the end of the next line appears to be consecutive, hence also referring to the past; the turn to future thus does not seem to take place until *'d* in l. 20; with it, the contents also become consoling, warning, and admonishing.

The history of certain other terms is quite as instructive. First of all, let us take *mwrh* (varr. *mwry*, *ywrh*) *ṣdq*, commonly translated, 'Teacher of Righteousness'; but the attribute, since often appearing without the article, may rather be adjectival, hence 'correct', 'right', 'just'; therefore we adopt the rendering, 'right teacher'. The title does not appear in W, nor in MFC nor M, which indicates—according to our chronological scheme—that it was coined rather late. In fact, it may first have been used in HC, where in some passages it seems to refer to a definite single person. This is the case, above all, in xi 4-6, where it is stated that the Wicked Priest pursued the Right Teacher to swallow him in his house of exile; this well fits the relationship of Menelaos and Onias III. The title of a 'right teacher' fits the latter very well also because of his firm stand for the traditional faith and practice of religion. The other passages in which a single individual may be meant are ix 9-10 (largely analogous to that mentioned above), v 9-11, and ii 1-2 (? the text not entirely preserved). On the other hand, in vii 4 at least it seems to be used rather as a more general, collective title, referring to a teacher of the existing sect; therefore we assume that the original text of the document has not been preserved untouched, but in later times has been subjected to revision(s?) more or less extensively—just as we found it to be with Z [5]. In the fragments of commentaries on Micah and Ps xxxvii it also apparently refers to a teacher of the sect in general, while in Z—the only other document in which it is attested—it does not appear to refer to a living person, but either to an earlier leader of the sect (Z a i 11) or a future personage (Z a vi 10-11, Z b l. 3 from end). On the other hand, another title of a 'teacher of the community' appears to be more contemporary in Z b (in which alone it occurs), referring to a person which apparently has been active in the 'new covenant' in the land of Damascus (see i 33 to ii 1). It thus seems that the title of the 'right teacher' was originally an honorary name assigned to Onias III, but suffered 'inflation' later on, being transferred first perhaps to some more able and eminent leader of the sect, then to his successors and finally came to mean any one of them in retrospect. However, with the calamity suffered in connection with the First Revolt, those that escaped to the Damascus region may have regarded the title as too pretentious and again dropped it from everyday use. Thus, it cannot have been an official title for a very long period—perhaps not at all.

The picture obtained from the use of various names for the *congregation*. The main terms are two: *'dh* 'congregation' in the proper Biblical sense, and *yḥd* (var. *yḥyd*), which rather corresponds to 'community'. The latter does not appear in W nor in H, which thus are wholly on the Biblical ground still; however, even the former occurs but twice in H, in hymn no. 3 and in a small fragment. On the other hand, *yḥd* alone occurs in HC (once only) and M (the one occurrence of *ʿdh* in v 20 is in a non-technical expression), while MFC and Z have both. However, they are not comparable to each other; in MFC the term *yḥd* appears to be in the course of developing to an independent, substantival expression, but has not yet totally lost its adverbial and adjectival character. It seems to be on the verge of becoming a substantive in the expression *ʿṣt hyḥd* 'the communal council', as well as in *ʿdt hyḥd* which combines both of our main terms and makes the shift to the mere *hyḥd* well understandable, since the two expressions appear to be synonymous and *ʿdt* therefore redundant. However, the fact that, when combined with some other substantive, *yḥd* still follows the rule of congruence: *šwlḥn yḥd*, but *hšwlḥn hyḥd* shows that the adjectival character was still felt; *ʿṣt hyḥd* may therefore be comparable to constructions like *yom hašševiʿi* in the Bible [6], even if congruence in gender is lacking. This again may be due to its earlier use as an adverb. On the other hand, in Z the distinction is of another nature: *ʿdh* is used exclusively in Z a; the other term, which here has the variant form of *yḥyd*, quite as exclusively in Z b. The variant suggests that the term at this time was pronounced *yâʾed*, cf. the SamH forms of roots II gutt [7] and below. The development of the terms can thus be summarized as follows: originally the sect referred to its collective body as *ʿdh*, 'congregation', a term inherited from Biblical Hebrew; this term alone appears to have been in use when W was written; MFC represents the transitory stage to the properly sectarian designation *yḥd*, and perhaps H and HC belong to the same stage; for although in H, *ʿdh* only is used as the term proper, *yḥd* appears in a close connection with it in iii 22: . . . *byḥd ʿm ʿdt* . . ., and the occurrences being only two, the one-sidedness could be accidental; in HC, again, the only occurrence is in *ʿṣt hyḥd* particularly characteristic of MFC. On the other hand, at the time of the compilation of M, *yḥd* has become fully established, reflecting the closed character of the sect; in connection with the migration to the Damascus region this character seems to have been missed, in so far as the migrants appear to dwell in several 'camps', *mḥnwt* (see Z a vii 6, xii 22sq., xiii 20, xiv 3.7 sq); the abandonment of the term *yḥd* may be in connection with this and not in a preference for *ʿdh* as a result of theoretic speculation, as other terms —such as *qhl* 'crowd', 'assembly', *ḥbr* 'comradeship'—also appear in the same meaning. Again, in Z b (ii 25 sq.) it seems to be presupposed that *all* the members of the sect are living in *one* 'camp' (*mḥnh*); whether this is meant in the concrete literal sense or not, the same idea was apparently enough for the reintroduction of the term *yḥ(y)d*. Observe that outside Z, the term *mḥnh* is used only in a military sense or in connection with travelling, never referring to the permanent dwelling places of the sect; and apart from MFC ii 15, only in W.

The term *kwhn hr(w)'š*, literally 'priest, the head', sometimes used in the Bible to designate the High Priest, occurs only in W; outside it, a term which could refer to the High Priest occurs only in MFC ii 12: *hkwhn rw'š kwl ʿdt yšr'l* 'the priest, the head of the whole congregation of Israel', in the discussion of a hypothetical case. Accordingly, it seems that the sect had interest in High Priesthood only in its initial phases, when it expected the majority of the people to join them, the High Priest included—and perhaps Onias III actually was associated with the initial movement. The term *hkwhn hršʿ* 'the wicked Priest', occurring several times in HC, could also contain an allitterative allusion to *kwhn hr'š* and thus refer to his status as High Priest. The term *mšyḥ* (var. *mšwḥ*) "Messiah" can in some texts refer to High Priest, but it is used in a different sense, viz. referring to a single future person.

Finally, we come to the use of different divine names. The Tetragram is nowhere attested outside Biblical texts. This links up very well with the practice of the latest Biblical period; Eccl. and Esth. do not use it at all, and Job and Dan. are also remarkably shy; the latter has three instances, all in references to older Biblical texts, the former originally probably only in the prose sections. The normal Rabbinical substitute *'dwny* is used almost exclusively in H, as a vocative; the only other instances are in a Biblical quotation in Z a xi 18, and in a hymn in W xii 7. 17. The use of *'lhym* 'God' is still more infrequent: apart from a Biblical quotation in M viii 15, the only other real attestations are in W again, x 4. 7, which also follow the wording of the Biblical pattern passages (Dt. xx 3, Nm. x 9, respectively) almost literally. The singular form, *'lwh*, again appears only in the Biblical text (i 11) of HC. In short, the only divine name used really copiously and in all the main documents is the ancient common Semitic divine name *'l*, normally translated 'God'. Identified in the Priestly Code with *Yahwae*, it appears to have come more into use in the post-exilic literature, such as Psalter and Job, the latter preferring it to any other divine name. Deutero-Isaiah also uses it relatively often, and this fact, in the light of the predilection for the Book of Isaiah among the Biblical books in the sect, may have had the decisive influence on the choice of the substitute for the Tetragram; *'lhym* was naturally more common, but its plural form might have been felt objectionable.

According to the results of this examination, then, the sectarian documents would have originated in the following order: first W, then MFC, then M, later on Z a and finally, as a revision of the latter, Z b. H and HC seem to have been written originally about the same time as MFC, but the latter has been subjected to a revision at a later date, while H, being a collection, could have obtained additions over a longer period. From the historical allusions and implications it seems that W and MFC cannot have been written later than the early Maccabaean period, while Z a derives from the period between the destruction of the temple and the Bar Cochba revolt, and Z b has been written after the latter.

II [7b]

Due to the lack of vowel signs proper and also any other kind of tradition of the exact pronunciation of the text, the purely philological investigation cannot be carried very far into details. Moreover, the results obtained will be affected by the fact that we only rarely have the original documents at our disposal. However, the latter handicap is not as serious as it might seem, since the interval between the origin of the document and that of the present manuscript is relatively short (compared with the state of things regarding other ancient documents), and the scribes in their work generally are conservative, so that they often preserve features which have been dropped from the contemporary everyday usage; and since we in these documents generally have to do with a language which was becoming increasingly only literary, this argument should have still more weight there. Therefore we may assume that, where the document has not been preserved in autograph, the linguistic stage it reflects is earlier than the time the present copy was written. Purely scribal features—such as the development of the special final forms of some letters—however, must be left out of consideration, since such *formal* characteristics are more susceptible to individual changes. As to different hands appearing in one and the same manuscript, only the first hand is generally taken into consideration. Where deviation from this principle appears, it is expressly stated.

We start with a feature, which partly appears to be orthographical, but can also reflect phonetic development, viz. the use of certain letters to indicate vowel sounds. Due to the lack of any other kind of indication of vowel sounds we must take the distinctive criterion from elsewhere and suppose that an ʾAlaef, He, Waw, or Yod is used to indicate a vowel in cases in which, judging from the two most important Hebrew dialects or traditions known to us, viz., Tiberian Hebrew [8] (TibH) and Samaritan Hebrew [9] (SamH), either a vowel or at most (a consonant temporarily created as a glide or as an element of) a diphthong, probably has stood; thereby it should not be considered impossible that one and the same vowel can be represented by more than one letter in writing.

If we, then, first try to reconstruct a chronological development of the use of the vowel consonants by means of the above mentioned documents plus the dated ones, we see that the use of vowel consonants in W and MFC is practically identical, even if, because of the small size of MFC, this similarity should not be pressed too much. In both, the vowels corresponding to TibH Šuraeq, Ḥolaem and Ḥiraeq are practically regularly indicated, and additionally the stem vowel in Qal preformal [10] 3rd pers. pl. which in TibH normally is reduced to Shwa. Of characteristic pronominal forms, only 3rd pers. pl. is attested in MFC; in both documents, its shorter form (corresponding to TibH *-am*) is—with one exception, W i 12—always written without a final He, while the longer one (TibH *-haem*, *-haen*) in numerous cases is provided with it. Thereby it is remarkable that in MFC the forms provided with the final letter practically all occur in the *first* half of the document (in W, they are more evenly distributed). The conjunction *ki* is also regularly written with final ʾAlaef. On the other hand, when comparing W with H we find certain differences. True, the use of Waw and Yod within words is about the same, but *ki* appears in H occasionally without the final ʾAlaef and the 3rd pers. pl. suffix is written regularly without final He; the only exception is in the short form, written *-mh* in xiii 10; moreover, even the suffix of 2nd pers. sg.m., which in W regularly appears as *-kh* is not infrequently written with a final Kaf only; and in ii 22 vii 29 curious mixed forms appear, with He after a final Kaf. Other forms with non-Tiberian final He are similarly more sparse in H. Turning to HC, the final He has totally disappeared, but ʾAlaef is still normally attached to *ki*; on the other hand, it is interesting to note that the suffix of the 3rd pers. sg. m. after *ʾl* and *ʿl* is sometimes written with the mere *-w*, but once *-yhw*. The name of Jerusalem, which in W regularly ends with *-lym*, is here quite as regularly *-lm*;

and the name of Kittim, in W written *ktyym*, appears here as *kty'ym* (MT ktiv mostly *ktym*). On the other hand, in M the final He is quite regular, occasionally even augmented by an 'Alaef (*hy'h'* viii 13, etc.), and the final 'Alaef of *ki* and *mi* is apparently also omitted only quite accidentally. The suffix of 3rd pers. sg. m. after plural forms is here often *-yhw*, and only occasionally *-w*. In the documents datable to the Bar Cochba period all these phenomena are completely absent; instead, we find other constructions which will be dealt with later on.

The general trend of the development is clear; in the passage of time, the number of the vowel consonants used appears to be *reduced*. True, this is in contradiction to the prevalent theory according to which the vowel consonants continually increased, assuming new functions and gaining in regularity, until the introduction of the vowel signs proper. However, so little is known of the actual development of the pronunciation of Hebrew during the relevant period that a proper designation for that 'theory' would be hypothesis or perhaps rather surmise; in most expositions it appears to be based on the tacit assumption that the pronunciation of Hebrew or at least its vowels did not change during the relevant period at all. At most, it is supposed, there can have been parallel traditions, 'standard' and 'substandard', or 'pure Hebrew' and Hebrew influenced by Aramaic, 'the language of the Scripture' and 'the language of the learned', 'The Holy Language' and 'the language of Mishnah', etc. Whatever you will, only that the Holy Tiberian Hebrew *must* remain the Norm and Canon according to which *any* other form of Hebrew is to be judged, sentenced and executed—if at all possible.

Since the Qumran texts do not seem to fit this schema very well, they are now supposed to represent a special 'freak' form within the 'substandard'. Assuming this, let us see whether we can find any regularity at all in this freak 'sub-substandard'. If we suppose that the reduction of vowel consonants within it is a regular trend, then the order of the documents thus far dealt with should be: 1-2) W and MFC, 3) M, 4) H, and 5) HC, then the Bar Cochba documents. In the first part, however, we arrived at the conclusion that H and HC originated before M, and about the same time as MFC. However, as we found there, HC apparently has been revised later on; and since a revision is a relatively independent work, it is possible that he who undertakes it also transforms the orthography more than a normal copyist; so it was actually to be expected that HC would reflect the stage of development of the time of the revision. Again, H being a collection would not represent any *one* stage, but cover a longer period. Finally, MFC is so small in size that it can only be dated roughly on this kind of evidence.

Some smaller fragments show affiliation to some of these documents. The Deuteronomy fragment, 1Q[4], appears to have had final He even after the short form of 3rd. pers. pl. masc., so it possibly could antedate W. Taken as a whole, 1Q appears to exhibit mostly characteristics of W, MFC, and H. In the 'small caves' apart from 2Q, on the other hand, only a very few traces of them can be discovered; 5Q13 has most instances, viz., *-mh* for 3rd pers. pl. masc. suffix three times, and *-kh* for the 2nd sg. m. twice (?l. 8 uncertain). 3Q15 has some characteristics of the Bar Cochba documents, but these do not properly belong to the sphere of orthography. In the Biblical fragments of 2Q, instances of all the forms with final He attested in W are to be found, in 2Q23 even the verbal ending *-tmh* (= SamH — *timma*, TibH *-taem*)—but the form of the corresponding suffix is *-km* in that fragment.

1QIs b, like Z a and Z b, being orthographically comparable to MT, Is a remains to be dealt with. We find in it all the possible uses of the final 'Alaef and He familiar from the other documents, as well as an analogous use of Yod and Waw inside the words; besides, pronominal (and verbal) forms of 2nd pers. sg. f. with a final *-y* are attested. Alongside these, however, forms without these vowel consonants are frequently used[11]. The distribution of the 'fuller' forms is again interesting: the number is relatively much smaller in chapters i to xxxiii than in xxxiv to end, and particularly marked is the increase in ch. xxxiv, which even otherwise seems to be the beginning of a new section[12]. Since it is now proven quite possible or even probable that chapters xxxiv and xxxv come from the pen of the same author as those from xl onwards[13], we could perhaps assume that our copyist had two different exemplars from which he copied the text, the first of them representing a stage when only the present 33 chapters from the beginning had been united into one whole, while the second one extended over the whole present book. However, naturally it is to be assumed that the first exemplar is the older one; and keeping to our principle that the copyist largely imitates the pattern of the model exemplar, it seems that in the older exemplar there were fewer such forms than in the younger one. Even the sudden increase in ch. xxxiv and subsequent decrease are best understood from the presupposition that the scribe was used to manuscripts in which such 'fuller' forms did not occur very much; in the exemplar for chs. i to xxxiii he had become accustomed to use them to some extent, and when in the complete exemplar he found them to a much larger extent (perhaps regularly), he first followed the pattern closely, but soon relapsed nearer to his normal habit. It is to be observed that even in the first half they occur more frequently in the initial chapters even if the difference is not so marked[14].

Keeping to the theory of the 'freak' character of DSS, we could account for this opposite tendency by the supposition that the exemplars used by the sectarian scribe of Is a were inherited from a pre-sectarian phase of textual transmission, in which the use of vowel consonants had been steadily increased. Leaving the matter to rest on that assumption for the time being, we proceed to study the phonology.

The relatively great age of Is a —or in any case of the exemplars from which it is copied—provisionally established, it is most convenient to start with it. In the consonantism proper, it is almost exclusively the gutturals on which reliable conclusions can be drawn. Their confusion with each other is practically completely documented; true, we do not find an instance of ʾAlaef and Ḥeṭ being interchanged in writing, but in the light of the fact that there are instances of every guttural being omitted in writing, and others in which they are obviously quiescent, this may be ascribed to the relative accuracy of the copyist who, in spite of numerous minor mistakes, yet appears to have been relatively faithful to his model exemplars. Examples: ʾAlaef omitted: *zwt* i 12 et al., *ydymw* i 18, *hbyw* xvi 3, *nspym* xiii 4, *tntw* xxxvi 16, etc.; He omitted: *kmpkt* i 7, *wʾzynw* viii 9 xxviii 23, *mtlwt* xxx 10, *lšʾwwt* xxxvii 26, *lšmyʿ* lviii 4, etc.; Ḥeṭ omitted: *whzyqh* (!) iv 1, *rbwt* xxi 15, *ṣṣḥwt* lviii 11; ʿAyin omitted: *yšyhw* i 1, *wyšh* (Tib. *wyʿś*) v 4 xlviii 14, *bynyhm* ix 7 xvii 4, *ybwr* xxviii 15; ʾAlaef quiescent: *kmpʾkt* i 7 sm; *zʾwt* iii 6 et al.; *nwʾm* iii 15 et al.; *hyhʾ* v 1 et al.; etc.; He quiescent: *mhʾwyby* iii 1, *whʾrṣ* viii 23, *rwḥhw* xxxiv 16, *hhṣyl* xxxvi 19, etc.; Ḥeṭ quiescent: *mbṭḥm* xx 5 (cf. *-ṭnw* v. 6); probably *wyzḥ* v 29 (but *wywḥ(z)* cannot be excluded); and perhaps *šḥwd* v. 23 et al.; in *šwḥwd* xlv 13 it may represent a glide, cf. below; ʿAyin quiescent: *yrʿ* (fem.) xv 4, *hyʿr* (= MT *hʿyr*) xxxii 19, *pwʿlty* xlix 4, *šmʿwʾ* (= MT *šmwʿ*) lv 2, *pwʿltmh* lxv 7; ʾAlaef confused with He: *ḥwṭh* i 4, *nh* v 3 et al., *hyk* xiv 12, *hnšʾ* xxxiii 10, *hwrrṭ* xxxii 38, *hkn* xl 7; *ybnʾ* v 2, *whyʾ* viii 14, *ʾnh* viii 18, *ʾwšyʿnw* xxxvii 20, *ʾḥšyty* xlii 14, *ʾds* lv 13, etc.; ʾAlaef confused with ʿAyin: *ʾṣwt* xxv 1, *wʾth* xxviii 22;

He confused with Ḥeṯ: *hgwrh* iii 24, *hrbwt* xxi 15 sm, *nrhb* xxx 23, *mhšwkym* xlii 16, *w'šytḥw* v 6, *tptḥ* xxx 33; He confused with ʿAyin: ʿ*msym* lxiv 1; Ḥeṯ confused with ʿAyin: *šʿys* xxxvii 30; *sḥwrh* liv 11. As can be seen, the confusion is much further advanced regarding ʾAlaef and He than Ḥeṯ and ʿAyin, which suggests that the two latter ones, which originally probably were pronounced deeper in the throat, had persisted longer than the other ones, and therefore were etymologically better in the memory of our scribes; the fact that mistakes in them almost regularly occur in rare words and forms is better in accordance with this assumption than with the usual hypothesis according to which only a part of them were quiescent, while in other words and forms they were still pronounced; as is well known, it is in the most usual words that the phonetic developments are completed most rapidly. It is interesting to see that there is not much difference in this respect between the two halves of the ms.: in the second half, the total number is slightly higher (ca. 54% of all), but of those involving Ḥeṯ and ʿAyin, the majority are in the first half (but their number is too small for the law of averages to begin to function); accordingly, the confusion may be mainly the work of the scribe of Is a. So we conclude that the latter, normally at least, did not pronounce the gutturals, but the writers of the model exemplars probably still did.

What can be concluded about the pronunciation of vowels is partly tied up with the gutturals. Above, it was already mentioned that in *šwḥwd* xlv 13, *ḥ* may represent a glide between the two vowels. To judge from TibH and SamH [15], the word goes back to a prototype +*šuḥd*, early modified by the guttural to +*šoḥd*. The quiescization of the guttural yielded +*ŝōd*, which under a double peak accent appears to have yielded +*šóʾod* [16]. The normal consonant text, *šḥwd*, however, suggests that the long vowel usually was not split—this instance could be due to a pausal accentuation, the word standing immediately before the concluding formula, *ʾmr Yhwh ṣbʾwt*. Theoretically, there is another possibility, viz. that the first *o* would have dissimilated into another vowel, as has happened in SamH in the cases of a double peak accent; but this assumption implies development having proceeded father than with ʾAlaef or He in a comparable position, as we shall see presently, and also farther than in SamH [17], therefore this assumption is hardly credible. As already hinted, such vocalisation is normally indicated only in the neighbourhood of an ʾAlaef or He. Examples: *rʾwš* i 5 and frequently, *rwʾš* i 6a. fr.; *wywʾmr* viii 1 et al.; *nw'm* iii 15 et al.; *mw'd* xvi 6, *mw'dh* (in the second half only) xlvii 6 et al.; *'whwl* xvi 5 sm; *thww* xl 17 = *twh* xlix 4; there is an instance of ʿAyin too, *pwʿlty* xlix 4, cf. *pwʿltmh* lxv 7, *pwʿwl* lix 6. The fact that ktib *rwš*, *zwt*, etc. appears too may seem to indicate that actually only one vowel was pronounced. However, this is by no means certain, as we do not know the quality of the supposed glide in every case with certainty, and cases in which the consonant text, when deviating from MT, does suggest something, it appears to be *w* rather than '. Ktib like *thww* can hardly be said to represent +*tố'ū*, but rather +*tốwwū*, and *twh* does not contradict this, unless perhaps as regards the final vowel (= +*tốwwō*?). Similarly, *rwš* can represent a pronunciation +*rốwwoš*; however, the fact that in the vast majority of cases it is the guttural which is written may indicate that the glide originated as an ', but later on (perhaps starting from the III *w* nouns? the final vowel in +*to'u* can have coloured the first one darker) was replaced by *w*. At the time of our scribe this stage would have been reached, but not yet so established that it would have generally replaced the earlier ktiv. Another possibility is that the overlong forms had begun contracting again, or that besides them, a monosyllabic form had been preserved under a lighter stress (in st. cstr. and comparable positions), as seems to have been the case in SamH [18].

Apart from the vowels provided with a double peak accent, certain other deviations from TibH require comment. One of them appears to be closely related to it, viz., the appearance of an ending *'y*, *yy* or *y'y* where the written MT normally has only one Yod. Mostly this appears in plural; besides the very common *gw'ym* (= MT *gwym*), we find *nkry'ym* ii 6, *plštyym* xi 14, *kśdyym* xiii 19, *ʿwʿyym* xix 14, *ktyym* xxiii 1. 12, *kl'ywt* xxxiv 6; in singular, there appear *'yy* xx 6, and perhaps *g'y* xxviii 4 (but this could be a simple transposition of the quiescent 'Alaef). The monstrous-looking *'yy'mym* xxxiv 14 may also belong to this category. In TibH, the pl. forms written *-yym* are invariably pronounced *-iyyîm*; but here, the occasional appearance of 'Alaef indicates that this was not at least uniformly so. The sg. of *gw'ym* being *gwy*, ' is here obviously a glide; and since it seems that the quality of the glide normally corresponds to the stressed vowel rather than to the unstressed one [19], we may conclude that the stress was on the penultima, and that the colour of *o* at the time the glide was created was nearer to *a* rather than *u* [20]. Now it seems that in post-exilic Hebrew generally a long *e* and *i* vowel which bore the word stress under certain conditions[21] was developed into a diphthong, *-ay*; that it could occur in pl. forms like ours is indicated by SamH *šelišâ'em*, pl. of *šelîši* [22]. The form of the suffix of 3rd sg. m. after pl., *-yw*, in which *y* is quiescent, shows that quiescization of Yod in pl. forms was not foreign to the Jerusalem dialect, either. Accordingly, we may suppose it to have taken place here as well, and assume that ktiv like *nkry'ym* represents the true pronunciation better than the earlier *kšdyym* etc.: *+nokrâ'em*, *+kašdâ'em*, etc. However, it is well possible that the original glide was preserved for a longer time in numerous instances; this appears to have been the case in *kl'ywt* (= *+kulâyot*) at least. On the other hand, the development of *qṣ'wwt* xli 5 (elsewhere without ') is obscure; in TibH it is corresponded by *qeṣôṭ*, in SamH, by *qáṣṣot*. This makes it probable that *w* is a glide; the fact that the word occurs only in st. cstr.—i.e., relatively unstressed —might have made the choice freer. The sg. forms *g'y* and *'yy* (perhaps even *nk'y* lxvi 2?), if they can be regarded as authentic, similarly point to an ending *-ay*. SamH furnishes us with a parallel, *riggalâe'i* Ex xii 37, Nm xi 21; but being a military term, it could be due to an Aramaic influence. Finally, it seems that, like in TibH [23], the process could be applied to a long *e* within a word, if the starting point for *'yy'mym* be the TibH *'emîm*; the resulting initial sylable *'ay-* being followed by a consonant, a svarabhakti could have developed after SamH pattern[24]: *+'áymem* through *+'áyyamem* and *+'ayyámem* into *+'ayyâmem*. The prevalent *yrwšlym* besides *yršlm* (cf. MT qre/ktiv) may owe its existence to the same development.

Another phenomenon numerous enough to be dealt with in this survey is the appearance of *w* presumably as a vowel consonant where TibH has an *a* vowel (i.e., Qamaeṣ or Pataḥ) or a murmuring vowel (Shwa). This phenomenon, however, does not appear to be uniform in origin. First of all, DSS seem to have preserved a number of old *o* vowels which in MT have been reduced. This is true, e.g., of the forms of imperative pl. m. and sg. f., preformal pl. 2 & 3 m. and sg. 2 f. in which the 2nd rad. apparently regularly was pronounced with a full vowel, even if in a number of cases Waw is lacking even where it is corresponded by an *o* vowel in sg. in TibH.[24b]. Examples: imp. *drwšw* i 17 ii 18, *'mwrw* iii 10; *šp wṭw* v 3; *ḥšwpy*, *'bwry* xlvii 3, etc.; pref. *yḥpwrw* i 29; *ymšwlw* iii 4, *ypwlw* iii 25, *yrbwṣw* xiii 20, etc.; as can be seen, the *o* vowel has further spread in the intr. verbs as well. Other forms comparable to these: coh. *'šqwth* (= MT ktiv) xviii 4; suffixed: *ylkwdh* xx 1, *'ṣwrnh* xxvii 3, and even *t'kwlnw* xxxi

8, etc. The fact that in MT a full vowel appears in these forms only when it is stressed again suggests that the word stress lies on the penultima. True, naturally DSS need not follow Masoretic rules; but the distribution of the vowel consonants in the next group also gives a similar impression. It is a question of nouns in which a Waw appears in the place of a TibH Shwa or other comparable vowel. Characteristic instances are: *bywmy* i 1 sm; *swdm* i 9 et al.; *ʿwmrh* i 9 et al.; *tḥwt* iii 24, *rwmlyh* vii 1. 15, *mśwrh* ix 5, *dwdnym* xxi 13, *ʾrmwnwtyh* xxxiv 13 sm; *rwksym* xl 4, *ʿwmsym*, *nwśʾym* xlvi 3, *ʾwqdh* liv 12, *ḥwzyr* lxv 4 et al.; etc. In most of these instances, there is a form with an *o* or *u* vowel in the relevant position in other forms in Hebrew or in related languages; as regard *bywmy*, it is the *o* vowel of the sg. which has here penetrated the pl. form, just as in Aram; for *swdm* and *ʿwmrh*, we have the transcriptions Sodom and Gomorra; for *tḥwt*, the nearest form seems to be Aramaic again, *teḥoṯ*; but we can perhaps also compare the twofold pronunciation of this word in SamH, one of which appears to go back to +*tuḥt* which with the quiescization of the guttural would yield +*tût* (or rather +*tôt*, via +*toḥt*) which also fits the ktiv; however, in SamH this pronunciation is restricted to the local meaning 'under, beneath' [25]. In *rwmlyh*, the meaning of the first part is unknown; *mśwrh* corresponds to the TibH *miśrā* which deviates from the normal pattern of formation of nouns from continuable roots, and the DSS form could therefore be more regular, going back to +*ma-śurra*(*t*), cf. the Tiberian *miśmoraeṯ*, etc. On the other hand the first vowel of the place name Dedan appears to have been originally *a*. In *ʾrmwnwtyh*, the *o* indicated by the first *w* has been inherited from sg. again; to *rwksym*, we may compare TibH *rukse* Ps xxxi 21, even if semantic connection is obscure (understood as a metaphor?); in *ʿwmsym*, *nwśʾym* we may see ancient nouns of patient of the type +*qutal* [26]; in *ʾwqdḥ*, Waw apparently represents a prothetic vowel which in TibH appears as *ae*, but cf. the tendency of Qof to prefer Ḥaṭef Qamaeṣ to a simple Shwa even there; for *ḥwzyr*, there are parallels from several Aramaic dialects and Akkadian. What interests us properly in this connection, however, is the position of the vowel consonant. With few exceptions, it is written in a syllable which in the basic form of the word appears to be penultima; and apart from them, normally only permanently long vowels are marked with vowel consonants. It is a general linguistic observation that the word stress tends to lengthen the vowel on which it lies, therefore, assuming that it here lay on the penultima [26b], no deviation from the general principle of marking only long vowels was *initially* necessary, as the practice mostly is confined to open syllables; later on, it appears to have spread to closed stressed syllables too to some extent. In *ʿwmrh*, the prototype may have been bisyllabic[27], so that it belongs to this category too; and in *ʾrmwn-*, the afformative may have been assimilated to the one deriving from a proto-Semitic *-ān* in which the vowel, accordingly, was permanently long. Moreover, there are numerous cases in which obviously unstressed short vowels have been written with a vowel consonant; therefore this group need not be a total exception.

Occasionally, other vowel consonants occur, mostly in comparable positions. Examples: *ʿʾwn* i 15b, *yʾtwm* i 17.23, *tyʾmynw* xxx 21 (apparently to indicate meaning), *klʾywt* xxxiv 6 (pl. tantum), *ʾyyʾmym* xxxiv 15 (ditto), *hwlykty* xlii 16 (cf. SamH Qal *ʾalikti*[28]), *špʾym* xlix 9 (a collective pl.); etc.

On the other hand, it is not clear, whether the marking of the vowels in the final syllables of certain verbal forms has anything to do with their length. This is especially true of the Qal preformal sg. and 1st pl. and n. act. of the verbs with *o* as the stem vowel. We could perhaps assume that, following the analogy of H-stem, 3rd and 2nd pl. as well as hollow roots, III vowel, and III guttural verbs (in which latter the last radical had become quiescent), the stem vowel tended to be lengthened generally at a time when the quality of word stress allowed that; or also, that the vowel of H-stem under a different kind of stress was shortened [29] (as it has happened in SamH) and its *mater lectionis* thus becoming a sign for a different *semantic class* (causative), its analogy could have achieved the generalization of Waw to mark still another semantic class (transitive) in distinction to the intransitive verbs which remained without a special indicator. Or finally, it could mark the beginning of the shift of the word stress to the final syllable, under the influence of Aramaic, the semantic analogy of placing the word stress uniformly on the stem vowel at this stage providing a satisfactory excuse.

In the other main scrolls, little additional material is offered; however, interesting evidence of continuous development can be found. First of all, in W, the situation is comparable to Is a in all essentials; some interesting details seem to indicate slightly earlier stages still. Eg., *rôš* (TibH) is never written without ʾAlaef; and besides *rʾš* and *rwʾš*, *rʾwš* (marking the unstressed vowel) occurs only once (v 12). The adjective 'first' derived from it is *regularly* written *r'yšwn*, which is completely parallel to SamH *ra'īšon* [29b]; in *rbw'wtm* xii 4, the split caused by the double peak accent is also apparent. The name of Jerusalem is regularly written *yrwšlym*. In the numeral *m'ywtyw* iv 2, the stem may, accordingly, have been split into two syllables too: *me'iy-*? In MFC hardly any relevant material is present. In H, an interesting new phenomenon presents itself; besides *wyšmwrhw* in fragment 3, 7 (B), which follows the earlier pattern, we find *'dwrškh* iv 6, and n. act. *ldwrškh* ib. 16; in these forms, the stem vowel is thus transferred to the first radical, when the verb is provided with a suffix. [29c] Considering that this never occurs in 3rd and 2nd pers. pl. of preformal and that the guttural (in *-hw*) was probably quiescent, this seems to indicate that the transfer took place only when the third radical was followed by a consonant. True, this seems to be contradicted by *wyšwm'wny* iv 24; but here again, the third radical is a guttural and therefore silent, so the transfer could be in connection with that. However, due to the scanty material these are but surmises. In HC, it is again the 2nd radical only after which Waw appears indicating the stem vowel; on the other hand, 'Alaef appears regularly in the gentilic nouns: *kšd'ym* ii 11, *kty'ym* ib. 12 et al. The confusion of the form of the 3rd pers. sg. m. suffix after pl. nouns with that after sg. nouns, which appears sometimes in Is a, e.g., *qwdšyw* lxiii 10, *ḥwmltyw* ib 9, *ydyw nṭwyh* v 25 et al; etc; is here shown to belong definitely to this category by different forms in which it appears: *'lw* viii 5 bis, *'lw* ib 7, but *'lyhw* xii 11. A pronunciation which can cover all of them can only have been *-āw*; this is well in accordance with the fact that in Is a only the form after sg. has suffered alterations. On the other hand, ktiv like *'lw* suggests a subsequent monophthongization of all the forms. This is supported by the fact that the pronoun for 3rd pers. sg. is regularly written without a final He: *hw'*, *hy'*, as the masculine mostly even in H: the final vowels start being reduced and partly dropped.

In M however, the pronominal forms still have full vocalization about as in Is a; in the 3rd sg. the final He can even be augmented: *hy'h'* viii 13. As regards the sf. of 3rd sg. m., confusion prevails with obviously quiescent Yod and He; *'wwnwtw* iii 7.8, *'ynyw* v 5, *'ḥyhw* vi 10, *pyhw* vii 9 ix 25, *ṣdqwtw* xi 3, etc. On the other hand, double peak accent seems to have disappeared; the vowel adjoining to a guttural is never written twice, and besides forms like *yw'klw* vi 2, *zw't* ix 20, others like *ywmrw* vi 13, *rwšw* vii 7 appear; true, these could still be explained by the supposition that the glide ' has turned *w* in the meantime; but the analogy of *ršyt* (besides *r'šyt*) makes the alternative of monophthongization more probable; and the ktiv *b'wpy*ʿ x 2 (for TibH *b^e^hofiac*), which hardly can have been pronounced otherwise than *bofi* corroborates this. The strange vocalization of *rwḥwm* 'their spirit' may simply indicate a pronunciation *+rūwwam*, the latter Waw being accordingly consonantal; *mtwḥt* vii 13 apparently stands for *+mittōt*, etc

As regards Z, the relatively long interval between the compilation and latest copying could have had more influence on the shape of the text than in the case of the other documents; therefore we do not use it in this part. In the fragments found in Qumran (6Q15), characteristic forms are almost lacking; but the suffix of 3rd pers. pl. m. appears regularly without a final He, and *ryšwny(m)* (cf. Z a vi 5) has an 'Alaef above Yoḏ, written by a later hand.

So we finally come again to the documents datable accurately to the Bar Cochba period. In the texts from Wadi Murabbaʿat, the characteristic pronominal forms, sf. of 2nd sg. m. included, regularly appear written without a vowel consonant; the controversial 2nd pers. sg. m. of the afformative conjugation is also regularly written without a final He, as in MT ktiv. Found in the immediate neighbourhood of the texts which use a phonetic spelling for any conceivable final (and other) vowels, and with the tendency to reduce vocalization in earlier texts established, the most plausible explanation for the absence of such *matres lectionis* is that there were no final vowels to be indicated in these forms. The only alternative, viz., that there would have been an ancient, well established model text of which these documents were copies suffers, above all, of completely lacking documentation for periods earlier than this. Moreover, such a rigid pattern would be natural only in Biblical manuscripts in which it could be copied from an earlier exemplar, but in these documents it is used everywhere, casual documents and private letters included, and what is more, it is extended even to the 1st pers. sg. of afformal, where Yod is occasionally omitted (e.g., text 24E l. 5.7: *ḥkrt*). Obviously, all the inflectional vowels that were not absolutely essential to the understanding of the speech tended to be omitted; this is understandable only if the word stress had become so heavy or sharp that the stressed syllable was becoming more and more prominent at the expense of the others. This links it up with the contractions, which are also a clear indication that the omission of final *matres lectionis* cannot be an indoctrinated theory; had he learnt that part of artificial rules so well, how is it possible that he made such gross mistakes in another respect? Generally, the contractions consist of the omission of the initial ʾAlaef of the sign of object, its Taw being then prefixed to the following word which is provided with the article the He of which is likewise omitted; *tʿpr* = *ʾt hʿpr* 24E l. 8, *tḥkyr* = *ʾt hḥkyr* ib. 10, *tšmym* = *ʾt hšmym* 43 l. 3, etc. The pronunciation may have been *taššamaim* or something like it. The presence of the article, however, is not necessary, cf. *tmy* = *ʾt my* 44 l. 8; it also indicates that the sound represented by Taw was syllabic, hence apparently a spirant. To this, a mistake in the famous copper scroll (3Q15), can be compared: in col. i l. 3, the scribe started *ʾrwh-*, but observing his double mistake, wrote anew: *ʾrbʿyn*. This implies, first that *b* even after a consonant had become a spirant, secondly that the resulting spirant was phonetically identified with the sound represented by Waw, and thirdly, that the confusion of the gutturals continued. This last is naturally also indicated by the above mentioned contractions, and others like *šbʿšrh* 3Q15 4, *ʿlyʾh* ib. x 1 also imply it or their general weakening. Such features seem to point to the Bar Cochba period as the time of the writing of the copper scroll as well; and another feature now to be discussed also seems to link it up with the documents definitely datable to it.

This is the appearance of the letter Samaeḵ in various places in which Šin earlier has been used. The only instance familiar to me in the main sectarian scrolls is *nsgbh* H vi 25 (corrected into *nšgbh*) of the root written *śgb* in TibH [30]. As is known, in TibH, the letter Šin represents two different sounds which in vocalised texts are distinguished from each other by means of diacritical points, and generally it is assumed that this represents the original state of things, since in some other Semitic languages two different sounds appear as counterparts of it, roughly corresponding to the division in TibH. Lately, however, it has become increasingly evident that such correspondences are far from regular [30b], and it seems to the present writer that the relations of different Semitic sibilants are yet to be worked out [31]. There are also theoretical considerations against the assumption that Šin throughout the Biblical period represented two different sounds. Since the recognition of the existence of phonemes as groups of phonetically distinguishable sounds the interchange of which does not affect the meaning of the words, it has been relatively easy to recognize that the writing systems based on the alphabetic principle use such phonemes as basic units, modifying the alphabet adopted according to the needs of the phonemic system of the language. As a general principle, every sound phoneme nowadays has its own mark, may it consist of one, two or even more letters; if additional circumstances must be taken into account, it means that the writing system has abandoned the alphabetic principle and fallen back to the partly logographic, partly syllabic level familiar from the writing systems used before the invention of the first alphabet, as has happened to the present-day English orthography. In no language, however, is this state of affairs original; at the time of the adoption of the alphabet, it was modified till it was sufficiently adapted to the phonemic system prevalent at the time so as not to confuse the meanings of different words. In the ancient times, this appears to have taken place regularly by means of adding new signs for sounds that did not exist in the language from which the alphabet was borrowed. In the Semitic languages, it was generally possible to omit signs for vowels, since the vocalization mostly followed definite pattern discernible from the consonantal 'skeleton' and/or the syntactical connection; where this was not the case (as e.g. in certain plural forms), an allusion by means of certain consonant signs appears to have been sufficient. In any case, there is no evidence to a supposition that two different consonant phonemes would have been originally marked by one and the same sign in any Semitic language [31b]. Moreover, the reason for this is evident; since consonants in the Semitic family are the bearers of the basic meaning of the word, such a combination would have quickly led into confusion. So the only possibility is that the two sounds would have been preserved as allophones of one and the same phoneme. However, such persistent allophones appear to be positional in character; one of them appears in a phonetical environment in which the other(s) never occur, and vice versa. This is the case with the Bega̲dkefaṯ; the explosive pronunciation appears in geminates, after another consonant, and after a major juncture, the spirantical one anywhere else. The exception from this rule, viz. the cases of spirantical pronunciation after a consonant where a vowel recently has disappeared from between the two seems to indicate that even after an alteration in the original conditions the difference can persist; but the exception from the exception, viz. in cases where the explosive pronunciation reappears (prep. *l* + n. act., etc.) shows that it does not last long—unless the difference develops phonemic, as in some cases in Modern Hebrew. Since there does not appear to be any such positional distinction between the two pronunciations of Šin, the natural conclusion is that it represented originally only one sound. This corresponds to the position in SamH still today: Šin is always pronounced as the sibilant proper. And since the writing with Šin is wholly consistent throughout the properly sectarian scrolls in spite of their outspoken phonetic character—the one instance in H can well be late because of the nature of this document as a collection—, the natural conclusion here is that the sect still consistently pronounced Šin in one way only, up to the latest times. How, then, the change presupposed in TibH did take place?

The correction of *nsgbh* into *nšgbh* in H vi 25 gives a hint. It shows that the pronunciation with *s* in this particular word at least was not unknown, but was considered incorrect by the sect. Now we know that the sect militated against any foreign influence, and it is well possible—if not probable—that the use of Hebrew in its writings was due to this reason. It is therefore natural to assume that they saw in the new pronunciation foreign influence, and we need not go farther than Aramaic to discover a plausible source; as you can see in any etymological dictionary of Hebrew, for almost any TibH root containing Šin there is an Aramaic equivalent with Samaek. Some cases in which there is no attestation may be accidentally so, and in others, where Aramaic has a different root in that meaning, the influence of some other, semantically and phonetically closely related root may have caused the change (e.g., *ʿsq* 'to busy himself with' for *ʿsh* 'to do'). Such exceptions only confirm that it cannot be a question of a purely etymological phonetic development. So we can safely conclude that the split of Śin from the original Šin took place under the influence of Aramaic some time before the Bar Cochba period, and that the sound from the very first was identified with that of Samaek̲—a Śin sound, distinct from both Šin and Samaek̲, never existed in Hebrew. The roots in which an original Šin in these documents appears replaced by Samaek̲ are all frequently used, viz., *nśʾ*, *ʿśh*, and *ʿśr*; a possible exception is *kśb*, if Bar Cochba's original surname *kwsbʾ*, as it appears in these documents, is to be combined with TibH *kaeśaev* 'young ram'.

Another characteristic feature of these documents is that the verbal forms which we found practically regularly written plene in the earlier documents, never appear so here. We found it probable there that the plene writing was a consequence of penultimate stress; accordingly, its absence here may mean that the stress has been shifted away from the second-last syllable. Where, then? It may be unnecessary to consider more than one possibility: to the last syllable. Naturally not in all the inflexional forms, but in those relevant here, viz., the imp. and pref. forms provided with a vocalic afformative or with a suffix. The semantic analogy of having the word stress on the stem vowel again has given way to the positional one, and since the moving force of the development, viz., the Aramaic influence, determined the direction of the shifts towards the end of the words, it appears that in this connection the place of the word stress in TibH was determined in most forms. Thus, it can be traced directly to the position of stress in Aramaic around the beginning of our era.

III

Most of the relevant morphological items have been mentioned already in connection with phonology. We can therefore deal with them more briefly. To begin with pronomical elements, the only variations in 1st pers. sg. are: 1) the attachment of an ʾAlaef to the subject form [32] of the suffix. According to my notes, this occurs exclusively in the second half of Is a [33], where it is extremely common (34 instances); the single instance of *ʾnyʾ* for the separate form in lxvi 9 may be an unconscious imitation of it. 2) The omission of Yoḏ in the form attached at the end of verbal stems to form the 1st pers. sg. of the afformative conjugation in the documents of Bar Cochba period. True, this is not very common, but its very appearance presupposes a phonetic reason as well, as there is no precedent to it in Hebrew. The presence of Aramaic influence in these documents makes it probable that it was the moving force here too, but had the final vowel been clearly pronounced, there is hardly any doubt that it would have been regularly written too, in the light of the established Hebrew tradition and the fact that in the vast majority of cases it is still written even here. It may be significant that it is dropped only in relatively fixed formulas or technical terms in which there is no doubt as to the identity of the person referred to, e.g. *ʾny mrṣwny ḥkrt hmk* 'I, of my own desire, take in rent from you . . .' (text 24C l. 5 sq. et al.). In 1st pers. pl., no variations appear apart from the attestation of the Biblical *ʾnḥnw* also in H fragm. x 6 and in Z b ii 29 (here, besides *ʾnw* in the preceding line); *ʾnw* appears also in W and M, and in some fragments.

In the 2nd pers., there are again variations. True, the sg. m.

separate form is everywhere *'th*; the one instance of *'t* in H v 32 may be due to an oversight, since *'th* is attested twice in a similar phrase in the very same psalm. The sg. f. separate form is attested only in Is a li 10.12 *'ty*, and in *'th* ib. 9. In the former, we have a form identical with SamH and presupposed proto-Semitic one, in the latter, apparently confusion with masc. (the form looks like having been corrected into *'ty*; at first, the scribe apparently took the reference to be to God Himself). In the verbal afformatives, *-th* is the normal form for masc. in Is a and all the properly sectarian scrolls where it appears; in H, however, *-t* is already occasionally attested (Z is not taken into account, apart from some special cases, for the same reason as in part II), and in the documents from Bar Cochba period it becomes the rule without exception. In Is a, mixed practice also appears, particularly in the first half, apparently due to the influence of the model exemplar; as a matter of fact, the present writer cannot regard one single instance of *-t* from the second half [34] as demonstrably 2nd. masc. It could be that the scribe, being uncertain of interpretation, left most of such forms deliberately without a *mater lectionis*. A comparable picture is obtained from the suffixed form, but here, the mere *-k* is slightly more frequent than *-t* in verb, and also occasionally attested in the second half without doubt. In the properly sectarian documents, the long form *-kh* again prevails, *-k* appearing in H besides it; the one instance of *-k* in M (ii 8) besides regular *-kh* is again obviously due to oversight. As regards sg. f., the situation is very interesting again: apart from xxii 1, where *-ky* occurs in an interjectional expression, and *-ty* in a subsequent verb plus xvii 10 *škḥty*, I cannot find the forms with final *-y* outside the second half of Isaiah, where again there is no certain instance of *-t* in a fem. form, either, and only a few of *-k* in the suffix [35]. When combining this with the analogous phenomenon in 1st sg. suffix (see above), we cannot escape the conclusion that all these forms are due to the influence of the model exemplar in the second half of the book; they were apparently becoming obsolete at the time our scribe was at work, but were not yet so totally forgotten that he would have wilfully omitted them when finding them in a model exemplar. That being so, it is hard to accept the thesis that the 2nd f. sg. forms would be due to Aramaic influence [36], were it so, we should expect their usage to increase and become regular in the latest documents, rather than their being dropped at the very threshold of the development. So they must be genuine Hebrew elements inherited from earlier times; as is known, even in MT some instances are still preserved of them [37].

Turning to plural, only the masc. is preserved, of all the forms according to my notes—this means anyway that if some instances of fem. are found, they all must be without a final vowel consonant. In the separate form, *'tmh* only is attested in Is a (only twice in the first half); in W, two instances of *'tm* occur besides two longer ones; elsewhere, no attestations. In the verbal afformative, in the second half of Is a *-tmh* alone occurs; in the first half, four instances of it besides many more of *-tm*; in W also, the latter is in majority; elsewhere, no attestations. In the suffix again, the distribution is more even, even if *-kmh* is definitely more clearly in majority in the second half of Is a than *-km* in the first half. In W again, both forms exist side by side (see, e.g., p. x beg.). In some Biblical fragments, 1Q27 l. 1 (besides *-km*), and 1Q29 l. 3 there are further examples of *-kmh*, elsewhere no attestations. So it seems that in the forms of 2nd pers. masc. the final vowels were more persistent than in fem. and the 1st pers.; and in sg. masc. also more so than in pl.

In the 3rd pers., confusion is considerable, apparently due to the quiescization of the gutturals. We cannot pay attention to insignificant variants here [38]. In sg. separate forms, the distribution in Is a is almost as clear-cut as one could wish; *hw'h* and *hy'h* occur only in the second half, and apart from two examples of *hw'*, and one of *hy'*, these shorter forms are found only in the first half. In the sectarian documents proper, the longer forms occur in W (besides one example of *hw'*), M, sporadically in H, and in the fragment 4QF1; *hw'/hy'* in HC, preponderantly in H, and in the other fragments. In the suffixed forms, those after sg. and pl. nouns are largely confused, apparently indicating identical pronunciations; in masc., *-yw* for *-w* is very common particularly in the second half of Is a, while *-w* after a pl. can be documented with certainty only in the first half. In fem., again, *-h'* for TibH *-ah* is only found a few times in the second half, and for TibH *-ha* also only there, but definitely in majority. Among the sectarian documents proper, similar forms are found in W (f. *-hh* xviii 10), HC (mainly *-w* for *-yw*), and M (mostly *-w* or *-yhw* for *-yw*) [39]. Elsewhere it is mainly the 'normal' TibH forms that are met. In fem., the tendency towards reducing vocalization with the complete model exemplar of Is a is clear, but the masc. variation is not so easily digested. It seems, however, plausible to assume that the use of *-w* for normal *-yw* must be interpreted differently in early documents than in later ones; we can assume that the model examplar for the first half of Is a did not use quiescent consonants to any large extent, and that, therefore, the writing of *-w* for *-yw* simply meant that *-y-* in this connection had become or was becoming quiescent. The practice, however, was not generalized, perhaps since the forms after sg. and pl. were continually apart phonetically. *-w* for *-yw* in later documents would represent the tendency towards monophthongization accomplished in SamH, while *-yhw* suggests that there was a competitive drive to preserve the diphthong—as has happened in TibH. In Is a, a third variant still occurs sometimes, its form being *-why* after pl. nouns, *-hy* after pl. verbal forms [40]. The former is identical with the corresponding Aramaic form, and therefore it is normally declared as a plain Aramaism; but its complete absence from the sectarian documents proper makes me again suspicious about that. It is again mostly (after verbs, always) found in the second half of Is a; perhaps we could assume that it originated after verbs in pl. by the time the complete model exemplar was written, by way of dissimilation: *ū-hū* to *-ū-hī*, and supported by the Aramaic analogy was transferred to nouns also; but when the vocalization began to be reduced and gutturals became quiescent, the final *-hi* was dropped. In such a case, the mere *-w* after pl. nouns could be the outcome of this form. True, in Hebrew it is normally the first of two similar vowels that is dissimilated, but contrary cases also occur [41], and perhaps the Aramaic analogy determined the direction of the development in that phase already. So we can perhaps term it as an early half-Aramaism.

In pl. separate forms only the long ones, *hmh* and *hnh* are attested in Is a—the text in xxx 7 is uncertain—and in all the sectarian documents proper apart from W vii 2, where *hm* may be attributed to a slip of the scribe, and sporadic occurrences in H and the fragmentary commentaries on prophets from 4Q. In fem., only the long form is attested. Turning to suffixes, we find the TibH *-ām* replaced by *-mh* again almost exclusively in the second half of Is a; of the two occurrences in the first half, *bmh* in vi 13 is in a very difficult context, so it is uncertain whether the scribe regarded it as a pronominal construction; in xi 6, it stands in a pause. In W, it occurs once, in i 12, besides a large number of the short form, so it could be a slip to the contrary; in H, there is also one attestation, in xiii 10, in the other main scrolls, none at all, but in the fragment 5Q13 it appears three times, and in 2Q Nm xxxiii 52 once. *-hmh* for TibH *-hm* (and occasionally *-m*) is more widespread; it appears in both halves of Is a besides *-hm* (in the second half, the latter is rare); in W, there are five attestations (vii 7. 14 ix 6 xi 9 xvi 3), so it cannot be a slip, although *-hm* is much more numerous; it also occurs in MFC (e.g., i 5 twice) besides the shorter form; in HC xii 14 (but Mem has final form; a slip?) besides many instances of *-hm*; in M also once, viii 21; and in 1Q27 l. 1. The fem. form *-hnh* occurs four times in Is a: iii 16, xxxiv 17 (twice; 2° sm), and xxxvii 27, besides two occurrences of *-hn* (iii 17, xi 7).

In the other word classes, there is not much remarkable development between different scrolls. In the pl. masc. and sg. fem. forms of imperative and preformal we already found plene writing of the stem vowel practically regular in Is a and the sectarian scrolls proper from W to M. In the documents dated to Bar Cochba period and 3Q15, on the other hand, we do not find a trace of it, and the same appears to be the case with Z in general, even if there are a few exceptions in Z a: *wyʿbwrw*, *wygwdw*, cf. H-stem *wypyrw* (all i 20). Accordingly, by this time the word stress in these forms seems to have shifted to the last syllable, but in Z a—which we found to be the earliest of this group—the stem vowel is not yet totally reduced, and the scribe, influenced by the orthography he had seen in the older documents, still occasionally marks it. The evidence from the forms in which the stem vowel stands in the last syllable (i.e., n. act., imp. sg. m., pref. l. sg. and pl., 2. sg. m., 3. sg.) points to a comparable conclusion; the plene writing is extremely common in all the documents, and in the second half of Is a practically exclusive, but in the first half so many defectively written forms occur that they cannot be regarded as chance products [42]. The only consistent conclusion is therefore that it is due to the influence of the model exemplar, which accordingly may have been written at a time when the word stress even in these forms was not yet on the last syllable. The fact that H-stem forms often are also written without Yoḏ [43] could be interpreted as a sign of the stress lying on the preceding syllable, but the phenomenon is too sporadic and other explanations too often possible [44] for it to be taken into consideration here.

In the nominal flexion there is hardly any general phenomenon regular enough for mentioning here. As regards the stem formation, in H—mainly in hymns i to iii—a number of forms appear which may have some significance. I mean the use of type +*qtwl* (= the normal shape of n. act.) in a half verbal sense in connections in which the Bible normally has a noun of the type +*qutl*; e.g., *gdwl* i 32 xiv 23bis xvi 12; *ʾrwk* i 6 xvii 17; *ḥzwq* ii 7; *ʾmws* ii 8; *smwk* ii 9; 36; *ʿrwι* ii 18; *lhwb* iii 30. This seems to be a further indication of the origin of the normal type of n. act. from the *+qutl* type noun [45], and at the same time may mark the shift of the stress in this verbal noun to the last syllable, probably following the example of the form to which the prep. *l* was fixed—in this, the Waw regularly appears after the second radical, cf. above. Purely non-verbal nouns retain it after the first radical, e.g., *bwqr* xii 6, *qwdš* xiii 1; so *'wrk* xiii 12 etc. too. In a 2Q fragment, Jer. xlii 9, the word for God is written *'lwhymh*, which reminds of *mayma ṭahorîma* etc., in a text with Palestinian punctuation [46]; among the adverbs, *m'wdh/mw'dh/m'dh*—occurring only in W xii 12 xix 5 and H fragm. x 10 outside the second half of Is a—apparently has the same final vowel. Perhaps the final 'Alaef in the conjunction *ky'*—and the interr. pron. *my'*—also is a *mater lectionis* for some such vowel: *kîyya*, *mîyya*? [47]

IV

In syntactical matters, we again confine ourselves to the sectarian scrolls proper; for although in the Biblical texts there are many syntactical differences to MT [48], we must anyway suppose that a model exemplar which ultimately must have been more or less common to both has strongly influenced the present syntactical constructions, too. Of the properly sectarian documents we also omit H and HC, the former since in a work of poetical character several untypical constructions may be expected to be met with, and the latter, since it partly consists of Biblical text, partly appears to be revised at a later time to an unknown extent, and in some passages is also rather fragmentary. The remaining documents, to be utilized here, are accordingly; W, MFC, M, Z a, and Z b [49].

Within the scrolls themselves, not much development can be observed. The main rule of the word order, that the most emphasized or otherwise important part of the sentence is mentioned first, is regularly followed. Nominal sentences appear fairly often, more often with a copula than without it. The normal conjugation referring to the future is the preformative one, although the afformative conjugation preceded by *w-* also occurs rather frequently throughout the documents. Outside Z, the preformative conjugation with *w-* is not often used; in a future sense it appears in W vi 10 M ii 16 iv 21 vii 23 x 2, in Z a slightly more frequently, e.g., ii 2.14, and in Z b ii 2. 33tris; referring to past, in W x 2 xvii 6 M iii 18 iv 18. 26; in Z fairly frequently, e.g., Z a i 4. 7. 8bis, etc.; Z b ii 9. 18. 19, etc. The normal conjugation referring to past is the plain afformal; only in Z b i 34 ii 11. 23 it has this reference when provided with the conj. *w-*. On the other hand, the plain afformal also refers to the future in W xi 6bis. 7 Z a ix 7; but the two first instances are in a Biblical quotation and the third probably influenced by that example; while in Z a ix 7 the syntactical position is rather complicated and the scribe therefore could have erred regarding the temporal reference of *ʿnh*, particularly since there is another instance of afformal just preceding and semantically parallel to this one. The reference to present or indefinite time is normally made by preformal; the rare occurrence of this usage in the two oldest documents (only W x 8 MFC i 5) is due to the fact that they deal mainly with future things, with occasional references to the past. The only example of afformal in an indefinite sense is *spr* Z a ix 4; it could also be result of a syntactical mistake, an afformal —with *w-*—preceding being taken for a parallel instance, though actually it refers to relative future (compared with the verb preceding it). The noun of agent (and patient) can, and often does, naturally refer to the present or indefinite time too, but since it is often (also without copula) used of future and past as well, this ability is not properly characteristic of it, but rather the fact that it fairly regularly refers to a permanent or continuous state or action; this use again occurs through all the documents. Besides it, a frequentative sense appears in M i 20. 24 ii 10 Z a iv 18bis ix 14 Z b ii 2; the only remaining instance is *hʿmdym* Z a iv 4, and even it refers to future. In a frequentative sense, we find also afformal with *w-* in M ii 5bis vi 4 Z a xii 3 Z b ii 31. 32, and preformal in M ii 19-24. Noun of action is mostly used with the prep. *l-* in a final sense—this combination hardly appears in another sense at all—, but the use with the prep. *b-* in a temporal sense also goes through all the documents. The noun of verb, on the other hand, seems to occur only in W i 8 (taking up and confirming the sense of a preceding verbal form) outside Biblical quotations. Normal preformal appears to be used in a jussive sense in *yškyl* Z a xiii 7.

As to the syntactical combinations, the most interesting phenomenon is the tendency to use identical verbal forms in parallel functions in subsequent sentences. A preformal is normally continued by another preformal, and when a transition to *w*-afformal occurs (the verb being most emphasized), normally a series of these follows; and the same is the case with afformal and w-preformal referring to the past, even if the latter forms real series in Z only. Within such series, a 'plain' verbal form could occasionally be provided with *w-* too, and so the twofold reference to both past and future of w-afformal and -preformal could arise; the earliest instance of w-preformal referring to future, *wyhyw* W vi 10 has a half jussive sense, which also probably facilitated the development, and the first w-afformal referring to past, *wšbw* Z b i 34, is in an adversative parallelism with a preceding plain afformal, which may be why the scribe felt that it lacked a consecutive sense. Jussive forms are also normally followed by other jussives, so in W xvii 8 M ii 2-4. 5-6. 8. 9. etc. Z a xiii 7-9; the only exceptions are again in W, xii 13 xix 6, where a w-afformal follows. On the other hand, the rule of cohortative being followed by another one (W xiii 12-13 xiv 12-13) has no exceptions, nor that of imperative continued by imperative, W xii 9-14 xiv 16 xix 5. 7 Z a i 1 iii 7 (the last one in a Biblical quotation). The negation *bl* is also taken up by *wbl*, M viii 7-8. The adverb *bṭrm* is only combined with an afformal to refer to the past, Z a ii 7; *'ẓ* with preformal occurs with the same reference in Z b ii 17.

To assess the significance of these data we have to compare them with the two other well-known old syntactical structures of Hebrew, viz., those of Biblical Hebrew (BH) and Mishnaic Hebrew (MH) [50]. In most respects, we find Qumran Hebrew (QH) to lie syntactically between these two entities. The use of preformal to refer to the present, which is so common in BH and QH, is totally absent in MH; on the other hand, afformal with reference to the future or indefinite time, absent from MH, is also disappearing here. The noun of agent, again, is used wholly in analogy with the Biblical language, apart from the creation of a frequentative usage starting in M, while only W has preserved a trace of the affirmative use of the noun of verb, common in the early BH, but wholly absent in MH. The construction *l* + n. act. in a final sense is common to both BH and MH, though more exclusive in the latter; *b* + n. act. in a temporal sense does occur in BH, but is relatively less frequent than in QH, while in MH it is totally absent. The consecutive Waw, so common in BH, occurs often here also, but relatively much less frequently than in the Bible, and in a reversed proportion: in BH, the w-preformal is much more frequent than w-afformal, while in QH, the latter has upper hand (particularly outside Z); in the normal MH, it is never used. The tendency to continue with the verbal form already used also prepares the way to the MH usage; but the ability to make change still preserves something of the BH variability. The fact that in W a couple of Biblical traits are found which never return in the other documents is another indication of its greater age and perhaps somewhat different background; while the revival of w-preformal and ʾz̧ + preformal referring to the past in Z may be an indication of an environment in which Hebrew was not generally spoken in any form, which enabled the increase in the influence of the Biblical language to take place—the non-Biblical traits found there seem to corroborate this.

V

The order and approximate dates of the origin of the documents dealt with thus seem to have been the following: 1) the manuscript which served as a model exemplar for the scribe of Is a in the first half of the latter. The fact that it appears to have comprised only chapters i to xxxiii, the last of which also represents the last section which with some probability can be attributed to the eighth-century prophet Isaiah seems to presuppose relatively great age for it; also the fact that vowel consonants sporadically appearing in the Book of Ezekiel appended to certain pronominal forms seem to have been present in it, if not in identical, in any case comparable connections, rather favours than prevents an early date. The contents of ch. xxiv to xxvii, in my opinion, do not prevent such an early date either; it is well known that in connection with the exile and the upheaval following it apocalypticism flourished, and even if these chapters in some respects rise above the elements generally assigned to that period, the parts of the book normally assigned to Deutero-Isaiah also represent the peak of prophecy in some respects anyway. It is well conceivable that the man who, in the prime of his life, had apocalyptic inclination enough to produce passages like Is xl 3-5 xliii 18-20 liii 7-12 lv 12-13 xxxiii-xxxiv can well have, after many frustrations, in his old age—perhaps in connection with the Zerubbabel revolt—produced these chapters. On the other hand, however, it is well known that numerous mistranslations of the LXX presuppose a text about as devoid of the vowel consonants as the Canaanite inscriptions; therefore we must suppose that different kinds of orthographical traditions were in vogue in the early times, and transitions between them naturally possible; so it could have been such a transitional text. Therefore a date between fifth and third centuries seems possible; the presence of Deutero-Isaianic material in it on the one hand, and its limited extent on the other, may make an early fourth century date most probable. 2) The model exemplar for the latter half of Is a. The use of vowel consonants appears to have been at its peak, and judging from W (cf. the next item), it cannot have been written later than the beginning of the second century. 3) The original W document; on the grounds given in section I, it cannot have been written later than in the early phases of the Maccabaean revolt, but due to the lack of any allusions to this, probably has been written slightly earlier, perhaps in late 170's. The use of vowel consonants has diminished; at least the 1st, and 2nd fem. sg. pronominal elements seem to have lost their final vowels, as also some adverbs etc. 3) The original MFC document; this follows the pattern of W so closely that they hardly can be distinguished. 5) The earliest parts of H, at least hymns i to iii; the reduction in vowel consonants is continued, and the actual shift of the word stress to the last syllable (in n. act.) begun. Contemporary to this again may be 5) the original form of HC, on terminological grounds given in section I, as well as historical allusions connected with them. Both these items still apparently belong to the middle parts of the second century. Next to them, and not much later, 7) Is a must be placed. The final vowel consonants are being left out of use, but have not yet been forgotten. 8) The use of vowel consonants in M is so consistent that the document preserved to us may well be one of the earliest; on philological and historical grounds it could be assigned anywhere from the late second century B.C. to the beginning of our era. 9) The present shape of HC, and the preserved exemplars of W, MFC, and H, to judge from their inconsistent use of vowel consonants with a clear tendency to decrease, appear to be somewhat later. 13) The original document of Z a, on terminological and historical grounds datable to the time after the First Jewish Revolt, probably towards the end of the first century. 14) The documents from the Bar Cochba period; the use of vowel consonants has reached its minimum, which is slightly beyond that normally found in MT, and the same can be said of the degree of the influence of Aramaic; the stress also appears to have shifted to the last syllable in a continuously increasing degree. Finally, 15) Z b is datable after this period on terminological and historical grounds.

It is a fact that sharp or heavy word stress tends to reduce the vocalization of the words, in the first place that of the unstressed syllables. The reduction in the use of vowel consonants is most naturally combined with it. A good working hypothesis to explain the above mentioned phenomena would therefore be the supposition that the word stress was growing lighter in the post-exilic period until ca. 200 B.C., then began to grow heavier or sharper, reaching the peak during the Bar Cochba revolt. As we know, this period was also historically very troublesome, and unstable social conditions normally create tension among the people, which again, due to psychic factors, can have parallel influence on their speech too; and heavy or sharp stress is easily conceivable as an expression of psychic tension or pressure. The contractions in the Bar Cochba documents are parallel to this; and the tradition about the origin of the Masoretic text of the Hebrew Bible preserved in Sifre Dt. 356, Mass. Soferim VI 4, Yer. Ta'anith IV 68a fits this schema strikingly well. According to it, MT was based on three manuscripts preserved and found by chance; accordingly, the probability is that these manuscripts were relatively young, and the story shows that Aramaic influence had penetrated at least one of them, to the extent that a genuine Hebrew word had been replaced by a purely Aramaic one. The variation between *m'wnh* and *m'wn* may also reflect the reduction of the final vowels; in these mss., accordingly, it was not yet complete, whilst in the Bar Cochba documents it apparently is so. On this basis, the MT is reported to be established, probably towards the end of the first century, and so the subsequent development, as reflected in the Bar Cochba documents, did not have any influence on it. The afformative vowel of 1st sg. was preserved in writing, since at the time the model exemplars were written it had not yet been dropped; on the other hand, those of the 2nd pers. were omitted, since they had become quiescent earlier. The replacement of Šin by Samaek in the 'Šin-roots' was just beginning, therefore it is confined to scattered variants here and there in the present MT; had it been based on mss. written during the Bar Cochba period or later, we apparently would have quite a number of the commonest of these roots regularly written with Samaek. The same appears to be the case with the intrusion of the Aramaic and Greek vocabulary; therefore their extent in BH is so strikingly small when compared with MH, though the latter also ceased to be used as a spoken language only a few decades—anyway, less than a century—later even among the learned. And finally, it also strikingly explains the deviation from the normal ultima stress in the 1st and 2nd pers. sg. of afformal. To attribute it to the analogy of 3rd sg. m. is not very plausible—why didn't 3rd sg. f. and 3rd and 2nd pl. follow the same analogy? No, but just as the earlier penultimate stress in 2nd. pl. m. (*qataltímma*, cf. SamH) became ultimate through the omission of the final vowel—and so strengthened the analogy drawing the stress to the ultima even in the other forms—, so the penultima stress in *qatálta*, *-ti* became ultimate when they were replaced by *qatált*. They were again provided with final vowels so late that a renewed Aramaic influence did not have time enough to transfer the stress to the ultima except to a limited extent, and this was apparently utilized to create a difference between 'plain' afformal provided with the conjunction *w*-, and 'consecutive' one, though in some other forms it was nearly completely generalized [51]. So it seems that the scribe of Is b and other similar texts [52] did *not* follow the established pattern of the model text, but *contributed to the creation* of such a pattern; and MT is not based on an older and better preserved text than Is a, but has descended from a similar text by way of orthographic changes following an analogous phonetic development; and Qumran texts are not written in a 'substandard' Hebrew degenerated by Aramaic influence, but represent a phase in the development of Hebrew *less* influenced by Aramaic than the Masoretic text and Tiberian Biblical Hebrew—let alone MH.

Melbourne 1963

NOTES

[1] The fact that the title is used without an article suggests that *ṣdq* is used adjectivally, which is why this translation is preferred; and also that it is a general title, not assigned to a certain individual (cf. below).

[2] To me, the word looks like *hqʾl* rather than *hqhl*; and since the Qof is somewhat exceptional in shape and size, I think the best way of emendation is to leave it out; perhaps it was an unintentional stroke in the model exemplar of the present ms., and the scribe was hesitant about what to do with it. In the preceding sentences, as is seen, I assume that both *swkt* and *skwt* were read in one way, *sukkoṭ*. The former could represent the old orthography from the time the stress lay on the penultima (cf. sections IV-V).

[3] Why *hrʾšwn* should be 'ungrammatical' (Rabin), I do not understand, as *qṣ*—to the best of my knowledge—appears as masculine throughout the history of Hebrew. Rather, the construct state *pqdt* before the adjective attribute is somewhat peculiar, but in no way unparallelled, either; cf. *yom hašševici* Gn. ii 3 etc.

[4] Naturally this does not refer to identical *individuals*, but the leading circle. Perhaps the copper scrolls were also delivered by them to Bar Cochba to finance the revolt?

[5] For the same reason, the title of 'The Wicked Priest' could in some other passages refer to later persons—it could have become a general title for the Jerusalem High Priest.

[6] Cf. n. 3.

[7] See my *Grammar of the Samaritan Dialect of Hebrew* § 27.

[7b] This and the next section cf. GOSHEN-GOTTSLEIN in *Scripta Hierosolymitana*, 4 (1958) p. 101-37, who adds many interesting details; but his purely synchronistic approach makes him assume double tradition instead of diachronic development and deny the occurrence of such transitory phenomena as double peak accent.

[8] This is our designation for the form of Hebrew represented by MT Qre.

[9] See my *Materials for a Non-Masoretic Hebrew Grammar* vols II-III.

[10] For my terminology, see the Introduction to vol. II of my *Materials*.

[11] For details, see KUTSCHER, *The Language and Linguistic Background of the Isaiah Scroll*, p. 95-140 etc.

[12] As has been generally observed, the style of writing is slightly altered; in my opinion, this could have been caused by a change of pen, which may presuppose a major break in work.

[13] Cf. POPE in JBL LXXX/1952 p. 235-43; also EATON in VT IX/1959 p. 151 sqq; etc.

[14] Cf. n. 11.

[15] The references to SamH are to my *Grammar of SamH* (= *Materials* III).

[16] Cf. my *Grammar of SamH* § 119*cc*; the earlier guttural may have kept the colour of the vowel close enough to *a* for the glide to become ʾ (and not *w*).

[17] In SamH, effects of double peak accent occur only alongside ʾ, *h*, *ū*/*w*, and *ī*/*y*.

[18] Cf. my *Grammar of SamH* § 119*cc*; subsequently, the shorter forms have gained ground both in SamH (see ib. *ff*) and TibH (cf. *soḏ*, *ḥeq*, etc., in which only the simple length is found, as against *moṯ*/*mawaeṯ*, *beṯ*/*bayiṯ* etc.); and the same could be the case in Qumran Hebrew already.

[19] Cf. SamH *galûwwem* and TibH *geluyîm* both from +*galū-im*; and notes 16, 18.

[20] Cf. n. 16.

[21] Cf. my *Grammar of SamH* § 119 *cc-ee*.

[22] See my *Vocabulary to SP* (= *Materials* II), root *šlš*.

[23] And perhaps SamH; but here all certain cases of *e* appear contracted.

[24] Cf. my *Grammar of SamH* § 76*b*.

[24b] Cf. R. MEYER in V.T. 3 (1953) p. 225-35; BUSH in RQ 2 (1960) p. 502-7.

[25] See my *Vocabulary to SP*, root *tʾ3t*.

[26] Cf. ʾ*ukkal* Ex iii 2; and my *Grammar of SamH* 12.

[26b] I am happy to see that on this point I agree with BEN ḤAYYIM, *Scripta Hierosolymitana*, 4 (1958) p. 202 ff., but unfortunately his faiture to see the subsequent shift in later documents makes him assume a genetic relationship with Sam H.

[27] Cf. my *Vocabulary to SP*, root ʾ*4mr*.

[28] Cf. ib. root ʾ*2lk*.

[29] Cf. BEN-HAYYIM in *Melanges de Philosophie et de Litterature Juives* III/1958 p. 98 sq.

[29b] See my *Vocabulary to SP*, root *rʾš* I; the var. *raišon* is from rapid recitation.

[29c] Cf. GOSHEN-GOTTSLEIN in RQ 2 (1959) p. 44sq.

[30] The strokes between *h* and *š* in *hšrym* W iii 3 do not look like a letter to me; and the meaning, hence root of *spwt* ib. v 12 is uncertain; *š* for *s* occurs in HC i 11; *mʾšw*. In Is a, *s* for *š* appears twice; *lḥswp* xxx 14, *sʾy* xlix 18.

[30b] Cf. GORDON, UHB, I 5, 1.4.21; ASA *swk*, = *śwk*; *śfq* = *śpq*, etc. besides more regular *š* = *ś*, and the next note.

[31] Cf. Ar. *šʾf*, which hardly can be distinguished from Hebrew *šʾp*/*šVp*: *šbk* = *sbk*; ʾ*ašǧa*ʿ 'mad' with *šgʿ*; *kšf* 'to disclose' with *kšf*, etc.; the story in Jdg. xii 6 which is exactly opposite to the present-day situation in SamH; the correspondence of Samaeḵ by *x*, Šin by *s* in Greek; etc.

[31b] The *ṣ* in the Semitic name of Tyrus could have been phonetically different

from that in Sidon, standing as it does before a back vowel, but still part of the same phoneme.

[32] I.e., the one which is mainly used with nouns, and with n. act. indicates *sbj*.

[33] KUTSCHER (*Language and Linguistic Background*, p. 134 sq.) does not give other examples from Is a, either; of the two p. 136, *py*ʾ (HC ii 2) does not contain the suffix, and in ʾ*py*ʾ M x 19, the final ʾ*Alaef* seems to be erased.

[34] In all the possible 13 instances, syntactical connection is obscure.

[35] See KUTSCHER, *Language* etc. p. 158 for details.

[36] See KUTSCHER, ib. p. 143, 159 sqq.

[37] Remarkable is that in SamH, -*kī* as a real suffix is extinct (just as masc. -*ka*).

[38] For details in Is a, see KUTSCHER, *Language* etc. p. 350 sqq.

[39] Since *w* and *y* are alike in M, -*yhw* could be read also -*why* (= Aram.); but since this is not found in the other sectarian documents proper, while -*yhw* is, (HC xii 11, besides Is a lxii 9), we prefer this reading (cf. below on -*why*). The word in MFC i 7 which HABERMANN reads *ywmwy* is in BARTHELEMY-MILIK's photograph *ywmyw*. What WERNBERG-MØLLER in RQ 2 (1960) p. 223-36 says about the distinction of *w* and *y* in M serves only to indicate that the difference between the two sounds (probably non-phonemic at the time) was still felt, but not consistently (cf. ib. p. 225).

[40] See KUTSCHER, *Language* etc. p. 161 sq. for details.

[41] E.g., *lūlē* from *lū lō*.

[42] See KUTSCHER, *Language* etc. p. 103.

[43] Cf. n. 29.

[44] Cf. KUTSCHER, *Language* etc. p. 112.

[45] Cf. my *Grammar of SamH* § 11*a*.

[46] See my *Materials* vol I p. 36, 53, 58, etc.

[47] Cf. the suffixed *panaya* in MT, Ex xx 3 Dt v 7, which also obviously reminds of the kitiv -*y*ʾ of the same suffix in the second half of Is a (cf. above, with n. 33).

[48] KUTSCHER, *Language* etc. p. 266-342 et al.

[49] This last only where it substantially differs from Z a.

[50] According to SEGAL, *A Grammar of Mishnaic Hebrew* (Oxford 1958). CH. RABIN in *Scripta Hierosolymitana*, 4 (1958) p. 144-61 comes largely to similar results apart from the basic Jewish assumption of the existence of two kinds of Hebrew side by side, which makes him see the diachronic development as an advancing process of misture.

[51] Such as the suffix of 2nd sg. m.; cf. also my article, 'Spoken Hebrew from the Tenth Century A.D.', *Abr Nahrain* 1963.

[52] I.e., the scroll of Minor Prophets, those from 6Q, etc.

APOSIOPESIS IN THE O.T. AND THE HEBREW CONDITIONAL OATH

BY

A. D. CROWN

Aposiopesis may be defined as "a rhetorical device which consists in suddenly breaking off speaking in the middle of a sentence", [1] because the speaker is unable or unwilling to continue: the sudden halt in speech also breaks the thought of the sentence. As an example we might cite (in English), "When I looked into the room the first thing I saw . . . but I dare not describe that dreadful sight". [2]

According to *GKC* [3] aposiopesis is the concealment or suppression of entire sentences which are of themselves necessary to complete the sense and therefore must be supplied from the context. *This is especially frequent after conditional clauses.* [4] *GKC* cites a number of examples of alleged aposiopesis and in particular reference is made to three paragraphs dealing with special cases of this device. [5] The said paragraphs discuss (a) the abridgement of conditional clauses whether in the protasis or in the apodosis [6]; (b) the omission of a verb on which the accusative (sometimes indicated by אֶת) depends; [7] and (c) incomplete, i.e. elliptical sentences when either the subject or the predicate must be supplied from the context. [8]

However, it should be noted immediately, that by definition many of the examples put forward in *GKC* must be disregarded, for there is a failure to distinguish between true aposiopesis and simple ellipsis in syntax. The essence of an aposiopesis is not so much the omission of a word or words but a marked break in the thought, a break which may be so extreme as to approach an anacoluthon, and the two may, in fact, be confused. [9]

The break in thought in an aposiopesis can scarcely be filled by reference to the context: the lacuna must be bridged by individual interpretations which may, of course, differ.

Where there is lacking a word or a group of words that would otherwise be required to complete the grammatical construction or fully to express the sense, but which can readily be inferred from the context, the device employed is an ellipse rather than an aposiopesis. [10]

The majority of the verses, cited by *GKC* as aposiopesis fall into the category of ellipsis, leaving uncertain the question of whether true aposiopesis is to be found in the Old Testament.

The author of this paper undertook a sample study of all forms of ellipsis in the Book of Genesis to see how far the contention could be maintained that aposiopesis is a common device in Hebrew. *The study does not claim to be exhaustive* but most of the examples to be found in Genesis were recorded. (It should be noted that even simple ellipse may be a point of interpretation; for example in the phrase וְאֶת־רַעֲבוֹן בָּתֵּיכֶם קְחוּ וָלֵכוּ׃ [11] "take (food for) the famine of your households and go," the word וָלֵכוּ may well be interpreted as, "go your way" [12] i.e. an example of ellipsis).

More than two hundred ellipses were found in Genesis, [13] yet despite the claim for frequency in *GKC* not one aposiopesis was found that could, unequivocally, be maintained to be such. Four doubtful cases were found, two of which have commonly been noted as aposiopesis. The first of these verses [14] need not be discussed in detail since versional evidence suggests that the text is corrupt. [15] If one accepts the agreement of four versions against the Masoretic Text, the lacuna disappears.

The second verse [16] reads in full

וַיְדַבֵּר אֶל־עֶפְרוֹן בְּאָזְנֵי עַם־הָאָרֶץ לֵאמֹר אַךְ אִם־אַתָּה לוּ שְׁמָעֵנִי נָתַתִּי כֶּסֶף הַשָּׂדֶה קַח מִמֶּנִּי וְאֶקְבְּרָה אֶת־מֵתִי שָׁמָּה׃

and is translated by the *AV* ". . . but if thou *wilt give it* I pray thee, hear me; I will give the money for the field . . .", adding the words, "*wilt give it*". The verse can be viewed in two ways, either as containing a hypothetical clause אַךְ אִם־אַתָּה, broken after the protasis to be resumed with a second hypothetical clause, לוּ שְׁמָעֵנִי, i.e. an aposiopesis where an apodosis is missing, [17] or else as containing a protasis followed, after an aposiopesis, by a desiderative clause. That לוּ can hardly be a hypothetical particle is shown by the imperative which follows it; an imperative can follow לוּ only when that word is a desiderative particle. [18] In this case one may need to see no more than an anacoluthon reading אַךְ אִם־אַתָּה as parallel in intention (even though not completed) to לוּ שְׁמָעֵנִי [19]. On the other hand the accents suggest that both אִם . . . לוּ are connected to make one idiom even though this would be unique in the O.T. Perhaps there was seen here a parallel to the Aramaic אִלּוּ or אִילוּ [20] which appears to be compounded from אִם (= אִן = הֵן) and לוּ. [21] In this case the best translation would be, "If you would but listen to me, . . ." leaving no necessity to postulate either an anacoluthon or an aposiopesis.

The third case is more difficult to resolve. The text reads: [22] —

וַיֹּאמֶר אֵלָיו לָבָן אִם־נָא מָצָאתִי חֵן בְּעֵינֶיךָ נִחַשְׁתִּי וַיְבָרְכֵנִי יה׳ בִּגְלָלֶךָ :

The verse falls into two, apparently disjunctive portions. The first clause is customarily translated, "If I have found favour in your eyes" and is usually the protasis of a conditional sentence. The second clause is translated by the *AV* "I have learned by experience (*RSV* "by divination") that the Lord has blessed me for thy sake". The latter phrase appears not to be an apodosis but seems to start the thought afresh leaving a lacuna that is filled by the *AV* with the words "*tarry*: *for*". Apparently here is a classic aposiopesis: [23] yet the verse is more troublesome than that, as is shown by the contradictions in *GKC* when discussing its problems. [24] The Septuagint turns the second half of the sentence into a complete apodosis, by rendering the word נִחַשְׁתִּי οἰωνισάμην ἄν "I would have taken omens", but this, though it clears up the grammatical difficulties, does not make good sense. The use of the consecutive imperfect after נִחַשְׁתִּי suggests that there is a close connection between these two words [25] allowing the translation, "I have found by divination that Jahweh has blessed me because of you", but the break between the first and second clauses is still complete and the sentence remains unintelligible so long as אִם is regarded as a hypothetical particle. אִם may, however, be used as a desiderative particle [26] or (though less probable) as a direct interrogative [27] and despite the customary rendering of אִם־נָא מָצָאתִי חֵן it must be suggested that only one or other of these usages will make the sentence intelligible without recourse to imaginative reconstruction. The *RSV* translates אִם וכ׳ as a desiderative construction, but its paraphrase "If you will allow me to say so" appears to be without justification since it has no parallel. From the verses subsequent to this it appears that Laban is asking Jacob to give him a second chance to prove his good will, requiring the sense in this verse of, "May I (still - עוֹד) find favour in your eyes (for - כִּי) I have learned by divination . . ." etc. The syntax is incomplete but this does not justify the view that we must find here anything more than simple ellipsis.

The fourth doubtful case is said [28] to contain a suppressed apodosis, and since, if this were the case, the missing words could not be supplied by reference to the context we must again consider here the presence of an aposiopesis. The relevant part of the verse [29] reads:

לוּ יִשְׂטְמֵנוּ יוֹסֵף וְהָשֵׁב יָשִׁיב לָנוּ אֵת כָּל־הָרָעָה וכ׳

Neither the *AV* "Joseph will peradventure hate us and will certainly requite us all the evil . . ." etc., or the *RSV* regard this as a genuine case of a hypothetical sentence, since the context implies that the danger was real and therefore לוּ is being misused [30], i.e. the clause is read as though the word לוּ were really אוּלַי. In any case even if one were to regard לוּ as a hypothetical particle in this context, the sense of the verse is completed by the statement "and will certainly requite us . . ." etc., and thus this clause would need to be taken as the apodosis, whatever the grammatical difficulties. It is doubtful whether there is any justification in looking here for an aposiopesis.

Nowhere else in the Book of Genesis did there appear a verse in which the ellipsis could not easily be supplied by reference to the context. Every case observed fell into one of the following categories.

(a) Condensations of well-known expressions or interjections, to give only the essential meaning, i.e. brachylogy. [31] For example there is the common use of הִנֵּה (or הִנְנִי) without subject or copula. [32] Perhaps, also to be regarded as a brachylogy rather than as an ellipse is the omission of a noun governed by a numerical adjective particularly where the noun is a measure, weight, or statement of time. [33] e.g. בָּרִאשׁוֹן = בַּחֹדֶשׁ הָרִאשׁוֹן. [34] The same brevity of expression is, however, found even where the noun is not common or even a specification of mensuration, so long as the noun is readily understood from the context; e.g. תַּחְתִּיִּם שְׁנִיִּם וּשְׁלִשִׁים, [35] where the word 'storey' is omitted.

Another form of condensation of expression which, because of its frequency, may be regarded as brachylogy rather than ellipsis is the common omission of the noun governed by a demonstrative adjective leaving the adjective with the appearance of being a demonstrative pronoun or even a demonstrative adverb.

E.g. וַיִּתֶּן־לִי גַּם־אֶת־זֶה = וַיִּתֶּן־לִי גַּם־אֶת־[הַבֵּן הַ·] זֶה. [36] The reverse construction is frequently found where the demonstrative adjective is omitted, it apparently being felt that the effect of the article is sufficient to imply the demonstrative force. E.g. הַבָּנוֹת בְּנֹתַי [37] = הַבָּנוֹת [הָאֵלֶּה] בְּנֹתַי.

(b) The ellipse of the pronominal object of verbs is particularly common, [38] but does not seem to be limited to verbs of speaking, sense or motion, as suggested by *GKC* or Davidson, [39] but apparently may happen with any transitive verb since the omission of the pronominal object occurs with שחת [40] נכר [41] ידע [42] צלח [43] (hiph'il) and חלל. [44] Less frequent is the ellipse of the object (rather than the pronominal object) of a verb [45], e.g. וַיְבַקֵּשׁ לִבְכּוֹת [46] = וַיְבַקֵּשׁ [מָקוֹם] לִבְכּוֹת. Despite Davidson [47] if the lost object is not part of an oft-repeated phrase, or if it is not part of an idiom, and hence has to be supplied by reference to the context of the verb (as in the example above) rather than by reference to the verb itself, this usage must be regarded as ellipsis rather than brachylogy. Note that no case of ellipse of the object was found where there was a real danger of ambiguity. In the example above, the words "and he went to his room" occur in the same sentence, and there is little room for doubt as to what is missing.

On the other hand if the lost object is implied in the verb and is unmistakeable without further reference the condensed expression must be regarded as a brachylogy. Such cases are found with the verbs יָלַד [48] (frequently), שָׁאַב, [49] שָׁבַר, [50] טָרַף [51] where the object of the expression can hardly be mistaken.

(c) Another common form of ellipse is the omission of the subject or pronominal subject of a verb, particularly with the participle or the infinitive construct, where the subject has been previously stated or is readily inferred from the context [52].

עָשׂוּ מִלְחָמָה אֶת־ [53] = עָשׂוּ [הַמְּלָכִים הָאֵלֶּה] מִלְחָמָה אֶת־ This type of ellipse is common where a word would be repeated שֶׁקֶל כֶּסֶף עֹבֵר לַסֹּחֵר [54] = שֶׁקֶל כֶּסֶף [כֶּסֶף] עֹבֵר לַסֹּחֵר and it may well have been the desire to avoid such repetition that has led to the loss of the subject even where partial ambiguity could result, e.g. וַנֹּאמֶר אֶל־אֲדֹנִי לֹא יוּכַל הַנַּעַר לַעֲזֹב אֶת־אָבִיו וְעָזַב אֶת־אָבִיו וָמֵת : ... אֶת־אָבִיו [וְאָבִיו] מֵת :

[Gen. 44: 22].

(d) The ellipse of the verb before the accusative where the verb is repeated within the same verse, or in an adjacent verse or where the verbal idea is obviously in the speaker's mind and can be supplied by reference to the context. [55]

E.g. אִם־מִחוּט וְעַד שְׂרוֹךְ־נַעַל וְאִם־אֶקַּח וכ׳ = אִם־[אֶקַּח] מִחוּט וְעַד וכ׳ [56]

or אִם־הַשְּׂמֹאל וְאִם־הַיָּמִין = אִם־[תִּקַּח] הַשְּׂמֹאל וכ׳ [57].

The sudden change from narrative in the third person to direct speech without an introductory כִּי אָמַר [58] falls within this category.

So-called aposiopesis in the partial suppression of the protasis or apodosis of a conditional sentence is usually ellipsis of the verb to a greater or lesser degree. [59] This can be shown by reference to Gen. 4: 24 where only the verb יֻקַּם is lacking to complete the apodosis. The omission is almost certainly to avoid the repetition one would find if the sentence were complete.

By extension, where the verb in the protasis of a conditional sentence is modified or limited by an adverbial clause or other words which are essential to the sense of the verb, these may also be omitted to avoid repetition. For example

וְעַתָּה אִם־יֶשְׁכֶם עֹשִׂים חֶסֶד וֶאֱמֶת אֶת־אֲדֹנִי הַגִּידוּ לִי וְאִם־לֹא הַגִּידוּ לִי [60]

Here the second protasis is parallel to the first in sense and the negative לֹא which is usually attached to the verb is sufficient in itself to bring to mind the verb and its modifying clause. There is no need to regard this verse and like cases as anything other than ellipsis.

(e) The ellipse of adjectives where their presence would be pleonastic, e.g.

וְיִשְׂרָאֵל אָהַב אֶת־יוֹסֵף ...... וְעָשָׂה־לוֹ כְּתֹנֶת פַּסִּים : כְּתֹנֶת פַּסִּים [רַבִּים] = [61]

(f) The omission of the relative pronoun [62].

It appears from the foregoing analysis that those paragraphs cited in *GKC* as dealing with *various kinds* (sic) of aposiopesis, namely contraction in conditional clauses, condensation of well-known expressions or interjections and omission of verbs in fact deal with various types of ellipse or brachylogy. So far as has been determined above aposiopesis is rare and no case of it occurs in the Book of Genesis.

It remains to be seen whether the "classic" cases [63] bear examination. *Ex.* 32: 32.

וְעַתָּה אִם־תִּשָּׂא חַטָּאתָם וְאִם־אַיִן מְחֵנִי נָא מִסִּפְרְךָ אֲשֶׁר כָּתָבְתָּ :

The *AV* translation is "Yet now, if thou wilt forgive their sin—and if not, blot me, I pray thee, out of thy book which thou hast written".

The words וְאִם־אַיִן, an elliptical protasis, presuppose that the first part of the sentence is also a protasis and, therefore, the first אִם־ cannot be interpreted in any other way than as a conditional particle. Since the first protasis has no words intervening between it and the second protasis an apodosis is missing. However, three versions [64] insert the word שָׂא completing the condition. Whilst it might be possible to suggest that the versions have glossed over a difficulty by deliberately inserting this word, it could equally well be maintained that a word has fallen out of the canonical text. This verse then must be rejected as an example of an aposiopesis.

Numbers 5: 20

וְאַתְּ כִּי שָׂטִית תַּחַת אִישֵׁךְ וְכִי נִטְמֵאת וַיִּתֵּן אִישׁ בָּךְ אֶת־שְׁכָבְתּוֹ מִבַּלְעֲדֵי אִישֵׁךְ׃

The *RSV* renders this as, "But if you have gone astray though you are under your husband's authority and if you have defiled yourself and some other man than your husband has lain with you." The suggestion that there is a marked break in the thought in this sentence or even the omission of a word or words depends, in part, upon the interpretation of תַּחַת and also upon the view that this sentence which is a protasis is not completed by the following verse. However, verse 21, whether misplaced or superfluous, does act as the apodosis to verse 20. If one views the word תַּחַת as meaning "in place of" then one must also complete the thought with the words "to another man" or "with another man". However, the word אִישֵׁךְ + תַּחַת may be translated either "whilst married" or "whilst under your husband's authority". [65] In any case if the text were incomplete the missing words could readily be supplied (as in the *AV*) by reference to the context, i.e. ellipsis rather than aposiopesis.

Whilst the use of וְכִי suggests that reference is being made to a second category of sin in the second clause, i.e. a complete suppression of the details of the general term "going astray" mentioned in the first portion of the sentence, only one type of straying, namely sexual intercourse, is implied in the whole passage from verse 11 onwards. Moreover, the clause from וַיִּתֵּן (so delicately translated by the *RSV*) is a circumstantial clause explaining why the woman has become unclean, namely the contact with semen. Thus וְכִי must be seen as an extension of the first clause, i.e. ultimate to it. The verse thus should be translated "But if you have gone astray whilst married, becoming unclean, in that some man other than your husband has put his sperm into you" verse 21. "Then . . .". Again it is difficult to maintain the assertion that this verse contains an aposiopesis.

Judges 9: 16.

See above and note 9.

1 *Sam*. 12 : 14 : 15.

אִם־תִּירְאוּ אֶת־יה׳ וַעֲבַדְתֶּם אֹתוֹ וּשְׁמַעְתֶּם בְּקוֹלוֹ וְלֹא תַמְרוּ אֶת־פִּי יה׳ וִהְיִתֶם גַּם־אַתֶּם
וְגַם הַמֶּלֶךְ אֲשֶׁר מָלַךְ עֲלֵיכֶם אַחַר יה׳ אֱלֹהֵיכֶם : 15) וְאִם־לֹא תִשְׁמְעוּ בְּקוֹל יה׳ וּמְרִיתֶם
אֶת־פִּי־יה׳ וְהָיְתָה יַד־יה׳ בָּכֶם וּבַאֲבֹתֵיכֶם :

That the presence of an aposiopesis in verse 14 is a matter of interpretation [66] can be seen when one compares the translation of the *AV* with that of the *RSV*. The syntax of verse 14 is grammatically correct, namely a conditional sentence complete with protasis and apodosis. The problem arising here is that the apodosis presents what has been termed "an identical proposition" [67] with the protasis, hence the view that וִהְיִתֶם marks not the conclusion of the condition but an extension of the protasis. However, this view firstly makes the protasis unconscionably long, and secondly ignores the basic "Deuteronomic" pragmatism of verses 14 & 15. The contrast between vv. 14 & 15 demands that verse 14 be complete in itself or else the explicit statement of the perils of apostacy in verse 15 loses its force. The root היה can denote the idea of existence as a synonym for חיה [68] an interpretation which the thought of the verse demands [69]. It may well be for this reason that some MSS begin the apodosis with וִחְיִתֶם, [70] though the emendation is not necessary. The evidence is such that one cannot unequivocally claim an aposiopesis here, but at best one must regard the case as doubtful.

2. *Sam*. 5: 8.

וַיֹּאמֶר דָּוִד בַּיּוֹם הַהוּא כָּל־מַכֵּה יְבֻסִי וְיִגַּע בַּצִּנּוֹר וְאֶת־הַפִּסְחִים וְאֶת־הַעִוְרִים שְׂנֻאֵו
נֶפֶשׁ דָּוִד עַל־כֵּן יֹאמְרוּ עִוֵּר וּפִסֵּחַ לֹא יָבוֹא אֶל־הַבָּיִת :

This sentence is so difficult of interpretation that even to postulate an aposiopesis would hardly solve its problems. The Chronicler [71] found it necessary to alter this text, possibly because of its unintelligibility. The Interpreter's Bible suggests that the words "whoever would smite the Jebusites" would be the beginning of a general amnesty on the Jebusites and the rest of the verse is a corruption of some threat of punishment for breach of the amnesty. The suggestion is not impossible. Equally valid is the opinion which sees in this a brief statement that David's men captured Jerusalem via a watercourse [72], but this does not solve the problems of the relationship of the clause following עַל־כֵּן with the first part of the verse. There is certainly no legitimate basis in this text for the *AV* translation of this verse with an aposiopesis by the insertion of the words "he shall be chief and captain". The *RSV* translation . . . "whoever would smite the Jebusites let him get up the water shaft to attack the lame and the blind who are hated by David's soul" . . . is closer to the Hebrew text and resolves the problem by postulating an unusual ellipse of an infinitive construct after וְיִגַּע. However, the relationship of the final clause עַל־כֵּן is thereby still left unresolved.

The *DNV* translation [73] "whoever will defeat the Jebusites must force a way in by the water course; David has a vigorous aversion to the lame and blind", offers a reasonably satisfactory explanation which needs no recourse to either ellipse or aposiopesis though it somewhat strains the meaning of the vocabulary. The probabilities of textual corruption here are such that one could not reasonably claim or easily refute the claim, that this verse contains an aposiopesis.

2. *Sam*. 23: 17.

וַיֹּאמֶר חָלִילָה לִּי יה׳ מֵעֲשֹׂתִי זֹאת הֲדַם הָאֲנָשִׁים הַהֹלְכִים בְּנַפְשׁוֹתָם וְלֹא אָבָה לִשְׁתּוֹתָם
אֵלֶּה עָשׂוּ שְׁלֹשֶׁת הַגִּבֹּרִים :

The omission of the verb in the question, הֲדַם etc., is nothing more than ellipsis: there is no break in the thought though the expression is not complete. If one accepts the question as "shall I drink" then the verb אֶשְׁתֶּה is missing. However, the Chronicler's insertion of this verb [74] makes the sentence unwieldy and it may be that the question was the rhetorical "Is this not the blood of" etc., i.e. הֲדַם should be read as . . . הֲזֶה דַם. [75] However, the reluctance of Hebrew to repeat a word or phrase in the same verse has been noted above, and in view of the preceding demonstrative pronoun the compression or ellipse would take place.

Ps. 27: 13. לׅוּלֵׅאׅ הֶאֱמַנְתִּי לִרְאוֹת בְּטוּב־יה׳ בְּאֶרֶץ חַיִּים :

Apparently an incomplete hypothetical sentence introduced by לוּלֵא with no apodosis. However, the evidence suggests that the verse should be regarded as an asseveration as in the *RSV*. The Masoretes seem to have regarded the particle לוּלֵא as doubtful (the heavy dotting around the word) and it is missing in a number of versions. לוּלֵא may be a corruption of לִי, אֵלַי, or עָלַי [76] and thus belongs to the preceding verse where the word וִיפֵחַ, (whether its root be a verb פוח or an adjective יָפֵחַ) [77] needs a first person singular pronoun to complete the parallelism with the rest of the psalm.

1 *Chron.* 4 : 10.

וַיִּקְרָא יַעְבֵּץ לֵאלֹהֵי יִשְׂרָאֵל לֵאמֹר אִם־בָּרֵךְ תְּבָרְכֵנִי וְהִרְבִּיתָ אֶת־גְּבוּלִי וְהָיְתָה יָדְךָ
עִמִּי וְעָשִׂיתָ מֵּרָעָה לְבִלְתִּי עָצְבִּי וַיָּבֵא אֱלֹהִים אֵת אֲשֶׁר־שָׁאָל ׃

Despite the reservations of *GKC* where this verse seems to be regarded [78] as the protasis of an incomplete conditional sentence, few commentators, or translators, regard it as such. [79] The particle אִם־ is regarded as being a desiderative rather than an hypothetical [80] being translated as "would that"; the thought is thus complete in itself. The context does not require any other interpretation of the verse than as a desiderative sentence.

Daniel 3: 15.

כְּעַן הֵן אִיתֵיכוֹן עֲתִידִין דִּי בְעִדָּנָה דִּי־תִשְׁמְעוּן קָל קַרְנָא מַשְׁרוֹקִיתָא קִיתְרֹס שַׂבְּכָה
פְּסַנְתֵּרִין וְסוּמְפֹּנְיָה וְכֹל זְנֵי זְמָרָא תִּפְּלוּן וְתִסְגְּדוּן לְצַלְמָא דִי־עַבְדֵת וְהֵן לָא תִסְגְּדוּן
בַּהּ־שַׁעֲתָה תִתְרְמוֹן לְגוֹא אַתּוּן נוּרָא יָקִדְתָּא וּמַן־הוּא אֱלָהּ דִּי יְשֵׁיזְבִנְכוֹן מִן־יְדָי ׃

This verse is probably the most time-honoured example of an aposiopesis in the *OT*. Again the first part of the verse is seen as an incomplete conditional clause containing a protasis but no apodosis. The conditional particle is thus attached to the verbs תִּפְּלוּן, וְתִסְגְּדוּן, i.e. "if you will fall down and worship . . ." etc. Both the *AV* and *RSV* supply the apodosis "*well*" [81] or "well and good". It may well be unnecessary to complete the condition in this way. The conditional sentence in Aramaic is normally expressed by the hypothetical particle הֵן with the imperfect in the protasis followed by the imperfect in the apodosis. [82] However, an alternative method seems to suggest itself as in verse 17 of Daniel where the conditional clause is constructed of הֵן + אִיתַי + participle in the protasis and the imperfect in the apodosis. Despite the translations of the *AV* and *RSV* which have ignored the true meaning of the conditional (since it seems to question the power of God) the force of this construction has long been recognized. [83] In verse 15 the same construction may be found. The adjective עֲתִידִין may in fact be a passive pe'al participle used in a parallel way to פָּלְחִין in verse 14. The pronominal suffix on אִיתַי suggests that אִיתַי is being used as a copula with a participle. [84] In this case the verb תִּפְּלוּן etc. must be read as the imperfect beginning the apodosis, and the thought and syntax are complete without the need to postulate an aposiopesis.

Of all the verses cited in *GKC* as classic examples of an aposiopesis not one can, with certainty, be said to exhibit this device. Though it is not impossible that the versional discrepancies and textual disagreements have arisen because of the desire to fill gaps in the text it may equally well be possible that the alleged lacunae were never present in the first place and that aposiopesis is a device rarely, if ever, used. Whilst the *OT* is an admirable body of literature it has a prime purpose that is remote from that of the literary author and it is conceivable and probable that some literary devices are never employed in its pages.

Yet, if this be the case, the text of the *OT* presents some serious anomalies. The conditional oath in its full formula כֹּה יַעֲשֶׂה־לִּי יה׳ וְכֹה יוֹסִף אִם־, "So may the Lord do to me and more also if..." (in all its variations [85]) does not state the punishment for a breach of the oath but leaves it, so it seems, entirely to the imagination.

Moreover, there are numerous clauses beginning with the particle אִם which are regarded, probably rightly, as asseverative statements. [86] Yet basically such clauses seem to have evolved from the conditional oath, and these are now mere truncated relics, the protases of oaths without any apodoses. It is as though the speaker in each case were afraid to utter the maledictory apodosis for fear of the possible consequences and has thus deliberately chosen to utter only part of the oath. [87] Are all of these asseverations to be regarded as cases of aposiopesis?

Now the oath is essentially a conditional self imprecation, a curse by which a person calls down upon himself something evil in the event of what he says not being true. [88] The purpose of the oath is to demonstrate good faith, whether it be in a promise to another or in a statement of intention before another (or to oneself), hence without a positive suggestion of evil consequences, even if the word be the simple term רָעוֹת [89] the oath can hardly have had much, if any, force and validity. In the ancient near east where written and engraved materials or even tombs were protected by maledictory clauses, the imprecations were frequently written out in full, but even in their shortest form there was at least a general indication of consequence. [90] It is thus unlikely that we can see the full Hebrew conditional oath formula as only "neutral and evasive as though the oath-taker is reluctant to define the curse", [91] but rather we should expect it to define, explicitly the punishment involved. Moreover, we should expect to find in the punishment or curse, something so well known and so deadly that there was no need to refer to it by name and even a danger in referring to it. Only in this way can the asseverative statement be fully explained.

The full formula, כֹּה יַעֲשֶׂה־לִּי יה־וְכֹה יוֹסִף אִם־ is a reversal of the usual order of the conditional sentence since in every case the apodosis, the result of the condition, is stated before the protasis. Normally, the demonstrative adverb כֹּה points to something that is to follow, whilst something previously expressed is indicated by its equivalents כֵּן or כָּכָה. [92] In every case in the *OT* where the parallel phrase כֵּן יֵעָשֶׂה or כָּכָה יֵעָשֶׂה is used, the phrase emphasises what has gone. [93] It is thus unlikely that the formula with כֹּה can look back to what has gone before or even express in a vague fashion something generally understood but not said, since either the word כֵּן or כָּכָה would be expected in the formula. On the other hand, since this formula in itself is the result of the condition it cannot look forward to something yet to come, unless a gesture follows or accompanies the words כֹּה יַעֲשֶׂה.

Now there is abundant evidence in the *OT* that a gesture accompanies the taking of the oath, namely, the raising of the right [94] hand [95]. Whilst this action is explained in the text as raising one's hand to Jahweh, it was obviously of a much deeper significance since the very act of raising up one's hand without uttering any words was regarded as a binding oath [96] and Jahweh himself, in his anthropomorphic acts could raise his hand in such a fashion. [97] Thus the verb נָשָׂא, to lift, can also mean to swear. [98] As a corollary of this argument it is most probable that the taking of the oath *always* involved raising the hand, hence we must expect this action in the case of the full conditional oath. Perhaps this full formula explains the real significance of the hand raising, since this act must also demonstrate the punishment involved. The gestures of punishment which one can demonstrate by raising the hand are few, limited perhaps to the act of rending out the tongue, [99] putting out the eyes, or more likely the running of a finger across the throat.

As a secondary consideration which may well strengthen the probability that the act of raising the hand originally involved the suggestion of throat cutting it should be noted that the taking of an oath involved, of necessity, invoking the name of Jahweh [100] and hence, unless some other punishment were explicitly stated in words, the penalty of death would be involved (for an offence against Jahweh) and presumably, a ritual death. Whilst the killing of a criminal in the *OT* is said to have been done by strangulation, burning, stoning or beheading [101] the ritual slaughter of animals or even persons involved the action described by the use of the verb שָׁחַט. [102] A preliminary analysis of this verb suggests that it is never used indiscriminately for "killing" but that it means, exclusively, the act of cutting the throat [103].

However, the running of the finger over the throat must have involved some considerable danger through homeopathic or imitative magic [104] even though the oath-taker be guiltless of breaking the oath.

The dangers involved in oath-taking are clearly demonstrated by 1 Sam. 25: 22 where the word לְאֹיְבֵי has an obvious prophylactic purpose, thus the ritual of running a finger over the throat would have to be indicated symbolically in order to avoid unnecessary self-destruction. The nearest symbolical act is that of raising the hand: even this act may become transmuted through fear of the consequences and by Talmudic times it was sufficient for a person taking the oath to say "by my right hand". [105]

It is only by postulating some deeper meaning to the act of hand raising which must have accompanied the asseveration that one can explain the implied apodosis in the asseverative sentence. The penalty which would normally be described in the apodosis must have been commonplace, so as to be readily perceived, yet deadly, and it may not be impossible that the asseverative sentence is a truncated form of the full formula discussed above. If the above reconstruction is correct, the missing apodosis which, on the face of things is the result of aposiopesis in each asseverative clause, can be seen as the act of raising the hand. So commonplace would this act have been that one is tempted to view asseverative clauses as elliptical rather than as aposiopeistic.

In conclusion it would appear doubtful whether one could substantiate the claim in *GKC* that aposiopesis is a common device in the *OT*. It is doubtful whether the device is used at all.

NOTES

[1] H. C. Wyld & E. Partridge, *The Universal English Dictionary*, London, 1961.
[2] *Ibid.*
[3] Gesenius, Kautzsch, Cowley (afterwards *GKC*), *A Hebrew Grammar*, 2nd. ed. 1960.

[4] *GKC*, p. 505, para. 176(a) my italics.
[5] *GKC*, para 159 dd, 117 l., 147.
[6] *GKC*, para 159 dd, p. 498.
[6] *GKC*, para 117 l., p. 365.
[8] *GKC*, para 147, p. 469.
[9] Cp. Ju. 9: 16, 19; & *GKC* para 167a.
[10] Cf. *The Oxford Dictionary*.
[11] Gen. 42: 33.
[12] Cp. *RSV* and *AV*.
[13] Gen. 1: 10, 12, 17, 20, 25, 30; 2: 5, 19; 3: 6, 12, 13; 4: 7, 20, 24, 25; 5: 3, 29; 6: 4, 15, 16, 19; 7: 23; 8: 5, 13; 9: 2, 4, 21; 10: 21; 11: 4; 12: 19; 13: 9; 14: 2, 14, 23; 15: 13; 16: 14; 17: 16, 17; 18 : 1, 6, 8, 9, 10, 27, 28, 29, 30, 31; 19: 1, 2; 20: 7, 14, 16, 17; 21: 14, 26, 33; 22: 1, 6, 7, 13; 23: 1, 14, 16; 24: 11, 14, 19, 20, 28, 30, 33, 41, 43, 44, 45, 49, 55, 60, 67; 25: 8, 28; 26: 7; 27: 1, 5, 10, 14, 18, 25, 42, 46; 28: 11, 15, 16; 29: 5, 6, 7, 32; 30: 27, 28, 30, 35; 31: 11, 21, 26, 31, 33, 34, 37, 39, 40, 42, 43, 52; 32: 18, 29; 34: 7; 35: 22; 37: 3, 10, 13, 15, 16, 21, 25, 28, 32, 33; 38: 9, 12, 17, 18, 19, 21, 22, 24, 26, 28; 39: 4, 9, 11, 22, 23; 40: 17, 20; 41: 1, 3, 15, 34, 38, 43, 51, 57; 42: 5, 16, 18, 28, 29, 30, 33, 36; 43: 5, 7, 14, 27, 30; 44: 1, 22, 27, 31; 45: 22, 23, 24; 46: 2; 47: 12, 17, 22, 26; 48: 9, 14, 19; 49: 4, 24; 50: 15, 18, 20, 23.
[14] Gen. 17: 16.
[15] Cf. Kittel, *Biblia Hebraica*.
[16] Gen. 23: 13.
[17] Cf. Skinner, *ICC*, Genesis, on Gen. 30: 27, where he cites this verse as an aposiopesis.
[18] Cf. *GKC* para. 110e, and paras. 159 l, m, x, z.
[19] Cf. *BDB* אִם 1 b(3).
[20] Cf. M. Jastrow, *Dictionary of the Talmud* etc., אִילוּ.
[21] *Ibid*., אִילוּ and אִין. Also Ezek. 3: 7.
[22] Gen. 30: 27.
[23] Cf. *GKC*, para 159 dd.
[24] Cp. *GKC*, para 111 l., 120 f, and 159 dd.
[25] Cf. A. B. Davidson, *Hebrew Syntax*, para 146 R. 4.
[26] *BDB* אִם lb (3).
[27] Cf. Gen. 38: 17 and *BDB* אִם 2a (a).
[28] *GKC* para 159 dd and Skinner, *ICC*, *op. cit.*
[29] Gen. 50: 15.
[30] Cf. *GKC* para 159y.
[31] Cf. *GKV* para. 147b.
[32] E.g. Gen. 18: 9; 22: 1.
[33] Cf. *GKC* para. 134n.
[34] Gen. 8: 13; see also 8: 5; 44: 27; 20: 16.
[35] Gen. 6: 16.
[36] Gen. 29: 33; cf. also 38: 21, 22.
[37] Gen. 31: 43 + three times. Cf. also Gen. 31: 52.
[38] Cf. Davidson, para. 73, R. 5.
[39] *GKC* para. 117 f.
[40] Gen. 38: 9.
[41] Gen. 38: 26.
[42] Gen. 28: 16.
[43] Gen. 39: 23.
[44] Gen. 49: 4.

[45] Cf. Davidson, para. 73 R. 5.
[46] Gen. 43: 30.
[47] Davidson, para. 73 R. 5.
[48] Gen. 20: 17; 17: 17 etc.
[49] Gen. 24: 19, 20.
[50] Gen. 42: 5, 41, 57.
[51] Gen. 31: 39.
[52] *GKC* para. 116 S.
[53] Gen. 14: 2.
[54] Gen. 23: 16.
[55] *GKC* para. 117 l.
[56] Gen. 14: 23.
[57] Gen. 13: 9; cf. also Gen. 24: 57; 27: 42.
[58] Gen. 41: 51.
[59] Cf. *GKC* para. 159 dd.
[60] Gen. 24: 49.
[61] Gen. 37: 3; cf. also Gen. 41: 3.
[62] Cf. Davidson, para 143 f; little need be said in addition to the survey in Davidson.
[63] Cf. *GKC* para. 167.
[64] Cf. Kittel, *op. cit.*
[65] Cf. *BDB* p. 966 שָׂטָה and p. 1065 תַּחַת 1c (b).
[66] Cf. also H. P. Smith, *ICC* Samuel, p. 88.
[67] *Ibid.*
[68] *BDB* היה III, 1.
[69] Cf. Dt. 4: 1; Amos 5: 14.
[70] Cf. *ICC*, *op. cit.* and cp. Kittel who ignores the versional evidence.
[71] 1 Ch. 11: 6.
[72] Cf. A. R. Hulst, *Old Testament Translation Problems*, Brill, 1960, p. 31 f.
[73] Dutch New Version, quoted from Hulst, *op. cit.*
[74] 1 Chron. 11:19.
[75] Cf. *ICC*, Samuel.
[76] Cf. E. G. Briggs, *ICC*, Psalms.
[77] Cp. *BDB*, פוח with B. Davidson, *Hebrew and Chaldee Concordance*, London, 1876, and adjective, יפח p. 381, col. 2.
[78] *GKC*, *op. cit.* para. 167.
[79] Cf. *RSV*, *AV*, *ICC*, Chronicles.
[80] Cf. *BDB*, *op. cit.*
[81] Cf. also, A. A. Bevan, *A Short Commentary on the Book of Daniel*, Camb. 1892; J. A. Montgommery, *ICC*, Daniel. Note that H. H. Wright, *Daniel and its Critics*, London, 1906, and R. H. Charles, *A New Commentary on the Book of Daniel*, ignore the alleged aposiopesis.
[82] Cf. K. Marti, *Biblisch-Aramäische Sprache*, Berlin, 1896, and also Dan. 2: 5, 9.
[83] Cf. the long note in the *ICC* Daniel, *op. cit.* and also Dupont Sommer, "Une inscription Araméene inédite de Sfiré", *Bulletin du Musée de Beyrouth* XIII, 1956, p. 27, line 11. הן אי]ת י יקתלן את תאתא
[84] Cf. F. Rosenthal, *A Grammar of Biblical Aramaic*, Wiesbaden, 1963, para. 95.
[85] This oath occurs eleven times in all, each occurrence being in the historical books of the O.T., viz. 1 Sam 3: 17; 14 : 14; 20: 13; 25:22; 2 Sam. 3: 9, 35; 19: 14; 1 K. 2: 23; 20: 10; 2 K. 6: 31; Ruth 1: 17.
[86] Cf. S. H. Blank, "The Curse, Blasphemy, the Spell and the Oath", *HUCA* vol. 23, pt. 1, p. 90 f. cf. also *BDB* אִם.
[87] Blank, *op. cit.*

[88] Westermarck, *The Origin and Development of the Moral Idea*, vol. II, p. 118.
[89] Cf. C. Fensham, "*Malediction and Benediction in Ancient Near Eastern Vassal Treaties, and the Hebrew O.T.*" *ZAW* Band 74, 1962.
[90] *Ibid.*, p. 6.
[91] Blank, *op. cit.*, p. 90.
[92] *BDB*, *op. cit.* כֹּה p. 462.
[93] Dt. 3: 21; 7: 19; Josh. 10: 25; 1 Sam. 1: 7; 2 Sam. 9: 11; 12: 31; 1 K. 2: 38; 1 Ch. 20: 3; Job 1: 5; Jer. 28: 6.
[94] Ps. 144: 8.
[95] Gen. 14: 22; Dt. 32: 40; Dan. 12: 7.
[96] Ezek. 20: 5; 1 K. 8: 31.
[97] Ezek. 20: 5.
[98] *BDB*, *op. cit.* נָשָׂא 1b. p. 670.
[99] Ps. 137: 5.
[100] Cf. A. Guillaume, *Prophecy and Divination*, p. 257 f. and also C. Fensham, *op. cit.* p. 3, who points out that in every case of a malediction in the Ancient Near East the gods were involved.
[101] Midrash Rabbah, vol. II, 22 (to Ruth I. 17).
[102] Gen. 22: 10.
[103] Consider also the ritual of killing animals for food, by the Jews—שְׁחִיטָה (cutting the throat exclusively). The basic meaning of שָׁחַט seems to be 'to draw across finely'. Cf. 1 K. 10: 16.
[104] Cf. Pritchard, *ANET*, p. 353. & *Homeopathic Magic in the Hittite Oath* Westermarck, *op. cit.* pp. 77-80.
[105] Nazir. 7.

A MEDIAEVAL ARABIC TREATISE ON VENESECTION

BY

M. J. L. YOUNG

ABR NAHRAIN III

LIST OF ERRATA

p. 37, line 27, *instead of*: practise *read*: practice
p. 38, line 15, *instead of*: bloodvessels *read*: blood-vessels
p. 38, line 32, *instead of*: visble *read*: visible
p. 39, line 27, *after*: patient *insert*: to
p. 41, lines 21-23, *change as follows*:

The two veins of the tip of the nose: it is said that the harm which venesection of these causes is greater than its benefit.

The four veins of the lips: these are four veins, a pair of which are in each lip. Bleeding from them is useful for ulcers of the mouth, aphthai and ailments of the (unreadable) and lip.

p. 42, line 12, *instead of*: laneet *read*: lancet
p. 42, running title, *instead of*: reatise *read*: treatise
p. 43, line 20, *instead of*: phlemboto- *read*: phleboto-

NOTES

Note 1 *should read*: Ar. Qīfālāni. A. Fonahn, Arabic and Latin Anatomical Terminology, chiefly from the Middle Ages (Videnskapsselskapskrifter II Hist.-Filos. Klasse, 1921, No. 7) Kristiana, 1922, p. 123.

Notes 12-16: change order into 12, 14, 15, 13, 16.

Note 26 *should read*: Ar. fās. This presumably refers to a type of instrument with a short blade already known to the Greeks, for an illustration of which, see The Legacy of Greece, ed. by R. W. Livingstone, Oxford, 1921, plate facing p. 240.

Note 27 *should read*: Ar. nāṣūr. E. W. Lane, An Arabic-English Lexicon, London, 1863, (Reprinted New York, 1955), Bk. I, Pt. 8, p. 2790.

Note 28 *should read*: Ar. dam'ah. P. Sbath and M. Meyerhof, Le Livre des Questions sur l'Oeil de Honain ibn Iṣhāq, Cairo, 1938, p. 135.

Note 37 *should read*: Ar. khazz. Al-Munjid fī'l-Lughah wa'l-Adab wa'l-'Ulūm, Beirut, 1956, p. 173.

Caption for Plate I, first line, *read*: Facsimiles of Folios.

ABR-NAHRAIN

AN ANNUAL PUBLISHED BY THE DEPARTMENT OF SEMITIC STUDIES UNIVERSITY OF MELBOURNE IN ASSOCIATION WITH THE DEPARTMENT OF SEMITIC STUDIES UNIVERSITY OF SYDNEY

EDITED BY

J. BOWMAN

ASSOCIATE EDITOR

E. C. B. MacLAURIN

ASSISTANT EDITOR

A. D. HALLAM

VOLUME V

1964-1965

LEIDEN
E. J. BRILL
1966

ABR-NAHRAIN

ABR-NAHRAIN

AN ANNUAL PUBLISHED BY THE DEPARTMENT OF SEMITIC STUDIES UNIVERSITY OF MELBOURNE IN ASSOCIATION WITH THE DEPARTMENT OF SEMITIC STUDIES UNIVERSITY OF SYDNEY

EDITED BY

J. BOWMAN

ASSOCIATE EDITOR

E. C. B. MacLAURIN

ASSISTANT EDITOR

A. D. HALLAM

VOLUME V

1964-1965

LEIDEN
E. J. BRILL
1966

PRINTED IN THE NETHERLANDS

CONTENTS

EDITORIAL NOTE

The publication of this fifth volume of Abr-Nahrain has been possible by money made available by the bequest fund of the late Professor M. D. Goldman, first Professor of Semitic Studies at Melbourne University, and by the generous subsidy of the Australian Humanities Research Council. We acknowledge our great indebtedness for this aid.

The present volume of Abr-Nahrain marks as it were the end of an era. In volumes 1-4 Professor A. Guillaume was a contributor. Now, alas, he is gone, having died last December. We were honoured to have had him publish first his admirable Arabic contributions to Hebrew Lexicography in our pages.

Professor Guillaume, as well as being one of the greatest Arabists and Islamic Scholars of the twentieth century, was a very fine Hebrew Scholar. I understand he died at his desk, whilst writing on the Arabic background of the Hebrew Book of Job.

After service in Egypt during the First World War, he was Professor of Hebrew and Arabic at Durham, then Principal of Culham, near Oxford. During the Second World War, he lectured for sometime at Beirut University.

After the War, he was Professor of Hebrew at London, then Professor of Arabic and Head of the Middle Eastern Section at the London School of Oriental Studies. After retirement, he was a visiting Professor at Princeton, then at Leeds, where your Editor was proud to be his colleague.

In this present volume, we have three important articles:

First is the continuation of Dr. Daniel Leslie's important researches on the Chinese Hebrew Memorial Book of the Jewish Community of K'aifeng. We are happy to state that in the forthcoming numbers of Abr-Nahrain, there will be further contributions on this theme by Dr. Leslie.

The second contribution, Homer and Ugaritic Literature by A. F. Campbell, S.J. was written prior to the publication of *Hellenosemitica* by Michael C. Astour, therefore, Fr. Campbell was naturally unable to refer to it. However, in the next volume of Abr-Nahrain he will write a lengthy article reviewing that work.

The third contribution in this Volume is by Rabbi S. Coleman, on the Dialogue of Habakkuk in Rabbinic Doctrine. It is similar to the researches he published in his book *Hosea Concepts in Midrash and Talmud*, Bloemfontein, 1960. We are confident that these three articles in themselves make a memorable volume of Abr-Nahrain.

It is my pleasant duty to welcome my colleague, Mr. A. D. Hallam, as the new Assistant Editor of Abr-Nahrain. He will replace Mr. W. Culican, to whom we express our gratitude for services rendered.

Editor,
John Bowman
Professor of Semitic Studies,
University of Melbourne.

THE CHINESE-HEBREW MEMORIAL BOOK OF THE JEWISH COMMUNITY OF K'AIFENG

BY

DANIEL LESLIE

Part II

TABLE OF CONTENTS (continued)

E. The clans

a The Surnames

The 1489 inscription writes of 70 surnames *hsing* 姓 as coming to China from 'India' [1], presumably to K'aifeng during the Sung (960-1279), and probably during the earliest part of the dynasty before 1126 [2]. However only 17 surnames are actually enumerated (including 3 duplications presumably of different families), and some scholars [3] suggest reading 70 (七十) as 17 (十七).

[1] T'ien-chu 天竺. However this probably means no more than that they came from west of China. There can be little doubt that they came from Persia. There are several Hebrew-Persian manuscripts from the community. The mention of 27 rather than 22 letters of the (Hebrew) alphabet, and of 53 rather than 54 sections of the Law (see, e.g., two vertical tablets, White II p. 143, 152) is also strong evidence. It is of course possible that they came from Persia to China via India.

[2] For K'aifeng was no longer the capital of the Sung, rulers only of South China after 1126. We are concerned here with the entry of the K'aifeng Jews, not with the first entry of Jews into China, which was probably considerably earlier. For the K'aifeng Jews, Williams (White, III p. 108) writes: 'The fact that these Jews still used the Seleucid era, or "Era of Contracts" rather than the "Era of the Creation", is an indication that they entered the country before the tenth century'. Laufer (White III pp. 9-10), arguing that their language was New Persian rather than Pehlevi or Middle Persian, writes that their immigration into China could hardly have taken place before the tenth century. In both cases the arguments apply better to the date of their *lack of contact* with Persia rather than their *entry* to China. We cannot take too much notice of the fact that some of the Rabbis are called *Shaliaḥ* שליח (also miswritten as שליע, שליחי), translated as 'envoy' by Williams and White. The *Jewish Encyclopedia* IV p. 38 (following Elkan N. Adler 'The Persian Jews: Their Books and their Ritual' *Jewish Quarterly Review* X, 1898 pp. 584-625) writes 'The שליח ('messenger') who signed his name as copyist upon the Pentateuch was the typical transmitter of Persian rites, rituals, and writings to these Chinese Jews'. Nevertheless these same rabbis were described as *Sopher* ספר 'scribe', *Melamed* מלמד 'teacher'. It is quite feasible that *Shaliaḥ* is to be taken as 'leader of prayers' rather than 'envoy'.

[3] See Ch'en Yüan (*Tung-fang Tsa-chih* 17, 5, p. 117); D. MacGillivray 'The Jews of Honan: a tragic story of submergence (a fresh study of the Stelae)', *Journal of*

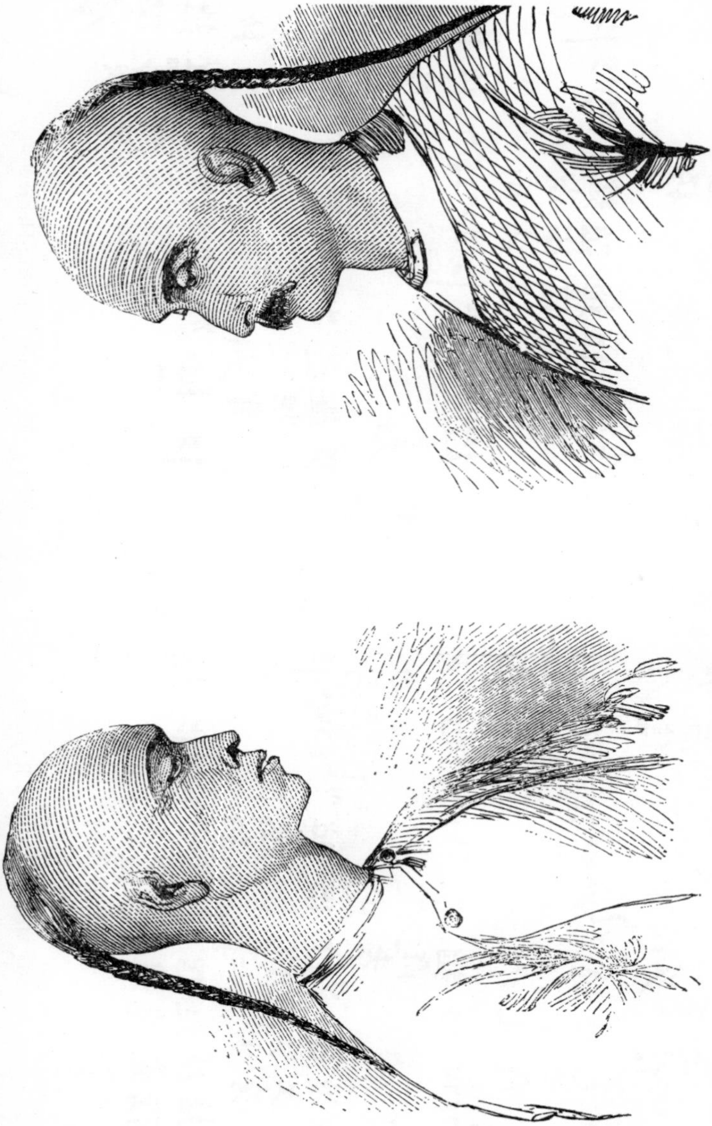

'Two K'aifeng Jews' (from *The Illustrated London News*, Dec. 13, 1851)
Can one see non-Chinese features in these Nineteenth Century assimilated Jews?

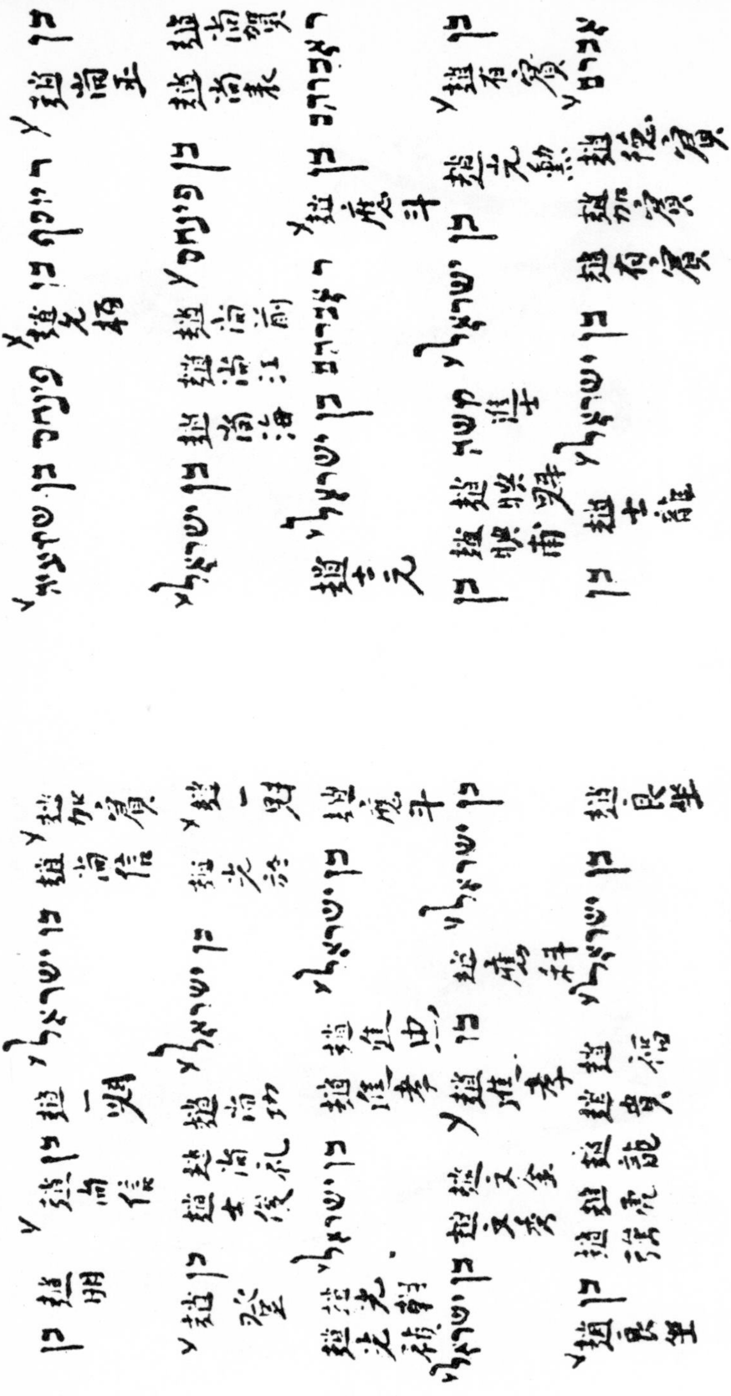

'Moses, *chin-shih*; Register of Men' (p. 54, White p. 55, of the Chinese-Hebrew Manuscript).

The 17 surnames are:

Li 李 (twice)	Yen (or An) 俺	Ai 艾
Kao 高	Mu 穆	Chao 趙
Chin 金 (twice)	Chou 周	Chang 張 (twice)
Shih 石	Huang 黄	Nieh 聶
Tso 左	Po (or Pai) 白	

The 1489 inscription mentions only three individuals before the Ming dynasty (1368-1644): Lieh-wei Wu-ssu-ta 列微五思達 (probably Levi the Oustad) of 1163; Yen (or An) Tu-la 俺都剌 (probably a transliteration of Hamdullah or Abdullah) of 1163; and a further, otherwise unnamed, Wu-ssu-ta (the Oustad?) of 1279. Though Yen 俺 may be taken as a surname, one of the 17 mentioned earlier, it is significant that these names are all transliterations [4]. We cannot be too sure that the 17 surnames mentioned in the 1489 inscription as for the Sung do not rather reflect the actual situation of the early Ming.

Referring presumably to the period between 1368 and 1489, fourteen men are mentioned by the 1489 inscription as being *Man-la* [5]. For this period we also have others mentioned who are fairly clearly Jews[6]. The following (Jewish) surnames are found:

the North China Branch of the Royal Asiatic Society 59 (1928), pp. 22-49, especially p. 29; A. C. Moule, *Christians in China before the Year 1550*, London, 1930, p. 2 footnote 3, and also in *T'oung Pao*, 28, 1931, p. 126. White II, p. 20, and Löwenthal (*Monumenta Serica* 12, 1947, p. 107) reject this change. They cite the 1679 inscription which mentions (for 1163 apparently) 'Believers with 73 surnames (*hsing* 姓) and over 500 families (*chia* 家)'. However the 1679 text is the least reliable, and it is quite possible in any case that its composer understood the 七十姓等 of the 1489 inscription as '70 odd surnames' and changed it to '73 surnames'. In fact the meaning of the 1489 inscription is rather '70 clans as hereby enumerated' (17 were in fact enumerated). As Moule notes, why were the 3 duplicates mentioned, if 17 was an incomplete listing?

[4] For the arguments in favour of reading Oustad, and Hamdullah or Abdullah, see my article 'Some notes on the Jewish inscriptions of K'aifeng', *Journal of the American Oriental Society*, 82, no. 3, 1962, pp. 346-361, esp. pp. 351-353; and Löwenthal, *Monumenta Serica* 12, 1947, pp. 103-106. My arguments in favour of Hamdullah rather than Abdullah are not justified. Abdullah might feasibly have been used by Persian Jews; and though the phonetic fit for Hamdullah is stronger, that for Abdullah is possible. Moreover Professor Herbert Franke of Munich has pointed out to me Pelliot's footnote on p. 84 of L. Hambis, *Le Chapitre CVII du Yuan Che*, 1945, Leiden, which reads 'Amdula est la forme mongolisée de "Abdullah" '.

[5] *Man-la* is a title used for leading members of the community. We shall discuss later its possible connotation as 'rabbi' or as 'mullah'.

[6] The decision as to whether a particular man mentioned is Jewish or not is usually easy. Some are mentioned as *Man-la*'s; others as having repaired the

Li (9 individuals, all *Man-la's*)
Ai (3, including 2 *Man-la's*)
Chang (2, including 1 *Man-la*)
Chin (5)
Shih (1)
Yen (2, including 1 *Man-la*)
Chou (1 *Man-la*)
Kao (4)
Chao (2)

The two men of the Chao clan, Chao Ying (of Ning-po?) mentioned as bringing a copy of the Law from Ning-po during 1457-1465, and Chao Chün, who brought the stone for the 1489 inscription, may have been members of the Chao clan named as one of the 17 (or 14) original surnames. Alternatively, as seems more likely, they may have been related to the physician Yen Ch'eng, who was granted by Imperial favour the surname Chao in 1423. We cannot really be sure that prior to this date there were any Jews named Chao. All we can say is that no Jews with the surname Yen are mentioned thereafter.

Mentioned also are four men, whom we may take to be non-Jews, with surnames Ts'ao 曹, Fu 傅, and Wu 吳 (2).

The 1512 inscription mentions only Jews with the surname Chin (3 individuals).

It also mentions five men, who are unlikely to have been Jewish, with the surnames Hsü 徐, Tso 左, Kao 高 [7], and Chang 張 (2).

It seems fairly clear that by 1489, and probably even by 1368, there were only eight surnames of importance in the community (counting Chao and Yen as one).

Turning now to the 1663 inscriptions, we find only seven surnames mentioned as contributing money to rebuild the synagogue (after the inundation of 1642) [8]. These surnames include in fact all the Jews

---

scrolls; others as believers; others as having assisted in the building of the synagogue. Those mentioned solely as having written special incriptions, seal characters, and characters in vermilion (for the engravers), and also the stone-cutters, are almost invariably non-Jews.

[7] We can be fairly sure that these three famous scholars, all holders of the *Chin-shih* degree, were not Jews of K'aifeng. The fact that the surnames Tso and Kao are possible Jewish ones is deceptive. If it is argued that they might have been Jews from other communities, then the fact that they have these surnames loses most of its significance, for other Jewish communities may have adopted other surnames. The two men named Chang were the engravers of the characters, and might possibly have been Jews.

[8] These seven surnames are confirmed by visitors to the community, from Gozani in 1704 and onwards, to the 1919 K'aifeng conference with representatives of these seven clans (see White I p. 42, III pp. 219-220). Ricci however, writing in 1605, mentions ten or twelve Jewish families in K'aifeng (see Löwenthal, *Folklore Studies* V, 1946, p. 394; but cf. p. 397, where Ricci talks of six or eight families!).

mentioned in both the 1663 inscriptions, the 1679 inscription, and the smaller tablets mostly from 1663-1688.

Leaving out those names already mentioned in the 1489 inscription, these comprise:

Li 李: 6 individuals, including the *Chang-chiao* 掌教 'Leader of the Religion', and 1 *Man-la*.
Chao 趙: 14 individuals.
Ai 艾: 11 individuals, including 1 *Man-la*.
Chang 張: 1 *Man-la*, and one other who may not have been Jewish.
Kao 高: 5 individuals
Chin 金: 2 individuals
Shih 石: 1 *Man-la*

The 1663 and 1679 inscriptions also mention non-Jews with the surnames Hou 侯, Liu 劉, Wang 王, Han 韓, Li 李, and Ch'eng 程.

It is time now to turn to the evidence of the Register. The men's Register gives only these seven surnames, though several others are found in the Register of Women. Our table No. 4 (*Abr Nahrain*, Vol. IV p. 37) makes clear that a large number of the wives came from these 7 surnames. Out of a total of 380 wives mentioned, 235 are of these seven Jewish clans, 52 are of unknown clan, and the remaining 93 may be tabulated as follows:

Li	6 'daughters of Adam'
Chang	2 'daughters of Adam'
Kao	1 'daughter of Adam'
Chao	4 'daughters of Adam'
Chou 周	2 'daughters of Israel'
Tso 左	1 'daughter of Israel'
Huang 黃	1 'daughter of Adam'
Po 白	3 'daughters of Adam'
Yen	—
Mu	—
Nieh	—
Other surnames	73 'daughters of Adam'

Clearly the only Jewish surnames (of the original 17 or 14) which survived into the fifteenth to seventeenth century A. D. besides the seven of the Register of Men are Chou and Tso. This is confirmed by the solitary Chou (a *Man-la*) of the 1489 inscription. The Huang and

Po wives are labelled as non-Jewish [9], though, of course, their ancestors might have been Jewish. For women of non-Jewish origin, no information is available about their father. We can however make some attempt to date them by their husbands and sons where mentioned. Of those surnames (apart from the seven) used by earlier Jews, one wife, 'daughter of Adam', surname of origin Po, can be dated, for she was grandmother of Chang Wen-jui. This puts her in the seventh generation, fl. approx. 1580 (see later for the justification of this dating).

b *Marriage and Assimilation* [10]

The 90 'daughters of Adam' of known clan come from 47 different surnames (see White, III pp. 188-190). The main ones are:

Chao 趙 4 wives or mothers (besides the Jewish ones)
Ch'en 陳 7 wives or mothers
Chu 朱 7 wives or mothers
Hsü 許 5 wives or mothers
Li 李 6 wives or mothers (besides the Jewish ones)
Wang 王 5 wives or mothers

Laufer (White, III p. 12) writes that 'it appears that many of these women were Mohammedans or of pure Chinese stock'. There is however no reason to consider intermarriage with the Moslems as greater than with other Chinese. In the nineteenth century, when the Chinese Protestant delegates in 1850-51 and the Reverend Martin in 1866 visited the community, there was no love lost between the Jews and their Moslem neighbours. The fact that the two sects were accepted as related by the other Chinese proves nothing.

From the Register, we can discover the extent but not the development of intermarriage. Presumably the original settlers brought few wives with them. Certainly by the Ming dynasty, Jew was marrying Jew as our tables 4-6 (*Abr Nahrain*, Vol IV, pp. 37/38) show. Only 113 non-Jewish wives are registered, as opposed to 267 of Jewish origin.

[9] Missed by Laufer (White III, pp. 11-12); and by Löwenthal (*Monumenta Serica* 12, 1947, pp. 105-106) who criticizes White for not labelling Chou, Tso, Huang and Po as Jewish surnames.

[10] I have not seen the work by Ch'en Tseng-hui 陳增輝, *Yu-t'ai-jen hua-hua k'ao* 猶太人華化考 (The assimilation of the Chinese Jews), Peiping, 1946 (M.A. thesis, Yenching University).

In the case of the 90 'daughters of Adam' of known surname, 37 are mentioned together with husband or son (or grandson), as opposed to 5 only of the 50 'daughters of Israel' of known surname of origin. This enables us to date several of them with reasonable accuracy. Most of the dateable women are of the 8th-10th generations (but this applies also to the Jewish women). We may suppose that the 23 Hebrew-named 'daughters of Adam' were of earlier generations. In any case only certain clans noted husbands and sons of the women.

There is little doubt that the assimilation of the Chinese Jews increased in the eighteenth century. Ricci [11] described his visitor, the Jew Ai, in 1605 as 'a Jew by profession of his faith, nationality, and features' whose 'face was quite different from that of a Chinese in respect to his nose, his eyes and all his features'. By the nineteenth century, when the next wave of visitors to the community started in 1850, it is difficult to accept that the Jews were any longer distinguishable by physical appearance (See plate VII).

Ricci (Löwenthal, *op. cit.*, p. 396) writes of 'Gentile wives and relatives': this is supported by our 8th and 9th generation 'daughters of Adam' of about Ricci's time. Brotier's statement (White, I. p. 63) that 'They receive no proselytes, they never marry with the Gentiles' seems to be an exaggeration of Gozani's 1704:

> These families marry one among another, and never with the *Hui-hui*, or Mohammedans, with whom they have nothing in common, either with regard to books, or religious ceremonies [12].

A further deduction from our table of intermarriage is even more significant. The K'aifeng Jews intermarried with non-Jews, and with Jews of the 7 surnames (apart from 2 Chou and 1 Tso wives). We must conclude that *by this time* (*the seventeenth century*) *there were no Jewish communities* (*in Ningpo or elsewhere*) *in contact with our K'aifeng Jews*. For there can be little doubt that our Jews of K'aifeng would have intermarried with any other available Chinese Jews. The only alternative (hardly credible) is that all the Jews of China had adopted

---

[11] I quote the translation of R. Löwenthal, *Folklore Studies* V, 1946, pp. 394, 397. White I, pp. 31-37, quotes from A. C. Moule, *Christians in China before the Year 1550*, 1930, N. Y. Cf. also *Fonti Ricciane*, edited by Pasquale M. D'Elia, 1942, Rome, II pp. 314-325.

[12] I quote White I p. 42, who is quoting John Lockman, *Travels of the Jesuits*, London, 1762, vol. II pp. 11-22, which is based upon the French of the first edition of the *Lettres edifiantes et curieuses*, Paris, 1707, vol. VII, pp. 1-28, itself translated from Gozani's Portuguese original. Brotier's Memoir is found in the 1781 edition of the *Lettres edifiantes et curieuses*, Paris, vol. XXIV, pp. 56-100.

the same (seven) surnames, or stemmed from one immigration. This is only partly confirmed by Ricci who wrote in 1605:

> They number only a few families and, as far as we know, they have no synagogues elsewhere except in Kaifeng fu, the capital of Honan province, and in Hangchow fu, the capital of Chekiang province.

and:

> They lived there (in K'aifeng) for 500 or 600 years and many more families of their co-religionists with a synagogue stayed in Hangchow, the capital of Chekiang, and also in other parts, but (there) without a synagogue. However, they gradually vanished by dying out.

Brotier (see White I, p. 52) whose work is based on letters by Gozani (1704), Gaubil (1723) and Domenge (1722), wrote in 1770 that 'their colonies in Hang-chow, Ningpo, Peking, and Ning-hsia, have even disappeared. . . only those of Kaifeng Fu are now known'.

There is no hint of any other Jewish communities in China in the 1663 incriptions. But in the 1489 inscription we read that Chao Ying of Ning-po brought a copy of the Law to the synagogue at K'ai-feng from Ning-po during the *T'ien Shun* period 1457-65, and that four K'ai-feng Jews obtained a further copy [13] also from Ning-po. Moreover the 1489 inscription mentions Chin Hsüan and his younger brother Chin Ying of Ning-hsia (in Kansu), and their great-uncle (Chin) Sheng who had been 'lieutenant of the *Chin-wu* advance guard of the Imperial escort' (White II, p. 14). The 1512 inscription mentions Chin P'u of Wei-yang (Yang Chou) and Chin Jun of Ning-hsia.

This evidence is not conclusive, for all these Jews had K'ai-feng surnames, and were closely associated with the K'ai-feng community. We cannot be quite sure that any other communities were flourishing in the fifteenth century.

It is interesting to note the two versions given by Brotier (see White I, pp. 52, 65) for the origin of (presumably the same?) oldest scroll of the Law. (Quoting Gozani?) he writes of a Pentateuch obtained, prior to the time of Wan Li 1573-1620, 'from a Mohammedan whom they met at Ning-hsia in the Province of Shensi. A Jew of Canton, being about to die entrusted it to him as a precious relic'. Quoting Gaubil, he writes that 'the Jews from Hsi-yü (the west? i.e. Persia?) being arrived in the midst of these circumstances, they had of them a Bible, together with other books'. This is given as about the time of the burning of the synagogue in the period of Wan Li 1573-1620.

---

[13] See Leslie, *Journal of the American Oriental Society*, 82, 1962, p. 354, footnote 31.

These stories cannot be corroborated[14]. It seems probable that by this time the K'ai-feng community was already isolated.

F. Genealogies

a White's Erroneous Family Trees

White was the first to appreciate the genealogical value of the Register. He has constructed, III pp. 158-60, a family tree for the Li clan spanning sixteen generations. Unfortunately this is based on incorrect identifications. White has joined together a Jewish family for the 3rd to 7th generations, with a non-Jewish family for the 7th to 18th generations. The central figure in White's discussion is Li Kuang-t'ien, 'Hero of the Defence of Pien 1642', whose story is found in the *Shou Pien Jih-chih* 守汴日志 (Diary of the Defence of Pien), and White has devoted well over twenty pages to him and his family (see III pp. 103-4, 149-53, 158-60, 201-8, 221-4, 128-36). *This man and his family were not Jews*. He himself was never mentioned in any of the Jewish sources, which would be most surprising were he to have been a Jew.

White's argument is based on the following erroneous identifications.

(i) Li Kuang-tso, the elder brother of Li Kuang-t'ien, and a *Chin-shih* of 1649, figures twice in the Jewish inscriptions, though not in the Register. In the 1663a inscription, he is mentioned as having written the characters in vermilion (for the engravers). He is also the author of a four character horizontal tablet (*pien*) in 1670. In both cases, there is no reason to assume that he was Jewish, for such honours to (and by) the synagogue were normally given by such non-Jewish high officials. Of the eleven persons who wrote such *pien* (from 1656-79), nine held non-Jewish surnames, one was our Li Kuang-tso, and the last only was a Jew, Chao Ying-tou, *magistrate* and honorary *Chin-shih*. Almost all are known to have been high officials and scholars of the time. Similarly the composer of the 1663a inscription, Liu Ch'ang, and the writer of the seal characters at the top, Hou Liang-han, whose names appear alongside that of Li Kuang-tso, were non-Jewish high officials invited to honour the community by performing those tasks. The three corresponding scholars for the 1512 inscription, Tso T'ang of Chiang-tu, Kao Fang of Huai-nan, and Hsü-ang of Wei-yang, are also most unlikely to have been Jews, even though two of them had possible Jewish surnames. Not one of

---

[14] Cf. Tobar, pp. 93-4, who doubts both stories.

these high officials and scholars is mentioned elsewhere in the inscriptions. The main argument that Li Kuang-tso was Jewish is his surname. But there were perhaps more men surnamed Li in China than all the Jews in the world at the time! Ch'en Yüan (*Tung-fang Tsa-chih* 17, 5 p. 118-9), though he looks on Tso T'ang as probably of Jewish origin, states bluntly that Li Kuang-tso was not a Jew.

(ii) Li Jung (*Chü-jen* of 1600) was the father of Li Kuang-t'ien. A quite distinct Li Jung of nearly two hundred years earlier is mentioned in the 1489 inscription.

(iii) Li Ying-yüan, the great-grandfather of Li Kuang-t'ien, obtained his *Chin-shih* in 1553. His father is known from the Hsiang-fu gazetteers to have been named Li Yu. White identifies this Li Ying-yüan with a man of the same name in the Register. He writes (III p. 135):

> In the Codex it states that Li Ying-yüan was the eldest son of Li Yü-ch'un (C 34, 139), by which it may be accepted that Li Yu and Li Yü-ch'un are one and the same person.

Such an identification merely serves to provide its own disproof. We may anticipate slightly and give the approximate dates of 1640-50 for the Li Ying-yüan of the Register.

We need hardly add that such a famous family of scholars and officials would have been mentioned in the inscriptions were they Jewish.

White's work on the Chinese Jews and their genealogies is of permanent value. But in this case he has created a completely mythical story.

White (III p. 163) has also constructed a family tree for the Chao clan extending over eleven generations. This too is largely mythical. Once again White has joined two families together. The key links are missing and the act of faith required to jump them is too great. In fact his first seven generations are almost certainly not of the Chao family at all. I have given earlier (*Abr Nahrain*, Vol. IV, p. 28) the reasons for transferring this family from the Chao to the Li. White has three arguments in favour of continuing the lineage. The first is his mistaken belief that R. Moses, the Physician (No. 186) (of the Li clan) is Moses, the *Chin-shih* (No. 273) (of the Chao clan), a most unlikely possibility. The second is his missing link imagined before Moses the Physician, based on the fact that he has the same name as a Moses the Physician of eight generations earlier. Thirdly, he takes the first Moses the Physician (No. 192) as Chao Ch'eng (formerly Yen Ch'eng), a physician according to the inscriptions, and founder of the Chao clan.

This triple speculation is not merely worthless, but certainly incorrect.

b *The Family Tree of the Ai Clan*

White's two extended trees, for the Li and Chao clans, are incorrect. For neither of these clans can we discover trees of more than eight generations (see below). There is however one remarkable family tree which covers almost all the 164 members of the Ai clan included in the Register of men, and extends over eleven generations.

We may note here that such family trees, although often given in Chinese Genealogical Registers *Chia-p'u*, are not given in our Memorial Book as such, but have to be reconstructed from the father and son relationships, and by inference from the order of entry in the Register. The following family tree, though one or two of its later entries may be out of place, is almost entirely reliable, in particular for the first nine generations. The tailing off for the 10th and 11th generations is of course due to the nature of the Register as concerning only the dead.

c *The Chao Clan*

White's most successful suggestion is that Moses, the *Chin-shih* 進士, No. 273 of the Register, is the scholar and official Chao Ying-ch'eng 趙映乘, a believer and Hebrew scholar according to the synagogue inscriptions, and an official and holder of the *Chin-shih* degree according to the inscriptions and non-Jewish Chinese sources. The essential passage in the Register (see plate VIII) reads: 'Moses, *Chin-shih*, Chao Ying-k'uei, Chao Ying-fu, son(s) of Abram'.

Now the only Jews of K'ai-feng (or elsewhere) known to have received the doctorate degree *Chin-shih* are Chao Ying-ch'eng and his younger brother Chao Ying-tou 趙映斗 [15].

It is very common (in the Register, and in general for Chinese families) for brothers to share one character in their personal names;

---

[15] Chao Ying-ch'eng is recorded in the exam lists as a *Chin-shih* of 1646, exactly as is stated in the 1663a, b and 1679 inscriptions. Chao Ying-tou is recorded by the gazetteer as a *Pa-kung* 拔貢, a high grade degree just below the doctorate. He is nowhere mentioned as a *Chin-shih* other than in the Archway inscriptions of 1678 (White II pp. 111-15) where we read of Chao Ying-ch'eng 'recipient of the doctorate' (賜進士) and Chao Ying-tou 'recipient of an honorary doctorate' (思進士). We do not know why he was thus honoured. For further examples of such honorary doctorates, see Shang Yen-liu 商衍鎏, *Ch'ing-tai K'e-chü K'ao-shih Shu-lu* 清代科舉考試述録, Peking, 1958, p.84.

and Moses, (Ying-   ) presumably the eldest son, is far more likely to have been Ying-ch'eng, also probably the eldest son.

White is clearly right that Moses, *Chin-shih*, son of Abram, brother to Ying-k'uei 映魁 and Ying-fu 映甫 (from the Register) is Chao Ying-ch'eng 映乘, son of Chao Kuang-yü 光裕, and presumably brother to Ying-fu 映黻, Ying-tou 映斗, and Ying-kun 映袞 (all of whom appear in the Hsiang-fu gazetteers).

Our family tree given below shows that it is not difficult to match up Abram with Kuang-yü, and to solve the difference between the brothers of the Register and those of the gazetteer.

Chao Ying-tou is mentioned in the 1663a inscription as 'younger brother' *ti* 弟 to Chao Ying-ch'eng, and also elsewhere to Chao Ch'eng-chi 承基, an army officer. These three contemporaries (fl. 1642-1653) are all called *chiao-jen* 教人 'believers'. Chao Ying-ch'eng is known from non-Jewish sources to be a son of Chao Kuang-yü. That Ying-tou is brother to Ying-ch'eng is confirmed by the Chao Archway panel in the synagogue where the two are coupled with Chao Kuang-yü in such a manner as to make it obvious that they were his sons. It seems probable that Chao Ying-tou was merely a 'younger cousin' (*ti* 弟 might have this meaning) of Ch'eng-chi.

Chao Ying-k'uei is not known other than from the Register, where he also appears as father to Hananiah (No. 296). (Chao) Ying-fu 映甫 is probably identical to Chao Ying-fu 映黻 of the gazetteer, as suggested by White. His widow from the Kao clan mourned him for over 40 years [16]. He presumably *died young*. Neither of these figure in the inscriptions.

Chao Ying-tou and Chao Ying-kun, on the other hand, appear prominently in the 1663 and 1679 inscriptions, both being alive at this latter date, as opposed to Chao Ying-ch'eng, who probably died in about 1657 (see below, Pt. 3). (Chao) Ying-tou is mentioned as the husband of two women of non-Jewish origin in the Register of women, though he does not appear in the Register of men. We may assume that these two younger brothers were still alive when the Register was closed (around 1663?) and thus do not appear in the Register of men.

We shall be dealing with these brothers and their dates again in greater detail in our Part 3 when we try to identify them in the local gazetteers.

---

[16] See Hsiang-fu gazetteers, 1739, ch. 15, p. 72b; 1898, ch. 18, p. 20b; K'ai-feng-fu gazetteer 1695, ch. 27, p. 47b. Cf. also Ch'en Yüan (*Tung-fang Tsa-chih* 17, 6 p. 122).

Tree No. 3 : *Shih family* 1

Generations: 7 8 9 10 11

- Berachah (7)
  - Job (8)
    - R. Eliezer (9)
    - Berachah (9)
      - R. Joshua (10)
        - Chung-yü (11)
      - Tzu-te (10)
        - Chung-p'u (11)
        - Chung-pi (11)
      - Tzu-ch'un (10)
      - Tzu-hsiu (10)
    - BTL·L (9)
      - Tzu-cheng (10)

Tree No. 4 : *Shih family* 2

Generations: 7 8 9 10 11

- Moses (7)
  - Levi (8)
    - Joseph (9)
      - Simcha (10)
        - Sheng-ming (11)
      - Tzu-ch'iang (10)
      - Tzu-hung (10)
      - R. Judah, the Scribe (10)
    - Issachar (9)
      - Mordecai (10)
    - Solomon (9)
      - (Mattithiah?) (10)
      - Tzu-ai (10)
      - Tzu-teng (10)

Tree No. 5 : *Chang family* 1

Generations: 5 6 7 8 9 10

- rachah (5)
  - Akibah (6)
    - Gershon (7)
      - Phinehas (8)
        - Wen-chün (9)
          - T'ien (10)
          - Mei (10)
          - Hsing (10)
          - Wang (10)
        - Wen-yao (9)
          - Chih (10)
          - Fa (10)
          - Sheng (10)
      - Mordecai (8)
        - Wen-chi (9)
        - Wen-hsin (9)
      - Chü-te (8)
        - Wen-hsiang (9)
  - Jeberech (6)

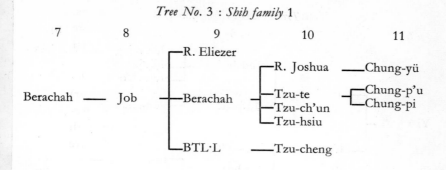

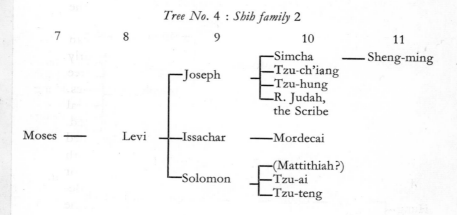

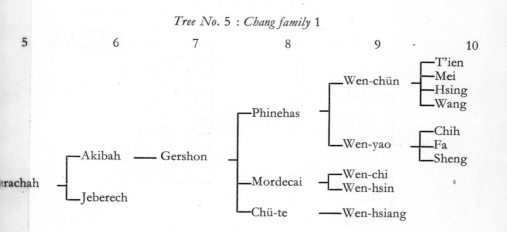

Tree No. 6 : *Chang family* 2

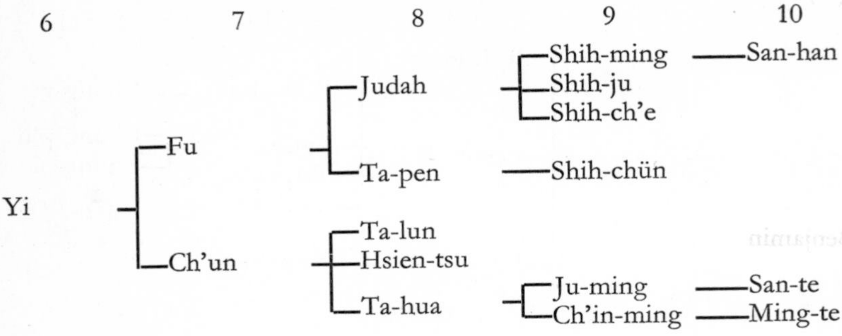

Tree No. 7 : *Chang family* 3

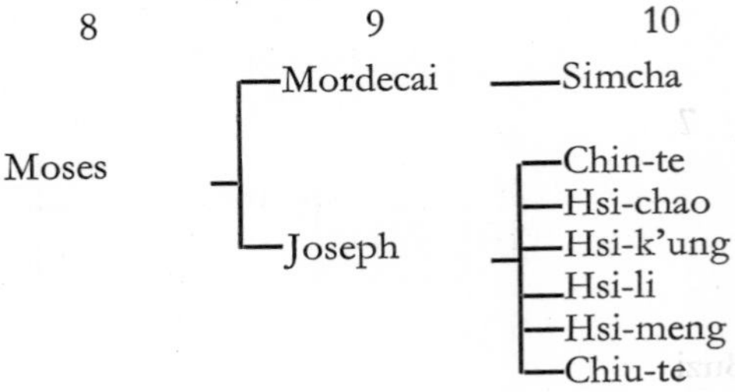

Tree No. 8 : *Kao family* 1

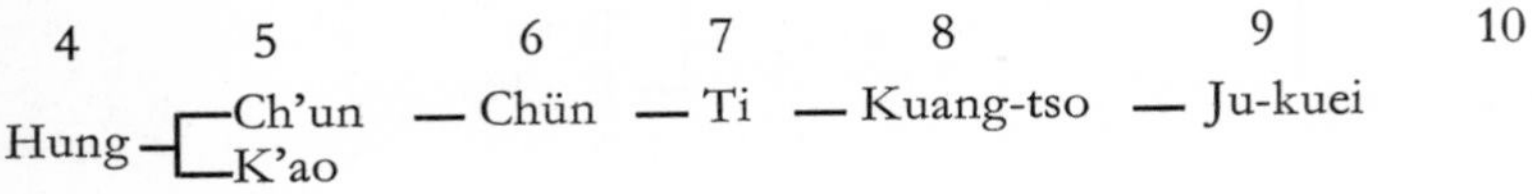

Tree No. 9: *Kao family* 2

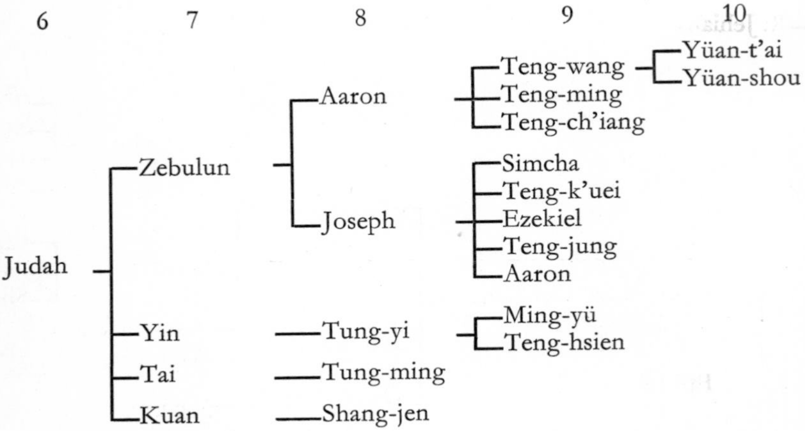

Tree No. 10 : *Kao family* 3

Generations: 7 — 8 — 9 — 10 — 11

- Benjamin (7)
  - Joseph (8)
    - Yi-kuei (9)
    - Tse-kuei (9)
    - R. Jinnon (9)
    - Yün-kuei (9)
  - Issachar (8)
    - Yüeh-kuei (9)
      - Chi-tsu (10)
    - Cho-kuei (9)
      - Sheng-tsu (10)
      - Chi-tsu (10)
    - P'an-kuei (9)
    - Kung-ch'en (9)
  - Joshua (8)
    - Lun-kuei (9)
      - Yüan-p'u (10)
    - T'an-kuei (9)
    - Judah (9)

Tree No. 11 : *Kao family* 4

Generations: 7 — 8 — 9 — 10 — 11

- Buzi (7)
  - Reuben (8)
    - R. Jacob (9)
      - R.BTL·L (10)
  - Simeon (8)
    - Joshua (9)
      - Ch'ung -ch'en (10)
    - Solomon (9)
      - Ch'ung-chieh (10)
    - R. Mordecai, The Scribe (9)
      - Ezekiel (10)
      - Samuel (10)
      - R. Issachar (10)
      - Joseph (10)
  - Levi (8)
  - Issachar (8)
    - Asah(?) (9)
      - Yüan-chi (10)
        - Jacob (11)
      - Moses (10)
        - Chi-yüan (11)

Tree No. 12 : *Li family* 1

Generations: 3 — 4 — 5 — 6 — 7 — 8 — 9 — 10

- Moses, e ysician (3)
  - R. Jehiah (4)
    - R. Isaac (5)
      - R. Elidad (6)
        - R. Abishai, The Teacher, The Envoy (7)
          - R. Abdiel (8)
          - R. Jacob, The Teacher, The Envoy (8)
            - R. Shadai (9)
            - R. Jeremiah, The Scribe, The Teacher, The Envoy (9)
              - Chin-ch'ao (10)

Tree No. 13 : *Li family* 2

Generations: 7 — 8 — 9 — 10 — 11

- Ephraim (7)
  - Phinehas (8)
    - Hsiang (9)
      - Tzu-hsing (10)
        - Ssu-jen (11)
    - Ch'a (9)

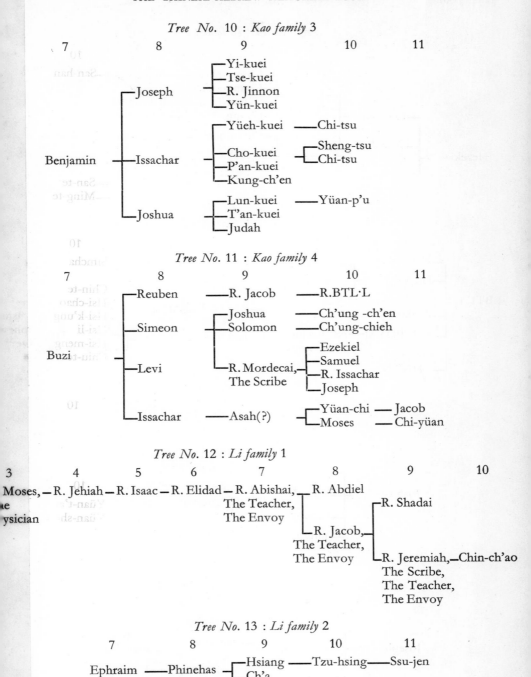

Tree No. 14 : *Li family* 3

Generations: 5 — 6 — 7 — 8 — 9 — 10

- Hezekiah
  - Obadiah
    - Kuo
      - Chung-cheng — Ming-wang
        - Shih-chün
        - Fa
      - Chung-ch'en
      - Chung-hsin — R. Simcha
      - Chung-ch'eng — Ming-kao
    - K'un
    - Lin
      - Chung-jen — Ming-hsing — Joshua
      - Chung-yi
  - Joseph
  - Gad

Tree No. 15 : *Li family* 4

Generations: 5 — 6 — 7 — 8 — 9 — 10 — 11

- R.BTL·L
  - R. Eber
  - Hayyal(?)
    - Samuel
    - Joseph
    - Judah
  - Amram — Jesse
  - R.SLPDYM — R. Ezekiel, The Scribe
  - YḤNTN

- (8)
  - R. BTL·L — Moses — Hui (alive?)
  - Jacob — Joseph
    - Ch'ung-p'u
    - Sheng-hung
  - Yu-hsiu (nephew (alive?)

Tree No. 16: *Li family* 5

Generations: 8 — 9 — 11 — 11

- Joshua
  - Samuel
    - Ch'eng-ai — Yen-nien
    - Ch'eng-chün
  - Yü-ch'un
    - Ying-yüan
    - Ch'eng-yin
  - Eleazar
  - Ying-ch'un — Ch'eng-shih

Tree No. 17 : *Chin family*

Generations: 7 — 8 — 9 — 10

- Joseph
  - Fu — Ying-wen
  - Mordecai
    - Ying-tou
      - Chih-lin
      - Chih-hsiu
    - Ying-hsüan — Issachar
  - Shou

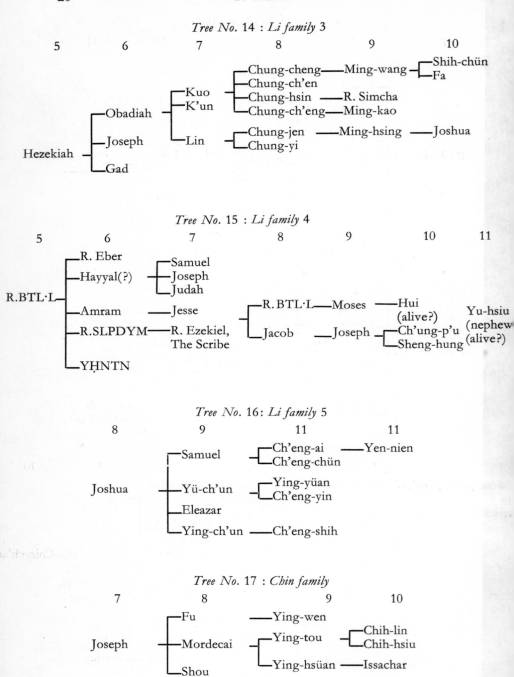

Chart No. 4: Matching Family Trees

	Ai	Chao	Shih 1	Shih 2	Chang 1	Chang 2	Chang 3	Kao 1	Kao 2	Kao 3	Kao 4	Li 1	Li 2	Li 3	Li 4	Li 5	Chin
		(E)	(B)	(B)		(e)	(f)		(2) (3)							(Y)	

relationship between named and identified individuals; those with brackets involve usually the assumption that men of similar name within one clan are of the same generation. The * refers to similar named members of two families within the same clan.

G. The Generations

a *Family Relationships*

We have seen the family trees based on the Men's Register. From the Women's Register, we can obtain little to aid us in tracing genealogies, for the women transferred from one clan to another on marriage. In any case, no personal names are given for the women other than Hebrew names. But we can give father-in-law to son-in-law, and maternal grandfather to grandson, in those cases, comparatively few, where both the fathers and the husbands or sons of the women of the Register are mentioned. The woman herself drops out of the equation. This information is of almost no value for extended family relationships. But it is of enormous value in helping us to equate generations from one clan to the next.

Here is all the information obtainable.

List No. 4
Fathers-in-law and Sons-in-law

	Father-in-law	Son-in-law	Page
(a)	Ai Ho	(Li) Yen-nien	68
(b)	(Ai) Rabbi Mordecai	(Li) Chien-huan	71
(c)	(Ai) R. Judah	(Chang) Teng-ti	84
(d)	Ai Sung-hsüan	(Chang) Hsing	85
(e)	(Ai?) Issachar	(Chang) San-chi	85
(f)	Ai Hsin-so	(Chang)Hsi-chao	86
(g)	Ai Yung-shun	(Chin) Kuang	102
(h)	(Li) Simcha	(Ai?) Ting	81
(i)	Li Chung-ch'eng	(Chang) Wen-chi	83
(j)	(Li) Ithamar	(Chang) Ta-lun	84
(k)	(Li) Joshua	(Chang) Ta-pen	84
(l)	(Li) Moses	(Chang) T'ien	84
(m)	(Li) R. Simcha	(Chang) Fa	85
(n)	Chang Wen-chün	Chin Chih-jui	102
(o)	(Kao) Zebulun	Li Shu	69
(p)	Kao Cho-kuei	(Chang) Mei	84
(q)	Kao Tien	(Chang)Hsi-k'ung	86
(r)	Kao Yang-chih	(Chang) Hsi-li	86
(s)	Kao Ying-kuei	(Chang) Li	85
(t)	Kao Yüan-shou	(Chin) Kuang	102
(u)	(Chao) Phinehas	(Li) Shou-chiao	68
(v)	Chao Kuang-hsün	(Kao?) Teng-k'uei	93
(w)	Chin Yu-hsin	(Chang) Wen-hsiang	83
(x)	Chin Ying-tou	(Chang) Chih	84
(y)	(Chin) Mattithiah	(Chang) Hsin-yü	85
(z)	(Shih) Joseph	(Li) Tzu-hsing	70

	Father-in-law	Son-in-law	Page
(A)	(Shih) Joseph	(Li) Hsing-wu	70
(B)	Shih Tzu-li	(Ai?) Tzu-cho	80
(C)	(Shih) Solomon	(Chang) Sheng	85

In the above list and the one to follow, the surname of the older generation is usually given for the man himself or equally reliably for his daughter. That of the son-in-law or grandson is rarely given but is deducible from the clan pages. However these surnames also are entirely reliable in the case of Li or Chang members, and to a considerable extent for the others given here.

List No. 5
Maternal Grandfathers and Grandsons

	Maternal Grandfather	Grandson	Page
(D)	(Ai) Jeremiah	(Chao) Tsʻui	94
(E)	(Ai) Putiel	(Chao) Yüan-hsing	96
(F)	Li Shih-ch'eng	(Ai?) Fa-chih	80
(G)	Li Chiu-chou	(Chang) Wen-jui	83
(H)	(Li?) R. SLPWDYM	(Chang) Chü-jung	83
(I)	Li Chung-hsin	(Chang) Hsiu	83
(J)	(Li) Jacob	(Chang) San-kuei	86
(K)	Li Wang-ch'en	(Chang) Hsiu-chi	86
(L)	(Chang) Joseph	(Li) Yen-shou	68
(M)	(Chang) Mordecai	(Chao) Chien	94
(N)	Kao Kuan	(Chang) Lung	96
(O)	Chao Teng	(Ai?) Wei-yi	80
(P)	Chin Lu	(Chang) Wen-chi	83
(Q)	(Chin) R. Joseph	(Chang) Mei	83
(R)	Chin Shih 石	(Chang) Chiu-te	84
(S)	Chin Teng	(Chang) San-shan	84
(T)	(Chin) Mordecai	(Kao?) Yüan-pi	93
(U)	(Chin) Jesse	(Chao) Yün-chung	94
(V)	(Shih) Joseph	(Li) Yüan-liang	70

In addition, we may note the following relationships:

(W) (Kao) Benjamin, great grandfather of (Ai?) Fa-chih, p. 80.

(X) Li? (or Ai?) Ithamar, maternal grandfather of (Chang) Wen-chün, p. 83.

(Y) Ai? (or Shih?) R. Judah, maternal grandfather of (Li) Chʻeng-hsien, p. 68.

Besides the Register, we have two further sources for finding relationships between individuals. The first, the local gazetteers, will be utilised when we try to identify individual Jews. The information obtained from the second source, the Chinese inscriptions of the synagogue, is given below.

List No. 6
Family Relationships in the Inscriptions

	Person	Relationship	Person	Source
1.	(Ai) Ts'ung-sheng, Yung-yen, Hsien-sheng, Ta-sheng, Fu-sheng,	sons 子	of Ai Ying-kʻuei	1663 b
2.	Ai Hsien-sheng	grandson 孫	of Ai T'ien	Vertical Tablet
3.	(Chao) Ying-tou	younger brother 弟	of Chao Ying-ch'eng	1663a
	(cf. the Archway inscriptions and local gazetteers).			
4.	(Chao) Ying-tou	younger brother (or cousin?) 弟	of Chao Ch'eng-chi	1663a
5.	(Chao) Yüan-chien	nephew 姪	of Chao Yün-chung (Chao) Yün-ch'eng (Chao) Ying-kun	1663b
6.	(Chao) Yüan-min, (Chao) Yüan-chien	elder sons 長子		1679
	(Chao) Wen-lung, (Chao) Wen-feng	grandsons 孫		
7.	(Chin) Ying	younger brother 弟	of Chin Hsüan	1489
8.	(Chin) Sheng	great uncle 佰祖	of Chin Hsüan	1489
9.	(Kao) Tung-tou	father 父	of Kao Hsüan	1663a
10.	(Li) Yu-hsiu	nephew 姪	of Li Hui	1663b

b *Matching Generations*

We have two main sources for matching generations from one clan to another (and finally all to the Ai clan tree taken as standard): the father-in-law, son-in-law and maternal grandfather, maternal grandson relationships given above; and our knowledge of contemporaneity and actual dates of individuals from the inscriptions and gazetteers. From the 1663 and 1679 inscriptions and the Hebrew-Persian colophons (see below in our Part III), we may label the following groups as contemporaries.

List No. 7
Contemporaries

1. Ai Hsien-sheng
   Chao Ch'eng-chi
   Chao Ying-ch'eng
   (all friends of Liu Ch'ang, died 1670).

2. Ai Hsien-sheng
   Chao Ch'eng-chi
   Chao Ying-ch'eng
   (Chao) Ying-tou (younger brother)
   Chao Yün-chung
   (Kao) Tung-tou and son Kao Hsüan
   Kao Teng-k'uei
   Kao Wei-p'ing (a Scholar)
   Li Chen (Leader of the Religion)
   Li Ch'eng-hsien
   Li Ch'eng-chün (from 1663 b)
   Li Fa-t'ien (a Scholar)
   (all were active in 1642-1653 at the time of the inundation of K'aifeng, according to the 1663 a inscription).

3. Ai Ta-sheng, brothers, sons and nephews
   Ai Wei-yi and family
   Chang Wen-jui and family
   Chao Yün-ssu
   Chao Ying-ch'eng
   Chin Ying-hsüan and family
   Kao Teng-k'uei
   Kao Teng-k'o
   Li Hui, and nephew (Li) Yu-hsiu
   Shih Tzu-chün
   (all restored scrolls after 1642, according to the 1663 b inscription).

4. Ai Sheng-chih
   (Ai) Shih-fang
   Ai Shih-te
   Ai Wei-yi
   Ai Ying-k'uei and his sons (Ai) Ts'ung-sheng, Yung-yin, Hsien-sheng, Ta-sheng, Fu-sheng
   Chao Yün-chung
   (Chao) Yün-ch'eng
   (Chao) Ying-kun and (their?) nephew (Chao) Yüan-chien
   Chao Ying-ch'eng
   Chin Chih-feng
   Kao Teng-k'o

Kao Teng-k'uei
Li Hui
(all contributed to rebuilding the synagogue in 1653, according to the 1663 b inscription).

5. Chao Ying-tou
Chao Ying-kun
Chao Yüan-feng
Chao Yün-ch'eng
(all alive in 1679).

6. (Li) Rabbi Jacob, son of Rabbi Abishai, son of Rabbi Eldad; and his son Rabbi Shadai
(Kao) Rabbi Mordecai, son of Simeon
(Ai) Rabbi Akibah, son of Aaron, son of Ezra
(Kao?) The youth Simcha, son of Joshua, son of Joseph
(Kao) Rabbi Jacob, son of Reuben, son of Buzi
(Kao?) Mordecai, son of Benjamin, (son of Buzi ?)
(all signatories of the Hebrew-Persian Colophon dated as 1622-1626).

7. (Ai) Shadiavor, son of Bethuel, son of Moses
(Ai) Rabbi Akibah, son of Aaron, son of Ezra
(Chang?) Mordecai, son of Moses
(all signatories of a further undated Hebrew-Persian colophon).

We are now in a position to attempt to match the generations of the different clans. Some of our matching is hypothetical, based on several hints, rather than on an actual relationship between two given men. One key assumption is that men of similar name within one clan are of the same generation (though not, apparently, if of similar or even identical name in different clans).

The following chart (No. 4) gives (without all the evidence) the linkages (of father-in-law, son-in-law; maternal grandfather, maternal grandson; contemporaneity) which have enabled us to match the generations of the genealogical trees given above. Those given in brackets can only be taken as probable links: for we have (in these cases) made the jump from one man to another man of the same clan with similar name, but otherwise unknown to be related.

Some of the clans are clearly related by marriage. Chang family 1, for which there is most information, is related to the Chin family; to Li family 3 and family 4; to Kao family 3; and to Shih family 2. These relationships are confirmed by the lists of contemporaries, which also enable us to match Chang family 1 and its associates with the Ai and Chao families, many of whose members (or at least similar named men) are mentioned in the inscriptions as contempories. This gearing of alll the clans to the Ai clan may be wrong by one generation for several families. In any case contempories may be of different generations as well as ages. Members of the younger branches of the clan will often be many years younger than seniors of the same generation. We have attempted to keep this in mind (and will return to the problem when we come to the dating of identified individuals), but obviously all our calculations are approximate and somewhat hypothetical. Though generations may overlap in age, this is a less worrying problem than one would expect, for Chinese custom frowned strongly on marriage outside one's own generation, that is to say, that once two families had undertaken one bond of marriage, further marriages would confirm in generation to the generations of the first marriage relationship.

From these linkages and the genealogical trees we can construct the 5th column of the following essential chart. The dates in the 6th column are based on individuals mentioned in the synagogue inscriptions as alive at the dates given.

Chart No. 5
Common Characters in the Personal Name

Clan	Character	Number in Register	Number in Inscriptions	Probable Generation	Approximate Dates Alive
Ai	Hsien — 先	4		9th	
	Hsin — 新	7		9th	
	Sheng — 生	4	1	10th?	1653
	Shih — 士	4		10th	
	Shih — 世	2	2	11th	1653-1676
	Tzu — 自	5		11th?	
	Wei — 惟	3	1	9th	1642-1653
	Yi — 一	5		10th?	
	Ying — 應	4 (+ 1?)	1	9th	1653
	Yung — 永	2	1	10th?	1653
	-sheng — 生		4	10th	1642-1668
Chang	Hsi — 希	4		10th	
	San — 三	5		10th	
	Shih — 世	5		9th	
	Ta — 大	4		8th	
	Wen — 文	6	1 (+ 1?)	9th	1642
Chao	Kuang — 光	6	1	9th?	
	Shang — 尙	9		10th?	
	Shih — 士	3		10th?	
	Wen — 文	3	2	12th?	1679
	Ying — 應	4			

Clan	Character	Number in Register	Number in Inscrip-tions	Probable Gener-ation	Approximate Dates Alive
Chao	(Cont'd.)				
	Ying — 映	3	3	10th	1642-1679
	Yüan — 元	3	3	11th	1653-1679
	Yün — 允	5	3	10th	1642-1679
Chin	Chih — 之	4	1	10th	1653
	Ying — 應	14	1	9th	1642
Kao	Teng — 登	6	2	9th?	1642-1653
	Tung — 東	7	1		1642
	Wen — 文	4			
	Yüan — 元	4 (+ 2?)		10th?	
	-kuei — 桂	12		9th?	
Li	Ch'ao — 朝	3		9th	
	Ch'eng — 承	8	2	10th	1642
	Chi — 計	3			
	Chin — 進	4			
	Chung — 中	11		8th	
	Ming — 名	12		9th	
	Shih — 世	4		8th?	
	Yang — 養	4			
Shih	Chung — 中	3		11th	
	Teng — 登	3			
	Tzu — 自	10	1	10th	1642

Several of the families and their generations can stand alone, for we can date (approximately) a known individual of the family tree. The dating of others depends entirely on the hypothetical equating of generations and generation names, based on the above two charts. The whole structure, to be convincing, should not involve inconsistencies. In fact there are at least two possible contradictions:

1. Ai Wei-yi, who, together with his family, restored a scroll after 1642, according to the 1663b inscription, and contributed funds to the synagogue in 1653, is almost certainly of the 9th generation. But the linkage O, (p. 80, no. 500) reads: Chao *shih* (née), mother of (Ai) Wei-yi, *chaf* daughter of Chao Teng. This would imply that Ai Wei-yi was of the 11th generation, for Chao-Teng (father of Shang-kung, Shang-li and Shih-chün) was probably of the 9th generation.

   On p. 80, no. 501, we find: Chao *shih* (née), mother of (Ai) Wei-yi, *chaf* daughter of Adam.

We are entitled to consider no. 500 as perhaps a mistake and to ignore it. It is also possible to consider Chao Teng as of the 7th generation, with one slight inconsistency elsewhere in our matching.

2. For the various Kao families, we have assumed that the generation name Yüan- is always found in the 10th generation. Several of our linkages fit this well. This puts Kao Teng-k'uei, alive in 1642-1653, in the 9th generation, which fits the lists of contemporaneity quite well. It puts Kao Tung-tou and his son, Hsüan in the 8th and 9th generations, which is quite feasible, as would be their placing in the 9th and 10th generation.

   There are two possible contradictions here:

   a. Linkage v, (p. 93, number 629) makes Kao Teng-k'uei son-in-law of Chao Kuang-hsün, if my suggestion that p. 93 is of the Kao is accepted; and Chao Kuang-hsün is probably of the 9th generation, for Abram (Chao Kuang-yü) is father of Chao Ying-ch'eng and his brothers of the 10th generation. However, Chao Kuang-yü had a brother Ming-yü, and -yü is the common generation character, not Kuang-.

   b. According to linkage o, (p. 69, no. 389), (Kao) Zebulun is father-in-law of Li Shu, who is probably of the 9th generation, for he is father of Li Ch'eng-yeh. But our tree puts him as generation 7 of Kao family 2.

These few possible contradictions should not be taken too seriously, but on the other hand we clearly cannot be sure that our reconstructions are correct in all instances.

The detailed discussion of dates (both of the manuscript and of the generations) will be taken up in the following sections, when we try to identify individuals in the Register with those of the synagogue inscriptions, local gazetteers, and Hebrew-Persian colophons, all of which provide some accurate dates, though unfortunately rarely of birth or death. One of the main purposes of constructing the genealogical trees and matching the generations is to provide a firm base for such identifications.

(*To be continued*)

HOMER AND UGARITIC LITERATURE

BY

A. F. CAMPBELL, S. J.

In recent years, a considerable amount has been written about the similarities between the civilizations of Greece and the Near East. [1] Apart from the works which, at least in part, deal with this subject specifically, a growing number of references to it occurs in books and articles on the Aegean or the Orient in antiquity.

Cyrus Gordon has been one of the chief proponents of the thesis that close cultural similarity existed between the Aegean and Semitic worlds, going so far as to assert that "Greek and Hebrew civilizations are parallel structures built upon the same East Mediterranean foundation." [2] In *Before the Bible*, he attempts to bring together all the evidence that can be adduced to link not merely Greek and Hebrew civilizations, but Greece and the whole of the fertile Crescent from Mesopotamia to Egypt.

This article intends to deal with only a small section of so wide a field. On the Greek side, the subject has been confined to the Homeric epics and on the Semitic, to the poems of Ugarit. To assess Gordon's thesis on the basis of these two alone, would be unfair, though not as unfair as it might seem at first sight, since these two do play very important roles in his exposition. But the subject has so far been treated on a broad plane, and it should be worthwhile to give detailed examination to a small but important section of it.

It is an important section chiefly because Ugarit was in a favourable position to act as a medium of transmission to or from Greece. Relationships between literatures do not grow up in the abstract, they presuppose contact between peoples, and the possibility of this must be carefully evaluated. [3] The establishment of close links between the Aegean world and the Levant in the 2nd millennium B.C. has been one of the major contribution of archaeology in the last quarter century. The empire of the Mycenaeans with its control of the sea was a channel ready for the spread of cultural ideas from Syria to Sicily. Trading stations with little or no permanently resident population existed in the west, in Egypt, Gaza and Caria. At Miletus, Ugarit and throughout Cyprus the Mycenaeans established permanent colonies. [4]

A considerable trade must have passed through Miletus, probably coastal trade carrying products to Troy, Smyrna, Kolophon and other sites on the coast at which Mycenaean III A-B pottery has been found, and to the Mycenaean sites on Rhodes and Kos. [5] It would seem that Mycenaean trade did not penetrate inland to the Late Bronze Age sites of Central Anatolia, so that direct and continued contact between the Mycenaeans and the central Hittite kingdom is not strongly suggested. [6]

The case of the settlement at Ugarit was different. It was in close contact with the wealthy settlements at Enkomi, Kition, and Paphos in Cyprus, which because of its wealth of metal ore and its intermediary position in the ivory trade occupied an important economic position in the Levant. [7] Contact between the Mycenaeans at Ugarit and those at Enkomi was close and sustained, but the pottery shows that it was Ugarit rather than Cyprus which had the closest contact with the Mycenaean homeland. [8]

Ras Shamra occupies a privileged position. It has one of the few natural harbours on the Syrian coast; it is only a day's sail from Cyprus; it served as a terminus for caravan routes leading to Palestine in the south, Mesopotamia and the Hurrian-Mitannian territories in the east, and Asia Minor in the north [9]. A measure of its importance to the Mycenaeans is the fact that the Hittites, in their conquest of this part of the Syrian coast, left Ugarit alone, according to Schaeffer, chiefly out of respect for Mycenaean interests there. [10]

Ugarit had adapted the cuneiform script to form a consistent and widely used alphabetic system of writing. Cypro-Minoan script was also used for keeping trade tallies, and Akkadian, Hurrian and Sumerian were used for commercial and administrative documents [11]. Although a few examples of the Ugaritic-type alphabetic script have been found elsewhere, no other city in Canaan was as advanced as Ugarit in this respect. The possession of a written language and literature gives Ugarit an important role if there is to be transmission of religious and cultural ideas.

Furthermore, Ugarit was a centre of nature mythology with a mixed Hurrian and northwest Semitic population [12]. Mons Casius (Jebel Akra), which dominated the city, held an important position not only in Ugaritic belief but also in Hurrian mythology [13]. Ugarit was therefore in a position to combine the beliefs and ideas of its native Semites with those of the Hurrians as well as the Mesopotamians further east.

The links outlined so far suggest the possibility of cultural contact within the framework of the Mycenaean period. Although Homer is not Mycenaean literature, links between Homeric and Ugaritic literature could follow from the sustained contact between Mycenae and Ugarit. However, in view of the commonly proposed eighth century date for Homer, and the fact that Greek trade was almost equally extensive in the Mycenaean times and in the eighth and seventh centuries B.C., the latter period must also be considered [14].

Greek traders at this time were in contact with the Lydians and possibly with the Urartians at Trapezus in the Trebezond, both of whom may have had a common Hurrian substratum linked with the Hurrian influences in Ugaritic literature. During the same period, Greek traders were in contact with the Levantine coast, as shown by Al Mina and Tell Sukas for example. Proto-geometric sherds have been found not only on the Ionian coastbut also at Tell Abu Hawam in Palestine, so that the beginnings of the renewed trade with the Levant may be pushed back earlier than the eighth century. [15]

A third possibility, intermediate in date between these two, is provided by the Philistines, who were among the Sea Peoples, and formed an enclave of Aegean origin on the south coast of Palestine. As a sea-going people, they could have been a convenient means for transference of Canaanite ideas to Homer and the Bible alike [16].

Contact between the realms of Homer and Ugarit is, therefore, quite possible. If it took place in Mycenaean times, any borrowing on the Greek side would have to have become part of the tradition that culminated in the epics of Homer, while on the Ugaritic side, the borrowing would be from the beginnings of the epic tradition. If the contact is placed later, it is supposed that the Ugaritic poems lived on as Canaanite literature beyond the date at which the tablets we have were destroyed.

Literary Themes

Helen of Troy and the Epic of Kret

The Iliad is the great narrative of an expedition of the princely lords of Achaea, an expedition gathered, equipped and launched to bring back from Troy Helen, wife of Menelaus [17]. C.H. Gordon asserts that the epic of Kret is a parallel to this in its theme [18]. It is clear that, at least in part, the Epic of Kret is the story of an armed expedition on a large scale to lay siege to a city and gain a wife [19]. But there are two points about it which Gordon appears to take for granted, and which are nevertheless open to question.

Regarding the first, abduction of the wife, all the text says is that she went away, she departed [20]. With the Helen of Troy motif in mind, we might ask whether she went or was abducted [21].

The second and more fundamental point concerns the identification of the departed wife with Hurrai of Udm. Gordon makes no attempt to prove this identity, but merely takes it for granted [22]. There do not seem to be any positive grounds in the text to justify this identification.

This, of course, lessens the similarities with the story of Helen of Troy. Still, the basic elements remain: the loss of a wife, the armed expedition on a grand scale, the siege of a city, and the winning of a bride [23].

Achilles and Briseis, Kret and Hurrai

Similarities between the theme of the Iliad and the theme of the Kret epic may have prompted another comparison which Gordon discusses. He proposes that Kret's demand for Hurrai is paralleled by Achilles' demand for Briseis, and that these are examples of the theme of uncompromising and unbribable love for a particular woman [24].

At first sight, however, the situations do not appear to be exactly parallel. Kret is demanding a girl and refusing to take gifts in her place (K I vi 16-35, CML 35); Achilles is nursing his wrath over the loss of a girl and refuses to be placated even when gifts and the girl as well are offered to him. (Il. 9:131-2, 378)

Kret's position is quite clear. Pebel attempts to buy off the besiegers with gifts, without specifying the purpose of the siege; Kret replies that he has no use for Pebel's gifts, but that he wants what is not in his house, he wants the wench Hurrai. And with no further ado, as far as we know, he gets her. (K I iv 49f, CML 35f.)

The story of Achilles and Briseis is rather more complicated, chiefly by the fact that Achilles' wrath is provoked not only by his loss of Briseis but also by his loss of honour because of the insulting treatment meted out to him by Agamemnon. In a "shame culture" this is naturally a weighty motive for his anger [25].

These two elements are not perfectly integrated in the story [26]. It seems likely that there is more behind this episode than first meets the eye. Scholars differ in their opinions [27].

This is not the place to make a thorough investigation of the Achilles-Briseis episode. We are attempting to evaluate its similarities with Kret's actions in seeking Hurrai for his bride. One basic similarity is clear: both Kret and Achilles refuse the gifts that are offered them. One obvious difficulty is equally clear: the girl Briseis is included among the gifts that Achilles refuses — at least so we must presume from Il. 9: 273 f., although Achilles makes no mention of her in 9: 378 f. when he rejects the gifts.

It seems a reasonable hypothesis to suggest that Agamemnon's seizure of Briseis may have provided the main reason for Achilles' wrath in an earlier version of the incident. In that case, if Agamemnon offered to return Briseis at the start of Book 9, there would be no reason why Achilles should not be back in the Achaean battle line by the end of that Book. By giving more emphasis to the insult to Achilles' pride, an excuse can be provided for extending the incident and allows the Patroclus story to be included [28].

What should be said of Gordon's parallel? As the text stands, it is slight — the refusal of gifts in the context of a woman loved — and bedevilled with various possible interpretations. There remains the thought that a closer parallel lying behind our present text cannot be precluded.

Mythological Themes

Mt. Olympus and Mt. Saphon

In the course of a discussion on similarities in gods and mythology, Gordon remarks:

> One of the most intimate bonds between religion among the Greeks and among the people of Western Asia is the prominence of mountains as the abode of the gods. Olympus is for the Greeks what Saphon is for the Canaanites: the sacred mountain abode of the pantheon. [29]

Gordon goes on to say that different mountains have been regarded as sacred, according to the vagaries of local cult. It is reasonable enough that gods should be considered as dwelling where their work is visible and that weather gods should be placed on the highest mountain in a locality, around which the storm clouds gather and from which bad weather can naturally be thought to emanate [30]. More important might be similarities in the designation of one mountain for the whole pantheon.

Homer's view of Mt. Olympus as the mountain of assembly for the pantheon is seen at its best in the final scene of Book I of the Iliad. For then "unto Olympus fared the gods that are for ever, all in one company, and Zeus led the way." (Il. 1: 494-5) There Zeus has his own palace where the gods gather: ". . . and Zeus went to his own palace. All the gods rose together from their seats before the face of their father." (Il. 1: 533-4) It was apparently in Zeus' palace that the daylong banquet was held, with feasting and music and song provided by Apollo and the Muses. (Il. 1: 601-4) There, on Olympus, the gods had their own palaces: "But when the bright light of the sun was set, they went each to his own house to take their rest, where for each one a palace had been built with cunning skill by the famed Hephaestus, the god of the two strong arms." (Il. 1: 605-8) It is so much the mountain of the assembled gods, that, according to Nilsson, only in two passages does Zeus alone dwell on Olympus. Both are similes, referring to Zeus as weather god; neither suggests that Zeus is the sole inhabitant of Olympus [31].

At first sight, Saphon, the mountain which Gordon claims was the Canaanite Olympus, does not seem to be quite the same communal centre of divine life. It would seem rather to be the seat of power of Baal, and the traffic to and fro that the texts record is no more than the coming and going of those who have business with him. A closer inspection of the texts shows a situation more closely resembling that of Olympus.

In the Baal and Anat cycle there is reference to a great banquet for Baal at which "a sweet-voiced hero sang in honour of Baal in the recesses of the north". (B V i 20 f., CML 83) Unfortunately no guest list for the banquet is given so that we do not know who were present. In connection with another banquet, the phrase "pḫr m‘d" is used four times. (B III* B 12, 14-15, 18, 29. CML 79-81) It can be translated "full convocation" [32], "convocation of the assembly" [33], "the assembled body" [34]. Here, clearly, there is an Olympian assembly of the gods; unfortunately the place name given is enigmatic, "the mountain of L1, ǵr 11"[35]. Later in the same poem, when Baal's palace has finally been built, there is a banquet on Mt. Saphon to which all the gods, "the seventy sons of Athirat", are invited and at which the festivities are on an Olympian scale. (B II vi 35 f., CML 99 f.)

There is also the episode of Athtar, towards the end of the Baal-Anat cycle. Baal's death is announced and Athtar is nominated as the new king[36]. Athtar goes up to the recesses of Saphon and sits on Baal's throne; but he has to return shamefaced, admitting, "I cannot be king in the recesses of the north" i.e. on Mt. Saphon, for he was too small for Baal's throne, his feet did not reach the footstool nor his head the top. (B III i 11-37, CML 111). This episode provides fair grounds for attributing to Baal, the lord of Saphon, a hegemony over the other gods [37].

The conclusion is therefore justified that Mt. Saphon had a very similar place in Canaanite religion to that of Mt. Olympus in Greek religion.

However, in evaluating these similarities, the question of their significance must always be considered. Frequently, it is difficult to know whether we are merely dealing with two instances of a general pattern or with a significantly isolated parallel phenomenon [38].

Storm gods naturally dwell on mountains, and on that account may be expected to draw other deities mountainwards as well, as Nilsson suggests of Olympian Zeus [39]. This may weaken the value of the similarity between Mt. Olympus and Mt. Saphon in Homeric and Ugaritic literature. It remains true all the same that this is a feature they have in common, and it is a cogent argument against the conception of Olympus as a singularly Greek possession.

Hephaestus and Kathir-and-Khasis

Gordon notes the following points which he considers as parallel between Hephaestus and the Ugaritic Kathir-and-Khasis. The latter comes from Caphtor, even as Hephaestus has connections with Cretan Ida. Both gods are associated with fire. The role of both in the pantheon requires them to make fine weapons, jewellery and furnishings for the gods, and they are also the architects and builders of the gods' palaces [40].

The Caphtorian origin of Kathir-and-Khasis is provided by a passage in the Baal-Anat cycle. Referring to Kathir-and-Khasis it says, "Caphtor is the throne on which he sits, Ḥkpt, the land of his inheritance" [41]. But there is reason to doubt any link between Hephaestus and Crete. Gordon merely says that Hephaestus is of particular interest since he "has connections with Cretan Ida" [42]. But L. Malten states bluntly, "From Crete too, the god is completely absent" [43]. According to H. J. Rose, industrial Attica worshipped the divine smith with considerable zeal, but Crete, always backward in classical times, apparently never reverenced him at all [44].

It seems that Gordon must forego his claim to link Hephaestus with Cretan Ida, although there is agreement on the Oriental origin of the god[45]. He is on safer ground when he notes the connection of both gods with fire. In Homer fire can be called not only "the flame of Hephaestus" [46], but by inverting the process of metonymy the name of the god is itself used for his attribute [47]. The taming of the raging Scamander by the wondrous-blazing fire of Hephaestus is another example [48]. This "tour de force" is compared by Gordon with an episode in the building of Baal's palace on Mt. Saphon by Kathir-and-Khasis. They apparently collected an adequate supply of the choicest cedars from Lebanon. A mighty fire then burned in the palace for seven days; and when on the seventh day it was put out the silver had turned into plates and the gold had turned into bricks. (B II v 16 f., CML 99) [49] The two scenes show that both Hephaestus and Kathir-and- Khasis were masters in the use of fire; they do no more than that since the scenes themselves are quite dissimilar.

Kathir-and-Khasis made the composite bow over which Anat quarrelled with Aqhat. (A II v 11 f., CML 53; cf. A II vi 19 f., CML 55) Similarly, Hephaestus made the armour for Achilles (Il. 18: 368 f.), made the sceptre for Zeus which had been handed down to Agamemnon (Il. 2: 100 f.), and made the aegis for Zeus that Apollo bore as he led the Trojans. (Il. 15: 307 f.) The description of Hephaestus in his workshop (Il. 18: 372 f.) is reminiscent of the passage describing Kathir-and-Khasis at work among the bellows, tongs, the gold and silver, and the fine pieces of workmanship (B II 21 f., CML 93). That Kathir-and-Khasis built Baal's palace has already been noted. So too Zeus has his chamber made for him by Hephaestus (Il. 14: 338), and each of the Olympians had his palace, built by Hephaestus (Il. 1: 607 f.).

The similarities between Hephaestus and Kathir-and-Khasis are marked. Perhaps they go no further than is to be expected of the characteristics of the craftsman god; but then at least we must say that the craftsman god was conceived in similar fashion at Ugarit and in Homer.

The Mythology of the Divine Succession

"One of the main themes in the mythology is kingship among the gods. Just as Zeus wrested the kingship of the gods from Kronos, and the latter from Uranus, Baal wrested the kingship from the sea-god Yam" [50]. C. H. Gordon does not deal with this point intensively, but it has considerable ramifications that are relevant to the present subject.

What traces of the Ouranos-Kronos-Zeus succession are there in Homer? Zeus is constantly referred to as the son of Kronos, but nowhere in the Iliad or the Odyssey is the story of the succession told. Yet the number of references to the fate that Kronos has suffered make it clear that Homer is well aware of the story, even though he did not see fit to tell it [51].

The succession of Ouranos (?), Kronos, and Zeus and the fact that Kronos and his fellow gods were imprisoned in Tartarus by Zeus forms part of the common background knowledge of the Homeric epic. What parallels to this can be found in the Ugaritic poems? [52] Gordon, in the passage quoted earlier, says that in the Baal and Anat cycle it is told how Baal wrested the kingship of the gods from the sea-god Yam. As a parallel to Zeus' usurpation of power from Kronos, this strikes one as odd; since El had been the senior god, it would be expected that Baal should have to wrest the kingship of the gods from him and not from Yam.

The problem proves to be a complex one. T. H. Gaster interprets the Baal epic as a nature myth, the theme of which is the alternation of the seasons. Baal is the god of the rain, Yam the god of the sea and lakes and rivers, and Mot the god of death, of all that lacks life and vitality. "Baal, Yam, and Mot are thus the direct equivalents of the classical Zeus, Poseidon and Hades. Their three-cornered contest for dominion over the earth represents, however, more than a mere conflict of natural forces; what it symbolizes and allegorizes is, specifically, the alternation of the seasons in the Syro-Palestinian year" [53]. According to Gaster's interpretation, any parallel with Homer would not be in the framework of the relationship between the generation of Kronos and the Olympians, but would have to be sought in connection with the Olympians themselves [54].

A. S. Kapelrud lays considerable stress on the change in leadership among the Ugaritic gods, holding the view that it is clear that there was a long drawn out struggle between Baal and El as to who was to be the leading god in the pantheon [55]. None of the gods achieves complete victory; El still seems to be nominal head of the pantheon, while Baal is actual head of the gods. "There can, however, be little doubt that El has receded very much in the background, though he has in no way disappeared" [56].

Kapelrud cites the parallel cases in the stories of Kumarbi and from the *Enuma eliš*: the Weather God (Teššub) overthrew Kumarbi by defeating Ullikummi; and Marduk became head of the Mesopotamian pantheon by vanquishing Tiamat [57].

In discussing Baal's role as a fighter, Kapelrud distinguishes three types of battle in Near Eastern myth. In the first, one god defeats another and replaces him; in the second, a god battles with a monster and is rewarded for defeating it; in the third, the ousted god seeks a champion to defeat his successor for him. [58] He classifies the Baal-Yam combat as one of the third type: Yam is assisting El to dispose of Baal, their rival [59]. M. H. Pope, agreeing almost entirely with the position outlined by Kapelrud, suggests that the episode may actually be represented in the extant Ugaritic texts by the fragmentary fifth column of the text VI AB [60].

The contrary opinion is championed by J. Gray:

> The element of conflict between El and Baal has, we think, been greatly overemphasized by Nielson, Kapelrud, Cassuto and Pope. There is admittedly a certain amount of evidence for such a conflict. . . . Elsewhere in the texts, however, El shows no antipathy for Baal . . . . [61]

Careful examination of the texts does not provide a clearcut solution; too much is dependent on interpretation. There is evidence of enmity between Baal and El and likewise of harmony between them. Where the emphasis is to be laid must depend on the answers to a number of questions of interpretation.

Allied with this problem are the questions of how much belongs to a single poem and how much is from fragments of other poems or from earlier periods in the development of the myths. [62]

This discussion of the theories and interpretations of the Baal texts and the relationship of Baal and El is necessary to provide a background against which a number of alleged parallels can be considered. The possible parallels fall into three groups: concerning the relationship of Zeus and Kronos, Zeus and Poseidon and Hades, and Zeus and Typhoeus.

We have seen that Homer was aware of Zeus'victory over Kronos; it would appear that in the Ugaritic texts Baal has superseded El in the fertility cult. It is possible that we even possess a fragmentary text telling how Baal tied and bound El. [63]

If the combat between Baal and Yam is considered as a separate episode, and not as a part of Baal's battle with El, then both this fight and Baal's battle with Mot (B I* i-vi; III vi. CML 103 f., 115) should be compared with the relations of Zeus, Poseidon and Hades with one another. Possibilities for establishing a parallel are provided by the story of how the other Olympians, Hera, Poseidon and Pallas Athene, put Zeus in bonds, and how he was released only because loyal Thetis called Briareus-Aegaeon to his aid [64].

According to Iliad 15: 189 f, the division of authority between Zeus, Poseidon, and Hades was entirely peaceful, done by casting lots. Nevertheless, the fact that Poseidon is brought to comply with Zeus' order by threat of physical violence also suggests that the superior might of Zeus may have had something to do with it.

If, however, Baal's combat with Yam is seen as part of his struggle with El for sovereignty among the gods, a parallel to it can be sought in the Zeus-Typhoeus battle, for Typhoeus represents the old guard in a last effort against the new overlord of the gods.

The Iliad mentions it in a simile: "And the earth groaned beneath them (the marching Danaans), as beneath Zeus that hurleth the thunderbolt in his wrath, when he scourgeth the land about Typhoeus in the country of the Arimi, where men say is the couch of Typhoeus." (Il. 2: 781-3). Hesiod elaborates the story, making Typhoeus the progeny of Earth and Tartarus, and describing in detail the fight in which Zeus overwhelmed the monster with his thunderbolts (Theogony 820 f.) [65]. H. J. Rose felt that the groundwork for the picture of this extraordinary creature must be Oriental and not Greek [66], and the discovery of the Hittite version of the Hurrian myth of Ullikummi gives confirmation to this [67].

Prince Yam, Judge Nahar, is a more imposing figure than the monster Typhoeus; it is not impossible that instead of being El's champion against Baal he is Baal's rival for dominion among the gods.

However, the similarity with Typhoeus is increased if we accept the identification of Yam with the sea-dragon, Lotan [68]. Even without this identification, the two battles have much in common. Both Zeus and Baal are weather gods fighting to secure their claims to kingship among the gods; neither ultimately kills his adversary; both use weapons supplied by the divine smiths, and the weapons themselves are similar — thunderbolts in one case, self-propelling maces in the other. If the identification of Yam and Lotan is accepted, then both gods were involved in combat with a many-headed monster, and this in the context of conflict over the kingly succession among the gods [69].

Comparisons can therefore be made on three levels: the replacement of Kronos by Zeus and of El by Baal; the relationship of Zeus with Poseidon and Hades and of Baal with Yam amd Mot; the battle between Zeus and Typhoeus and between Baal and Yam.

What does this amount to ? Put in a nutshell, probably this: that just as clear links have been perceived between Hesiod and the Hittite versions of Hurrian myths, so in Homer and in the Ugaritic myths vestiges of similar stories can be traced. Not too much weight should be laid on these because Homer gives merely passing reference without going into detail, and because the significance of the Ugaritic parallels depends considerably on their still-disputed interpretation, and finally because such stories of the gods belong to a number of mythologies. On the positive side, it is justifiable to say that affinities appear between the mythological situations in the Ugaritic poems and underlying Homer.

The Elysian Plain and the Field of El

F. Dirlmeier compares the Islands of the Blessed and the Elysian plain with the Field of El in the Ugaritic texts [70]. The first reference to the Elysian plain is in the Odyssey [71]. From it we can gather that the Elysian plain was at the bounds of the earth and was cooled by blasts of the West Wind which Ocean sent up. The Ugaritic references which all repeat a five line formula, inform us that the Fields of El are at the source of the two rivers amid the channels of the two oceans [72]. The verbal similarity is too slight to carry any weight, and an etymological link has not been established [73].

Warlike Goddesses

Gordon wishes to parallel Anat's battle tactics with those of the battle between Odysseus and the suitors. "Brawl tactics, specifically the throwing of furniture, are famous from Odysseus' battle against the suitors in his halls at Ithaca" [74]. The following lines give some idea of Anat's fighting:

> She smashed seats over the warriors; tables were smashed over the soldiers, stools over the heroes. Anat fought hard and gazed (on her work), she battled and regarded (her work), she became excited (and) her heart was filled with laughter. Anat gave (her) self up to rejoicing when she plunged both (her) knees in the blood of the guards, (her) skirts in the gore of the warriors, until she was sated, ... (BV ii 20-29, CML 85)

There is no parallel to this in the battle against the suitors. Eurymachus urges them to hold tables before them as a shield against Odysseus' arrows. (Od. 22: 74) Not only is this a most natural thing to do, but it is also a purely defensive move, while Anat's use of the furniture is solely offensive. The suitors do not indulge in furniture throwing.

If there is a Homeric parallel to Anat's behaviour, specifically the joy that she takes in battle, it is far more likely to be found in Iliad 21: 385 f. Nevertheless, although this may be the Ionian genius at its most dismal [75], it is still a good deal more sophisticated than the bloodbath in which Anat luxuriates.

Father of gods and men: Zeus and El

Gordon also parallels Zeus as father of men and gods and El, father of the seventy gods and father of mankind.

The concept of fatherhood is probably to be defined in terms of the pater familias, the on with authority, who is protector and ruler of the family. The myths do ascribe actual paternity of some of the gods to Zeus, including pre-Greek and immigrant gods; the Ugaritic texts assign all the gods to the family of El, with the possible exception of Baal. [76]

It seems likely that both the Greek and Ugaritic forms of expression derive from a similar and natural attitude towards the head of the pantheon, thinking of the pantheon in the terms of a family relationship [77].

Importunate goddesses

One final parallel in the realm of mythology may be cited, which is raised by Dirlmeier and apparently also by W. Baumgartner and O. Eissfeldt [78]. In the Iliad, Thetis goes to Zeus and begs him to give might to the Trojans until the Achaeans honour Achilles. Zeus hesitates, but on her importuning assents and bows his head. (Il. 1: 497-530) In the poem of Aqhat, Anat, after being insulted by Aqhat, goes to El, and although the text is damaged it is clear that she is seeking his permission to punish Aqhat's presumption. It would seem that El at first is unwilling, but when threatened with violence, he graciously yields his consent. This is a small matter but it does indicate a similar view of the working relationship between members of the pantheon and its head [79].

Miscellaneous Parallels

Divine ancestry

Gordon claims that "some divine ancestry was necessary for anyone who claimed membership in the Mycenaean aristocracy. This is repeatedly borne out in Homeric epic. . . ". [80] He discusses various ways in which divine descent may be claimed. Among the parallels he alleges to this, only a few concern Ugarit. Kret is the son of El, and even so he is menaced by death; so too Sarpedon, son of Zeus, cannot be spared his fate [81]. In another place he mentions that Kret is referred to as the "lad of El" and "Hector . . . boasts of being the son or lad of mighty Zeus" [82].

It is quite correct that El is frequently referred to in the Kret epic as Kret's father. The formulae used in the final tablet, are even more emphatic. Kret's claim to be the son of El, the lad or servitor of El (K I i 40, CML 29 etc) has to be taken seriously, and raises the question of the mortality of one of divine descent [83].

On the other hand, it is not easy to determine what importance should be given to the different claims to divine descent in Homer[84].

The episode with Sarpedon indicated that the Greeks too were troubled by the problem of divine descent and mortality, at least within the epic framework. Hera points out to Zeus: "If thou send Sarpedon living to his house, bethink thee lest hereafter some other god also be minded to send his own dear son away from the fierce conflict; for many there be fighting around the great city of Priam that are sons of the immortals. . . ." (Il. 16: 445-9)[85].

Probably all that can be safely said here is that both at Ugarit and in Homer the problem of divine lineage and human mortality is preserved in the epic literature [86].

The Restraining Goddesses

H. T. Wade-Gery is taken to task by Gordon over the scene in which Achilles was pondering whether to draw his sword on Agamemnon, and Hera sent Athene to restrain him. (Il. 1: 188 f.) According to Gordon, this scene is singled out by Wade-Gery as exemplifying the innovations of the poet of the Iliad, whereas in fact it is anticipated at Ugarit [87]. Gordon says that Achilles was restrained by two goddesses and compares this to a scene where Baal was restrained by two goddesses from striking inviolate messengers. (B III*B 36 f., CML 81) However, Achilles was restrained by Athene alone, who had been sent by Hera [88], and to make matters worse the key lines of the Ugaritic text are damaged and the restorations differ radically [89]. The parallel is, therefore, at best doubtful.

Verbal Parallels

Some of the formulae in Homer were paralleled by Gordon from Near Eastern literature [90]. Only two of these are from Ugaritic texts. One is a common phrase recurring nine times in the Iliad: "ἄλλο δέ τοι ἐρέω And another thing will I tell thee." (Il. 1: 297 etc.) The Ugaritic phrase is "ʾap. mṯn. rgmm. ảrgm. argmk, Moreover I will tell a tale repeated." (B II i 17, CML93; A II vi 38, CML 55) Since mṯn can be considered as equivalent to ἄλλο and ảp to δέ, the correspondence is verbally quite close.

Twice in Book XVI of the Odyssey the formula is used: "Οὔ πω πᾶν εἴρητο ἔπος, Nor yet was the word fully uttered." (Od. 16: 11 and with slight change 16: 351; cf. also Il. 10: 540) In Ugaritic the phrase is: "bph. rgm. lyṣả. bšpth. hwth, The word verily came forth from his mouth, the speech from his lips." (A I iii 7, 21, 35; CML 63)

Dirlmeier accepts both of these; but the second does not correspond closely in form, and I doubt whether much weight should be given to such similarities [91]. Another verbal practice which is very common in Ugaritic is the climaxing of a number by a higher one. In the Iliad, an example of this may occur when "brazen Ares bellowed loud as nine thousand warriors or ten thousand cry in battle." (Il. 5: 859-61; 14:148-9) [92]. On the other hand, it could be argued that it is merely an addition to fill out the line and has no climactic sense. That such a line goes back to a climactic phrase is possible but unproven [93].

The Catalogue of Ships

Gordon and Dirlmeier are of the opinion that a jejune listing of palaces in the Baal-Anat cycle and the total mobilisation demanded by Kret's expedition throw light on the problem of the Catalogue of Ships in the Iliad [94]. But the list quoted is a mere half dozen lines, (B II iv 51-7, CML 97); such lists are common in the Ugaritic poems and can hardly be compared with Homer's Catalogue of Ships. Furthermore, it fits naturally into its place in the logic of the story, precisely as does the mobilisation required for Kret's expedition.

Universal human phenomena

Under this heading we may mention a few parallels briefly. Gordon notes that Odysseus, after being shipwrecked and buffeted by the sea, comes to a river mouth and prays to the river as to a god and a king. (Od. 5: 441-53) [95]. He sees in this a parallel to the position of Yam at

Ugarit. The traces of an earlier animistic attitude towards rivers and springs occur a number of times in the Iliad, but this attitude and its counterpart at Ugarit are surely examples of a universal religious phenomenon. The similarity would have to be more detailed to be of value [96].

Both Homeric and Ugaritic gods are feasted with roast meat and wine and entertained with song [97]. It would be an interesting study to discover whether these are modelled on sacrificial offerings or banquets among men. But in either case, the similarity is hardly significant [98].

The fact that a host asks why his guest has come, that strife and lewdness during banquets is viewed with disapproval is surely not to be regarded as a matter of significance. So too, the fact that a son may relieve his aged or weakened father of his kingship is no more than an admission that kingship was held by might [99]. It might be a particularly urgent matter at Ugarit, since the fertility of the land was bound up with the king's health.

These, and some other minor points mentioned by Gordon, may be classed as phenomena too common among peoples to be of significance in this context.

Conclusion

The literary themes discussed, Kret's siege of Udm in quest of Hurrai and his refusal of gifts in her place, do not, I think, correspond closely enough with their Homeric counterparts to be evidence of connections between the two literatures. However, once it has been established on other grounds that literary themes were exchanged or borrowed from a third literature, then it would be possible to say that the story of an expedition and a siege to secure a wife was very probably one of these themes, and that possibly the refusal of gifts in place of the girl was another.

The similarities in mythology are more convincing. The correspondence is not always exact, and a certain allowance has to be made for the common evolution of religious thought. In my opinion, they can be taken as evidence for some form of contact, particularly those connected with succession and kingship among the gods. The question remains as to whether such contact was direct or indirect; did the transmission occur through Ugarit, or have both Ugarit and the Greeks derived these from other mythologies, the Hittite and Hurrian for example? A more broadly-based study would be needed to reply to this; unfortunately the material that has been considered does not provide an answer.

What has become of Gordon's thesis that the Greek and Hebrew civilisations are parallel structures built upon the same East Mediterranean foundation, the international order that he envisages during the Amarna period? If the evidence of Ugarit as an intermediary is valid, there can have been little more than the exchanges in myth, literature and language that would be expected when different people mingle with one another. The pattern of archaeology allowed us to expect such exchanges might take place; the texts show that there is evidence that some did take place. But much more evidence must be adduced before we can talk meaningfully of structures or foundation.

The poems of Homer and Ugarit are only a part of the Greek and Near Eastern literatures. Before definitive conclusions can be formulated about the affinities existing between them, studies will need to have covered much more of both fields. Gordon casts his net far wider than Homer and Ugarit, but he does not go into detail and his presentation is marred by inaccuracies and the absence of critical judgement. Ultimately an assessment of the relationship between Greece and the Near East will have to be made. It would not be confined to literature alone, but with the evidence of art, archaeology, and philology, of anthropology, folklore, and comparative religion. The results of the limited investigation that has been undertaken in this article could then be placed in a more accurate perspective.

Sept. 1964

LIST OF ABBREVATIONS

AJA	"American Journal of Archaeology"
ANET	"Ancient Near Eastern Texts", ed. J. B. Pritchard, 1955 (1st. ed. 1950).
BSA	"Annual of the British School at Athens"
BTB	"Before the Bible", C. H. Gordon, London, 1962.
CML	"Canaanite Myths and Legends", G. R. Driver, Edinburgh 1956.
FMTH	"From Mycenae to Homer", T.B.L. Webster, London, 1958
Handbook	"A Handbook of Greek Mythology", H. J. Rose, London, 1953. (1st. ed. 1928).
HHI	"History and the Homeric Iliad", D. L. Page, University of California, 1959.
HM	"Homer and Mycenae", M. P. Nilsson, London 1933.
HUCA	"Hebrew Union College Annual"
JCS	"Journal of Cuneiform Studies."
JNES	"Journal of Near Eastern Studies"

JSS	"Journal of Semitic Studies"
Leaf and Bayfield	"The Iliad of Homer", W. Leaf and M. A. Bayfield, London 1908-1911.
MPL	"Mycenaean Pottery From the Levant", F. H. Stubbings, Cambridge, 1951.
OLZ	"Orientalistiche Literaturzeitung"
Rh. Mus.	"Rheinisches Museum für Philologie"
RSV	The Holy Bible: Revised Standard Version
Thespis	"Thespis", T. H. Gaster, Doubleday, New York, 1961. (1st. ed. 1950)
UL	"Ugaritic Literature", C. H. Gordon, Rome, 1949

REFERENCES

[1] Albright, W. F., "Some Oriental Glosses on the Homeric Problem" in *AJA* 54 (1950) pp. 162-176.

Astour, M. C., "Greek Names in the Semitic World, and Semitic Names in the Greek World", in *JNES* XXIII 3 (1964), pp. 193-201.

Barnett, R.D., "Ancient Oriental Iufluences on Archaic Greece" in *The Aegean and Near East*, ed. S.S. Weinburg, New York, 1956.

Davis, S., "New Light on Linear A" in *Greece and Rome*" 6 (1959), pp. 20-30.

Dirlmeier, F., "Homerisches Epos und Orient" in *Rh. Mus.*, 98 (1955), pp. 18-37.

Driver, G. R., review of *Before the Bible* in *JSS* VIII, 2(1963) pp. 277-82.

Dunbabin, T. J., *The Greeks and their Eastern Neighbours*, London, 1957.

Eissfeldt, O., "Recht und Grenze archaeologischer Betrachtung des Alten Testaments" in *O.L.Z.* 49 (1954) col. 101-8.

Gaster, T. H., *Thespis*, 1st. ed., 1950; Doubleday ed., New York, 1961.

Gordon, C. H., review of *ANET* in *AJA* 56 (1952), pp. 92-4.

Gordon, C. H., "Homer and Bible" in *HUCA* 26(1955), pp. 43-108.

Gordon, C. H., "Minoan Linear A" in *JNES* 17(1958) pp. 245-55.

Gordon, C. H., *Before the Bible*, Collins, London, 1962.

Gordon, C. H., "The Dreros Biligual" in *JSS* VIII, I(1963), pp. 76-79.

Lesky, A., review of "Homer and Bible" in *Gnomon* 29 (1957), pp. 321-5.

Priest, J. F., "ὅρκια in the *Iliad* and Consideration of a Recent Theory" in *JNES* XXIIII, 1(1964), pp. 48-56.

Webster, T. B. L., *From Mycenae to Homer*, Methuen, London, 1958.

[2] Gordon, C. H., *Before the Bible*, (above, note 1), p. 9.

[3] C. H. Gordon, *Before the Bible*, (above, note 1), devotes a chapter to channels of transmission, but at no stage does he discuss transmission between particular peoples at specified places between precise dates. Instead, he discusses possible means of transmission: invasion and conquest, commercial and colonial activity, specialist guilds of priests, craftsmen, singers, and so on. Gordon admits that his survey is far from exhaustive.

[4] Miletus appears in Hittite documents as a fortified outpost of the overseas power of Ahhijava. "There can be no doubt that the city known to the Hittites as Millawanda was Miletus. Founded by Cretans at the end of the Middle Minoan period, the place was in the fourteenth century an outpost of the king of Ahhijava, but later it became a vassal kingdom of the Hittites." G. L. Huxley, *Achaeans and Hittites*, Oxford, 1960, p. 15.

Huxley's work allows us plausibly to identify Ahhijava with Mycenae itself, but it should be noted that this conclusion does not spring solely from his investigation of the Hittite texts, nor from archaeology alone. The Hittite texts justify the conclusion that the king of Ahhijava must be taken to be a ruler of the Achaean Greeks of the Mycenaean Age. It is the evidence of archaeology and of Homer that leads Huxley on to the conclusion that the centre of Achaean power was Mycenae. (*Ibid*, p. 23 f., 25, 29, 44.) For a contrary view, see D. L. Page, *History and the Homeric Iliad*, Univ. of California, Berkeley. 1959, Ch. I. He concludes that Ahhijava is Rhodes. (p. 15) For the controversial question of Agamemnon's position, see the article by G. M. Calhoun in *A Companion to Homer*, ed. A. J. B. Wace and F. H. Stubbings, Macmillan, London, 1962, p. 434. M. C. Astour (above, note 1) p. 194, argues against any permanent stay at Ugarit by Mycenaean merchants and against their integration into Ugaritic society. He bases this on the claims that no ethnic or geographical name of the Greco-Aegean world can be found in the Ugaritic texts. However, the archaeological evidence is strongly against Astour's position, and perhaps philologists will be able to explain the lacuna in the texts.

[5] F. H. Stubbings, *Mycenaean Pottery from the Levant*, Cambridge U. P., 1951, p. 5 f., 21 f.

[6] A Hittite religious text mentions that copper was brought from Alasiya, presumably Cyprus. (O. R. Gurney, *The Hittites*, Penguin, 1952, 2nd ed. 1954, revised 1961, p. 86) Note too that from the analysis of the Hittite texts, Page feels justified in saying, "We are now confident that Achaeans and Hittites were in contact for one hundred and fifty years (more or less) preceding the sack of Troy VIIa." HHI, p. 19. The absence of archaeological evidence at inland sites might suggest the qualification "sporadic contact" as more accurate.

[7] The Minoans reached Ugarit in the Middle Minoan period. (C. F. A. Schaeffer, *Ugaritica I*, Paris, 1939, p. 22, 54 f.) They left their mark both in imported objects and in the architecture of the stonevaulted tombs. However the Minoans do not seem to have established any position on Cyprus. (Stubbings, MPL, p. 103; cf. H. W. Catling and V. Karageorghis, "Minoika in Cyprus", in *BSA* 55 (1960) p. 109 f. for a catalogue of Minoan objects in Cyprus — one jar and several bronzes in Middle Minoan, a substantial number of Late Minoan vase finds.)

[8] The Mycenaean pots and tombs at Ugarit strongly suggest that we are dealing with metropolitan Mycenaeans. (Information from Mr. W. Culican; cf. Stubbings, *MPL*, p. 71 f).

The distribution of Mycenaean pottery in the Levant has been studied by Stubbings (MPL). Not all of it need have passed through Ugarit; the pottery at Gaza is mainly Cypro-Mycenaean, and Qatna and other Orontes towns may have been supplied through Alalakh. It is not certain either, that Ras Shamra was the only settled trading site. At Tell Sukas and near Beirut, Mycenaean burials with plentiful pottery and figurines suggest the possibility of settlements. The likelihood of a Mycenaean settlement of Al Mina has been proposed. (T. J. Dunbabin, *The Greeks and Their Eastern Neighbours*, London, 1957, p. 26-7.) Also a site which in the Tell el-Amarna letters appears to be more important than Ugarit, Tell Simiran, north of Latakia, is still unexcavated.

[9] T. H. Gaster, "Ras Shamra, 1929-39", in *Antiquity* 13 (1939) p. 304 f.

[10] Schaeffer, *Ugaritica I*, (above, note 7) p. 103-4.

[11] C. F. A. Schaeffer, *The Cuneiform Texts of Ras Shamra-Ugarit*, London, 1939, p. 37 f. G. R. Driver, *Canaanite Myths and Legends*, Clark, Edinburgh, 1956, p. 1. T. B. L. Webster, *From Mycenae to Homer*, Methuen, London, 1958, p. 9.

[12] Schaeffer, *Ugaritica I*, (above, note 7) p. 28 f

[13] cf. "The Son of Ullikummis", in *Ancient Near Eastern Texts*, ed. J. B. Pritchard, Princeton, 1950, 2nd ed. 1955, p. 121 f.

[14] Dunbabin (above, note 8) p. 19.

[15] R. D. Barnett, (above note 1), pp. 228 f, 235, (Trebizond, Al Mina, Tell Sukas); G. W. van Beek, BASOR, 138, 1955, pp. 34-38 (Tell Abu Hawam).

[16] cf. W. Culican, "The First Merchant Venturers" in *The Dawn of Civilization*, ed. S. Piggott, Thames & Hudson, London, 1961, p. 159. Schaeffer thinks that the Sea Peoples, among them the Philistines, may have contributed to the diffusion of Cypriot copper ingots during the twelfth and eleventh centuries when they occupied Enkomi and probably all Cyprus. (C. F. A. Schaeffer, *Enkomi-Alasia*, Paris, 1952, p. 28 f.) Note in this connection: "The so-called Oxhide ingots, it must be stressed, are no earlier than c. 1200 B.C. in Cyprus — their origin is not Cypriot, though it may well be Aegean." (H. W. Catling and V. Karageorghis, (above, note 7) p. 127, n. 203).

[17] There are several places in the Iliad where one would expect this theme to be stressed and it is not. This could be accounted for by Page's suggestion that it might be a storyteller's motif woven into the texture of the Trojan War at a time when the royal house of Mycenae was extinct and the past no longer vivid in memory but merely a theme for poetry. He agrees with Gordon that it is a typical motif. (Page, *HHI*, p. 257).

[18] Gordon, *BTB*, p. 132 f.

[19] The armed expedition is: "a numerous force three hundred times ten thousand, pioneer(s) without number (and) veteran(s) without count, going by thousands (like) sheets of rain (?) and by ten thousands like (drops of) early rain. . . ." (K I ii 35-40, *CML* 31) Food was made ready, "bread for five (and) provisions for six months". (K I ii 30-1, *CML* 31) This mighty host marched till on the seventh day they reached Udm when siege was laid to the city. When Pabil, king of Udm, attempted to buy off the besiegers, Kret replied, according to the instructions given him by El in a dream: "What need (have) I (of) silver and yellow metal, (even) gold . . .? So shalt thou give (me) what is not in my house: give me the wench Huray the (most) gracious of the progeny of thy first-born. . . ." (K I vi 22-5, *CML* 35) And Hurrai is given to Kret for his wife, amid the lamenting of all Udm, grieved to see her go.

[20] ʾaṯt. ṣdqh . lypq
mtrḫt . yšrh
ʾaṯt. trḫ . wtbʿt (K I i 12-4, *CML* 29)

Ginsberg interprets this as meaning "to die" (*ANET* p. 143, n. 2), but Gordon asserts that this word for departed is never used as a euphemism for death. (*BTB*, p. 134) Driver notes: "Namely, she deserted him, though lawfully wedded to him." (*CML*, p. 29 n. 2) The meaning "she died" does not accord well with the parallel phrase, though it too is variously interpreted. The verb is "lypq": the "l" can be either negative or emphatic; the root meaning of the verb stem can be either from pwq = to obtain, or from npq = to go out, to take out. In the light of tbʿ attested in a number of passages as "to depart", the meaning "went away" seems most likely in this context.

[21] In the Iliad Troy is an object of enmity because of Helen's abduction of Paris. Quite an important element would go out of the epic if Helen had merely left Menelaus of her own accord and taken refuge in Troy.

The lines that follow (K I i 15-25, CML 29) are difficult to interpret; they tell in stylised phrasing of the death of Kret's offspring. If, as in Gordon's view, Hurrai is Kret's "destined wife to be", through whom he is to beget his progeny, these children are an obstacle that has to be explained. The alternative interpretation is that Kret has lost his wife and bemoans the destruction of his family by natural death, pestilence, sea and sword. The passage has to be left with certain obscurities.

[22] What grounds can be brought forward to justify the assertion, for the poem

is certainly not explicit on the point? There is the close juxtaposition of the passages on the same tablet so that no missing lines can have intervened. Then there is Kret's demand for "what is not in my house" parallel to "The wench Huray", and the fact that he can describe her beauty in some detail. These hardly constitute evidence. The description of Hurrai appears to be taken from statuary and is formal rather than objectively descriptive, and what is not in Kret's house may be his progeny. Webster notes the difficulty, but considers it is clear that such a poem could have inspired the story of Helen of Troy, and adds: "It was an act of poetic genius to identify the wife who had deserted with the woman to be won from the town." (*FMTH*, p. 87.)

[23] This is the reversal of the usual diplomatic procedure by which sieges were bought off and treaties were cemented by marriage.

[24] Gordon, *BTB*, p. 228.

[25] cf. E. R. Dodds, *The Greeks and the Irrational*, Univ. of California, Berkeley, 1951, p. 17, 28 f.

[26] Achilles says to Agamemnon: "By might of hand will I strive for the girl's sake neither with thee nor with any other, seeing ye do but take away what ye gave." (Il. 1: 298-9), and when Thetis leaves him he is described as "wroth at heart for the fair-girdled woman's sake, whom they had taken from him by force in his despite". (Il. 1: 429-30) At the embassy, in Book 9, he says: "Nay, for whoso is a true man and sound of mind, loveth his own and cherisheth her, even as I too loved her with all my heart, though she was but the captive of my spear." (Il. 9: 341-3) Ajax complains: "But as for thee, the gods have put in thy breast a heart that is obdurate and evil by reason of one only girl; whereas we now offer thee seven, far the best that there be, and many other gifts beside." (Il. 9: 636-9).

From these these examples, it is clear that the loss of Briseis still has a part in the story. But so too does the question of dishonour. When Achilles swears his solemn oath that the Achaeans will need him and will have to do without him, he concludes: "But thou shalt gnaw thy heart within thee in wrath that thou didst honour no whit the best of the Achaeans. " (Il. 1: 243-4). And to Thetis he complains: "My mother, seeing thou didst bear me, though to so brief a span of life, honour surely ought the Olympian to have given into my hands, even Zeus that thundereth on high; but now hath he honoured me, no not a whit. Yea verily, the son of Atreus, wide-ruling Agamemnon hath done me dishonour; for he hath taken away and holdeth my prize through his own arrogant act." (Il. 1: 352-6) In rejecting the embassy, he says to Odysseus: "Nay, not though he gave gifts in number as sand and dust; not even so shall Agamemnon any more persuade my soul, until he hath paid the full price of all the despite that stings my heart." (Il. 9: 385-7) And in 9: 648 and 16: 59 he speaks of being treated "as though I were some alien that had no rights."

Then there are a couple of passages in which Achilles' anger is apparently allowed to overwhelm any love he may have had for the girl. In rejecting the offer of Agamemnon's daughters from whom to choose his wife, he says: "Many Achaean maidens there be throughout Hellas and Phthia, daughters of chieftains that guard the cities; of these whomsoever I choose shall I make my dear wife." (Il. 9: 395-7) And finally, there is Il. 9: 334-7, where the reference is uncertain:

ἄλλα δ' ἀριστήεσσι δίδου γέρα καὶ βασιλεῦσι,
τοῖσι μὲν ἔμπεδα κεῖται, ἐμεῦ δ' ἀπὸ μούνου 'Αχαιῶν
εἵλετ' ἔχει δ' ἄλοχον θυμαρέα. τῇ παριαύων
τερπέσθω.

Leaf and Bayfield, along with many scholars, put a full stop after εἵλετ', and take ἄλοχον as referring to Clytemnestra. E. V. Rieu translates accordingly: "It is not as though he had no wife. He has one, of his own choice. Let him sleep with her and be content." (*The Iliad*, tr. E. V. Rieu, Penguin, 1950, p. 170). If, however, it is punctuated as above, with A. T. Murray (*The Iliad*, tr. A. T. Murray, Loeb, 1924) and L. A. MacKay, (L. A. MacKay, *The Wrath of Homer*, Toronto, 1948) and ἄλοχον is taken as referring to Briseis, then these lines must detract from the picture of Achilles longing for his beloved Briseis.

[27] For L. A. MacKay it is an ironic device, an imitative underplot in which Agamemnon offends Achilles in the same way that Paris has offended Menelaus (L. A. MacKay — above note 26 — p. 109). Achilles underlines this point himself in Il. 9: 337ff. D. L. Page, comparing Il. 9 and 16, especially 9: 378ff. and 16: 83-7, claims that the author of Book 16 could not have known Book 9 (Page, *HHI*, p. 297 f.).

[28] Il. 16: 83-7 seem to suggest that in the "insulted pride" version Briseis was not among the gifts offered, or that there was no embassy at all.

[29] Gordon, *BTB*, p. 232.

[30] M. P. Nilsson, *The Mycenaean Origin of Greek Mythology*, Univ. of California, Berkeley, 1932, p. 231.

[31] M. P. Nilsson, *Homer and Mycenae*, Methuen, London, 1933, p. 267. The two passages are Il. 13: 243; 16: 364.

[32] Driver, *CML*, p. 79.

[33] C. H. Gordon, *Ugaritic Literature*, Rome, 1949, p. 12.

[34] Ginsberg, *ANET*, p. 130.

[35] Ginsberg translates "LI" as "Lala", Gordon merely transliterates it as "LI", and Driver translates it as "El". In the Myth of Ullikummis III b, *ANET* p. 124, Mt. Lalapaduwa is one of the heavenly mountains.

[36] "This (the announcement that Baal the Mighty is dead) raises the question of a substitute for Baal, the dead king-god, and ʿAṯtar, the deity manifest in the bright Venus star, is put forward as a candidate, his qualification being the fact that as the brightest star in those latitudes he might match in some degree the lightning flash of Baal." (J. Gray, *The Legacy of Canaan*, E. J. Brill, Leiden, 1957, p. 55.) On the other hand, according to T. H. Gaster, the point of this episode is that Athtar is the god of artificial irrigation, and cannot take the place of Baal, the weather god, the god of rains, in heaven. He is confined to the exercise of his powers on earth. (T. H. Gaster, *Thespis*, 1st ed. 1950, Doubleday, New York, 1961, p. 126-7, 216.)

[37] Confirmation of Saphon's role as the mountain of the assembled gods is to be had from some biblical references. The plainest of these is Isaiah 14: 13: "I will sit on the mount of assembly in the far north" (RSV), literally, in the recesses, i.e. remotest or topmost parts, of Saphon. (וְאֵשֵׁב בְּהַר מוֹעֵד בְּיַרְכְּתֵי צָפוֹן).
This occurs in a passage that is redolent of Ugaritic mythology, and apparently refers to Athtar's attempt to sit on Baal's throne. cf. Gray, (above, note 36) p. 209; M. H. Pope, *El in the Ugaritic Texts*, E. J. Brill, Leiden, 1955, p. 102.

Psalm 48: 3 refers to "Mount Zion, in the far north, the city of the great King". (RSV) This is a strange description of Mt. Zion in the south of Palestine, but literally the phrase is not "in the far north" but "in the recesses of Saphon". The application of this description to Mt. Zion indicates that Saphon was considered the seat of divine power. A similar reference, though not so explicit, is found in Ezekiel 28: 14, 16.

It is worth noting that Eissfeldt considers the Hebrew word Saphon for North, has its meaning because the mountain Saphon was in the North. (L. Koehler and W. Baumgartner, *Lexicon in Veteris Testamenti Libros*, E. J. Brill, Leiden, 1958, p. 812.

[38] T. H. Gaster has amassed an array of comparative phenomena on the question of the heavenly abode of the gods. It is doubtful how much of it, under closer examination, would remain relevant to Olympus and Saphon. (*Thespis*, p. 181 f.) Gray, while paying tribute to Gaster's sensitivity toward primitive modes of thought and behaviour, criticises his methods for being somewhat Frazerian, suggesting that his arguments might be stronger if his analogies were more selective. (Gray, above note 36, p. 9).

[39] Nilsson, HM, p. 268.

[40] Gordon, *BTB*, p. 236-7.

[41] (B V vi 14-16, CML 91) The translation given here is Gordon's. (*UL*, p. 23-4) His note on "ḥkpt" in the glossary of the Ugaritic Manual is: "The abode of Kṯr-w-Ḫss in Caphtor, variant 'ḥqkpt' with foreign palatal intermediate between 'k' and 'q' written both ways as in the Caphtorian word for 'helmet' written either כובע or קובע. Note the stem 'kpt' in both 'kpt-r' and 'ḥ-kpt'." (C. H. Gordon, *Ugaritic Manual*, Rome, 1955, p. 263) Ginsberg's translation is substantially the same. (*ANET*, p. 138) However Gaster and Driver take a different view of "ḥkpt". Gaster agrees that "kptr" is Caphtor, probably Crete. He attributes the location of the seat of Kathir-and-Khasis on an Aegean island to the fact that during the 2nd millennium B.C. a great deal of the ceramic and metal ware in use of the mainland was imported from the Aegean or fashioned on Aegean models. He continues that in Aqhat II v 20 (*CML* 53) Kathir-and-Khasis are associated with a place called "ḥkpt". This, he says, is the Egyptian "Het ka Ptah", "sanctuary of Ptah", the regular name of Memphis, seat of the Egyptian potter god Ptah, whom he considers to have been understood as the corresponding Egyptian deity to Kathir-and-Khasis.)*Thespis*, 163-4)

Gaster makes no mention of the appearance of "ḥkpt" in parallelism to "kptr" in B V vi 14-16, a text which I think argues against his interpretation of "ḥkpt". Driver, however, accepts it and translates the lines: "(for) Crete (is) the throne on which he sits, Egypt the land of his heritage." On "Egypt" he gives a note: "Or 'Memphis', seat of Ptah Egyptian god of craftsmen." (*CML*, p. 91).

[42] Gordon, *BTB*, p. 236.

[43] L. Malten in A. Paulk and G. Wissowa, *Real Encyclopädie der Classischen Altertumswissenschaft*, Stuttgart, 1912, Vol. VIII, p. 314. "Völlig fehlt der Gott auch in Kreta."

[44] H. J. Rose, *A Handbook of Greek Mythology*, Methuen, London, 1st ed. 1928, 5th ed. 1953, p. 166.

[45] Rose, *Handbook*, p. 165; A. B. Cook, *Zeus*: *A Study in Ancient Religion*, Cambridge, Vol. III, 1940, p. 236.

[46] Il. 9: 468; 23: 33; 17: 88; Gordon, *BTB*, p. 236.

[47] Il. 2: 426. σπλάγχνα . . . ὑπείρεχον Ἡφαίστοιο — held them over the fire.

[48] Il 21: 341 f. As Leaf and Bayfield point out in regard to Il. 21: 331-2, the pairing of Hephaestus and Scamander in Il. 20: 73-4 is symbolic of the natural enmity of fire and water. It also serves to emphasise the close connection between Hephaestus and fire in Homer.

[49] An interesting query is whether this has any connection with Aaron's explanation for the making of the golden calf in Exodus 32: 24.

[50] Gordon, *BTB*, p. 178.

[51] cf. T. B. L. Webster in *A Companion to Homer*, (above, note 4) p. 146. The principal references from the *Iliad* are:
Il. 4: 58-61; 5: 385; 5: 896-8; 8: 477-81; 13: 345, 354; 14: 200-4, 194, 243; 15: 187 f; and also *Od.* 11: 306 f.

[52] We need to keep in mind here the difference between epic and myth. In Homer we can perceive the myth lying behind the epic poetry; in the Ugaritic

poems we are dealing with the actual myth. cf. Gray (above, note 36) p. 18 f.

[53] Gaster, *Thespis*, p. 125-6.

[54] Such a case might be found in the exchange of messages between Zeus and Poseidon, ending in Poseidon's grudging compliance with Zeus' wishes. (Il. 15: 157 f.) The parallel that Gaster himself draws is with Zeus' combat against Typhoeus. (Il. 2: 783).

Gordon argues strongly against the seasonal interpretation of the Baal cycle. He claims that the failing of Baal was not a seasonal feature but that it was the drought or famine of an abnormally bad year that reflected Baal's failing. (*UL*, p. 3-5) For a discussion of this issue cf. Gray (above, note 36) p. 11, 37; R. De Langhe: "Myth, Ritual and Kingship in the Ras Shamra Tablets" in *Myth, Ritual and Kingship*, ed. S. H. Hooke, Oxford, 1958, p. 133 f.

[55] A. S. Kapelrud, *Baal in the Ras Shamra Texts*, Copenhagen, 1952, p. 86.

[56] Kapelrud, *ibid*, p. 86. He mentions the evidence of archaeological remains for Baal's position in the pantheon. "The main temple in Ugarit was dedicated to Baal, and there can be no doubt that an intensive cult of this god took place there. Up till now no corresponding temple for Il has been found." (p. 86) To put this in its proper light, we must remember that in the preface to *Ugaritica I*, Schaeffer cautioned that then more than seven eighths of the city still lay hidden beneath the tell. "Plus des sept huitiemes de la grande ville sont encore enfouis dans le tell de Ras Shamra. . . . Le palais, point capital pour la connaissance du site, n'est pas encore mis au jour." Schaeffer, (above, note 7) p. VII.

[57] Kapelrud, *ibid*, p. 90-1.

[58] Kapelrud, *ibid*, p. 98-9.

[59] Kapelrud, *ibid*, p. 103.

[60] Pope, (above, note 37) p. 94. The text is *CML*, 72-7. He continues that even if this fragmentary column were to be otherwise interpreted, the hypothesis still would hold good that such an episode was recounted somewhere in the Ugaritic myths. The supposition that this episode is assumed as the background to much of the Baal-Anat cycle appears to give the best explanation of El's paradoxical status.

Pope fears that Baal's behaviour in "taking refuge with El" may cast doubt on this view. (p. 92, about B III* B, *CML* 79) The text says that Baal was standing by El, and this can be equally well construed as ministering to him, which is precisely what the younger gods in the Kumarbis story do for the god they are about to supersede. (*ANET*, p. 120)

Finally, Pope notes that B VI and B III* may be independent versions of more or less similar myths. (p. 93) Driver agrees with this (*CML*, p. 11); so, too, does Gray, (above, note 39) p. 20 n. 4.

[61] "Gray, (above, note 36) p. 115.

[62] The apparent supersedure of El by Baal in the myths of the fertility-cult probably reflects the fusion of two different strata of religion at Ras Shamra corresponding to a critical phase in the settlement of Ugarit, such as the irruption of tribal groups from the desert which is archaeologically attested throughout Syria and Palestine about the end of the third millennium." Gray, (above, note 36) p. 116.

[63] B VI v, CML 77. This is the text mentioned by Pope above. It contains the following phrases: "Hadad sought him . . . Forthwith he answered . . . I know (or: thou knowest) . . . thou boundest (bull El) . . . thou tiedst . . . between two stones. . . ." These lines are repeated a second time, 1. 17 f. If, in these phrases, "Hadad" (i.e. Baal) and "Thou" may be equated, it is clear that Baal tied and bound El. This is the simplest interpretation, but imaginative restoration of the broken lines could give different sense. Granted the correctness of the equation, the meaning and relevance of the tying and binding must be explained.

[64] Il. 1: 403. Briareus-Aegaeon is one of those interesting examples in which the gods use one name while men use another. Other examples in Homer are: Il. 2: 813; 14: 291; 20: 74; Od. 10: 305; 12: 61.

Two explanations are given of this phenomenon. C.M. Bowra thinks it likely that when Homer gives the human name he gives the old name, and when he gives the divine name he means the new name. The difference between old and new is presumably the difference between the language of the pre-Greek population and that of the Greek invaders. The explanation might be that when the Greek gods superseded those of the conquered peoples, Greek was spoken in the temples and high places. (cf. C. M. Bowra, *Tradition and Design in the Iliad*, Oxford, 1930, p. 152 f.) Stanford, commenting on Od. 10 :305, and Leaf and Bayfield, on Il. 20: 74, hold similar views.

T. H. Gaster, on the other hand, while lecturing in Melbourne, noted that the same practice is found in Hittite writings where the language attributed to the gods is an old Anatolian language. He suggested, therefore, that the "language of the gods" was an older language, no longer understood by the people, but preserved in cult or myth and so thought to be the language of the gods. However, the fact that in Homer the forms of the "Language of the gods" seem to be Indo-European while the forms of the "language of mortals" show pre-Hellenic features argues against adopting Gaster's view, and against Gordon's comments on the subject. (*BTB*, p. 238)

[65] The debt that Hesiod owes to Hittite-Hurrian mythology has been acknowledged by a number of scholars. (cf. Webster, *FMTH*, p. 85; F. Dirlmeier, (above, note 1) p. 18 f.,; H. G. Güterbock, *JCS*, 5(1951) p. 135 f., 6(1952) p. 8 f.; Huxley, (above, note 4) p. 42; Dunbabin, (above, note 8) p. 56.

Dunbabin considers that in the "Theogony" the closeness of Hesiod's version to the Hittite coupled with the undigested nature of much of it suggests transmission in the eighth or seventh centuries. Huxley thinks it possible that the matter was not digested because it was indigestible, and that therefore it might have been borrowed in Mycenaean times and handed down strange, horrible and unchanged.

[66] Rose, *Handbook*, p. 58

[67] H.G. Güterbock, "The Song of Ullikummi" in *JCS* V, (1951), VI(1952).

[68] This identification is suggested by Kapelrud (above, note 55, p. 102); Driver sees Lotan as typifying or representing Yam (*CML* p. 16, p. 103 n. 10). Gaster sees Yam as the Dragon of the Sea and makes much of the ritual battle of god v. dragon; he asserts the parallel with the fight between Zeus and Typhoeus, as well as claiming a number of other Near Eastern parallels. He does not, however, identify Yam with Lotan. (Thespis, p. 128f, p. 201 f.) The Ugaritic passages in question are B I+i 1-3, 27-30, CML p. 102f in which Mot refers to Baal's victory over Lotan, and B V iii 52f, *CML* p. 86 in which Anat seems to boast of her part in the victory over Yam.

[69] Gaster quotes a Phoenician version of the story, culled from later sources, in which Cronos fought the dragon Ophion. He considers it to be substantially the same story as that in the poem of Baal. (*Thespis*, p. 142) Another version, also from later sources (Apollodorus and Nonnos) locates the final encounter on Mt. Casius, the mountain of Jebel Akra, near Ugarit, which is known as Mt. Saphon in the Ugaritic poems. (Rose, Handbook, p. 59; Gaster, *Thespis*, p. 140.) In the light of this, Gaster allows himself to wonder "whether Il. 2: 783 does not refer, after all, to Syria (Aram) when it locates the discomfiture of Typhon 'ein Arimois'. (On Arimoi=Arameans, see Strabo, xvi, 4. 27.)" (*Thespis*, p. 152).

[70] Dirlmeier, (above, note 1) p. 27.

[71] Od. 4: 561-8.

ἀλλά σ' ἐς Ἠλύσιον πεδίον καὶ πείρατα γαίης
ἀθάνατοι πέμψουσιν. (Od. 4: 563-4)

Rose suggests that Elysion is a pre-Greek paradise which the Greeks identified with their own happy land, the Islands of the Blessed. (*Handbook*, p. 80) F. R. Walton suggests that it appears to be a survival from Minoan religion. ("After-Life" in *The Oxford Classical Dictionary*, 1949).

[72] B III; 4-8, CML 109. B III* c 4 f., *CML* 77; B II iv 20 f., *CML* 97; B V v 5 f., *CML* 89; B I* vi 1* f., *CML* 107; A II vi 46 f., *CML* 55.

[73] However: "Man darf also wohl die orientalische und die griechische Anschauung kombinieren." Dirlmeier, (above, note 1), p. 27. Schaeffer considers that the term "Fields of El" in the Ras Shamra texts "evidently provides us with the origin of the Elysian fields of Greek mythology." (Schaeffer, above, note 11, p. 61) For a further discussion of El's abode, together with an attempt to locate it geographically, see Pope (above, note 37) p. 61 f. R. D. Barnett proposes an indentification of the Elysian fields with the Egyptian "Fields of Alu" (Barnett, above note 1, p. 238, n. 133).

[74] Gordon, *BTB*, p. 187.

[75] Page, *HHI*, p. 193.

[76] cf. M. P. Nilsson, "Zeus" in the Oxford Classical Dictionary, 1949; Pope (above, note 37) p. 47.

[77] Kumarbis is also referred to as the "father of the gods". (*ANET*, p. 122) The Egyptian creation texts cited in *ANET* do not make any mention of the concept of fatherhood. (*ANET*, p. 1 f.) Nor does the idea appear to be present among the Babylonians and Assyrians. Ea may be referred to as the creator of men and the lord of men, Marduk may be referred to as lord and king of the gods and of heaven and earth, but the idea of fatherhood in any universal sense does not seem to occur. (E. Dhorme, *Les Religions de Babylonie et d'Assyrie*, MANA Tome 2, Part 1, Presses Universitaires de France, Paris, 1949, p. 35, 144.)

[78] Dirlmeier, (above, note 1) p. 26.

[79] "Eine Untersuchung des Typus der (den obersten Gott) bittenden Göttin in der altorientalischen und griechischen Literatur wäre erfordlich." (W. Kullmann, *Das Wirken der Götter in der Ilias*, Akademie-Verlag, Berlin, 1956, p. 21, n. 5.

[80] Gordon, *BTB*, p. 243. M. I. Finley speaks of it as a "sanction for aristocratic privilege, for rule by might, and an ideology that no one believes is an absurdity." (M. I. Finley, *The World of Odysseus*, 1st ed. 1954, Penguin 1962, p. 153.)

[81] Gordon, *BTB*, p. 149.

[82] Gordon, *BTB*, p. 245. cf. K I i 5, *CML* 29; Il. 13: 54.

[83] Kret's son, the hero Elhu, is troubled: if Kret is the son of El, how can he die? But if he is dying how can he be the son of El? "We rejoice in thy life, our father, we exult (in) thine immortality. . . . Shalt thou then die, father, like men?... How can it be said (that) Keret is a son of El, the progeny of Lutpan and Kadesh, or (that) gods die? The progeny of Lutpan shall surely live." (K II i 14-23, *CML* 41).

[84] In the Mycenaean tablets the "Wanax" and the "Lawagetas" each had a "temenos" which T. B. L. Webster interprets to mean that "both of them were in some sense divine, and this divinity survives in Homeric terminology — Zeus born, Zeus nurtured "(Webster, *FMTH*, p. 11.) But L. R. Palmer's view of the comparative unimportance of Zeus in the Mycenaean pantheon suggests a doubt as to the reality of this idea outside the epic framework. (L. R. Palmer, *Mycenaeans and Minoans*, Faber & Faber, London, 1961, p. 119 f. and esp. 131.)
G. M. Calhoun considers from the evidence of the poems themselves that there are serious objections to a Homeric nobility of birth claiming divine descent.

(Calhoun, in *A Companion to Homer*, (above, note 4) p. 438.) A satisfactory evaluation of the questions involved would demand a far broader study of the relationships of gods and men in ancient Greece and the Near East. The Hittite kings of the period of the empire were considered to be divinely favoured, and were styled "Hero, beloved of the god". (Gurney, above, note 6, p. 65) The fourteenth century ivory bed-panel from Ugarit showing a goddess suckling two princelings is well known.

85 Zeus here does not call Sarpedon his son, but "dearest of men to me"; however, it is stated clearly elsewhere, cf. Il. 12: 297; 15: 67. It is noteworthy that Homer does not deny divine descent to a Trojan. cf. Aeneas, Il. 2: 820. The episode of Ares' rage over the death of his son, Ascalaphus, is another manifestation of the same problem. (Il. 15: 100-41).

86 The question of descent has a rather quaint offshoot that can be briefly noted here. Penelope asks Odysseus to tell her his family tree, "for thou art not sprung from an oak of ancient story, or from a stone". (Od. 19: 163) Practically the same phrase occurs in the Iliad, 22: 126. Opinions on the passage differ, but it seems likely that it has some reference to an older folktale. The only Ugaritic link is the name "bn abn, son of a stone" occurring in a list of names. (Gordon, *Ugaritic Manual*, above, note 41, Text 64, 1. 24) It is not very much, except that Jeremiah castigates the house of Israel, their kings, their princes, their priests and their prophets "who say to a tree 'You are my father', and to a stone, 'You gave me birth'. (Jeremiah 2: 27). Webster discusses the religious significance of trees and stones. (*FMTH*, p. 41 f. and 53. cf. also B V iii 37-8, *CML* 87). Possibly the phrases have their origin in some common cultic practice; it would be remarkable if they were coincidental.

87 Gordon, *BTB*, p. 227. According to Gordon, this scene has been singled out. This is hardly fair to Wade-Gery, since the incident receives half a page in a fourteen page chapter devoted to "The Creative Poet" and it is not the sole example. (H. T. Wade-Gery, *The Poet of the Iliad*, Cambridge U. P., 1952, p. 41)

88 Although Achilles' words provide Gordon with some slight justification: "Needs must a man, goddess, observe the words of you twain." (Il. 1: 216).

89 Ginsberg has only one goddess involved, though allowing other possible restorations. (*ANET*, p. 130) Driver translates the scene with a considerable difference, making Baal gentle not angry, and mentioning the attack only as a possibility to be guarded against. (B III* B 36 f., *CML* 81) Gordon's own translation is in *BTB*, p. 180-1, and *UL*, p. 14.

90 Gordon, reviewing *ANET* in *AJA* 56 (1952) p. 92-4.

91 Gordon alleges a parallel between Greek and Hebrew to which Dirlmeier adds another of his own. χθιζά τε καὶ πρωίζ' (Il. 2: 303) תְּמוֹל שִׁלְשֹׁם In both phrases, "yesterday and the day before" = formerly. ὅρκια τάμνειν (cf. Il. 2: 124) כָּרַת בְּרִית Both use the verb "to cut" regarding a covenant or oath. The correspondence in this second case might be due to common cultic practice. cf. J. F. Priest, (above, note 1) p. 53 f.

92 ὅσσόν τ' ἐννεάχιλοι ἐπίαχον ἢ δεκάχιλοι
ἀνέρες ἐν πολέμῳ. (Il. 5: 860-1)

93 For a discussion of borrowed words, see Webster, *FMTH*, p. 66, Gordon, "Homer and Bible" in *HUCA* 26(1955) p. 60 f., Dunbabin, (above, note 8), and Astour, (above, note 1).

94 Gordon, *UL*, p. 6, 125; Dirlmeier, (above, note 1) p. 30. cf. also Schaeffer (above, note 11) p. 39 f., and Page, *HHI*, p. 158, n. 21, regarding actual lists of ships from Ras Shamra and the use that has been made of these.

95 Gordon, *BTB*, p. 236.

[96] An example that may prove to be interesting is the battle between the River Scamander and Hephaestus; it comes from a part of the Iliad that has a number of Near Eastern affinities.

[97] For Ugaritic examples see B V i 4 f., *CML* 83; B II vi 40 f., *CML* 101; K III iv 3 f., *CML* 39.

[98] For some idea of the sacrificial offerings of Mycenaeans cf. Palmer, (above, note 84) p. 119 f.; M. Ventris and J. Chadwick, *Documents in Mycenaean Greek*, Cambridge U. P., 1956, p. 125 f., 275 f. For those at Ugarit cf. Gordon, *UL*, p. 110 f.

[99] K II vi 25 f., *CML* 47; Od. 1: 188 f., 24: 205 f. Gordon, *BTB* 240; Finley, (above, note 80) p. 99 f.

THE DIALOGUE OF HABAKKUK IN RABBINIC DOCTRINE

BY

SHALOM COLEMAN

I

The book Habakkuk has been scrutinised closely in recent years as a result of the commentary on the first two chapters by the Dead Sea sect considered to be the oldest of its kind [1]. Brownlee, however, has already demonstrated the importance of examining the targum along with the commentary as an important source of knowledge in Jewish interpretation [2]. Early manuscripts of targum were probably in existence as far back as the middle of the first century of the common era [3], a date contemporaneous with that of the script of the Habakkuk scroll [4]. The importance of the targum, however, really presupposes the need for examining other branches of Rabbinic literature for a clearer understanding of the Prophet's message. It is not always sufficiently borne in mind that Midrashic exegesis stems from the oral law which goes back to the Sinaitic Revelation [5], and the Rabbis had many a tradition long before it was committed to writing [6]. While the Rabbinic treatment furthermore was intended to derive the principles of the Jewish faith, it was a serious attempt to explain prophetic teaching and develop from it concepts which break the bounds of parochialism and dogma [7]. The Rabbis, who succeeded the Soferic teachers, had received and transmitted knowledge through successive generations which had become essential to their interpretations [8]. Their conclusions on occasion have little or no apparent connection with the original text. Nevertheless they were offered as a genuine appreciation of the Prophet's message translating abstract and strange exhortations into a human experience of concrete reality. This is what the Rabbinic treatment of the prophets has achieved for the Jew, and with it defined the Jewish faith as a way of life capable of fulfilment [9]. The preservation of the Sinaitic Covenant and its practical application to the needs of every generation were the tasks of the Rabbis of Midrash and Talmud [10]. They were the disciples of the wise [11] who learned and taught the Scriptures in a manner so as to keep alive in every generation a faith at once enduring, progressive, and authoritative to Jewish circles. The Rabbis, as Herford has clearly demonstrated, were serious students of the Bible [12]. They kept Jewish religious development within the traditional framework of the covenant and the discipline it demands. In the long process a Rabbinic doctrine emerged, which became the heart and soul of Judaism for every generation. It is in the light of this doctrine that the Prophet Habukkuk has been chosen as a subject for discussion in order to help the search for the truth of his message.

II

The Midrash records in the name of R. Samuel son of Nahman [13] that "All the prophets foresaw the empires engaged in their subsequent doings (towards Israel)" [14]. It continues to say in the name of R. Joshua son of Levi [15], that "in the future the Holy One, blessed be He, will make the nations (that oppress Israel) drink the cup of staggering" out of the place whence judgement goes forth i.e. Eden [16]. Habakkuk is here quoted as providing the text referring to the nation Babylon [17]. "He is terrible and dreadful", says the Prophet, "his judgement and his destruction [18] proceed from himself" (1:7). To the Midrashic teachers, however, Babylon was a symbol in the exhortation of Habakkuk. "Thou hast shown Thyself exceedingly great against those that rise up against Thee," they quote the prophets as saying, "And who are they that rise up against Thee? They that rise up against thy children — against Pharoah and all his hosts. . . . Against Sisera and all his chariots. . . Against Sennacherib and all his troops. . . . . Against Nebuchadnezzar and all his multitude. . . . Belshazzar . . . of him it is said 'Woe unto him that giveth his neighbour drink . . . Thou art filled with shame instead of glory' " (Hab. 2:15-16).[19] The Midrashic teachers perceive a reference to the crossing of the Red Sea in Habakkuk: "And God made a tunnel through the waters, as it is said: 'Thou has pierced through for the sake of his tribes' (Hab. 3: 14)" [20]. . . "God flattened out the water into a level highway, as it is said: 'The mass of water into a level place' (Hab. 3: 14) [21]. "Behind the children of Israel he turned the seaway into clay, as it is said: 'Thou hast trodden the sea with Thy horses and made the mighty waters into clay' (Hab. 3: 15)". [22].
In their interpretation of this verse they declare that Pharoah was punished by the Holy One, blessed be He, in Person [23], which is explained as follows: "Pharoah went forth with fury, and so did

God as it says: 'Thou marchest through the earth in indignation' (Hab. 3: 12); with a bow, and so did God: 'Thy bow is made quite bare' (to fight with it) (Hab. 3: 9); with flashing spear: 'at the shining of thy glittering spear' (Hab. 3: 11)". "Pharoah rode first on a male steed, and if one may say so [24], God showed Himself on a male steed. Pharoah thereupon said: "Surely this male steed kills its rider in battle, I will therefore ride on a female steed." Pharoah then changed to a white horse, a red horse, a black horse, and if one may say so, God appeared on a red, white or black horse, hence it says: 'Thou hast trodden the sea with Thy horses,' (Hab. 3: 15) diverse [25] horses" [26]. In the Midrashic interpretation Habakkuk's reference was made through the attitude of the other nations towards Israel. Pharoah was the "wicked" in the verse "Thou breakest the head out of the house of the wicked" (Hab. 3: 13), [27]. He was "the head" of the enemies of God which the Prophet mentions [28].

While "head" of God's enemies is Pharoah, however, the Midrashic teachers eleborate the more direct association of Habakkuk with Babylon in the following passage: "Whence do we derive that the Holy One, blessed be He, showed Abraham the various captivities? Because it says: 'And lo, a dread, even a great darkness, fell upon him. . .' (Gen. 15:12). The word "a dread" [29] refers to Babylon because it says: 'They (the Kasdim) are terrible and dreadful. . .' [30]. Rab [31] explains the verse 'Woe unto him that giveth his neighbour drink that puttest thy venom [32] thereto' (Hab. 2: 15), to mean Nebuchadnezzar, acted in anger [33] against Zedekiah [34], and charged him for rebelling against God and himself" [35]. Nebuchadnezzar, the Midrash explains, was the wicked one, who acted shamefully to Zedekiah [36] bringing out Habakkuk's words: "that thou mayest look on their nakedness" (ibid.). R. Hanina, son of Isaac, then said: "(God said to him) For thine own honour and for the honour of thy father ye have not ascended the throne, but only because thy ancestor [37] paid honour to his ancestor" [38]. The Midrash goes on to explain that because Merodach-Baladan paid honour to God by rising from his throne and taking three steps [39], God promised to raise up from him three kings "whose empire shall extend from one end of the world to the other." These were Nebuchadnezzar, Evil-Merodach, and Belshazzar. Therefore God said to him: "Thou and thy noble grandfather and father ascended the throne only because thy ancestor honoured this man's ancestor and dost thou treat him with contumely: therefore 'Thou art filled with shame instead of glory' (Hab.2:16). 'Zedekiah, my son, is degraded as any man may be degraded, but as for thee 'filthiness shall be upon thy glory '(ibid) -vomiting above and shame below. When the two leaders of his legions saw that he was vomiting above and defiled below, they arose and made him rise from his throne and removed his crown from his head and stripped him of his purple robe and so it is written: 'And his glory was taken from him' " (Dan. 5: 20 [40]. The whole passage clearly explains the reference to Babylon represented in the Midrashic interpretation by Nebuchadnezzar and Belshazzar [41].

In this analysis Pharoah and Nebuchadnezzar claimed divinity and thereby brought evil on themselves [42]. Habakkuk supplies the passage in support of Nebuchadnezzar's claim [43]. The latter, the Midrash explains, knowingly tore the flesh of a living animal and ate it [44], and therefore transgressed the Noahide laws [45]. These laws were imposed upon all men, Jews and non-Jews alike [46], and Nebuchadnezzar, who did not observe them was therefore the "wicked" in the passage: 'wherefore lookest thou upon them that deal treacherously, and holdest thy tongue when the wicked devoureth the man that is more righteous than he?' (Hab. 1: 13). With reference to this verse, R. Huna [47] asks: "Can then the wicked swallow up the righteous? Is it not written further: 'There shall no mischief befall the righteous?' (Prov. 12. 21). You must, therefore, say: 'He swallows up the one who is only 'more righteous than he', but he cannot swallow up the perfectly righteous man' " [48]. The point here is that while Zedekiah was righteous he was not wholly righteous. Having kept company with Nebuchadnezzar, as a familiar neighbour [49], he was judged by his conduct [50], and for that reason was regarded also as "uncircumcised" in the words: "drink thou also and be as one uncircumcised" (Hab. 2: 16) [51]. To be uncircumcised was to be unreceptive and impenetrable [52], hence he was not the "perfectly righteous" to escape the devouring of the heathen. Through his lack of perfect righteousness, Nebuchadnezzar was punished on his account, therefore he was not permitted to enter the precincts of the Almighty [53].

The fact was that the heathen nations did not observe the Noahide laws; and since they therefore did not recognise the laws of social Justice, no liability was incurred in any suit for damage to the heathens [54]. The heathens could not claim the protection of a law which they neither respected nor recognised. Habakkuk, R Joseph learned, delivered his exhortation: "He stood and measured the earth

He beheld and made the nations to start up" (Hab. 3: 6), to explain that while "God saw that the nations did not observe even the seven precepts which the sons of Noah had taken up on themselves, and seeing that they did not observe them, He stood up and released them therefrom" [55]. To Rab this means: "He declared the shedding of the blood of heathens permitted in specified instances and He declared the appropriation of the property of heathens permitted" [56]. It was the treatment which Rabbinic doctrine offers from Habakkuk in his reference to the Chaldeans. It would also explain why the Covenanters speak of Kitteans "bent on destroying peoples far and wide and subduing them to their own domination" [57]. It teaches, furthermore, that the heathen nations were exiled because they had not fulfilled the Noahide laws. To the Midrashic teachers, all of them, like the Canaanites who did not accept the Noahide laws, were exiled [58]. They could not last [59]. R. Eliezar, son of R. Simeon, says: "and since they were unable to remain loyal to the seven Noahide laws [60], then how much more were they unable to stand by all the laws of the Torah" [61]. Hence they were granted exemption from the obligation of fulfilling them, yet at the same time there was some reward if they did in fact accept them [62]. The truth, however, is that the heathens had refused to accept the laws of the Torah [63], and as a consequence had become weak and were destined for Gehinnom [64].

III

In the Rabbinic treatment "the nations of the world were asked to accept the Torah in order that they should have no excuse for saying: 'Had we been asked we would have accepted it.' For behold, they were asked and they refused to accept it" [65]. After they had refused it, the Holy One, blessed be He, had given up hope of their accepting it and so they were abandoned [66]. R. Johanan [67] said that the Holy One, blessed be He, offered the Torah to the nations and in every tongue [68]. This made no difference. "None accepted it until He came to Israel who received it" [69]. R. Simeon b. Yohai [70] put it another way: "He rose and measured the earth" (Hab. 3: 6). "The Holy One. blessed be He, considered [71] all generations and He found no generation fitted to receive the Torah other than the generation of the wilderness" [72]. Israel was the elect of God, and when she received the Torah the whole world was tranquil [73]. Habakkuk, to the Rabbis, provides the support for their constant stress on the study of Torah as a means of Jewish survival. "Rab Judah [74] says in the name of

Samuel [75]: 'And thou makest man as the fishes of the sea. . . .' (Hab. 1: 14). Why is man here compared to the fishes of the sea? To tell you, just as the fishes of the sea, as soon as they come on to dry land, die, so also man, as soon as he abandons the Torah and the precepts." (Another explanation): "Just as the fishes of the sea, as soon as the sun scorches them die, so man, when struck by the sun, dies." [76] The Torah was the sign of the Covenant which God had made with His people Israel. It was the horn through which God had revealed Himself to them [77]. The Midrash explains that when the ministering angels heard the announcement of the Holy One, blessed be He, who intended to give the Torah to Israel, they said to the Holy One, blessed be He: "Sovereign of the Universe, Thou art He whose (אשר) majesty is over the heaven. It is Thy happiness (אשורך) [78], Thy glory, and Thy praise that the Torah should be in heaven [79]. He said to them: "What does it matter to you?" [80] They said: "Perhaps tomorrow Thou wilt cause Thy Divine Presence to abide in the lower world." Then the Holy One, blessed be He, replied to them: "I will give My Torah to the dwellers on earth but I will abide with the celestial beings". . . . Who stated this clearly? Habakkuk, as it says: "His majesty [81] covereth the heavens, and the earth is full of his praise" (Hab. 3: 3) [82]. The words "God cometh from Teman" (Hab. 3: 3) are furthermore explained to mean: "When God gave the Torah on Sinai, He displayed untold marvels to Israel with His voice. What happened? God spoke and the Voice reverberated throughout the world. Israel heard the Voice coming to them from the south [83], so to the south they ran to meet the Voice. From the south, it changed round to the north, so they ran to the north. From the north it moved to the east, so they ran to the east, but from the east it moved to the west, so they ran to the west. From the west it moved to the heavens. But when they raised their eyes heavenwards, it appeared to proceed from the earth, ... The Israelites were enquiring: "Whence cometh the Lord, from east or south?" . . . as it is written: God cometh from Teman [84]. The Rabbis have extracted a "brilliant description of a Theophany", to use Davidson's phrase [85], from Habakkuk's choice of words. To them, however, the giving of the Torah was only part of the doctrine they taught. The essential part was in learning its contents. To possess the Torah was not enough. "To understand, to discern, to mark, learn and teach, to heed to do and to fulfil in love all the words of instruction in Thy Torah" [86] — this was uppermost in their minds. Hence while Abaye [87] said:

"Nowadays the communities are accustomed to read for haftarah [88] a chapter from Habakkuk [89] on Pentecost" [90], the intention was to stress alongside the Sinaitic Revelation it expresses, the importance of knowing the Torah. To know its laws and judgements means constantly to repeat and practise them. In such a case Israel would be assured of the hereafter [91]. If she would only appear to be a student of the Torah, however, she was rejected. As R. Judah said: "Whoever elevates himself with the prayer-shawl of a sage [92], and is not himself a sage, is not permitted to enter the partition of the Holy One, Blessed be He" [93]. There was no compromise with pretentious and superficial learning in the Rabbinic doctrine of Talmud Torah [94]. Pretence leads to the imcompetent teacher, of whom R. Judah [95] said: "Woe unto him who saith unto wood 'Awake'. — to the dumb stone: 'Arise.' Can this teach? Behold, it is overlaid with gold and silver, and there is no breath at all in the midst of it" (Hab. 2: 19), and went on to exclaim: "but the Holy One, blessed be He, will call to account those who set them up, as it is written: 'But the Lord is in His holy Temple; let all the earth keep silence before Him' " (Hab. 2: 20) [96]. The incompetent teacher had led the people astray. They became confused when they were not taught aright [97]. The Midrash illustrates the point through a dialogue of Habakkuk with God [98] "When Habakkuk came to God and God asked him: What seekest thou? Habakkuk replied: 'What I spoke before Thee was spoken unwittingly'." The Midrash goes on to explain "when he saw Hananiah, Mishael, and Azariah, cast into the furnace of fire and they were delivered, and he saw (also) Hananiah son of Teradyon and his companions burned for the sake of the Torah and not delivered, he immediately raised a cry: 'It is partiality!' [99]. He said before Him: "Sovereign of the Universe these are righteous and those are righteous, these pure and those pure, these holy and those holy, (yet) these are delivered and those are not delivered, therefore 'the law is slacked and judgement doth not go forth' " (Hab. 1: 4). Ignorance had led Habakkuk to this conclusion. It led Israel to reject the Torah [100]. The Prophet, however, had admitted his cry was from ignorance. It was the question which burned deeply within him challenging God's ways, and from his prayer the sages deduced: "Had it not been for the prayer of Habakkuk, two disciples of the Sages would have to cover themselves with one garment (through poverty) and occupy themselves with Torah." [101] To the Midrashic teachers Habakkuk was deeply concerned with the revival of knowledge in the people as a deterrent against moral and spiritual corruption. God does not seem to heed the voice of the Prophet. The Torah has become ineffective [102]. It is numbed [103]. "Thereupon God revealed Himself to Habakkuk and said: 'Wilt thou raise a cry against Me? Is it not written "A God of faithfulness and without iniquity.'" (Deut. 32:4). It was at this moment that Habakkuk began to say: 'I spoke unwittingly as it is said 'A prayer of Habakkuk the Prophet, upon words spoken unwittingly' (Hab. 3: 1)" [104]. It led him to realise that all the commandments of the Torah were based on one cardinal principle: "but the righteous shall live by his faith" (Hab. 2: 4) [105].

IV

Habakkuk had addressed his doubts to God but not against God. He had chided God with words, say the Rabbis, and afterwards directed his prayers to Him [106]. His complaint is against the enemies of Israel for their excessive pride and cruelty [107]. Yet he is very conscious of Israel's backsliding. He perceives that he has judged the situation too hastily and now urges the people to remain confident in God's ultimate judgement. Evil after all cannot be triumphant. [108] Faith therefore becomes the keystone of his message. Faithfulness and righteousness often stand in parallel passages [109], but Habakkuk defined clearly that the faithful and the righteous are one and the same, and if Israel is to live righteously then faith is indispensable [110]. Davidson is right to observe that the Hebrew language really has no word for "faith" [111]. However, he does not go far enough. The root in Hebrew means "be steady, firm, trustworthy" [112] and develops into the meaning "truth" [113]. To Habakkuk the faithfulness by which the righteous shall live is therefore truth untarnished and uncompromising. It is his conclusion after a desperate struggle with doubt, and enshrines a sublime message in which human conduct is transferred from a concept of morality to that of the spirit, and in so doing transcends itself into unquestioned faith. The Midrash illustrates the point through Abraham and Sarah to whom the Rabbis apply the verse: "Although the fig tree doth not blossom, neither is there fruit in the vines" (Hab. 3: 17). The reference to "the fig tree", they say, alludes to Abraham [114] and "neither is their fruit in the vines" to Sarah [115]. Habakkuk's reference furthermore to "the labour of the olive faileth" (Hab. *Ibid.*), they explain, means "the faces of those angels who gave the good tidings to Sarah shone like an olive. But Sarah had doubted them." Were they lying? [116] (she soliloquised).

No, but "the fields shall yield no food": which means she had withered breasts [117]. "The flock is cut off from the fold and there shall be no herd in the stalls" (*Hab. ibid.*), tells the Midrashic teachers that she feared 'flocks' would be cut off from her and there would be no 'herd' in her stalls, i.e., she could not bring up children [118]. Even if Sarah had believed the tidings of the angels she still feared that she would be unable to suckle the promised child [119]. Hence at first her faith was not true. "Subsequently however, Sarah exclaimed: 'What? am I to lose faith in my Creator! Heaven forfend! I will not lose faith in my Creator, "For I will rejoice in the Lord, I will exalt in the God of my salvation" (Hab. 3: 18)" [120]. The Midrash illustrates Habakkuk's own inward self-search through the self-search of Sarah. Sarah had found true faith and so did Habakkuk. It was the faith which Israel had inherited from Abraham and Sarah [121], and which Habakkuk now wants Israel to recapture once again. It was a faith in which to sense the living God is to sense infinite goodness, infinite wisdom [122]. It is God's answer when uncertainty struggles within the human soul. The Midrash says: "The soul is a pure element in the body, and the Holy One, blessed be He, is the Pure One in the Universe; let the soul, which is pure in the body, come and praise the Holy One, blessed be He,who is the Pure One in the Universe, as it is said: 'Thou art of eyes too pure to behold evil'" (Hab. 1: 13) [123]. Habakkuk stresses that, through true faith, the soul of the righteous becomes synonymous with the purity of the righteous, and the purity in turn is bound up in the Pure One. This is the faith, says R. Isaac son of R. Marion, by which even the Righteous One, who lives forever, also lives [124].

The Midrash draws its conclusion from the passage: "I will take my stand upon my watchtower and station myself upon the rampart, and watch to see what He will say to me" (Hab. 2: 1) that Habakkuk deliberately prepared himself to receive a revelation [125]. He realised he must wait for a new encounter with God. His message becomes a 'revelation' when God reveals His Word in it. This is so aptly summarised in the following words: "The Prophet must wait in patience for Him and His clear command, whether this comes through vision or audition or through some inner consciousness, springing from the mysterious contact between the human and the divine" [126]. The following passage from the Midrash [127] clearly illustrates the point: "What did the Prophet Habakkuk do? He drew a figure of a circle and stood in the middle of it and said to the Holy One, blessed be He:

'Master of the Universe, I shall not stir from this place until Thou declarest to me how long Thou wilt continue to show forbearance to the wicked in this world?' The Holy One, blessed be He, replied: 'Thou hast cried out to Me, but hast not doubted Me. As thou livest, I shall answer thee and cause thee to understand: I show forbearance to the wicked in this world so they may come back to Me in repentance and their wilful sins will then be reckoned as unwilling sins'". Whereupon Scripture goes on with what Habakkuk said: "And the Lord answered me and said, 'Write the vision, and make it plain upon tables, that a man may read it swiftly'" (Hab. 2: 2). "Then Habakkuk said further: 'Long since I proclaimed the end, but the time set has passed by. Is there another vision for an appointed time?' (Hab. 2: 3). God replied: 'Even though I proclaimed the end to thee and the time set for it has passed, say not: "The end will not come", Wait thou for it.' Hence the verse concludes: "Though it tarry, wait for it, because it will surely come" (Hab. *ibid.*). In his dialogue Habakkuk finds the true faith for its own sake, which he defines for the righteous.

V

To the Midrashic teachers, the verse: "For the vision. . . wait for it, because it will surely come" (Hab. 2: 3) "pierces and descends to the very abyss" [128]. What they mean is that just as the bottom of an abyss cannot be reached, so is it impossible to grasp fully the implications of the passage. What R. Nathan [129], in whose name the Midrash is stated, asserts, is that all calculations of the Messiah are false. This follows from Rashi [130] who says: ". . . the advent of the Messiah is unknowable. Hence 'wait for it'." To Habakkuk "Redemption has an end" [131] and while God told Habakkuk to write down the events which were to come upon the latter age, He did not inform him when that moment of fulfilment would come, and although it may be protracted he urges Israel to have the faith of the righteous and deliverance will come [132]. H. Wheeler Robinson has caught the spirit of Habakkuk as his message has been treated in Rabbinic doctrine: ". . . the religion of Israel, which could give all to God and ask for no reward, confident of fellowship with Him. That is the triumphant note on which ends the Psalm of Habakkuk" [133]. With the coming of the Messiah the nations who opposed Israel [134] will depart crushed in spirit [135]. It is Habakkuk's reference to the future life as the Midrashic teachers see it. Rab Judah says in the name of Samuel: 'Why is it written' "And thou makest man as the fishes of the sea...."?

(Hab. 1: 14). This can be applied to the present world or to the future world. You can, in accordance with R. Hanina [136], apply this to the present world, for R. Hanina says: 'Everything is in Heaven's hands except cold and heat'... or according to R. Simeon b. Lakish [137] it can be applied to the future life for R. Simeon b. Lakish says: "There is no Gehenna [138] in the Future World [139], but the Holy One, blessed be He, brings the sun out of its sheath so that it is fierce: the wicked are punished by it, the righteous healed by it" [140]. Habakkuk is conscious of the wickedness of the enemies of Israel. They will be dashed to pieces in the hereafter [141]. "The Holy One, blessed be He, will punish from His supporting place" [142], which implies it is destined at an established and fixed time and will not be rescinded [143]. The time cannot be forced by excessive prayer [144], but it will not be delayed [145]. The prophets shall not make known the end [146]. They shall not say the end of the exile is too far off [147] for then all hope would be lost [148] and since, in Jewish doctrine, the end of exile is the beginning of the Messianic era [149], for this reason also it was not shown to them.

To the Midrashic teachers there is reward for all those who wait for the Lord's redemption [150]. They ask: "Since He (the Holy One, blessed be He) waits [151] and we wait, who delays its coming? The Attribute of Judgement [152] delays it. And since the Attribute of Judgement delays its coming then why do we have to wait for it? (i.e. it will come in any case and we therefore need not anticipate its coming)—In order to receive reward" [153]. The whole concept of reward and punishment, bound up with those of the Messiah and hereafter, are often found in the Midrashic analysis of the Scriptures and are really the whole source for the Pharisaic development. It is therefore all the more surprising that a scholar such as Klausner should have found it difficult to recognise Messianism in Habakkuk [154]. Klausner is not very convincing. He argues, that Habakkuk definitely does not prophesy against the people Israel but rather directed his 'hard' words against the Assyrians or against the Chaldeans, because of his love for Israel. He goes on to explain that Habakkuk prophesies "a day of punishment for the Assyrians (or the Chaldeans)," and says of this day (and not of the day of redemption, as the Talmud interprets): "Though it tarry, wait for it: because it will surely come, it will not delay." (Hab. 2: 3) [155]. Surely however the two events are identical. The Messianic period ushers in punishment for the wicked and righteousness becomes vindicated. This in effect is redemption. Mowinckel appears to have grasped the implication of the Midrashic treatment though his conclusion is his own when he declares "the tribulations of the Assyrian and Chaldean period would end with the victory of Yahweh, which was identical with the triumph of Israel" [156]. Habakkuk sees in the Chaldeans a nation appointed as the instrument of divine vengeance to chastise Israel [157], or in the opinion of Bewer "to establish justice in the world" [158]. This in no way suggests that such a Divine instrument, as the Chaldean, will receive any dispensation for his own evil in which might is his god. As Heschel puts it: "Is this the way of justice: that innocent men should perish so that the wicked may be punished?" [159]. It opens the door to the righteous and the wicked in Rabbinic doctrine as the Midrashic teachers perceive it in Habakkuk.

VI

The chief complaint of the Prophet is: "Wherefore lookest Thou when they deal treacherously and holdest Thy peace when the wicked swalloweth up the man that is more righteous than he?" (Hab. 1: 13). Whilst we have already learned [160] that it had enabled the Midrashic teachers to perceive a difference in the degrees of righteousness and wickedness, it had also provided them with God's answer to the problem of righteous suffering which stirred deeply within the soul of the Prophet. There are some righteous who are saved and yet others are not saved 'because justice doth not go forth plainly' (Hab. 1: 4). God replied: 'Because the wicked crowneth the righteous therefore justice goeth forth deviously' (*ibid.*). Consider Nebuchadnezzar, uncircumcised and unclean, and Daniel, holy and pure — yet Nebuchadnezzar will put fresh garments on a righteous man [161], as it is said: 'And he changed his prison garments' (2. Kings 25: 29), and will also put purple garments on Daniel! Pharoah, uncircumcised and unclean, and Joseph, holy and pure — yet Pharoah made Joseph ruler, arrayed him in vestments of fine linen, and put a gold chain about his neck! Ahasuerus, uncircumcised and unclean, and Mordecai, holy and pure — yet Ahasuerus will make Mordecai ruler, will array him in royal apparel and place a crown upon his head, as it is said: 'And Mordecai went forth from the presence of the king in royal apparel' (Est. 8: 15). And so 'Because the wicked crowneth the righteous, therefore justice goeth forth deviously' (Hab. 1: 4). Thereupon God revealed Himself to Habakkuk and said: "Wilt thou raise a cry against Me? Is it not written 'A God of faithfulness and without iniquity' (Deut. 32: 4)"? [162] which the Midrashic teachers explain: " 'A God of faithfulness': Just as punishment will be exacted of the wicked in the world to come even for a slight transgression which they commit, so too is punishment exacted in this world of the righteous for any slight transgression which they commit. 'And without iniquity': Just as the righteous will receive their reward in the world to come, even for the least meritorious act which they do, so too are the wicked rewarded in this world even for the least meritorious act which they do"' [163]. In the whole of the passage the Midrash is offering Habakkuk's prophetic thinking and is another reason for his confession: "I spoke unwittingly" [164].

The Midrashic analysis of the concept of the righteous and the wicked in Habbakuk extends from Israel and "the other peoples" in a national sense [165], to the individual in his attitude towards the national and communal interest. According to the Rabbis there is no real room for the isolationist no matter the degree of piety to which he attains or aspires, and time and again they stress the need for national and communal attachment and responsibility [166]. The following passage from the Talmud [167] makes this point particularly clear: "Our Rabbis have taught: When Israel is in trouble and one of them separates himself from them, then the two ministering angels, who accompany every man, come and place their hands upon his head and say, 'So and so who separated himself from the community shall not behold the consolation of the community'. . . . . He who shares in the distress of the community will merit to behold its consolation [168]. Perhaps a man will say: 'Who is there to testify against me? The very stones of his house and its beams testify against him, as it is written: 'For the stone shall cry out of the wall, and the beam out of the timber shall answer it'". (Hab. 2: 11) [169]. In Rabbinic doctrine Habakkuk provides the passage for declaring that no man may sin in secret because he is of the opinion that nothing exists to testify against him [170]. The evil impulse [171] is the source of temptation and "you will find that it is the evil impulse that accustoms man to sin, and it is he that slays him, as it is said: 'Out of itself proceed both its standard of justice and its (lust for) deception' (Hab.1:7)" [172]. It is the evil impulse which makes him the "haughty man" (Hab. 2: 5) who is not popular even in his own household [173], who is guilty of corruption in his business dealings [174], who is a drunkard [175], and so ultimately is driven out of society and his community. The Midrash shows in its discussion of the evil impulse that it is the obstacle which prevents all mankind from coming "under His wings" [176]. In other words, as Lehrman has rightly pointed out, when it is destroyed [177] "righteousness would prevail and suffering would be banished" [178].

To Raba the great teacher of Mahoza [179], Habakkuk helped him to compare the righteous in the presence of the Shechinah [180] with a lamp in the presence of a torch [181]. What he means to convey is that light emanates from the righteous, albeit a less luminous one than the Shechinah which fills the whole universe, yet close to it [182]. This is further brought out in the Midrash [183] which declares: "Though you will find that three legions of angels go before the Holy One, blessed be He.... yet which of the three dwells closest [184] to the Holy One, blessed be He? The one whose charge is righteousness [185]."

Rabbinic doctrine sets out to demonstrate that righteousness will receive its just reward as the wicked must ultimately be judged for wickedness [186]. When righteousness is not vindicated and wickedness is not adequately judged, then nature itself, declares Raba [187], rebels against the Holy One, blessed be He [188]. The wicked may well protest their innocence, but the truth is known. Hence R. Aibu [189] commenting on the passage: "the peoples labour for the fire and the nations weary themselves for vanity" (Hab. 2: 13), declares that "all the raging of the wicked — their wearying of themselves, is in vain" [190]. Only when they merit good through acts of righteousness will they have dominion, but wickedness reduces mankind — "they will go down" and become "as the fishes of the sea and as the creeping things that have no ruler over them" (Hab. 1: 14) [191]. Such is the method of the Midrashic teachers elaborating Habakkuk's own question, who finds no answer, but is nevertheless waiting for the coming vindication of God's justice. The Prophets in general and the Psalmist along with them, virtually repeat Habakkuk's burning question [192], yet none have put it with such intensity. Habakkuk sharply expresses the ethical and religious motif which in Midrashic analysis has crystallised into a doctrine of unqualified faith in God's justice which Habakkuk tells us is worth waiting for, and is immortality.

VII

The Midrashic teachers have discovered in Habakkuk several important principles which define the Rabbinic doctrine of God. The Holy One, blessed be He, they say, is the Habitation of the world. The world is not His habitation [193]. That is to say He is the Ultimate Source of all things and in whom all things exist [194]. "This is what the Israelites said: 'Of a truth, before Thou didst create Thy world Thou wast in existence and since Thou didst create it Thou art He who exists (forever), as it says: "He stood and measured the earth" (Hab. 3: 6)[195]. God is Eternal, Transcendental and Immutable. "Come and see that not as the attributes of the Holy One, blessed be He, are those of mankind. Man wounds with the surgeon's knife and heals with a plaster, but the Holy One, blessed be He, with what He wounds so He also heals. He punished the world with a bow as it is written: "Thy bow was made quite naked. . . . . (Hab. 3: 9) and He restored the world with it as it is written, "I do set my bow in the cloud" (Gen. 9: 13) [196]. God is from everlasting as it is said: "Art Thou not from everlasting O Lord My God, Mine Holy One? We shall not die" (Hab. 1:12) [197]. Hence R. Akiba [198] says: "Ye shall not behave towards Me," saith the Holy One, blessed be He, "in the manner in which others behave toward their deities. When good comes to them they honour their gods, as it is said: 'Therefore they sacrifice into their net. . . '(Hab. 1: 16) [199], but when evil comes to them they curse their gods" [200]. "Should I have brought good upon you," says theHoly One, blessed be He, "give thanks. Should I have brought suffering [201] equally give thanks" [202]. This was the unqualified faith demanded by the Prophet the reward for which was joy, the same joy of faith with which our fathers in this world, which is altogether night, believed' [203], and which is described in the words "and he believed in the Lord". This was the faith which Israel had inherited and concerning which it is written: "But the righteous shall live be his faith" [204]. Unlike the other nations, whose gods are "like mute stone [205] and mere make-believe, and others have to guard them from being stolen, and how then can they possibly give new life to those who are suffering [206] that they should honour them? The God of Israel is Living, Ever-existing, and Personal. In his comment on the verse: "But the Lord is in His Holy Temple" (Hab. 2: 20) R. Samuel son of Nahman [207] made the following observation: "Before the Temple was destroyed the Divine Presence dwelt therein, for it says: 'The Lord is in His Temple' (Ps. 11: 4); but when the Temple was destroyed, the Divine Presence removed itself to heaven, as it is said: 'The Lord hath established His throne in the heavens' (*op.cit.* 103: 19). R. Eleazar [208] says: "The Shechinah did not depart from the Temple, for it is said: 'And Mine eyes and My heart shall be there perpetually' (2 Chron. 7: 16). So it also says: 'With my voice I call unto the Lord and He answereth me out of His holy mountain' (Ps. 3: 5), for although it was laid waste, it still retained its holiness" [209]. Samuel's interpretation would account for the Midrashic statement: "Since the destruction of the Temple there has not been a day without curse" [210], and obviously refers to Israel's exile among the nations where they became vulnerable to persecution and suffering [211]. The curse refers to the darkness of this world [212] over which the wicked seem to prosper in their wickedness, which is at the root of Habakkuk's inward conflict, and which, as a result, would appear to indicate God's 'removal'. On the day of judgement, however, the idols will not deliver the wicked [213]. There is no escape from death. God has made death an absolute decree since the day Adam ate the forbidden fruit [214]. "Thou didst decree and say: 'Ye shall be holy unto your God' (Lev. 21: 6) which prompts Israel to cry out: 'Lord of the Universe! It is Thy desire that we should be holy; well remove death from us, as it says: "Art not Thou from everlasting.... we shall not die" (Hab. 1: 12). But God replied: 'This is impossible'. Thus — "O Lord Thou hast ordained them for judgement" (Hab. ibid.) [215]. Now let them therefore bring to an end from before Him all the idols of the earth [216] and be atoned for by their children in time to come" [217]. R. Hiyya bar Abba [218] recalls that "when they brought their offerings to the Temple one Arbelian s'ah of wheat yielded a s'ah pollen, one of first flour one cibarium [219], one flour of the second course [220] one s'ah of bran. . . see how wonderful the sacrifices were for them". Whatever they offered on the altar was a blessing for its species. The main object [221] of the altar, however, he went on to say, was but for the atonement of Israel [222]. The very word connotes 'forgiving the iniquities of Israel' [223], 'a good remembrance for Israel' [224], 'blessing for Israel' [225] and 'life for Israel' [226]. The Prophet Habakkuk in the Rabbinic treatment provides Israel with renewed hope through her atonement and return to the altar of the Lord [227]. "In the hereafter the Holy One, blessed be He, restores the blessings". [228] Israel must be conscious therefore once more of her obligation to the covenant, and as a token of her withdrawal from idolatry she was obliged to bring five of each variety of offering "so that the total might amount to fifteen in allusion to the Patriarchs and tribal ancestors whose number amounts to fifteen [229]. For even as the Holy One, blessed be He, had given an oath to the Patriarchs, so He gave an oath to the tribal ancestors as may be inferred from the text: "oaths unto the tribes, Selah"[230] (Hab. 3: 9) [231] Moreover, just as Thou hast sworn to the patriarchs and hast concluded a covenant with them [232], so hast Thou sworn to each of the tribes and concluded a covenant with them" [233].

While therefore redemption comes through the merit of Israel's ancestral patriarchs [234], it comes also through Israel's own complete penitence. As her father Abraham she must have control over all two hundred and forty eight members of her body [235]. When she is in full control of all her faculties she will atone fully for her sinfulness, and in her privation and suffering God will remember her (Hab. 3: 2) [236].

VIII

In this whole approach to God in Rabbinic doctrine taken from the Prophet Habakkuk, what stands out is the demand for earnest and contrite submission to God's ways whatever form they may take. It is the duty of Israel to have faith in the justice of these ways and be ready to submit to the Hand directing them. This requires an unqualified and unquestionable faith which alone defines the righteous, and while he may learn of the reward for the righteous and the punishment for the wicked in the hereafter, Israel must not force its coming. He must wait for it. It will surely come for "all the times appointed by God will come in due course, even as He has determined in His inscrutable wisdom" [237]. Israel will then realise her redemption and restoration for blessing. Idolatry will disappear and all men will bow in silence before God once more inhabiting the Holy Temple, and in whom all creatures of His creation become enveloped by His Divine Omnipresence.

NOTES

[1] Driver's obs. *The Hebrew Scrolls*, p. 19 *et seq.*; Matthew Black, *The Scrolls and Christion Origins*, p. 13; E. W. Heaton, *The OT. Prophets*, p. 22; Hugh J. Schonfield, *Secrets of the Dead Sea Scrolls*, p. 92; Eissfeldt, *Old Testament and Modern Study*, ed. H.H. Rowley, p. 146.

[2] *Journal of Jewish Studies* (*JJS*) VII, 3-4, p. 169 *et seq.*; v. also Wieder, *Habakkuk Scroll and Targum op. cit.*, vol. 4 No. 1 1953.

[3] Shab. 115a trans. H. Freedman, *Sonc. The Talmud Seder Moed*, II:565 n.1; *JJS*. VII *op. cit.*, p. 183 where this is discussed.

[4] Black *op. cit.*, p. 17

[5] Rashi on Lev. 25: 1, v. also Pentat. and Rashi's comm. trans. and annot. Rosenbaum and Silbermann, Lev. p. 195 on p. 113 n.1. v. also Eliezer Levi משנה מפורשת on Ab. 1: 1 p. 5; v. also Davidson's obs. Nahum, Habakkuk, Zephaniah, *Camb. Bible*, p. 66 *et seq.* on Hab. 1: 4.

[6] *JJS* VII *ibid.*, v. also Baba Bathra 12b דאמר גברא רבא מילתא ומתאמרת הלכה למשה מסיני· "the proof is that a great man makes a statement and then it is found that the same rule was a halachah communicated to Moses at Mount Sinai," v. also Eissfeldt *op. cit.*, p. 117.

[7] This is also the force of the dictum BB. 12a נטלה נבואה מן הנביאים וניתנה לחכמים. "Since the day the Holy Temple was destroyed, prophecy was taken away from the prophets and given to the sages". Having become the heirs of the

prophets, the teachings of the sages too contained concepts of a universal nature.

[8] The Soferim lit. 'book-men', commonly transl. "scribes", were founded as a group of teachers by Ezra v. Ab. 1: 1 Eliezer Levi *op. cit.*, p. 5 *et seq.*; v. also Baron, *A Social and Religious History of the Jews*, 1: 397 n. 20; Ginzberg, *On Law and Lore*, p. 3; and Lauterbach art. Midrash and Mishnah in *Rabbinical Essays*, (1951) p. 165; v. also Ned. 37b מקרא סופרים ועיטור סופרים וקריין ולא כתיבן וכתיבן ולא קריין הלכה למשה מסיני· "The textual reading as transmitted by the Soferim, their stylistic embellishments, words read in the text but not written, and words written but omitted in the reading, are all halachah communicated to Moses at Mount Sinai." v. also Herford, *Talmud and Apocrypha*, p. 69 *et seq.*

[9] Avodah Zar. 36a in the name of R. Simeon son of Gamliel and R. Eliezer son of Zadok: אין גוזרין גזירה על הצבור אא״כ רוב צבור יכולין לעמוד בה· "We make no decree upon the community unless the majority are able to abide by it." v. also Horay, 3b, Bab. Bath. 60b, Mid. Tehil. (Mid. T.) 137: 6, Yalk. Mal. 589.

[10] v. Herford, *The Pharisees*, p. 137.

[11] ie. תלמיד חכם v. Ginzberg, *Students, Scholars, and Saints*, (1928) p. 39 *et seq.* for the significance of this term.

[12] Herford adequately sums up his treatment of the sages in a foreward to Frankel's *Peshat* (Toronto 1956).

[13]A Palestinian Amora of the 3rd. c. CE. The function of the Amora was to expound aloud to the audience what the teacher (Tanna) had spoken concisely and in a low voice, v. Sonc. The Talmud Index. vol. p. 731 on Amora and p. 744 on Tanna.

[14] This is the meaning of בעיסוקן and refers to their conduct towards Israel. v. Mat. Keh. (comm. Issachar bar Ashkenazi, 16th.-17th. c.). Ets Yosef (comm. R. Enoch Zundel b. Joseph of Bialistock 19th.c.) renders 1). "in their prosperity" כדמתרגמינן לכל חפץ לכל עיסקא בהצלחתן 2) "in their oppression of Israel". To the Ets Yoseph (*EJ*) we translate "every desirable thing"— חפץ as עיסקא — "activity", v. Lev. R. 13: 5; v. also Lods obs. on the word of God which the prophets saw, in his *Prophecy in Ancient Israel*", p. 121 quot. Habakkuk, *Ibid.*, n. 32.

[15] A Tannaite teacher quoted by Tanhuma b. Abba, a Palestinian Amora of the 5th.c. CE, or by R. Menahema, a name of doubtful origin.

[16] so Jastrow, *Talmudic and Midrashic Dictionary*, 1701a on Gen. R. 16.

[17] Habakkuk speaks of כשדים Chaldeans, and in 1: 8 by a word play פשו for פישון one of the four rivers mentioned in Gen. 2: 11, the Midrash identifies the latter with Babylon, v. Lev. R. 13 and Ets Yoseph *ibid.*, also Gen. R. 16; v. however Davidson, Camb. Bib. *op. cit.*, p. 71.

[18] The rdg. שֵׁאתוֹ for שְׂאֵתוֹ (his dignity, *BDB. Lexic.* 673a) is noted by Gaster in the Habakkuk comment. transl. "Dreadful and awful it is: out of itself proceed both its standard of justice and its (lust) for deception." v. *Scriptures of the Dead Sea Sect*, p. 236, 249 n. 5. Israelstam in the Sonc. transl. v. The Midrash IV: 227 n. 4 renders "destruction" as in Lam. 3: 47 where the word is parallel with שבר. The *BDB* : 981a considers the word doubtful and renders "devastation", a transl. confirmed by the Kohler-Baumgartner Lexicon (*KB*) p. 939a from the root שאה rendering "desolation". In contrast Gaster's rendering from the root נשׁא used only in niph. and hiph. "beguile, deceive" (*BDB*: 674a, *KB*: 638b) presupposes an unusual nominal form for a ל״א verb. In fact there is no apparent reason for repunctuating the Masorah since the root נשׂא "lift up" as in the phrase נשא ראשו "he lifted up his head" (Zech. 2: 4) has the meaning of "pride", (v. also *KB*: 635b and *op. cit.* 913a "defiance"). We shall see infra (n. 172) that the Midrash in its treatment of the evil impulse would support Gaster's rend. in order to bring out the force of the supporting verse quoted from Habakkuk 1: 7.

[19] Mekh. Shir. 6. The passage also quotes Dan. 5: 30 to illustrate the point of Belshazzar. It may also be a reason for the *LXX* apocryphon making Habakkuk a contemporary of Daniel; v. art. Habakkuk, Emil G. Hirsch, *Jewish Encyc.* VI: 117.

[20] Mid. T. 114: 7 dealing with the ten miracles the Holy One, blessed be He, wrought for the sake of Israel at the Red Sea. The Midrash uses a play on the word מטה which means "tribe" as well as "rod, stave"; v. also Yalk. Hab. 565 whole passage. Mid. T. 136: 7, v. also Ab. 5: 4 in Sonc. Nez. VIII Ab. p. 60, *ibid.* n. 3, Mekh. Beshal. 4 and Lauterbach's obs. Mekilta 1: 220 n. 6.

[21] The Hebrew פרזו transl. "(head of) his villages". The Midrash quotes Zech. 2: 8 "Jerusalem shall be as extended as the flat countryside" — פרזות, v. Braude's transl. The Midrash on Psalms 2: 220, *KB*: 777b "open rural country".

[22] v. supra n. 20 for all refs. Mid. T. 106: 4, v. also Ackroyd's obs. *JJS* VII *op. cit.* p. 175n. 22.

[23] Sanh. 94b

[24] On the word כביכול an expression used to introduce an anthropomorphism v. Pentat. with Rashi's comm. *op. cit.* Exod. p. 241 on 77 n.6.

[25] This is the meaning of פגיין given by Mat. Keh. Jastrow emends to סגיין v. Dict. *op. cit.*, p. 1132b with the meaning "plenty" ie. plenty of horses, *op. cit.*, 967a u. סוסיא ref. Hab. 3: 8. Probably hapax legomenon here.

[26] Yalk. Hab. 565, Mid. T. 18: 14, 114: 7, 136: 7, Mekh. Beshal. 5, *op. cit.*7, Cant. R. 1.

[27] Mid. T. 68: 12.

[28] *ibid.* v. also Anderson, *A Critical Introd. to the O.T.*, p. 160.

[29] אימה זו בבל and is deduced from a similarity of phrases (גזרה שוה), the words אימה and איום v. next n.

[30] Ex. R. 51 v. EJ who explains that the ref. is "to Chaldeans who are Babylonians", and *supra* n. 17.

[31] A Babylonian Amora d. 247 CE. He founded the Sura Academy.

[32] *AV*. "bottle"

[33] The force of the word חמתך

[34] who is רעהו "his neighbour".

[35] This is based on 2 Chron. 36: 13 "And he (Zedekiah) also rebelled against King Nebuchadnezzar, who had made him swear by God", for an explan. v. Lam. R. 2: 18

[36] v. Yalk. Hab. 562 on Hab. 2: 16.

[37] The ref. here is to Merodach-baladan from whom Nebuchadnezzar was supposed to have been descended, and the passage to which the Midrash refers describing the incident is Is. 39: 1 "At that time Merodach-baladan the son of Baladan, King of Babylon, sent a letter and a present to Hezekiah".

[38] i.e. Hezekiah, v. prev. n. and for the whole pasage Est. R. 3.

[39] Three steps backward are still maintained at the conclusion of the recital of the litany of the Eighteen Benedictions (Amidah) as the respectful mode of retiring from a superior, v. Hertz, *Authorised Daily Prayer Book*, p. 157.

[40] Est. R. *ibid.*

[41] Hab. 2: 16. שתהגם אתה והערל זה נבוכדנצר · גם אתה זה בלשצר·

[42] Ex. R. 8. Breasted discusses the divinity of the Pharoah in his *Development of Religion and Thought in Ancient Egypt* p. 123, v. also Jastrow, *Hebrew and Babylonian Traditions*, pp. 151, 218.

[43] Hab. 2: 17 which is explained to mean: "to the cattle and the beasts he appeared in the form of a (female) beast." v. also Yalk. Hab. 562.

[44] Lam. R. 2: 18. The passage rds. יומא חד עליל לגביה ואשכחיה דתליש בשר ארנבא ואכיל כשהוא חי, א״ל אישתבע לי דלית את מפרסם לי, ואישתבע ליה · · · "One day he (Zedekiah) entered his (Nebuchadnezzar's) presence and found him

tearing the flesh of a hare and eating it while it was yet alive. The King said to him: 'Swear to me that you will not disclose this about me', and he swore. . ." That Zedekiah did reveal the matter is because the oath was invalid since it was made at the מזבח פנימי -the inner altar, in contrast to the "outer altar" in the court, v. Yefe 'Anaf comm. S. Yaffe on Est. R. 3, v. also *infra* n. 53.

45 The seven Noahide laws are enumerated in Sanh. 56a as "social laws" (ie. to establish courts of justice, to observe social justice as Nahmanides on Gen. 34: 13), "prohibitions against blasphemy, idolatry, adultery, bloodshed, robbery, and eating flesh cut from a living animal." The passage includes other prohibitions such as sorcery which applied also to the heathens.

46 שבע מצות שנצתוו עליהן בני נח Bab. Kam. (BK) 38a, v. Sonc. *AZ.* Nez. VII: 5 n. 7, cf. Maim. Guide III: 48.

47 Babylonian Amora 216-297 CE.

48 Ber. 7b צדיק ממנו בולע צדיק גמור אינו בולע v. Bab. Mets (BM) 71a, Meg. 6b, Yalk. Hab. 562.

49 The Midrash says: "Zedekiah used to enter and leave the King's presence without permission", which clearly indicates that he stood high in the favour of the King, Lam. R. 2: 18, Sonc. The Midrash VII: 177 n. 1.

50 אוי לרשע אוי לשכנו "Woe to the wicked and woe to his neighbour", Neg. 12: 6, Nu. R. 18: 4.

51 *AV*. "and let thy foreskin be uncovered". The word ערל is however oppos. to מהול. Here it is the character of an uncircumcised heart Jer. 9: 25, Ez. 44: 7, 9, cf. Lev. 26: 41, or 'uncircumcised' ear Jer. 6. 10 i.e. unreceptive.

52 This is the implication of Deut. 10: 16, 30: 6, v. Hertz, Pentateuch and Haphtorahs p. 881 on the last.

53 Shab. 149b where the discussion revolves around the dictum of R. Jacob son of Jacob's daughter, who said: "He through whom his neighbour is punished is not permitted to enter within the barrier (precincts) of the Holy One, blessed be He." Sonc. Moed 11: 761 n. 8. Zedekiah had violated the oath, *supra* n. 44, v. also Sonc. The Midr. VII. Lam. p. 177 n. 3.

54 *BK*. 37b Mishnah, v. Sonc. Nez. 1: 211 n. 6 where Kirzner cites Guttmann in the *Heb. Union Coll. Annual*, III: 1 *et seq*, who demonstrates that in ancient Israel the legislation regulating the protection of life and property of the stranger was on the basis of reciprocity. Where such reciprocity was not recognised, the stranger could not claim to enjoy the same protection of the law as the citizen. In our modern society too those who do not abide by the law are treated accordingly by the state in which they live.

55 There is a word-play here on the Heb. ויתר גוים "and He made the nations start up", so *BDB*. 684a u. root I. נתר (*AV*. transl. "and drove asunder the nations"), with a second root meaning "be free, loose" from which the Rabbinic Hebrew word מותר "is released" hence "is permitted" is a hophal derivative, v. Jastrow *op. cit.*, 946a, v. *BK*. 37b *et seq.*, AZ. 2b, Yalk. Hab. 563.

56 The Midrash provides appropriate texts to illustrate Rab's explanation of Hab. 3: 6, v. Lev. R. 13, Yalk. Hab. 563. For the historical origin of the law affecting the Canaanites, v. *BK*. 38a and all refs in Sonc. Nez. 1: 215 n. 4.

57 v. Gaster *op. cit.*, p. 235. The subject of כשדים and כתים has been thoroughly exhausted; v. Teicher's argument for a Christian origin of the Habakkuk scroll in *JJS* V, No. 2: 47 *et seq.* identifying the Kittim with Roman anti-Christian elements for whom the writer has but "horror and contempt as if the Romans were beyond the pale of humanity" *op. cit.*, p. 51, so also Anderson and Harrelson, *Israel's Prophetic Heritage*, p. 231; v. also Davidson, *Camb. Bib. op. cit.*, p. 71, Pfeiffer, *The Books of the O.T.*, p. 312, Anderson, *A. Critical Intr.*, *op. cit.*, p. 159 *et seq.* quoting also Duhm's emend. Kittim for Kasdim and wants "Cypriots" or

"Greeks", v. Lods, *The Prophets and the Rise of Judaism*, pp. 8-9, E. W. Heaton, *The O.T. Prophets*, p. 22. However within the framework of this art. the Kittaeans and all other enemies of Israel are envisaged in the Midrashic analysis of Habakkuk and his ref. to Chaldeans. This is particularly clear in Mekh. Shir. VI and Yalk. Hab. 561, v. also *AZ*. 2b.

[58] Yalk. Hab. 563, BK. 38a quot. Hab. 3: 2, 6, in a discussion on Lev. 11: 21 "to leap withal upon the earth" being a ref. to 'exile' שבע מצות שנצטוו עליהו בני נח לא קיימום עמד והגלה אותם מעל אדמתם.

[59] They were driven out i.e. forced to emigrate, v. Deut. 2: 10-23. The words והגלה אותם may refer here to the fact that they were exiled and dispersed from their land, but because they did not have a moral law such as was embodied in the Noahide laws, there was nothing to bind them together and so they disappeared altogether as a nation; this in contrast to Israel, who, despite her exile had, because of her loyalty to the Torah, been in the position of maintaining herself as a nation in exile. Hence "they could not last".

[60] לא יכלו לעמוד בהם lit. they could not stand by them.

[61] Yalk. Hab. 563 which also provides several parables to demonstrate the point.

[62] The Talmud, in a discussion, strengthens R. Hanina's dictum: גדול המצווה ועושה יותר ממי שאינו מצווה ועושה by declaring that while the heathen nations do not observe, and were therefore exempt from the obligation of observing the seven Noahide laws, "even if they did observe them, they would not be rewarded... what is meant by this is (not that they go altogether unrewarded as though they had not observed them at all, but) they are not rewarded as much as the one who does something he is commanded to do. They are rewarded as one who does something but is not commanded to do it." *AZ*. 3a, *BK*. 38a where the text is altered slightly. The important thing here is to stress that the merit is greater when the מצוה is performed in obedience to Divine command and not simply becaus econscience prompts it, v. Sonc. Nez. VII. *AZ*. p. 6 n. 1.

[63] Mekh. Bah. 1 on Hab. 3: 3-6, *AZ*. 2b.

[64] Yalk. Hab. 563 on Hab. 3: 6, v. Jastrow, *op. cit.*, 388a on התיר זונאות שלהם "He untied their belts" meaning He made them weak. R. Aha said: הקפיצן לגיהנם "He made them jump into Gehinnom" i.e. Hinnom's Vale, a glen south of Jerusalem where Moloch was worshipped whence it came to denote the place of punishment for the wicked in the hereafter.

[65] Mekh. *op. cit.*, Bah. 5. This is accompanied by a series of quotations from Scripture to illustrate the point.

[66] Lauterbach is probably right in his rendering of ויתר הגוים "abandoned the nations" to mean "gave up hope of their accepting the Torah", Mekilta *op. cit.* II: 235 n. 10.

[67] Johanan bar Nappaha, a Palestinian Amora d. 279 CE. and one of the principal teachers responsible for laying the foundation of the Palestinian Talmud.

[68] *AZ*. 2b, v. also Lauterbach *op. cit.*, p. 200 nn. 13-14.

[69] *AZ*. *ibid*.

[70] Tanna of the 2nd. c. CE. a distinguished student of Akiba, who taught at Tekoa and according to legend spent thirteen years in concealment from the Romans in a cave, during which time he wrote the "Zohar"- a loose exposition of the Pentateuch in Aramaic which appeared as a pseudepigraph and was destined to become the Bible of the mystics.

[71] lit. measured

[72] Lev. R. 13, Yalk. Hab. 563.

[73] Yalk. Hab. 563 on Hab. 3: 6 וכשקבלו ישראל את התורה שקט העולם quoting Ps. 76: 9 in support. The implication is two-fold: a) the earth feared and was still, and b) when Israel had received the Moral Law the world was calm as a result

of its profound influence regulating man's behaviour towards his fellow-man.

[74] not to be confused with Judah I, the Prince and Patriarch who, c. 212 CE. finally edited the Mishnah. Rab Judah is identified with Judah son of Ezekiel a Babylonian Amora 3rd. c. CE.

[75] a student of Judah I and contemporary of Rab (Abba Areka) supra n. 31. His fame spread as a scientist in the field of medicine and astronomy. He boasted that he was as familiar with the paths of the sky as with the streets of his native Nehardea. After the death of Rab he was the acknowledged spiritual head of Babylonian Jewry. He died 254 CE.

[76] *AZ*. 3b

[77] Lam. R 6 on 2: 3, Yalk. Hab. 563. The passage deals with ten horns of which קרן התורה is one based on Hab 3: 4 where נגה כאור · · · קרנים מידו לו are the qualifying words, cf. Pr. 6: 23 where Torah is light, and 2 Sam. 22: 3 and Ps. 18: 3 where God is מגני וקרן ישעי v. also Braude, *Midrash on Pss*, 2: 483 on Ps. 75 n. 13 where the author also makes the point that in the text the words קרנים מידו לו refer to "the horn of the Sanhedrin in Torah" ie. the whole success of the Sanhedrin lies in its fulfilment of the Torah, v. Mid. T. 75: 5 and Yalk. Sam. 84 where the text varies slightly.

[78] There is a play here on אשר and אשור since Hab. 3: 3 does not say "Thy majesty".

[79] i.e. the mundane world is not worthy of so sublime a charter as the Torah, and it should therefore be confined to the celestial world.

[80] that is to say it contains laws which are applicable to mortals not to angels.

[81] *AV*. 'glory', v. however *BDB*: 217a

[82] Cant. R. 8.

[83] This is the force of תימן which means 'south'. The Voice הקול is the same as thunderings — קולות used with ref. to the Giving of the Torah v. Ex. 20: 15 and elaborated by Job "God thundereth marvellously with His Voice" (37: 5). *EJ*. explains the whole passage to mean that God does not exist in any one place, but His glory fills the universe. Hence His Voice can be heard from all sides at one and the same time . . ישמע קולו מכל הצדדים בשעה אחת

[84] Ex. R. 5: 9. Furthermore the significance of "south" as pointed out by Lehrman is that facing east, south is on the right, and the Torah was given on the right (Deut. 33: 2), hence the Voice is heard coming first from the south, v. Sonc. The Midr. III: 86 n. 2.

[85] Nahum, Habakkuk, Zephaniah, *Camb. Bible*, p. 83.

[86] *Authorised Daily Prayer Book*, transl. S. Singer, New ed. 1962 p. 41.

[87] lit. "my father" whose name was Nahmani. He was an orphan reared by his uncle Rabbah son of Nahmani (309-330) whom he succeeded as head of the school at Pumheditha. He died 338 CE.

[88] lit. conclusion, a section from the prophetic books recited after the reading from the Pentateuch on Sabbaths, Festivals, and Fast days, v. Jastrow *op. cit.*, 360b and 102a u. אפטרה.

[89] Ch. III which describes the Sinaitic Revelation and is therefore associated with Pentecost "The Season of the Giving of Our Torah" — its name in the liturgy, v. Hertz Pentat. *op. cit.*, p. 1032, and *Camb. Bible*, *ibid.*

[90] Meg. 31a.

[91] The passage in the Talmud Meg. 28b and conclus. Nid. 73a is attributed to a baraita (extraneous Mishnah) in the name of Elijah and known as Tanna d'bei Eliyahu. The passage in full reads: כל השונה הלכות מובטח לו שהוא בן עולם הבא שנ׳ הליכות עולם לו אל תקרא הליכות אלא הלכות . . "Whoever repeats halachoth (Jewish laws) may rest assured that he is destined for the future world, as it says: 'His ways are everlasting' (Hab 3: 6). Do not read הליכות (lit. goings,

ways), but הלכות (laws)". For an appreciation of repunctuation as a method of Midrashic exegesis, v. the writer's *Hosea Concepts in Midrash and Talmud*" p. 29, 32. In Nid. 73a the rdg. varies slightly כל השונה הלכות בכל יום "whoever repeats halachoth every day . . ." and this is the text often found in the liturgy of certain congregations, eg. publ. Shapiro, Vallentine, p. 210; v. also Yalk. Hab. 563.

92 תלמיד חכם lit. disciple of the wise, v. supra n. 11.

93 Yalk. Hab. 562 on Hab. 2 : 5.

94 lit. study of the law and refers to an institution which caters for the training of Jewish children in Hebrew and Jewish religious subjects.

95 Judah b. Nahmani, a Palestinian Amora 3rd. c. CE. v. next n.

96 Sanh. 7b where we are told that "the members of Judah II's household once appointed an incompetent teacher, and the Rabbis said to Judah b. Nahmani, the Amora (whose function was to expound aloud to the audience what the teacher had spoken concisely in a low voice) of Resh Lakish: "Go and stand at his side as Amora; and standing by him, he (Judah) bent down to hear what he wished to teach, but the teacher made no attempt to say anything. Thereupon R. Judah took as his opening text . . . . Hab. 2: 19", v. Yalk. Hab. 562, Jastrow *op. cit.* 1695b and sources Yerush. Bik. 3. 65d top which reads: "R. Jacob (having to act as an Amora to an ignorant teacher) interpreted . . . ." on Hab. 2: 19.

97 v. Gaster *op. cit.*, p. 238 on Hab. 2: 1-2 where למען ירוץ קורא בו "refers to the teacher who expounds the law aright, for God has made him *au courant*. . .". The last phrase brings out the force of the root רוץ. Gaster is to be congratulated on this rendering.

98 v. Mid. T. 90: 7, Yalk. Hab. 562-3 on Hab. 1: 4; v. also Mid. T. 7: 17.

99 תגר v. Jastrow *op. cit.*, 1647a.

100 Gaster *op. cit.*, 235 on Hab. 1: 4

101 The text in Sot. 49a is quoted in the name of R. Elai b. Jebarekya, identified with Elai son of Berekiah, a Palestinian Amora of uncertain date. It was based on a homiletical repunctuation transferring בְּקֶרֶב שָׁנִים into בְּקֵרוּב שְׁנַיִם i.e. read not 'in the midst of the years', but in 'the drawing together of two' Hab. 3: 2. The word פעלך 'thy work' means the study of the Torah, and 'drawing together of two' means two destitute students sharing one garment, v. Rashi ibid. Jastrow *op. cit.*, 1368b u. קירוב; v. also Yalk. Hab. 563.

102 תפוג תורה Hab. 1: 4 v. *BDB*: 806a.

103 *BDB. ibid.* and Gaster's rend. *op. cit.*, 235.

104 Mid. T. 90: 7 a homiletical rend. of Hab. 3: 1 על שגינות lit. upon Shigionoth, some form of wild passionate songs, so *BDB*: 993b, or poem of irregular structure, v. Stainer, *The Music of the Bible*, p. 79n. From a root meaning "go astray, reel" *BDB. ibid.* The Midrash takes the word from roots meaning "commit sin, or error", hence "unwittingly, erringly" v. *BDB*: 992b u. שגג with possibilities of roots שָׁגָה, שׁוּג parallel to it.

105 Mak. 24a, Mid. T. 17: 25 in the Saloniki and Venice eds. and in all subsequent eds. down to the Warsaw ed. of 1865 with Padua's comm. It is not found in the Constantinople ed. nor in the Buber ed. (herein designated Mid.T.), v Braude *op. cit.*, 2: 439.

106 v. Mid. T 90: 2 רבנן ור׳ יהודה ב״ר סימון (רבנן) אמרו ארבעה הם שסידרו תפלה וקינטרו דברים לפני הקב״ה. "The Rabbis and R. Judah son of Simon. The Rabbis said: Four directed their prayers to God after having chided Him. "v. also M. Buber's ed. New York 1947 p. 193a n. 3, Yalk. Hab. 563; v. also G. A. Smith, *The Twelve Prophets* II: 130 *et seq.* who sees the point.

107 All this is borne out in Hab. 1: 12-17.

108 v. Emil G. Hirsch, art. Hab. *JE.* VI: 117

109 for example Is. 11: 5

[110] v. Lods, *The Prophets and the Rise of Judaism*, p. 236, cf. Rowley, *The Growth of the OT*, p. 119.

[111] Davidson, *Camb. Bible*, *op. cit.*, 76.

[112] v. *KB*: 60b. This is better than *BDB*: 52b "confirm, support".

[113] **אמת** *KB*: 66b and *BDB*: 54a.

[114] The Midrash here quotes Hos. 9: 10, v. *Hosea Concepts etc.* of the writer p. 66.

[115] cf. Ps. 128: 3.

[116] *EJ.* on Mid. Gen. R 53: 3.

[117] There is a play here on **שדמות** (fields) and **שדים מתין** (withered breasts) or **שדי מת** lit. breasts of the dead, a sign of one incapable of conception; v. Jastrow *op. cit.*, 49 u. **איילונית** v. *EJ.* on Gen. R. *ibid.*

[118] Gen. R. 53: 3, Yalk. Hab. 565.

[119] *EJ.* on Gen. R. *ibid.*

[120] Gen. R. and Yalk. *ibid.*

[121] Ex. R 23. The passage rds. **ובאיזה זכות אומרים ישראל שירה בזכות אברהם שהאמין בהקב״ה שנ׳ והאמין בה׳** (Gen. 15) **היא האמונה שישראל נוחלין בה ועליו הכתוב אומר וצדיק באמונתו יחיה·**

[122] v. Heschel on Habakkuk in, *The Prophets*, p. 143.

[123] *AV.* "Thou art of purer eys than to behold evil." The rdg. here is that of Israelstam and brings out the lesson of the Midrash better, Sonc. The Midr. IV: 58.

[124] Ecc. R. 3: 11 **אפילו צדיק חי העולמים מאמונתו הוא חיה** on Hab. 2: 4.

[125] Ta'an. 23a where the passage rds. **פעם אחת יצא רוב אדר ולא ירדו גשמים שלחו לחוני המעגל התפלל וירדו גשמים התפלל ולא ירדו גשמים עג עוגה ועמד בתוכה כדרך שעשה חבקוק הנביא שנ׳...** and Rashi explains this according to the Targum: **כמין בית האסורים עשה וישב·** "he made a kind of prison and dwelt there." v. also *JJS* VII *op. cit.*, 171 where Brownlee concurs that the speaker is Habakkuk. What is clear, as Lindblom too observes, v. *Prophecy in Ancient Israel*, p. 181 *et seq.*, is that some deliberate preparations were made, cf. Mid. T. 126: 2.

[126] H. Wheeler Robinson, *Inspiration and Revelation in the OT*, p. 166, who is speaking of all prophets but takes Habakkuk as his example.

[127] Mid. T. 77: 1, v. also Midrash Haggadol Genesis (*MHB*) ed. Mordecai Margulies, Jerus. 1947 p. 688 1.22. Yalk. Hab. 562, cf. Gaster *op. cit.*, 238 addressed to the men of truth.

[128] Sanh. 97b in the name of R. Nathan a Tanna 2nd. c. CE., Yalk. Hab. 562.

[129] the older contemporary of R. Judah the Prince.

[130] Sanh. *ibid.* R. Nathan severaly criticised R. Akiba's proclamation of speedy redemption, and also opposed the calculations of the pre-Hadrianic Tannaim; v. Klausner, *The Messianic Idea in Israel*, p. 403.

[131] *MHB* on Ps. 119: 96, p.683 **אין לך דבר בעולם שאין לו קץ** quoting Hab. 2: 3 in support of **לא אולה יש קץ**

[132] This is the substance of the commentary of the Dead Sea Covenanters, v. Gaster *op. cit.*, 238, though their address is to the men who carry out the Torah, while the Midrash embraces all Israel in the message of Habakkuk.

[133] *Inspiration and Revelation* etc., p. 245, cf. Ab. 1: 3

[134] The ref. here is to the Romans and Persians who were singled out more than the others, and were considered to be more important "because their reign will last till the Coming of the Messiah", *AZ.* 2b **מאי שנא הני דחשיבי ומאי שנא הני דלא חשיבי להו משום דהנך משכי במלכותייהו עד דאתי משיחא·**

[135] **פחי נפש** *AZ. ibid.* which Jastrow transl. "despair, disappointment" *op. cit.* 1152a u. **פחי**. Mishcon's transl. is given here v. Sonc. Nez. VIII: 4.

[136] Palestinian Amora 3rd.-4th. c. CE.

[137] Palestinian Amora 3rd. c. CE. brother-in-law of Johanan bar Nappaha, with whom he laid the foundation of the Palestinian Talmud. (**תלמוד ירושלמי**)

[138] or Gehinnom; v. Jastrow *op. cit.*, 236a, supra n. 64.

[139] i.e. Messianic era, so Mishcon *ibid.*

[140] *AZ.* 3b, Yalk. Hab. 562, cf. Gaster *op. cit.*, 240 "God will render His judgement in the midst of many peoples. Thence will he in turn transport him (the wicked) for the execution of sentence, and in their midst He will condemn him and sentence him to the fire of brimstone."

[141] Mekh. Shir. V quot. Hab. 3: 12 in a discussion on Ex. 15: 6 where the imperfect תרעץ implies hereafter, so also the words in Habakkuk באף תדוש גוים

[142] Yalk. Hab. 562. On the phrase עת״ד הקב״ה ליצרעממעמידו v. Jastrow 818a.

[143] following the Targum, v. *JJS.* VII *op. cit.*, 172.

[144] *MHB.* p. 833 1.8 quot. Hab. 2: 3 which rds. שלא תדחקו את הקץ "ye shall not force the end", and is one of the interpretations offered by the Midrash to the passage. Cant. 2: 7; v. also Keth. 111a.

[145] Keth. 111a.

[146] Keth. *ibid.*

[147] This according to a variant rdg. from the root רחק instead of (supra n. 144) דחק

[148] Maharsha (comm. R. Samuel Edels of Posen, Lublin and Ostrog, a master of the dialectic method, d. 1631) on Keth. *ibid.*

[149] Sonc. Nash. IV: 713 n. 13.

[150] v. Is. 30: 18 which is quoted in support of the dictum.

[151] Is. 30: 18.

[152] מדת הדין v. *infra.*

[153] Yalk. Hab. 562 כדי לקבל שכר which is the whole point of the Midrash.

[154] *The Messianic Idea in Israel*, p. 87.

[155] *ibid.*

[156] *He That Cometh*, p. 136.

[157] *The Prophets of Israel*, C. H. Cornill p. 78; J. Lindblom *op. cit.*, 255; Lods *op. cit.*, 233; Davidson *op. cit.*, 72.

[158] *The Literature of the O.T.* p. 140, v. also Heschel *op. cit.*, 141

[159] This is one of Habakkuk's searching questions. Heschel *ibid.*

[160] *supra* n. 48.

[161] Braude has dealt fairly fully with the difficulty of this passage in his endeavours to reconcile it with historical fact, v. *The Midrash on Pss*, 2: 494 n. 18. We are only concerned with the point the Midrash is teaching, and which the continuation of the passage brings out in full.

[162] Mid. T. 90: 7, v. also Heaton who recognises this point, albeit in passing, *The OT. Prophets*, p. 22

[163] Ta'an. 11a

[164] v. also *supra.* The Midrash is in Mid. T. 90: 7 quot. Hab. 3: 1.

[165] Mowinckel observes that Habakkuk is a representative of nationalistic religion, *op. cit.*, 136.

[166] cf. Ab. 2: 4 v. Sonc. Nez. VIII, Ab. p. 14 n. 7 which offers three interpretations; v. also Ab. 4: 7 in the *Authorised Daily Prayer Book*, new ed. p. 265 where the phrase אל תפרש מן הצבור is mentioned in the name of R. Zadok (probably a contemporary of Johanan b. Zakkai, a student of Hillel in whose name it was originally cited). It is however omitted in Mish. Ab. 4: 5, v. also Herford on this in his Pirke Aboth p. 102, cf. also Sanh. 27b. מלמד שכולן (כל ישראל) ערבים זה בזה· "teaching that all Israel are responsible for one another (to prevent wrongdoing)".

[167] Ta'an 11a where several scriptural illustrations are offered, v. also *MHB*: 716, 1. 9, also Hag. 16a.

[168] The sentence וכל המצער עצמו עם הצבור זוכה ורואה בכח מת צבור is omitted in the *Munich Codex*.

169 The Targum now becomes clearer in the light of Brownlee's remarks, *JJS op. cit.*, 174.

170 This is brought out more clearly in Hag. 16a. where the discussion revolves around the 'evil impulse', v. the whole passage from אם יאמר לך יצר הרע ... חטוא.

171 יצר הרע.

172 Ex. R. 30: 13 ... אתה מוצא יצה״ר הוא מרגיל את האדם לחטוא והוא הורגו The transl. of Habakk. here is that of Gaster, *op. cit.*, 236, which here agrees with *EJ*. משטפו הוא נקמתו וזינו ושאתו מל״ ישיא אתכם חזקיהו. "Its judgement (i.e. standard of justice) is its own vengeance and law", and שאתו has the meaning as in "let not Hezekiah deceive you" (2 Kings 18: 29). Lehrman's transl. "their law and their majesty", following the *AV*. "their judgement and their dignity", is, as he rightly puts it, "not clear", v. Sonc. The Midr. III: 367 n. 1.

173 This is brought out in Sot. 47b quot. Hab. 2: 5 (גבר יהיר) האי מאן דמיהר אפילו אאינשי ביתיה לא מיקבל שנ״ גבר יהיר ולא ינוה, אפילו בנוה שלו מעיקרא קפצה אפילו עליה לסום מיתזיל עלייהו. v. also Yalk. Hab. 562.

174 v. Bab. Bath. 98a quot. Hab. 2: 5 to demonstrate the dictum of R. Hiyya b. Joseph (Babylonian and Palestinian Amora, 2nd. c. CE) חמרא מזלא דמריה גרים. "the condition of wine depends on its owners luck, for it is said, "Yea, moreover, wine is treacherous if the man is haughty. . ." (Hab. 2: 5). A haughty person who boasts of that which he does not possess, is punished 'measure for measure' by having that which looks like wine turned into that which in reality is vinegar, v. Sonc. Nez. 111: 408 n. 6. The whole passage is a comm. on the Mishnah 97b-98a dealing with the sale of wine and it turned sour, v. also Yalk. Hab. 562; cf. also the comment in the Qumran text viii, 11 *et seq.* quoted by Brownlee in *JJS. op. cit.* p. 175 "He also took the wealth of the peoples to add upon himself the guilt of transgression. ."

175 Nu. R. 10 ... יהיר מנין שנ״ ואף כי היין בוגד יהיר "How do we know that he (the drunkard) is called haughty?"

176 Ex. R. *ibid.* ... אם בלעו הקב״ה ליצר הרע הרי הכל באין לתחת כנפיו

177 This may be the force of והקב״ה המיתהו which otherwise offers difficulties, v. Sonc. *ibid.* n. 8 and *EJ. loc. cit.*

178 Sonc. The Midr. III: 366 n. 7.

179 Except for six points of law the ruling of Raba was accepted as norm. He founded the school at Mahoza which grew famous when his colleague Abaye (*supra* n. 87), had died and the Pumbeditha school was closed. He died in 352 CE.

180 *lit.* Divine Presence, Omnipresence, an appellation of God in Rabbinic literature.

181 Pes. 8a where the discussion centres around what should be used for searching the leaven (בדיקת חמץ) on the eve of the 14th. Nisan, v. Mish Pes. 1: 1, Pes. 2a, also Yalk. Hab. 563.

182 Pes. Rashi *ibid.* מזיו של הקב״ה ילכו זהרורין להקרין פני הצדיקים ולא יהיה אורם שוה לאורו אלא כנר פני בפני האבוקה. "From the brightness of the Holy One, blessed be He, goes forth rays to make the faces of the righteous shine, but their light is not equal to His light but as a lamp (which pales) before the torch."

183 Mid. T. 5: 7 quot. Hab. 3: 5 to illustrate לפניו ילך דבר the other two are 'fire' as in Ps. 50: 3 and 'righteousness' as in Ps. 85: 14.

184 פנימית lit. innermost.

185 צדקה here must mean 'righteousness' and not 'charity', since it refers to Ps. 85: 14 צדק לפניו יהלך. Nevertheless from what follows "charity" is clearly the meaning, v. Braude's rend. however *op. cit.*, 1: 88.

186 v. Yalk. Hab. 562 כדר׳ שמעון בן לוי דאמר אין גיהנם לעתיד לבא אלא הקב״ה מוציא חמה מנרתקה ורשעים נדונין בה וצדיקים מתרפאים בה. "According to R.

to

ABR-NAHRAIN

AN ANNUAL
PUBLISHED BY THE DEPARTMENT OF MIDDLE EASTERN STUDIES
UNIVERSITY OF MELBOURNE
IN ASSOCIATION WITH THE DEPARTMENT OF SEMITIC STUDIES
UNIVERSITY OF SYDNEY

EDITED BY

J. BOWMAN

ASSOCIATE EDITOR

E. C. B. MacLAURIN

ASSISTANT EDITOR

A. D. HALLAM

VOLUME VI

1965-1966

TUTA SUB AEGIDE PALLAS · EJB ·

LEIDEN
E. J. BRILL
1967

ABR-NAHRAIN

ABR-NAHRAIN

AN ANNUAL
PUBLISHED BY THE DEPARTMENT OF MIDDLE EASTERN STUDIES
UNIVERSITY OF MELBOURNE
IN ASSOCIATION WITH THE DEPARTMENT OF SEMITIC STUDIES
UNIVERSITY OF SYDNEY

EDITED BY

J. BOWMAN

ASSOCIATE EDITOR

E. C. B. MacLAURIN

ASSISTANT EDITOR

A. D. HALLAM

VOLUME VI

1965-1966

LEIDEN
E. J. BRILL
1967

PRINTED IN THE NETHERLANDS

CONTENTS

EDITORIAL NOTE

In this Volume of *Abr-Nahrain* we have the third of Dr. Daniel Leslie's informative studies on *The Chinese-Hebrew Memorial Book of the Jewish Community of K'aifeng*. It gives us great insight into the structure of the Community, and who were its leaders. As promised in *Abr-Nahrain* Vol. V., Fr. A. F. Campbel S. J. has contributed a critical and stimulating review of *Helleno-semitic* by Michael C. Astour.

We have two new contributors to this present volume. They are Professor Sami Ahmed, Professor of History, University of Denver, U.S.A. who writes on the problem of succession to Esarhaddon. This is the first article published in *Abr-Nahrain* in the field of Assyriology. We hope it will be the forerunner of other such contributions. The other new contributor is Dr. S. A. A. Rizvi, Senior Lecturer in the Department of Asian Civilization, Australian National University, Canberra. Dr. Rizvi, formerly of the London School of Oriental Studies, is a well known historian and specialist in the Mogul period. A further article by Dr. Rizvi will appear as a sequel to this in *Abr-Nahrain* Vol. VII.

Dr. J. A. Thompson and your Editor did archaeological work last August in West Azerbaidjan. A report on the ancient Church/Monastery cut into the cliff face at Rasad-e-Khan, with plans of its cells and tunnels, will appear also in *Abr-Nahrain* Vol. VII. This was first identified by your Editor in November 1964. We hope to include a preliminary report on the ancient Khozi Syriac New Testament MS, also discovered by your Editor in Tabriz in 1964 and microfilmed in its entirety last August.

It is our pleasant duty to express our thanks to the bequest fund of the late Professor M. D. Goldman for their continued support, and also to the Australian Humanities Research Council, and Melbourne University Publications Fund, all of whom made the publication of this present volume possible by their financial contributions.

J. Bowman

Department of
Middle Eastern Studies
University of Melbourne

THE CHINESE-HEBREW MEMORIAL BOOK OF THE JEWISH COMMUNITY OF K'AIFENG

BY

DANIEL LESLIE

Part III

TABLE OF CONTENTS (continued)

Lists, Tables, Charts and Genealogies (continued)

H. Some Peculiarities of the Register [1]

Before we try to identify individuals and date the manuscript, that is to say its compilation and closure, we need to note some peculiarities of the text.

White has already noted that several entries are by a different (possibly later) hand. Some are added in the margins, others sprawling across corners; a few are in brackets or crossed out. Some whole pages are by a different hand than the others of the same clan. Most of these are clearly additions, several of which were probably added many years after the main entries were completed. The calligraphy, incidentally, also helps slightly in checking our clan pages. For example, the handwriting of the end of p. 92 is continued by p. 93, and, though other pages for other clans may also have been written in this handwriting, we may suppose both these pages are of the same clan, the Kao. This is equally so for pages 97 and 98, which I take as both belonging to the Chao.

In addition to the above added separate entries, we find several insertions above or below the line which we may take to be added brothers. As White and Williams have noted, most of these are clearly additions by a distinct hand. E.g. (Kao) Samuel (no. 229); Chang Mei (no. 175); Chang Shih-ch'e (no. 164); (Shih) R. Judah, the Scribe (no. 331); and (Chao) Manasseh (no. 263) (White, Williams, p. 93, "by the same hand", is clearly wrong for this last case; the *mem* מ is quite distinctive). It seems legitimate to assume that these entries (Chang Shih-ch'e of the 9th generation, the others of the 10th generation) are *late* entries; these men having died after the main body of the Register was completed.

In some cases the additions are put into the body of the entry, but the distinct calligraphy suggests they are additional. Examples of this are Kao Hsüan (no. 247), and Chang Chin-te and Chang Chiu-te (no. 173, added at the beginning and end of the entry). These are also probably of the 10th generation.

In two other cases of added brothers, (Kao) Ezekiel (no. 208), (Li) R. Jeremiah, the scribe, the teacher, the envoy (no. 187), the calligraphy seems the same, so we do not know whether these names (of the 9th generation) were added later, or just overlooked and immediately entered. The addition of R. (or Rabbi) to Eleazar (no. 105),

---

[1] This is an elaboration on my Part I, Ba, Ca. It is based on a microfilm and photocopy, not the original manuscript held in Cincinnati.

WDR (no. 88), and the three fathers, Akibah (no. 12), Jeremiah (no. 36), Joshua (no. 338), may simply be the correction of oversights. We may note here that rabbis were scrupulously labelled as such. So far as can be known, no mistakes were made. Isaiah, Gershon and Abdiel, of the Ai Clan, were labelled as rabbis for their own entries (nos. 56, 64, 78), but not when they are mentioned as fathers (nos. 64, 78, 83), but this is not surprising.

For these late entries, we may even hazard identifications with men of the Inscriptions. White [1] has reasonably suggested that Ezekiel, brother of Simcha, Kao Teng-k'uei, Kao Teng-jung, and Aaron, sons of Joseph (no. 208, 9th generation?), may be Teng-k'o, associated with Teng-k'uei in the 1663b Inscription, both active after 1642. Similarly (Shih) R. Judah. the scribe, brother of Simcha, Shih Tzu-ch'iang and Shih Tzu-hung, sons of Joseph (no. 331, 10th generation) may well be Shih Tzu-chün, the *Man-la* of the 1663b Inscription, active after 1642. I believe also that R. Jeremiah, the scribe, the teacher, the envoy (no. 187, 9th generation), is Li Chen, the *chang-chiao* "leader of the religion", active in 1642, 1653.

There are a large number of mistakes in the Hebrew of the introductory prayers, in particular in spelling. In the Register, too, several names are written wrongly or at least peculiarly, as White has noted. We may also note that several men in the Register are mentioned in a Hebrew-Persian colophon (see below), sometimes with slightly different spellings.

Of particular interest are YPRYM יפרים (24, 302, 647), presumably a mistake for Ephraim אפרים (written thus in 263); and אדידיה (56) for ידידיה (66) Jedidiah (the same man, according to my Ai clan tree). I have assumed a similar mistake of *aleph* א replacing *yod* י in 213, where I read אשעיה (Oshaiah) as Isaiah ישעיה; and equate the father (Kao) Oshaiah of 213 with (Kao) Isaiah of 203. This produces our tree no 18 (see below). This error may well be connected with Chinese phonetics.

Several cases occur of *heh* ה being written as final *mem* ם. E.g. ·BDYM עבדים (194) thought by White to be Obadiah עבדיה (199); ·LQNM אלקנם (51), clearly Elkanah אלקנה (47). This may help to

---

[1] White II, pp. 76, 91. His own arguments are however fallacious for picking on Ezekiel rather than Simcha or Aaron. He has overlooked the fact that Aaron had an uncle, Aaron, father of Kao Teng-wang, etc. (no. 209), clearly cousins of Aaron and Ezekiel (my tree No. 9). White, incidentally, misread Ch'en Yüan; there is no connection between the Teng-brothers and Kao Wei-p'ing.

explain the miswriting of Chao Liang-ching as GMLYN GYM (see below).

Mistakes in the Chinese characters are as follows:

a. Li P'iao 漂, son of Simcha (130), is presumably 標 Piao of 148 "Simcha, son of Israel, father of Piao", as White (III, p. 90) noted.
b. Kao Che-kuei (or Cho-kuei) 拆桂 (219) is written in two ways (拆桂 and 擢桂) when he is mentioned as a father (221). Each of these writings occurs in the Register of women (657 and 541 (櫂桂 to be precise) respectively). Presumably only one man is concerned.
c. Ai Yi-fan 以藩 (14) is almost certainly the father Ai Yi-fan 一藩 (20), as White assumed without query.[1]
d. Similarly Li Chi-t'ai 計太 (154) may possibly be the father Li Chi-t'ai 繼太 (153).
e. Chin Shih 石 (534, 655) is possibly a mistake for Chin Shih 士 (311).

To these, we may add the suspected mistakes between entries in the Register and (the same) men as given in the Inscriptions and local gazetteers.

a. Chao Kuang-yü 光於, son of Israel (279), may be Chao Kuang-yü 光裕 (Archway Inscriptions, etc.), father of Chao Ying-ch'eng.
b. Chao Ch'eng-chi 承吉, son of Chao Kuang-ch'ao (298), is probably Chao Ch'eng-chi 承基 (1663a, 1679 Inscriptions).
c. Shih Pin 賓, son of Israel (326), may be Shih Pin 斌 (1489 Inscription).
d. Chao Ying-fu 映甫 (273), son of Abram, is probably Chao Ying-fu 映黻 (gazetteers).

---

[1] White's translation and transliteration of the names in the Register has been accurately done. The following minor errors should be corrected (in addition to those White himself has noted, I, p. xvii):
p. 40, no. 87 (and p. 170): Ai Ying-k'uei should read Ai Ying-? (艾應爻).
p. 42, no. 144 (and p. 182): Li Chen 李貞 should probably read Li Yüan 李員.
p. 46, no. 205 (and p. 181): Kao Wen-ch'eng should be Kao Wen-ch'en 文臣.
p. 46, no. 223 (and p. 181): Kao Yüan-p'u 元甫 is best read as Kao Yüan-fu.
p. 52, no. 309 (and p. 177): Chin Sheng-she should be Chin Sheng-se.
p. 66, no. 597 (and p. 189): Lin should be Ling 凌.
p. 68, no. 634 (and p. 174): (Chao?) Hsing is best read as (Chao?) Ching.
p. 68, no. 640: ·Y ŠH should read ·Y SZ (Ai, third sister).
p. 169: Ai Yi-fan, no. 14, is 艾以藩, no. 20 艾一藩.
p. 182: Li Chi-t'ai, n. 153 is 李繼太, no. 154 is 李計太.

There are five cases of dead men labelled by their sons as well as by their fathers, (31, 32, 93, 148, 244). Two only of these sons also figure in the Register: Li Ch'ung-pu, son of Joseph (137), and Li Piao, son of Simcha (130). Li Hui (tree no. 15) and Ai Shih-k'o (tree no. 1) were of the 10th generation and presumably alive. Kao Tung-po, son of Solomon, was presumably alive. We must, it seems, give up the thought that Kao clan men named Tung- were of the 8th generation. (Cf. my new tree, no. 18, below, which puts them in the 9th generation).

White suggested (III, pp. 101-102) that only "some half a dozen" cases are found of Hebrew and Chinese names for one man appearing in the Register. Most of his examples are doubtful. He gives Putiel as Ai Hsin-ts'ai, almost certainly a mistake. He suggests "Hosea (is) Li Yao" as the marginal entry no. 156. More likely, however, is "Hosea הושע (or better Joshua יהושע), son of Li Yao". The entry is so close to the edge of the paper that "son of" may have dropped out. Moreover, on the previous page, same line, is found an inexplicable יה. We may confidently take this as the beginning of Joshua (a late entry?). Li Yao 李耀, son of Moses (no. 158), is, I suspect, a brother of Li Hui 李輝, son of Moses (no. 31), alive in 1653 and not registered. Joshua would then be 11th generation.

I do not think any men in the Register were knowingly given both Chinese and Hebrew names. But some men seem to have been entered twice, once with Hebrew name, once Chinese. We may suggest:

a. Chao Kuang-yü 光於, son of Israel (279), as being Abram (almost certainly Chao Kuang-yü 光裕), son of Aaron (260, and see also 273).
b. Judah, son of Chin Yu-hsin (322) as perhaps Chin Ying-yang, son of Chin Yu-hsin (323, *in brackets*).
c. Chao Liang-ching (GMLYN GYM), son of Adam (259), and father of Aaron (258), is probably Ezekiel, father of Moses, Aaron, and Moses SMN (257). Ezekiel does not figure as an entry in his own right.
d. Entry no. 233 "Kao Yin (blank) Zebulun" may perhaps be "Kao Yin is Zebulun". But once again "Kao Yin, son of Zebulun" (this time suggested by White) is more likely to be correct.

I am inclined to think that each K'aifeng Jew had both Chinese and Hebrew names. Here is a list (and cf. list no. 9) of those men whose parallel names we can suggest (based almost entirely on circumstantial evidence). There is no sign of any relationship between the Chinese and Hebrew name.

List No. 8

Chinese and Hebrew names of the same man

	Register (Hebrew)	Register (Chinese)	Inscriptions	Local Gazetteers or other Chinese source
1.	(Chao) Moses, (*chin-shih*)		Chao Ying-ch'eng	Chao Ying-ch'eng
2.	(Chao) Abram	Chao Kuang-yü	Chao Kuang-yü	Chao Kuang-yü
3.	(Chao) Aaron			Chao Tzu-ts'ai
4.	(Chao) Ezekiel	(Chao) GMLYN GYM (Chan Liang-chin)		Chao Liang-ching
5.	(Kao) Joseph		Kao Tung-tou	
6.	(Kao) Ezekiel		Kao Teng-k'o	
7.	(Shih) R. Judah, the scribe		Shih Tzu-chün	
8.	(Li) R. Jeremiah, the scribe, the teacher, the envoy		Li Chen	Li Chen?
9.	(Ai) Shaphat		Ai T'ien	Ai T'ien
10.	(Chin) Judah	Chin Ying-yang		

Some (Chinese) names appear twice: These are:

a. Kao Ti, son of Israel (250) (in brackets; additional entry); son of Kao Chün (253).

b. Chao Kuei, son of Israel (301) (additional entry?); son of Chao Liang-tso (287).

c. Chin Ying-hsüan, son of Israel (324) (in brackets, crossed out; additional entry?); son of Mordecai (307).
(The Chin Ying-hsüan of no. 319 is unconnected, with a different character for hsüan).

We may add:

d. (Chao) R. Abraham, son of Israel (270);
son of Chao Ying-tou (269).

In such cases, it seems probable that the entry, son of Israel, is a mistake; the same one man is referred to, once by a scribe who did not remember the man's father, the other time more accurately with the father's name.

White (III, p. 88) has equated Ai Shih-k'uei, son of Putiel (94), with Ai Shih-k'uei, son of Ai Hsin-ts'ai (17). Though the characters are identical, this is almost certainly wrong, for Putiel is son of Ezra (95), and Ai Hsin-ts'ai son of Judah (10). This is one of two cases of identically (Chinese-) named distinct men in the Register. The other is Kao Chi-tsu and his identically named cousin (nos. 220, 221).

We should note here that the Chinese personal names of men in different clans (as also Hebrew names) are often the same. Examples (besides over fifty cases of pairs) are:

a. Lung and Hu, brothers in the Chang, Chao, Chin and Kao clans.
b. Teng-k'uei of the Ai, Kao, and Shih clans.
c. Shih-chün of the Ai, Chao, and Li clans.

We are less sure whether one or two women are referred to in the following case:

a. No. 500: Madam Chao, mother of (Ai) Wei-yi, K daughter of Chao Teng;
   No. 501: Madam Chao, mother of (Ai) Wei-yi, K daughter of Adam.

For we also have other cases of "double" mothers:

b. No. 361: Madam Jen, mother of (Li) Fa-t'ien, K daughter of Adam;
   No. 391: Madam Chu, mother of (Li) Fa-t'ien, daughter of Adam.
c. No. 523: Madam Li, mother of (Chang) Wen-jui, daughter of Li Chiu-chou;
   No. 524: Madam Hsü, mother of (Chang) Wen-jui, daughter of Adam.
d. No. 536: Madam Chin, mother of (Chang) San-shan, daughter of Chin Teng;
   No. 537: Madam Chao, mother of (Chang) San-shan, daughter of Adam.

In all these cases, one at least of the mothers is a non-Jewess. Perhaps the Jewish mother was the first wife, the other a second wife, presumably the biological mother (more likely than wet-nurse). None of these four sons, incidentally, appear in the Register of men (the first three appear in the 1663 inscriptions as active around 1642-1653).

Besides the above possible cases of polygamy (normal in both Chinese and Jewish culture), we have:

Chang Mei, husband of six wives, one only Jewish;
Chang Chih, husband of two wives, one only Jewish;
Chao Ying-tou, husband of two non-Jewish wives;
Li Shao-t'ai, husband of (presumably) two wives of the non-Jewish Ch'en clan;
Chin Kuang, husband of two or three wives of the Kao and Ai clans (see Register, p. 102).

Except in this last case, once again only one wife was of Jewish parentage. We cannot be sure that these wives were concurrent, though the case of Chang Mei and the double mothers do perhaps suggest polygamy (as White, III, p. 24, assumed). Moreover, there are at least four cases of Chinese-named pairs of sisters and six cases of Hebrew-named pairs of sisters, one of three sisters, and one of four sisters, for whom marriage to one man seems likely. (Nos. 367, 368, 402, 706, 418, 424, 425, 599, 612, 658, 678, 707).

Over five men in the Inscriptions are found in the Register of men, six others in the Register of women, with their Chinese names. Seven of the above list are registered with Hebrew names. We cannot dismiss White's belief that others were also registered in this way. But we must emphasise that the Register must have been closed during the life time of most of those mentioned in the 1663 inscriptions; and these could hardly have been registered.

In the Register of women, Hebrew transliterations are used for five of the seven Jewish surnames and also for the following men. I accept White's transcriptions:

GYN SWM גין שום	(372)	for Chin Hsüan?
GYN PW· גין פוא	(373)	for Chin Fu, Register of men, nos. 303, 313, of women, no. 596.
GN GW DW גן גו דו	(404)	for Chang Chü-te, nos. 113, 163 (White III, p. 80, also gives Chang Chiu-te, nos. 173, 534, which is less likely, for the entry comes next to those of daughters of (Chang) Gershon and Mordecai, father and brother of Chang Chü-te).

Entry no. 110 of the Register of men reads:

"QR DŠ NYYN ·Š BRM SŠ Y·GW ŠŠ son(s) of Israel".

We can state definitely that these are four brothers, DŠ דש standing for *ta-hsiung* 大兄 "eldest brother", ·Š עש for *erh-hsiung* 二兄 "second brother", SŠ סש for *san-hsiung* 三兄 "third brother", ŠŠ שש for *ssu-hsiung* 四兄 "fourth brother".

The proof of this lies in the corresponding abbreviations in the Register of women.

We find, given in Chinese, 16 eldest sisters *ta-chieh* 大姐; 8 second sisters *erh-chieh* 二姐; 5 third sisters *san-chieh* 三姐; 3 fourth sisters *ssu-chieh* 四姐; 1 fifth sister *wu-chieh* 五姐; 2 sixth sisters *liu-chieh* 六姐; 1 seventh sister *ch'i-chieh* 七姐. These include first, second sisters (368 and 402); first, third sisters (706); second, third sisters (367); and second, sixth sisters (400).

We also find 23 DZ דז; 7 ·Z עז; 10 SZ סז; 2 ŠZ שז, 3 ·WZ עוז, which clearly refer to *ta-chieh*, *erh-chieh*, *san-chieh*, *ssu-chieh*, *wu-chieh*. These include first, third sisters (658); second, third sisters (599); third, fourth sisters (707); possibly first, second, third sisters (612); first, second, fourth, fifth sisters (678). I have no certain explanation however of the 2 cases of ·YZ עיז (though it may perhaps refer to a concubine's daughter).

My suggestion (in Part I, footnote 16) that DZ דז and SZ סז stand for *tzu* "child" (or White's "character") is completely wrong. My statistics, of the women especially, also require slight modification with these extra double and quadruple entries.

Entry no. 612 is difficult. I suggest reading DZ ·Y SZ דז עי סז as דז עז סז (eldest, second, third sister).

I have checked, incidentally, those fathers in the Register of women who have more than one entry for daughters registered. Striking cases are:

1. No. 678; (Li) Jesse: דז עז שז עוז (1st, 2nd, 4th, 5th sisters);
   680; (Li) Jesse: 六姐 (6th sister).
2. No. 564; (Chang) Asher: 四姐 (4th sister);
   585; (Chang) Asher: עוז (5th sister).
3. No. 658; (Ai) R. Mordecai: דז סז (1st, 3rd sisters);
   406; (Ai) R. Mordecai: 五姐 (5th sister);
   648; (Ai) R. Mordecai: עי שה (née Ai).

There are only three cases of possible contradiction:

1. No. 355, (Chang) Gershon: 大姐 (eldest sister), clan of marriage unknown;

402, (Chang) Gershon: 大姐，二姐 (eldest sister, second sister), married into Li clan.

2. No. 459, (Chao?) Shemaiah: Leah, married into Ai clan?
362, (Chao? or Ai?)
Shemaiah: Leah, married into Li clan.

3. No. 550, Issachar: שי שה דז (eldest sister of Ai or Shih Clan?), married into Chang clan;
665, (Ai) Issachar: דז (eldest sister), married into Chao clan.

This last case is possibly resolved by taking Issachar (550) of the Shih clan (שא), rather than the Ai (עי) (but cf. my Pt. I, footnote 15). But all three cases may feasibly be interpreted as the result of remarriage and double entry into the clan memorial registers of both husbands. It is unlikely that there were two separate men named Gershon in the Chang clan.

We have had some success in recognising Chinese names and even terms written with Hebrew letters. This encourages us to look for a Chinese origin of the name or term DW· MYN דואמין, which occurs in:

No. 424: Dosath (?) *chaf*, KRṬR *chaf*, Dosath (?) *chaf*, DW·MYN, daughter(s) of Hillel;
No. 434: N·Z, *chaf*, DW·MYN, daughter(s) of Hananiah.

White's view that DW·MYN is simply a further (unusual) Hebrew name goes against the fact that *chaf* (adopted?) follows each of the other names, but in neither case follows DW·MYN.

I suggest tentatively that DW·MYN דואמין (if Chinese, then Wade-Giles *tu-ming* or *tu-min*, *tuo-ming* or *tuo-min*) is 多名 *tuo-ming* or better still 等名 *teng-ming* [1], in either case to be understood as "and others".

I. Identification of Individuals

There are three main possible sources for identification (and hence dating) of the men of the Memorial Book: the Chinese inscriptions of the synagogue; Hebrew-Persian colophons to sections of the Torah; the Chinese local gazetteers (in particular of Hsiang-fu and K'aifeng fu).

White has already correctly noted many of the identifications from the inscriptions and the most important of the colophons. But his

[1] Cf. the *Chinese Repository* XIV, 1845, p. 325, where it is stated that the Chinese Jews pronounced תהו ובהו as *Theohung-vo-peohung*.

attempts to identify names in the Register with names in the Hsiang-fu gazetteers are mistaken, except in the case of those already figuring in the inscriptions. In some of these latter cases only, a few key dates not given by the inscriptions can be established from the local gazetteers.

a. *The 1489 and 1512 Inscriptions*

Possible identifications between men mentioned in the 1489 and 1512 inscriptions and in the Register are as follows:

1. Chang Hao, *man-la*, (fl. c. 1400-1450?), may be "Rabbi Chang Hao, son of Israel", Register, no. 200. It is quite likely that this name was recorded in the Register *because* he was mentioned in the 1489 inscription, though otherwise unknown. We may note, as a warning against facile identifications, a Chang Hao of identical characters, *kung-sheng* of 1659 (Hsiang-fu 1661 gazetteer, 4, p. 30a).
2. Kao Hung (Register, no. 251), father of Kao Ch'un and Kao K'ao, appears on our family tree no. 8 as of the 4th (or 5th?) generation (i.e. fl. c. 1450 or 1480). White's identification with the inscription Kao Hung, active in the synagogue around 1465-1488, is convincing. We have no signs that his associates (or brethren?) Kao Chien and Kao Jui appear in the Register. They might have been registered with Hebrew names, or have left inadequate posterity so their names were not preserved in the Register. In fact, very few men of these earlier generations are recorded.

   White (III, pp. 2-4; and cf. Wells Williams, *Chinese Repository* XX, 1851, p. 465, footnote) has suggested that the "ominous character for 'flood' (*hung* 洪)" at the top of page 51 (p. 52 in White III, pp. 48, 49) refers to the flood of 1642 (1663a inscription). The entries on the page cover six generations, extending from Kao Hung of c. 1465-1488 to about 1650. There is no guarantee that the flood of 1461 (1489 inscription) is not the one concerned, rather than that of 1642.

   In any case, the character 洪 *hung* ("flood, vast") is to be taken, I suspect, rather as an alternative name for Hung 鋐, which occurs vertically below the marginal 洪 (White's photo, III, p. 48). White's speculations as to dates deduced from this "flood" page are to be rejected. The date 1642 is in no way specially connected with our manuscript.
3. Chao Chün, brother of Chao Hung, sons of Chao Shang-cheng,

Register, no. 264, is most unlikely to be the Chao Chün of the 1489 inscription (*Chinese Repository, op. cit.*). According to my chart no. 5, his father was possibly of the (8th? or) 10th generation, fl. c. (1580? or) 1650. I doubt if any members of the Chao clan recorded in the Register lived before the 16th Century.

4. Shin Pin 石賓, son of Israel, no. 326, might feasibly be Shih Pin 石斌, active in 1457-1465 according to the 1489 inscription. The characters for Pin are unrelated. But this is an additional entry at the top of the Shih clan entries, ahead of Job and Levi of the 8th generation, the earliest we can date. Was his name added perhaps because he appears on the inscription, though otherwise forgotten?
5. White (III, p. 133) has identified Li K'un (Register no. 199; our tree no. 14 gives him as of the 7th generation, i.e. fl. c. 1550) as a civil official soon after 1472 (see, e.g., Hsiang-fu gazetteer 1898, 3, p. 33b). The date is wrong; officials of Hsiang-fu almost never came from Hsiang-fu; the 1489 inscription would presumably have mentioned him. The identification is to be rejected.

   Equally unfounded is White's identification of Li K'un's brother Li Lin (and several others) as among the "Martyrs", listed in the 1898 gazetteer, 16, pp. 77-83. Such identifications by name only are absurd.
6. White, III, p. 119, has also identified Chao Teng of the Register (nos. 280, 500) as a *chü-jen* of 1403, *chin-shih* of 1404, who rose to the rank of Prefect, dying c. 1444. He takes this man to be the grandfather-in-law of Ai Wei-yi, prominent in the 1663 inscription, active in 1642-1653. This is manifestly absurd. Our identification of Chao Teng's generation is uncertain, but he could hardly have been before the 17th Century.

   In fact, identification of men of early generations in the Register in the inscriptions (and even more so in local gazetteers) is a near hopeless task. Those named with Chinese names were almost all of later generations.

b. *Hebrew-Persian Colophons*

As White (III, pp. 2-4) points out, several names in the Register of men can be identified with names mentioned as authors of a short Hebrew-Persian Colophon (text and translation by R. J. Williams in White III, pp. 105-109) [1]. This Colophon ("appended to the Genesis

[1] It was first published in 1779 by Ignaz Koegler S. J. "Notitiae SS Bibliorum Judaeorum in Imperio Sinensi", *Journal zur Kunstgeschichte und allgemeinen Litte-*

section—book of the Torah" says White), gives the dates 1933 for the commencement and 1937 for the completion of the (copying of the) Torah, which (according to Williams) must refer to years in the Seleucid era (era of Contracts), and would be 1622 and 1626 A.D.

Williams's translation gives for the names mentioned:

> "Our master, our Rabbi, Rabbi Jacob, son of Rabbi Abishai, son of Rabbi Eldad, the scribe, the teacher, the envoy (HŠLYHY!).
> The envoy (HŠLYH!) Rabbi Shadai, son of Rabbi Jacob.
> *The leader*(?) *of* prayer, Rabbi Mordecai, son of Simeon.
> *The Shekhter*(?) Rabbi Akibah, son of Aaron, son of Ezra. The youth Simcha (ŠMHH!), son of Joshua (YHŠWY!), son of Joseph, made a free-will contri- bution (NDBḤ!)
> *Witness*(*es*): Rabbi Jacob, son of Reuben, son of Buzi;
> Mordecai, son of Benjamin, son of Buzi (BWZ BWY!)".

Rabbi Shadai (9th generation) and his father Rabbi Jacob, son of Rabbi Abishai, son of Rabbi Eldad, can be traced in the Register (White, nos. 187-192) three more generations back to R. Moses, the physician (הרפה) (See tree no. 12, and photo). With four generations involved, we can ignore the difference in spelling for Jacob יעקוב and יעקב, and also between Eldad אלדד and Elidad אלידד; and overlook also the fact that the titles of scribe ספר, teacher מלמד, and envoy שליח, שליחי, שליע (perhaps "prayerleader" or "representative" is better than Williams's "envoy"?) are given to different members of this family.

The 九爺 "nine sires" (rather than the misleading "nine officials" of White III, p. 91) presumably refer to the nine rabbis (of seven generations) of this family, recorded here in the Register. White's suggestion that these generations might cover a period of 200 years is not unreasonable; R. Moses, the physician, might well have been born around 1420-1450.

---

ratur, 7 (1779), pp. 240-252, 9 (1780), pp. 81-92. This was revised and printed as a book by C. T. von Murr, 1805, Halle. It was also published by James Finn as an appendix to his *The Jews in China*, 1843, London (and see also *Chinese Repository* XIV (1845), pp. 305-334, 388-395, esp. p. 323). My photo is taken from White III, p. 105. I quote the translation by R. J. Williams. The text is of considerable difficulty, being a peculiar mixture of Hebrew, Aramaic, Persian and Arabic, but written in Hebrew letters. Williams and White give the translation of Persian and Arabic words in italics, Hebrew and Aramaic words in roman type. Some of the errors in spelling may not have been in the original. The distinction between ח (ḥ) and ה (h) in particular is not always clear. In my opinion, some of the interpretations (notably of offices) are speculative. But the dates 1933 and 1937 are clearly given.

However, we must reject the whole of White's speculations (running throughout his work) that this R. Moses the physician was Chao Ch'eng the physician (fl. 1421-23) of the inscriptions. He bases this identification solely on the fact that both were physicians and may have lived around the same time. In fact, we can feel confident that this family of rabbis were of the Li Clan (our tree no. 12) and not the Chao.

Most of the others mentioned in the Colophon are also identifiable in the Register with a high degree of probability.

Rabbi Akibah, son of Aaron, son of Ezra, is almost certainly R. Akibah (no. 91) of the Ai clan tree, 9th generation.

Rabbi Jacob, son of Reuben, son of Buzi, is almost certainly R. Jacob (no. 226), of our Kao clan tree no. 11, 9th generation.

Rabbi Mordecai, the "leader of prayer", son of Simeon, is probably Rabbi Mordecai, the scribe (הספר), (no. 230), of the Kao tree no. 11, 9th generation (cousin of R. Jacob).

The youth Simcha, son of Joshua, son of Joseph, is probably Simcha (no. 214) of the Kao clan, our tree no. 18, 9th generation, cousin of Kao Tung-tou, oldish in 1642.

The second witness, Mordecai, son of Benjamin, son of Buzi, cannot be traced in the Register. The name Buzi occurs only in the Kao clan (tree no. 11). It is possible that Benjamin was the baby brother to Reuben, Simeon, Levi, Issachar (no. 224) (by another younger wife perhaps!?); but neither Benjamin nor his son Mordecai appears in the Register so far as we know. White gives בנימין בוז בוי but בנימין בן בוזי (Benjamin, son of Buzi) is also found.

The *Chinese Repository* (XX, 1851, p. 464) peculiarly, whilst missing some of these names, adds "Presented by Abram, son of Aaron". If correct, this would probably refer to Abram (Chao Kuang-yü), (no. 260), whose eldest son Chao Ying-ch'eng was born in 1619 according to our reconstruction. Does this in fact come from a different colophon (dated 1619?)?

We can trace children and nephews for most of these men of 1622-1626, but only for one more generation. This provides a large measure of support for a date of closure of the Register no more than 50 years later.

Further colophons (not mentioned by White) are also of interest. Two (undated ones?) were first published in the *Facsimiles of the Hebrew Manuscripts obtained at the Jewish Synagogue in K'ae-fung-foo*, Shanghai, 1851; and are mentioned by the *Jewish Encyclopedia* IV, p. 38, and by Wells Williams, *Chinese Repository* XX, 1851, p. 462.

They include the following genealogies:

a. Colophon to 13th Section of the Law (Exodus):
   1. Rabbi Akibah, son of Aaron, son of Ezra;
   2. Shadiavor, son of Bethuel, son of Moses;
   3. Mordecai, son of Moses.

Shadiavor שדיאור is undoubtedly Shadeur שדיאר (Register, no. 7), 10th generation in our Ai family tree.

Rabbi Akibah is clearly the same man as in the previous colophon, 9th generation of the Ai family tree, but of a cadet branch compared to Shadeur.

Mordecai, son of Moses, is probably of the Chang clan (no. 122), our tree no. 7, 9th generation.

All three are thus in the Register. This colophon must have been written shortly after the other one.

b. Colophon to 23rd section of the Law (Exodus):
   4. Rabbi Phinehas, the teacher, the son of Israel, the son of Joshua, the son of Benjamin.

We cannot trace a Rabbi Phinehas. The phrase "son of Israel" is in any case very peculiar here. No man named Israel is found in the Register. A Joshua, son of Benjamin, figures in the Kao clan, our tree no. 10, 8th (or 9th) generation. If connected, Rabbi Phinehas might have been of the 9th, 10th, or even 11th generation. He was perhaps alive at the time of closure of the Register. I suspect rather that two contemporaries, Rabbi Phinehas, son of Israel, and Joshua, son of Benjamin, were both concerned with this colophon.

There are three more colophons mentioned by Neubauer [1] which may provide further names. The dates 1930, 1931, 1932 (1619, 1620, 1621) are mentioned.

To sum up:

The Hebrew-Persian colophons offer striking evidence of the accuracy of our genealogical trees and also provide a powerful weapon for dating the various generations and the manuscript itself. We may add that our family trees and the identification of the rabbis and other individuals in the colophons confirm the dates 1622 and

---

[1] A. Neubauer, "Jews in China", *The Jewish Quarterly Review* VIII, 1895-6, pp. 123-139, esp. pp. 137-138. Cf. also E. N. Adler, "The Persian Jews: Their Books and their Ritual", JQR X, 1898, pp. 584-625, esp. pp. 624-625; and *Chinese Repository* XX, 1851, pp. 464-465.

1626 given by White and Williams for the commencement and completion of the copying of the scroll.

c. *The Inscriptions from 1663 to 1688*

We now come to the most interesting period of the community. The peak was undoubtedly reached in 1663 when the Jews were clearly respectable and flourishing. In this year an inscription was set up in the synagogue, and it was around this time that the Memorial Book, for all seven clans in one volume, was compiled. Several Jews of this time are identifiable in local gazetteers.

Here is a list of all the Jews mentioned in the two 1663 inscriptions, the 1679 inscription, and also in the dated and undated synagogue tablets written by Jews (mostly between 1670 and 1688) [1] (leaving out those names already figuring in the 1489 inscription). I have added (in brackets) three relatives of Chao Ying-ch'eng mentioned in non-Jewish Chinese sources. Probable and possible identifications in the Register and gazetteers are given in the last column.

List No. 9

Jews mentioned in the 1663 to 1688 Inscriptions

Surname and Name (and title or rank given in inscriptions)	Date of Inscription	Approximate date alive and active	Details of appearance in Register, Gazetteers
Ai Fu-sheng	1663b, 1688	1653, 1688 (10th generation)	
Ai Hsien-sheng (Official Physician)	1663a, b; tablet	1653 (10th generation)	
Ai Sheng-chih	1663b	1653 (10th generation?)	Men, no. 104; Women, no. 508, as husband.

[1] The horizontal tablets between 1656 and 1679 were written by scholars and officials, 12 by non-Jews, one only by the Jewish magistrate Chao Ying-tou (who incidentally alone wrote 謹 "respectfully") in 1670. The vertical tablets were mostly written by Jews ("believers" or "disciples"), the dated ones being in 1676, and 1688 (five by one man). In the 1663a inscription there is a significant remark (White II, p. 67) that these tablets have all been composed by officials of Honan. This is only slightly exaggerated, for almost all the "believers" were actually mentioned in the local gazetteers. One suspects that these tablets were connected with social honours received by the writers.

Surname and Name (and title or rank given in inscriptions)	Date of Inscription	Approximate date alive and active	Details of appearance in Register, Gazetteers
Ai Shih-fang	1663b	1653 (11th generation?)	
Ai Shih-te	1663b, 1676	1653, 1676 (11th generation?)	Hsiang-fu gazetteers, undated, youth at beginning of Ch'ing (1644-).
Ai Ta-sheng (*man-la*)	1663b	1642, 1653 (10th generation)	
Ai T'ien	Tablet	1573, 1605-7 (8th generation, tree no. 1?)	Hsiang-fu gazetteers, *chü-jen* in 1573. Pao-ying gazetteers, "Supervisor of Schools" 1605-1608. Met Ricci in 1605. Possibly Shaphat, Men, no. 67.
Ai Ts'ung-sheng	1663b	1653 (10th generation)	
Ai Wei-yi	1663b	1642, 1653 (9th? generation, cadet branch?)	Women, nos. 500, 501 as son.
Ai Ying-k'uei 應奎, *tzu* Wen-so	1663b, tablet	1653 (9th generation)	Hsiang-fu gazetteers, physician between 1644 and 1661. *Ju-meng-lu* mentions druggist Ai Wen-so. Probably *not* in Men, no. 87; Men, no. 81? or no. 78?
Ai Yung-yin	1663b	1653 (10th generation)	
Chang Wen-jui (*man-la*)	1663b	1642, 1653 (9th generation)	Women, no. 399, as grandson; nos. 523, 524, as son.
Chang Wen-te	1679	1679 (9th generation?)	
Chao Ch'eng-chi 承基 ("captain-adjutant" "major" "Lt-Colonel")	1663a, 1679	1653, 1663 (10th generation?)	Kansu gazetteer as "major", 1657-1661. Men, no. 298, written as 承吉.

Surname and Name (and title or rank given in inscriptions)	Date of Inscription	Approximate date alive and active	Details of appearance in Register, Gazetteers
Chao Kuang-yü 光裕 (given titles and ranks of Chao Ying-ch'eng and Chao Ying-tou)	1678	born before 1600 (9th generation, tree no. 2)	Hsiang-fu gazetteers, honoured (in 1646?) because of son Ying-ch'eng. Three Generations Examination Record of Chao Ying-ch'eng. Men, no. 273, as Abram, father of Moses, *chin-shih*, Chao Ying-k'uei and Chao Ying-fu; no. 260 as Abram; possibly no. 279, written as 光於. Hebrew-Persian colophon as Abram, son of Aaron?
(Chao Liang-ching) 良荆		(7th generation, tree no. 2)	Three Generations Examination Record of Ying-ch'eng. Men, nos. 258, 259 as GMLYN GYM; (no. 257 as the father Ezekiel?). Women, no. 634 as Ching 荆?
Chao Tso-mei (Literary Graduate)	Tablet	1729	Hsiang-fu gazetteers, recommended for post in Shantung, 1729.
(Chao Tzu-ts'ai)		(8th generation, tree no. 2)	Three Generations Examination Record of Ying-ch'eng. Men, nos. (257), 258, 260 as Aaron.
Chao Wen-feng	1679	1679 (12th generation?)	
Chao Wen-lung	1679	1679 (12th generation?)	

Surname and Name (and title or rank given in inscriptions)	Date of Inscription	Approximate date alive and active	Details of appearance in Register, Gazetteers
Chao Ying-ch'eng (*chin-shih*, Intendant)	1663a, b, 1678, 1679	1619-c. 1657 (10th generation, tree no. 2)	Hsiang-fu gazetteers, *chin-shih* 1646. Shang-hang gazetteers, Intendant, 1650-1653. Ch'i-chou gazetteers, Intendant,1656-1657. Ch'ing Veritable Records, Intendant in 1650. Three Generations Examination Record, 28 years old in 1646. Men, no. 273, as Moses, *chin-shih*; probably no. 299 as Moses, father of Chao Yüan-t'ing.
(Chao Ying-fu) 映黻		Died c. 1645-1655 (10th generation, tree no. 2)	Hsiang-fu gazetteers, widow honoured, circa 1690, after 44 years mourning. Men, no. 273, written as 映甫.
Chao Ying-kun	1663b, 1679	1653, 1679, 1695? (10th generation)	Hsiang-fu gazetteers, *kung-sheng* of (middle? of) *K'ang-hsi* period (1662-1723). K'aifeng 1695 gazetteer, as an assistant editor and salaried graduate.
Chao Ying-tou (honorary *chin-shih*, magistrate)	1663a, 1670, 1678, 1679, tablet	1653, 1670, 1679? (10th generation, tree no. 2)	Hsiang-fu gazetteers, *kung-sheng* in 1653. I-liang gazetteers, magistrate 1667-1669 approximately. Kun-ming gazetteers, magistrate 1663-1667. Women, nos. 673, 674, as husband.

Surname and Name (and title or rank given in inscriptions)	Date of Inscription	Approximate date alive and active	Details of appearance in Register, Gazetteers
Chao Yüan-chien	1663b, 1679	1653, 1679 (11th generation, Cf. tree no. 2)	
Chao Yüan-feng ("Subprefect")	1679	1679 (11th generation?)	
Chao Yüan-min	1679	1679 (11th generation)	
Chao Yün-ch'eng ("Confucian Scholar")	1663b, 1679	1653, 1679 (10th generation)	
Chao Yün-chung	1663a, b	1653 (10th generation, cf. tree no. 2)	Women, no. 637 as son.
Chao Yün-ssu	1663b	1642-1653 (10th generation)	
Chin Chih-feng	1663b	1653 (10th generation)	
Chin Ying-hsüan	1663b	1642-1653 (9th generation, tree no. 17)	Men, nos. 307, 321, 324.
Kao Hsüan (*kung-sheng*)	1663a, b, 1679	1642, 1652, 1653 (9th? or 10th? generation, tree no. 18)	Hsiang-fu gazetteers, *kung-sheng* of 1652. Men, no. 247.
Kao Teng-k'o	1663b	1642, 1653 (9th? generation, tree no. 9)	Possibly Ezekiel, Men. no. 208.
Kao Teng-k'uei	1663a, b	1642, 1653 (9th? generation, tree no. 9)	Men, no. 208; probably Women, no. 629 as husband.
Kao Tung-tou	1663a	1642 (8th? generation or 9th? tree no. 18)	Men, no. 247 as Joseph, father of Kao Hsüan; no. 213 as Joseph.
Kao Wei-p'ing (graduate)	1663a	1653	

Surname and Name (and title or rank given in inscriptions)	Date of Inscription	Approximate date alive and active	Details of appearance in Register, Gazetteers
Li Chen 禎 (*Chang-chiao*)	1663a, b	1642-1653 (9th generation, tree no. 12?)	Possibly Hsiang-fu gazetteers, *chü-jen* of 1615. Probably *not* Men, no. 144. Probably Men, no. 187 as R. Jeremiah, the scribe, the teacher, the envoy.
Li Ch'eng-chün	1663b	1642 (10th generation, tree no. 16)	Men, no. 128.
Li Ch'eng-hsien (*man-la*)	1663a, b	1642 (10th generation)	Women, no. 371 as son.
Li Fa-t'ien (graduate)	1663a	1653	Women, nos. 360 as grandson, 361, 391, as son.
Li Hui	1663b	1642, 1653 (10th generation, tree no. 15)	Men, no. 31, as son, presumably still alive.
Li Yu-hsiu	1663b	1642-1653 (11th generation, tree no. 15)	
Shih Tzu-chün (*man-la*)	1663b	1642-1653 (10th generation, tree no. 4?)	Possibly Men, no. 331 as R. Judah, the scribe.

d. *Ai T'ien, Ai Ying-k'uei, and their Family*

Pelliot and Ch'en Yüan both identified the K'aifeng Jew Ai who visited Ricci in 1605 as Ai T'ien 艾田 of Hsiang-fu, holder of the *chü-jen* degree of 1573. The Hsiang-fu gazetteers (1661, 4, p. 20a, 1739, 12, p. 24b, 1898, 4, p. 26b) write that Ai T'ien reached the rank of district magistrate. So far no confirmation of where and when he was appointed to this post has been found; it was not recorded in the 1585 K'aifeng gazetteer, 12. p. 59.

Ricci's description (see, e.g., Löwenthal 3, p. 397, possibly more convincing than the similar Ricci description on p. 394) mentions that the Jew Ai, about 60 years old, came from the capital of Honan (i.e. K'aifeng), held the literary licentiate's degree (i.e. *chü-jen*), had two brothers who were apparently rabbis, and had come to take a teaching post in a school in Yang-chou in 1605.

As noted by Ch'en Tseng-hui [1] in his excellent analysis, Pelliot overlooked that this Ai T'ien was mentioned in the Yang-chou gazetteers. He figures in the gazetteers of Yang-chou fu (1810, 37, p. 51a; and cf. 1733, 20, p. 81b) and of its district Pao-ying 寶應 (1690, 8, p. 5a, 1841, 11, p. 4b, 1932, 9, p. 40a) as a licentiate from Hsiang-fu appointed to an educational post as "schools supervisor" 教諭 for 1605-1607 (replaced in 1608).

Ch'en Tseng-hui also produces some circumstantial evidence to show that Ai T'ien might have taken an examination in Peking in 1604 for the teaching post (and not for the *chin-shih* degree as stated by Ricci). It is thus feasible that both dates, 1604 and 1605, given by Ricci in his two versions of the story, might be correct.

The identification is strikingly confirmed. Whilst agreeing with Laufer (White III, pp. 13-15; cf. Moule, White III, pp. 20-21) that some points of Ricci's story are peculiar, we cannot query the conclusion of Pelliot and Ch'en Yüan. The Jew Ai was Ai T'ien.

There is also a short vertical inscription from the synagogue written by Ai T'ien, "disciple of the religion", and recut by Ai Hsien-sheng (White II, p. 143). The latter is described as 本支孫 "a grandson of the main branch".

The 1663a inscription states that Ai Hsien-sheng, an official physician, was a friend of Liu Ch'ang, died 1670, and contemporary of Chao Ying-ch'eng, born 1619, died c. 1657. His father Ai Ying-k'uei 艾應奎 and the brothers Ts'ung-sheng, Yung-yin, Hsien-sheng, Ta-sheng, Fu-sheng were active in 1653; and Ta-sheng, a *Man-la*, had grown up children by 1653 (see 1663b inscription). Ai Fu-sheng was still alive in 1688 (dated vertical inscriptions; White II, pp. 145-152, Tobar, pp. 25-27, wrongly give 1668). Ai Ying-k'uei is the author of an undated vertical inscription.[2]

---

[1] Ch'en Tseng-hui 陳增輝, 關於利瑪竇集中之猶太人艾氏 ("On the Chinese Jew Ai in Matteo Ricci's *Opere Storiche*"), *Hsieh-ta Hsüeh-pao* 協大學報 I (1949), pp. 171-180, especially pp. 178-9.

[2] For the vertical inscriptions written by members of the Ai clan, see Ch'en Yüan 陳垣, 1920, 6, p. 122, 7, pp. 105-6; 1923, pp. 36, 56-59; White II, pp. 143-152, III, p. 112; Tobar, pp. 23-29. Of considerable interest is the reference, Smith, p. 75 (White I, p. 119), to a tripod, bearing an inscription "on a fortunate day in the third month of spring, in the time of Wan Li (A.D. 1572)". White converts this date to 1573. As Smith's dates are almost invariably wrong, many by one

There is no other known record in Chinese of Ai Hsien-sheng and his brothers. But the father, Ai Ying-k'uei, was well-known. He has a short biography in the Hsiang-fu gazetteers as a physician (1661, 5(2), p. 112a, 1739, 15, p. 53b, 1898, 17c, p. 28a). Ai Ying-k'uei 艾應奎, *tzu* Wen-so 文所, was a skilled doctor, who lived at the beginning of the Ch'ing dynasty (1644-, before 1661). He is also mentioned, as pointed out by Löwenthal, in a Chinese work of unknown authorship, supposed to be from around 1650, the *Ju-meng-lu* 如夢錄, a description from memory ("as in a dream") of K'aifeng before the 1642 flood. This work refers to the synagogue as in the Li 李 family lane, near the "earth" street. Ai Wen-so (i.e. Ai Ying-k'uei) is mentioned as living nearby and owner of a pharmacy.[1]

To return to Ai T'ien. It is thus hardly deniable that Ai T'ien, the *chü-jen* of 1573, was Ai T'ien of the synagogue inscription. Both would be of the same age as the Jew Ai, about 60 in 1605.

That Ai T'ien alone does not appear in the main inscriptions means nothing, for he apparently had less to do with synagogue affairs, and moreover the 1663 inscriptions are mainly concerned with the flood of 1642 and its aftermath. However, it does mean that others successful in Chinese society might not have been mentioned in the 1663 inscriptions.

But we do have one serious problem. Ai T'ien must have been dead long before the Register was closed (c. 1660-1670). Why does his name not appear in it? It is unreasonable to suggest that Ai T'ien did not appear in the Register because he was "expelled from the synagogue and almost excommunicated" (Ricci, Löwenthal, pp. 394, 397). As Laufer points out, Ai T'ien was sufficiently acceptable in the synagogue to have written a tablet, repaired by Ai Hsien-sheng, one

year, we may hazard the guess that this fortunate day refers to the *chü-jen* degree of Ai T'ien, obtained in 1573.

[1] Löwenthal, 1946, p. 388 (and cf. also White III, pp. 131, 150). Löwenthal cites the 1921 edition, pp. 35a-b, 40. I have seen the edition in the 三怡堂叢書, pp. 29a, 33a-b. It has a preface dated 1852 by Ch'ang Mo-lai 常茂徠 of Pien (i.e. K'aifeng). The term used for synagogue is *T'iao-chin-chiao Li-pai-ssu* 挑筋教禮拜寺 (Temple of Worship of the Religion that extracts the Sinews). That this is the synagogue is confirmed by Ricci's 1605 "the Jews they call the *hui-hui*, who extract the sinews from the meat which they eat" (Löwenthal, 1946, p. 394). Gozani in 1704 (White I, pp. 42, 44) also used the term *T'iao-chin-chiao*. The locality as given in the *Ju-meng-lu* fits the 20th Century site given by White in his map of K'aifeng (and cf. the 1898 Hsiang-fu gazetteer street maps; and also the description of the Protestant delegates in 1850, White I, p. 106).

of the leaders of the synagogue. We must assume that most men if not all had Chinese and Hebrew names; and that Ai T'ien was one of those who appear in the Register under a Hebrew name.

White has appreciated this difficulty. He writes (III, p. 21):

> "In the Chinese names of the Codex there is the name of Ai Ying-k'uei (No. 87) but the final character *k'uei* is differently written, and moreover he is recorded as being a son of R. Mordecai, and to identify Ai T'ien as R. Mordecai is at present an insurmountable difficulty. None of the five brothers is named in the list of Chinese names of the Codex, probably because the Codex was written some twenty years before the stone inscription, though it is quite probable that they are included in the list under their Hebrew names."

He tries again (III, p. 112):

> "None of these six names is found in the Codex; the five sons were probably not mature men when the Codex was written, and so would not be enrolled in the list."

These arguments are wrong. The Register was actually written no earlier than the 1663 stone inscription and certainly not twenty years earlier. It is likely that the brothers do not figure in the Register because some if not all of them were still alive in 1663 at about the time of closure of the manuscript. Certainly their father Ai Ying-k'uei, an old man in 1653, may well appear in the Register under a Hebrew name. But any guesses are speculative. White's identification of Ai Ying-k'uei 應奎 as Ai Ying-k'uei 應魁 (No. 87) is unjustified. The Register (No. 87) writes merely 艾應$^{\times}_{\times}$, where the $^{\times}_{\times}$ is most unlikely to be a Chinese character, and may perhaps be "so-and-so" (i.e. of unknown final part of the name).

If we look at our Ai family tree (*Abr-Nahrain* 5, 1964/65, p. 14), we see that three great-grandsons (9th generation) of R. Halpon (?) are named Ying- (應). We may assume that Ying-k'uei was of the 9th generation, and Ai T'ien of the 8th. Tobar, Ch'en Yüan, Laufer and White have all assumed that Ai T'ien was the grandfather of Hsien-sheng, and thus father of Ying-ku'ei. This is based on the interpretation of the expression 本支孫 "grandson of the main branch" (or perhaps "grandson of the same branch") as implying direct descent. We do not know for sure which part of the large Ai family tree would include Ai T'ien, and Ai Ying-k'uei and his sons. It is not unreasonable to suggest however that Ai T'ien is Shaphat (with two brothers as rabbis!) of the 8th generation on our tree. Ai Ying-k'uei would thus figure as one of his sons, perhaps R. Uzziel.

THE following is the original, from the "Notitiæ, &c.," of Kœgler :—

דר במדינת באל בין ליגנן שהר כודאי אזמד אסמאן הורה פונאח שח פרשח חמח ישראל סוהון מאן ניושת אול הורה צולי אלף תשעה מאח שלשים שלש מאהי אב חדא בשבא שלש רוזי ׳ ניושת הורה תאמן צלי אלף תשעח מאח שלשים שבע מאהי אייר ערבעה בשבא עשר שני רוזי ׳ מרינו רבינו רבי יעקוב בן רבי אבישי בן רבי אלוד חסמר חמלמד חשליחי : חשליה רבי שאדי בן רבי יעקוב ׳ ניושאו צלו רבי מורדכי בן שמעון בנישת רבי עקיבה בר אחרן בן עזרא נדר נדבה תבחור שמחה בר יחשוי בן יוסף ׳ נואה רבי יעקוב בר ראובן בן בוזי ׳ מורדכי בר בניסין בה בוי ׳ ברוך אתה בבאך וברוך אתה בצאתך ׳ כבד מאד במקניה בכסף לישועתך קויתי יהוה :

1. The Hebrew-Persian Colophon of 1622-1626 (Seleucid 1933-1937) (reproduced from White III, p. 105).

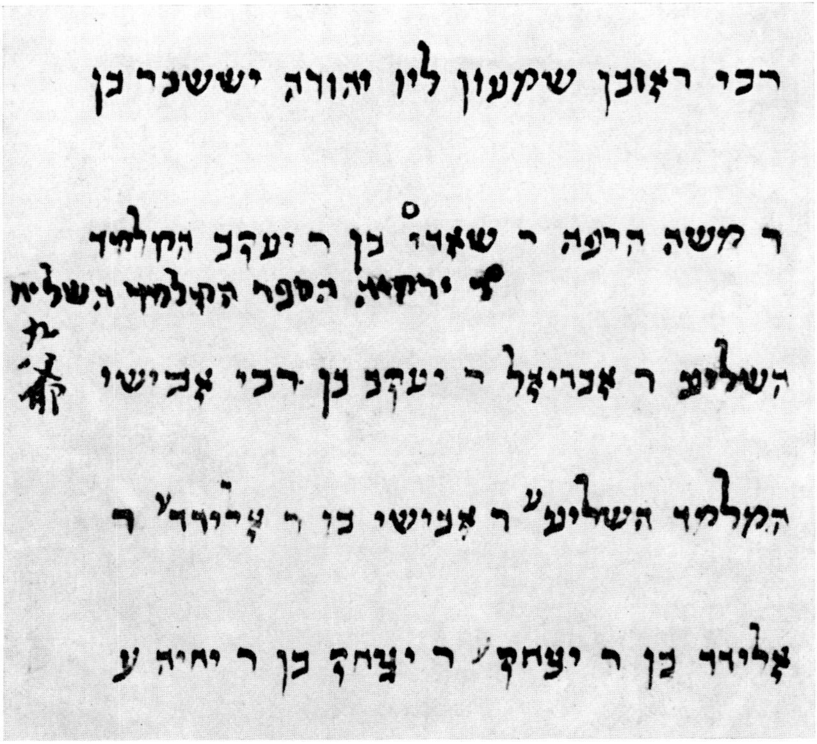
רבי ראובן שמעון לוי יהודה יששכר בן

ר משה הרפה ר שאול בן ר יעקב הקלמד
ירקא: הספר הקלמדי השליח

השליע ר אבריאל ר יעקב בן רבי אבישי

המלמד השליע ר אבישי בן ר אליודד ר

אליודד בן ר יצחק ר יצחק בן ר יחיה ע

3. "The Nine Sires" (p. 43, White p. 44 of the Chinese-Hebrew Manuscript).

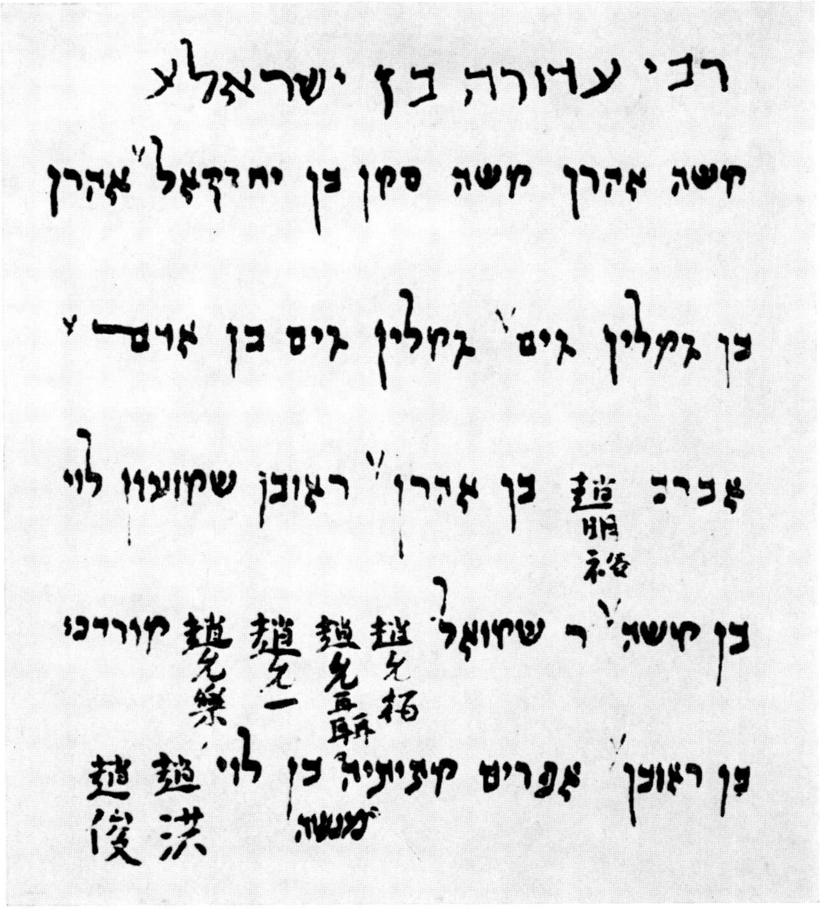

2. "GMLYN GYM" (p. 53, White p. 54 of the Chinese-Hebrew Manuscript).

I am not entirely convinced however that Ai Hsien-sheng, son of Ying-k'uei, was a direct grandson of Ai T'ien. The phrase "grandson of the main branch" might feasibly imply that he was not, Ai T'ien being Shaphat, of a minor branch of the clan, Ai Hsien-sheng being of the head branch. If so, it is possible that Ying-k'uei is registered as R. Abdiel, eldest son of R. Gershon, eldest son of R. Isaiah, eldest son of R. Halpon. Four of R. Abdiel's sons are registered. Were these four of Ai Ying-k'uei's five sons?

e. *Chao Ying-ch'eng and his Family* [1]

There can be little doubt that the main outline given by White for this man and his family is correct. His hypothesis that Ying-ch'eng is Moses, the *chin-shih* (Register, no. 273) is solid.

Chao Ying-ch'eng's history is obtained from several sources. He is prominent in the inscriptions of 1663a, b, and is mentioned in 1679 and on the Archway inscription of 1678, though he was almost certainly dead before any of these inscriptions. He is also the subject of several short biographies in the Chinese gazetteers:

a. *Honan Supplementary Provincial Gazetteer* 續河南通志, 1767, chap. 54, p. 1b; repeated almost identically in the 1898 Hsiang-fu District Gazetteer, chap. 15, p. 62a.
b. *Fukien Provincial Gazetteer* 福建通志, 1737, chap. 32, p. 33b; identical biography in T'ing-chou Fu Gazetteer 汀州府志, 1752, chap. 20, p. 32a; slightly different and abbreviated biography in the Fukien Provincial Gazetteer, 1829, chap. 140, p. 36a; a more detailed version in Shang-hang District Gazetteer 上杭縣志, 1760, chap. 7, pp. 9a-b.

Ying-ch'eng's offices are also recorded in the lists of officials given in various Fukien and Hukuang gazetteers. His degrees and ranks are also mentioned in Hsiang-fu and K'aifeng gazetteers. As a *chin-shih*, his "three generations" ancestry was recorded; and this has been quoted by Ch'en Yüan in his 1923 booklet, p. 37, though not in his 1920 works on the Jews.

The main facts of his career are as follows:

Chao Ying-ch'eng 趙映乘, *tzu* Han-chang 涵章, was born in 1619,

[1] This continues, with more details from the Chinese gazetteers, our section Fc "The Chao clan" in Part II. I hope to publish later full details of Chao Ying-ch'eng's many appearances in the local gazetteers; and also details of his writings.

chü-jen in 1645, *chin-shih* in 1646. His father was Kuang-yü 光裕, grandfather Tzu-ts'ai 子才, great grandfather Liang-ching 良荆.

He received a post (in 1646?) as *Hsing-pu Lang-chung* 刑部郎中 (department director in the Ministry of Justice), and then, in 1650, he was sent to be (military) intendant with the rank of Assistant Surveillance Commissioner 按察使司僉事 in the Chang-nan Circuit 漳南道 in Fukien, with headquarters at Shang-hang 上杭 in T'ing-chou fu 汀州府. He was replaced in 1653. It was in fact in 1653 that he returned to K'aifeng for the three years period of mourning for a parent.

He had been active in the Synagogue affairs in 1642. It was in 1653 that he again took an active part in collating and reconstructing the scrolls of the Law and in commencing the rebuilding of the Synagogue destroyed in the floods of 1642.

In 1656 (not at the beginning of *K'ang-hsi* as Ch'en Yüan, 1920, 17, 6, p. 122; 1923, p. 38, wrongly states), he was appointed as (military) Intendant 按察使僉事 in the Lower Chiang-fang Circuit 下江防道 in Hukuang Province (now Hupei) with Headquarters at Ch'i-chou 蘄州 in Huang-chou fu 黃州府. He was replaced in 1657. According to the biography in the Honan and Hsiang-fu gazetteers, he died in office, almost certainly in Chiang-fang in Hukuang. We may assume he died in 1656 or 1657, at the age of 38 or 39.

In the Register (no. 273), Ying-ch'eng appears as Moses, *chin-shih*, (older?) brother of Chao Ying-k'uei and Chao Ying-fu, sons of Abram. Our family tree (*Abr-Nahrain* V, 1964-65) gives the *probable* ancestors of Abram and also a *probable* son Yüan-t'ing, and grandson Wen-ch'ang, of Moses. Yüan-t'ing may perhaps have died youngish, Wen-ch'ang possibly as a child or infant, for he could hardly have been born before 1659 (40 years after the birth of his grandfather). As White has noted, this last entry was by another hand, and perhaps a late entry, so we cannot be dogmatic about its date of entry into the Register.

We do not know whether Ying-ch'eng had any other sons or grandsons. Chao Yüan-chien, mentioned in the 1663b and 1679 inscriptions was a nephew of Chao Ying-kun and may possibly have been a son of Ying-ch'eng.

I have given the father of Abram as Aaron. We must assume that Abram is Kuang-yü, Aaron is Tzu-ts'ai, and perhaps Ezekiel is Liang-ching.[1]

---

[1] We may note too a Chao Liang-tso of the Register with grandson Kuang-li

White's suggestion (III, p. 118) that Abram is R. Abraham, son o Ying-tou 應斗 (no. 269) is proved wrong by the "three generations" list. However, there is one other possibility of considerable interest.

GMLYN GYM, son of Adam (no. 259), father of Aaron (No. 258), rather than (or as well as?) Ezekiel (previous entry, father of Aaron!!), may be the grandfather of Abram (Kuang-yü), son of Aaron. That is to say that Chao Liang-ching 趙艮荆 is entered in the Register as GMLYN GYM. (Chan-ling Chin is the most literal transliteration). White suggested the romanization Chang Liang-chün. Surely this GMLYN GYM must stand for Chan Liang-ching, a mistake for Chao Liang-ching? This identification eliminates the absurdity of a man surnamed Chang or Chin appearing under the Chao clan. But the "son of Adam" also provides a serious problem. A mistake for "son of Israel"? Or the explanation of why Chao Ying-ch'eng was the first Jewish *chin-shih*?! Was his great grandfather a convert? It is however possible that Ezekiel was GMLYN GYM, a double entry having occurred by mistake. We may note that the first entry for the Chao clan wives (no. 634) gives Li *shih* (*née* Li), wife of (Chao) Ching 荆, "daughter of Israel". Was this Ching 荆 really Liang-ching 艮荆?

The career of Chao Ying-tou, younger brother of Ying-ch'eng, is also fairly well known. The inscription of 1663a says he entered Pien 汴 (i.e. K'aifeng) in 1653 (after the floods) to take his exams. In fact, according to the Hsiang-fu gazetteer of 1661, chap. 4, p. 30a, this is the exact year he received the *kung-sheng* 貢生 degree (not "about 1662", White III, p. 123).

Peculiarly the 1663a inscription does not mention this degree, nor do any other of the inscriptions (of 1670, 1678, 1679) in which he figures. The two 1678 Archway inscriptions call him a *chin-shih* "by grace" 恩進士. This degree must have been honorary, for he does not appear in any official *chin-shih* lists.

As noted by Fang Hao [1] in his excellent study, he was appointed district magistrate in K'un-ming 昆明, district of Yünnan-fu 雲南府 in Yünnan Province, in 1663, replaced in 1668. Thereafter, he was

(nos. 286, 287, 288). Perhaps these were related to Liang-ching and his grandson Kuang-yü.

[1] Fang Hao 方豪, *Fang Hao Wen Lu* 方豪文錄 ("Studies in the History of the Relations between China and the West"), 1948, pp. 277-280 (revised from his 1944 *Chung-wai wen-hua chiao-t'ung-shih lun-ts'ung* 中外文化交通史論叢, pp. 113-119).

appointed magistrate to the nearby district of I-liang 宜良, also in Yünnan-fu, in (1666 or) 1667 and replaced in 1669 (or 1671). Fang Hao has also noted a reference to Chao Ying-tou, magistrate of I-liang, as active in 1667 in the rebuilding of a Confucian "Palace of Learning" *Hsüeh-kung* 學宮. A tablet to this effect (though undated) still exists in I-liang with Chao Ying-tou's name and title *Wen-lin-lang* 文林郎 on it (see Fang Hao, p. 280).

In 1670, Ying-tou was back in K'aifeng, for he composed a dated horizontal inscription in the synagogue, being described as magistrate of I-liang, with the title of *Wen-lin-lang*. The 1678 and 1679 inscriptions add to this "with one grade higher" 加一級. He was presumably still alive in 1679, for he is prominently mentioned in the inscription of that date as the "builder" 建.

In the Register, he appears only as a husband of two women of non-Jewish origin (nos. 673, 674). We may assume he was alive when it was closed.

Ying-tou is called "younger brother" *ti* 弟 to Ying-ch'eng, but also to Ch'eng-chi (1663a Inscription). Chao Ying-ch'eng's father Kuang-yü was honoured with his (eldest) son's title *Feng-cheng ta-fu* 奉政大夫. The Hsiang-fu gazetteers do not mention here Ying-tou, but the two 1678 Archway Inscriptions (White II, pp. 111-115), describe Kuang-yü as holding the post and title of Ying-tou as well as those of Ying-ch'eng. It seems legitimate to assume Kuang-yü was also father of Ying-tou; and Ch'eng-chi merely a cousin (or second cousin) of the brothers. Whether these honours were posthumous or not is not clear. One parent had died in 1653, but this might equally have been the mother rather than Kuang-yü.

Kuang-yü 光裕 appears in the Register as Abram (nos. 273, and 260 [1]); and possibly, (a double entry by mistake?), as Kuang-yü 光於, son of Israel (no. 279).

The identification of further brothers is entirely circumstantial, but nonetheless convincing. The dates we can fix give an excellent fit.

Chao Ying-k'uei (no. 273) of the Register, brother of Moses, had a son Hananiah (no. 296), but is otherwise unknown.

Chao Ying-fu 映甫 (no. 273) is identified by White (and cf. Ch'en Yüan, 1920, 17, 6, p. 122, 1923, p. 38) as Chao Ying-fu 映黻 of the

[1] As brother of Chao Ming-yü 明裕, sons of Aaron. There is no reason to query the joint generation character -yü 裕 (mis-written? as 祫). But we must query whether 光 Kuang- was a generation character for the 9th generation as I have supposed.

local gazetteers, the husband of a woman *née* Kao (a Jewish surname), who mourned her husband for over 40 years. She was then honoured (around 1690 is a likely date—see neighbouring entries in the gazetteers) as a virtuous widow; Ying-fu thus presumably died youngish around 1650. The identification seems very probable. Neither Ying-fu nor Ying-k'uei appear in the synagogue inscriptions.

Chao Ying-kun 映袞 (滾 in the 1679 inscription) is mentioned as an uncle of Yüan-chien, and active in 1653 (1663b inscription). He was the composer of and (together with Chao Ying-tou) responsible for the mainly Chao clan 1679 inscription. It seems probable that he was a younger brother of Ying-ch'eng and Ying-tou. He is presumably also the *kung-sheng* of the (middle? of the) *K'ang-hsi* period (1662-1723), mentioned in the Hsiang-fu gazetteers; and also the scholar, one of the assistant editors of the K'aifeng prefectural gazetteer of 1695. So far, he is not known as holding any other posts. If he was a brother of Ying-ch'eng, born 1619, he must have been born 20 or more years later. He does not appear in the Register, presumably because he was still young and alive at its closure.

Chao Ch'eng-chi 趙承基, prominent in the 1663a inscription was probably a (second) cousin of the brothers Ying-ch'eng and Ying-tou. He was a captain-adjutant in K'aifeng some time after 1642 (1663a inscription), promoted to be major in (Hai-yüan district of) Ku-yüan in Shensi in 1657, being replaced in 1661 (Kansu provincial gazetteer 1900, 53, p. 13a). He was back in K'aifeng before 1663, for it was he who requested Liu Ch'ang to compose the 1663a inscription.

In the Memorial Register, we find a Chao Ch'eng-chi 承吉 (no. 298), son of Chao Kuang-ch'ao, who appears, with a brother Kuang-chen, as a son of Israel (no. 283). It seems probable that this refers to Ch'eng-chi 承基. Presumably his father was related, and of the same generation as Chao Kuang-yü, father of Ying-ch'eng and Ying-tou (contemporaries of Ch'eng-chi). We may assume that Ying-tou was not literally a "younger brother" of Ch'eng-chi, but merely a younger cousin or second cousin.

f. *Other Identifications in the Local Gazetteers*

Most convincingly identified in the Chinese local gazetteers are Ai T'ien and Ai Ying-k'uei, Chao Ying-ch'eng, Chao Ying-tou and their family, discussed above. For the identification of more than one individual of the family helps to corroborate the identification of the family as a whole. The following proposed identifications are of less significance for they stand alone.

1. Kao Hsüan, son of Kao Tung-tou, *kung-sheng* 貢生 (1663b, *kung-shih* 貢士 1663a), active in the community between 1642 and 1653, is, as noted by White, Kao Hsüan, *kung-sheng* of 1652 (Hsiang-fu 1661 gazetteer, 4, p. 30a; cf. 1739, 12, p. 43a, 1898, 4, p. 52b), one year ahead of Chao Ying-tou. In 1653, Kao Hsüan and other Jews presented a petition to the local authorities, requesting and obtaining permission to rebuild the synagogue. So far, no record is known of his obtaining an official post.

   White (III, p. 126; cf. II, p. 72) equates him with Kao Hsüan, older brother of Mattithiah and son of Joseph, Register, no. 247. This is to be accepted, Joseph being thus the Hebrew name of Kao Tung-tou. We may note that this entry is additional and may be a late one. White's further identification of this Joseph as (4th?) son of R. Mordecai, the scribe (no. 229, see also my tree no. 11) is almost certainly wrong. It is probable that R. Mordecai, identifiable in the Hebrew-Persian colophon as active in 1622-1626, was of the same generation as Kao Tung-tou, an old man by 1642. Far more convincing is that Kao Tung-tou was the Joseph registered in no. 213. I have reconstructed a further tree for the Kao clan which makes Joseph (Kao Tung-tou) older brother to Kao Tung-ming. It is partly based on rewriting Oshaiah אשעיה as Isaiah ישעיה (no. 203).

   We should note here that our Kao clan trees are the least reliable, and we cannot guarantee the generations proposed. However we fix them, contradictions turn up.

Tree No. 18: Kao family 5

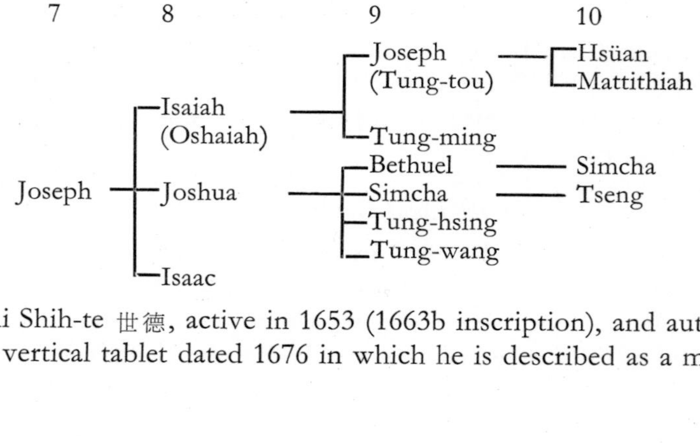

2. Ai Shih-te 世德, active in 1653 (1663b inscription), and author of a vertical tablet dated 1676 in which he is described as a member

of the religion, is identified by Ch'en Yüan as a virtuous youth whose family was honoured at the beginning of the Ch'ing (1644-1911) (see Hsiang-fu gazetteers, 1739, 15, p. 23a, 1898, 17b, p. 20b). This identification is acceptable but of little interest. The 1663b inscription also mentions Ai Shih-fang, possibly a brother of Ai Shih-te.

In the Register, we find also Ai Shih-ch'ang 世昌 (no. 20). According to my family tree for the Ai clan, he belongs to the 11th generation of a very junior branch. Ai Shih-te was presumably of this branch.

3. Li Chen 李禎, the leader of the religion *chang-chiao*, active in 1642 and 1653 according to the 1663 inscriptions, is equated by White with a *chü-jen* 舉人 of 1615, appointed district magistrate (Hsiang-fu gazetteers, 1661, 4, p. 21b, 1739, 12, p. 26b, 1898, 4, p. 28b). This is feasible, but there are strong arguments against. Would the head of the religion have left K'aifeng to become a magistrate? Perhaps before he became head of the religion. Would not his degree have been mentioned in the inscriptions? Not necessarily, for that of Chao Ying-tou (as of Ai T'ien) was not mentioned. We may discover one day where and when the Li Chen of the gazetteers was appointed magistrate, and this may be of help.

   White (III, p. 126) also identified him in the Memorial Register, no. 144. This is unjustified, for the Chinese character, though uncertain, is probably 員 Yüan, not 貞 Chen (note that the local gazetteers use both 禎 and 貞 for Li Chen, the *chü-jen*). This entry in any case is "son of Israel". But Li Chen, the religious leader, must have been called a rabbi and registered as such. Moreover, surely his father's name would have been known?

   I believe that Li Chen, senior by 1642, *was* registered, but with his Hebrew name. I suggest that he was R. Jeremiah, the scribe, the teacher, the envoy, son of R. Jacob, the teacher, the envoy (no. 187, see tree no. 12). His name, we may note, was added over the line to that of his elder brother R. Shadai (mentioned with his father R. Jacob in the Hebrew-Persian colophon dated 1622-1626). Their genealogy would then consist of a long run of senior rabbis.

4. Chao Tso-mei, literary graduate *hsiu-ts'ai* 秀才 author of an undated vertical tablet (not 1729 as given by White III, p. 120), is identified by White as the Chao Tso-mei mentioned in the table of special recommendations (薦辟表) section of the chapter of degree

holders in the Hsiang-fu gazetteers (1739, 12, p. 3b, 1898, 4, p. 3b). The 1898 gazetteer writes that he was appointed to Shantung. The date given is (after?) 1729.

The identification is likely, though by no means established. I have not managed to find any mention of his holding a post in the Shantung provincial gazetteers, in particular between 1729 and 1739.

Of some interest is that this is one of two (out of 17) vertical inscriptions which were apparently not recorded by the Jesuits (between 1704 and 1723), but only by the Protestant delegates in 1850. This is not conclusive for dating the tablet however, for the other one, also undated, by Chao Ying-tou, must have been composed in the 17th Century.

Chao Tso-mei does not appear in the Register.

Other identifications by White (III, pp. 209-210, etc.) are to be rejected. At best, they are based solely on an identity of name. In particular, he identifies Chang Ch'un, Chao Shih-yüan, Kao P'an-kuei, Li Hua, Li Hsiu, Li Lin, Li Yü of the Register in a long list of "martyrs" in the 1898 gazetteer (16, pp. 77-83). In the case of the brothers and poets Li Wei-chung and Li Wei-ho (see White III, pp. 133-4, 209-210), Li Jung and his sons (see my Part II), we can prove that White is wrong. Where there is no confirmatory evidence, of degree, date, locality, we can merely speculate. Of White's 34 odd identifications, only 12 are of interest, and have been dealt with above.

J. Dates

Individuals identified and dated, by means of the Hebrew-Persian colophons, the synagogue inscriptions or local gazetteers, may help to date their generation on the family tree and also the closure of the manuscript. The trees themselves may give us clues as to the date of closure of the manuscript and its earliest entries.

a. *Dating the Register*

We are now in a position to try to fix the date of closure of the Register. We must note however the definite possibility that odd entries, especially those which appear to be added, are later additions. It is probable, in any case, that the pages for the different clans differ somewhat. The Memorial Book as we have it today may be a copy and compilation from separate lists for each clan separately.

The basic evidence for closure must be the dates for individuals registered. The following men, identified in the Register and by some external source, were alive at the following dates.[1]

Some identifications are more reliable than others (see my List No. 9).

1.	Kao Tung-tou (as Joseph)	alive 1642
2.	Li Ch'eng-chün (late entry)	alive 1642
3.	Chin Ying-hsüan	alive 1642, 1653?
4.	Li Chen (as R. Jeremiah?) (late entry)	alive 1642, 1653?
5.	Shih Tzu-chün (as R. Judah?) (late entry)	alive 1642, 1653?
6.	Chao Ying-fu (映甫 for 映黻)	died around 1645-1655
7.	Chao Kuang-yü (Abram)	born before 1600; he or his wife died in 1653
8.	Kao Teng-k'o (as Ezekiel?) (late entry)	alive 1653
9.	Kao Teng-k'uei	alive 1653
10.	Ai Sheng-chih	alive 1653
11.	Kao Hsüan (late entry)	alive 1653
12.	Chao Ying-ch'eng (Moses, *chin-shih*)	alive 1656, died c. 1657
13.	Chao Yüan-t'ing (son of Moses) (late entry?) Register no. 299	presumably alive in c. 1659
14.	Chao Wen-ch'ang (Register no. 300, son of above) (late entry)	presumably not born before 1659. This is the only entry which requires a 12th generation on my trees.
15.	Chao Ch'eng-chi (承吉 for 承基) (late entry)	alive 1657-1660, probably 1663.

We may feel completely sure that the Register was not closed before 1642, and reasonably confident that entries were still being made in 1653. The key entry is that of Chao Ying-ch'eng as Moses, for we are certain that he was alive in 1656 and the entry bears no signs of being additional. The other entries (for the Chao clan) after 1653 seem to have been extras.

We can deduce little from the registered men of the 11th genera-

[1] We should add those of earlier generations whom we have managed to identify: Kao Hung, R. Chang Hao, possibly Shih Pin of the 15th Century; Ai T'ien (as Shaphat), fl. 1573-1605, Chao Liang-ching (as GMLYN GYM), fl. c. 1550, Chao Tzu-ts'ai (as Aaron), fl. c. 1580; and the rabbis and others mentioned in the Hebrew-Persian colophon dated 1622-1626.

tion (nos. 3, 4, 6, 20, 21, 140, 157, 237, 245, 265, 296, 297, 299, 338, 339, 345).

The only case of an entry of the 12th generation is: Chao Wen-ch'ang (no. 300, additional entry), son of Chao Yüan-t'ing (no. 299). He could hardly have been born (let alone died) before 1660, for his grandfather, Moses, was born in 1619, assuming my family tree is correct.

We must add Chao Wen-chin, Chao Wen-hsiu (no. 285), "sons of Israel". Were these also 12th generation?

Of the women of calculable date, several are of the 11th generation (nos. 380, 502, 616, 623, 675, 686, 693, 696, 697, 717). The very last entry in the Register, Madam Li (no. 717), eldest sister, daughter of Li Shih-kuei, is of the 11th generation.

Only one case exists of a woman registered of the 12th generation.

Madam Li, eldest sister, daughter of Li Yen-shou (no. 518, additional entry) was probably of the 12th generation, for Yen-shou's mother (no. 379) was daughter of (Chang) Joseph (no. 122), whom my tree no. 7 puts as 9th generation. Li Yen-shou is not registered, but was presumably of the same generation as Li Yen-nien (no. 140), son of Li Ch'eng-ai, brother of Li Ch'eng-chün (no. 128, additional entries, 10th generation, my tree no. 16), active in 1642 (1663b inscription). Madam Li could hardly have married and died before 1650.

Equally important for dating the Register are those known to be alive at about this time but not registered. It is true that some men were registered with Hebrew names and so we can never be quite sure that others in the inscriptions also do not figure in this way in the Register. But this seems most unlikely in the case of men whose names are given in Chinese in the Register of women. The following men named in the inscriptions are mentioned in the Register of women:

1.	Ai Sheng-chih	as husband	Alive in 1653, but registered (i.e. dead) in Men, no. 104.
2.	(Kao) Teng-k'uei	as husband	Alive in 1653, but registered (i.e. dead) in Men, no. 208.
3.	Li Ch'eng-hsien	as son	Alive 1642, *man-la*.
4.	Ai Wei-yi	as son	Alive, father of a family in 1653.
5.	Chang Wen-jui	as grandson, as son	Alive in 1653, *man-la* and father of a family.
6.	Chao Yün-chung	as son	Alive 1653.
7.	Li Fa-t'ien	as grandson, as son	Alive 1653, a graduate.

8.	Chao Ying-tou	as husband	Alive in 1670 and probably in 1679. *Kung-sheng* in 1653.

We may add (from the Register of men, no. 31)

9.	Li Hui	as father (still alive)	Alive in 1642, possibly 1653.

We may note that two of the three husbands were also in the Register of men; but none of the five sons. Incidentally, none of the fathers of the women are found in the inscriptions.

These unregistered men provide strong evidence that the Register, not closed before 1653, was closed before 1700, probably even before 1670 (apart from odd entries). Laufer's date of 1660/1670 is as accurate as we can get.

b. *Dating the Generations*

Dating of men other than those actually identifiable in the Inscriptions, local gazetteers, or the Hebrew-Persian colophons, must be based on rough and ready methods. I have assumed a 30-33 year difference between generations (father to son), but have not fully taken into account the problem of cadet families. The generations of some families are linked by marriage, others I have based on contemporaries (see my chart no. 4). This matching of all the other clans to the Ai clan is not entirely reliable. A further cause of errors is the insecurity of our Kao clan trees and their generations. For the women, the clan page of several pages is not established. In spite of these inaccuracies and approximations, I do not think we will have erred by more than 30 years in any individual case.

The Chao clan tree is the most accurately dated, for Chao Ying-ch'eng's dates are 1619-c. 1657. Ying-fu, his brother, married but died young, probably around 1645-1655. Ying-tou, a further brother, was mature in 1653, and still alive in 1670 and probably in 1679. Ying-kun (another brother?) was active in 1653, still alive in 1679 and probably in 1695.

I suggest, working backwards and forwards from this 10th generation:

generation:	7	8	9	10	11	12
floreat:	1510-1610	1545-1640	1580-1670	1615-1700	1645-1735	1675-1770

The dates of the Ai clan generations are somewhat more circumstantial, and complicated by the size of the tree. Based partly on the fact that Shadeur (Shadiavor), 10th generation, was contemporary with

R. Akibah, 9th generation of a cadet branch, active in 1622-1626, and partly on the likelihood that Ai T'ien, around 60 in 1605, Ai Ying-k'uei, an old man in 1653, and Ai Fu-sheng, active in 1653 and still alive in 1688, were 8th, 9th, and 10th generation descendants of R. Halpon (6th generation), I suggest (for the main branch):

generation:	6	7	8	9	10	11
floreat:	1465-1565	1500-1595	1535-1625	1570-1660	1600-1695	1630-1730

Similar, though less reliable dates may be established for the generations of other clans.

The dates for the earliest entries vary for each clan. Apart from odd entries that may feasibly be taken as men (of c. 1465) appearing in the 1489 inscription, only the Ai, Li, Chang and Kao clans extend back (on our trees) into the 15th century.

Amongst the earliest are:

1. (Chang) Berachah, son of Israel, no. 108, 5th generation on our tree no. 5, with sons Akibah and Jeberech.
2. Kao Ch'un, Kao K'ao, sons of Kao Hung, no. 251. Kao Hung, though not actually registered, lived in 1465.
3. (Li) R. BTL·L, no. 193, tree no. 15, and Hezekiah, no. 194, tree no. 14, with many sons, were of the 5th generation, though not actually registered.
4. (Li) R. Moses, the physician (not registered), no. 192, tree no. 12, with 8 generations recorded. His son R. Jehiah (4th generation) can be dated as fl. 1450-1500, for R. Jacob and his son R. Shadai (8th and 9th generations) were active in 1622-1626.

The first four generations of the Ai clan cover the 15th century. The father, R. Samuel, no. 45, unregistered, would have lived in the 14th century, and possibly his four sons too. There is hardly any possibility that any entries stem from before the Ming (1368-1644). For the Ai clan, it is feasible that all the entries fall within the Ming period. But this is quite impossible for the Chao and Kao clans (unless we ignore some late entries as additional).

c. *Dating the Clan Pages*

From the family trees we have constructed we obtain confirmation of the clan pages of the men. In particular, we see that Ai clan pages 26-27 are connected to pages 30-37; Chang pages 38-39 are continued by 42-43; Li pages 28-29 and 40-41 are closely linked to one another, and to p. 45; and p. 44 is linked by one link to p. 45 and one link to p. 29. We may declare pp. 44-45 as of the Li clan. Our trees also show that the separated pages of the Ai, Li and Chang clans are not distinct families, for all the pages of the clan are linked.

I have attempted to date the generations included on particular pages of the Register. Pages 30-37 of the Ai clan work steadily downwards in date, with pages 26-27 later entries; for the Li clan, pp. 44-45 seem to be the earliest, then 28-29, and lastly 40-41; for the Chao clan, there seems to be a downward, slightly irregular progression from p. 54 to p. 58; Chang pages 38-39, 42-43, work steadily downwards. Once again, the Kao clan pages are the least satisfactory. Some pages suggest that they are arranged approximately in order of death, others rather by families within the clan. Most family trees are entered by starting with the first recorded generation and working downwards to the youngest generation (e.g. Ai family); one or two only working backwards (e.g. Li family 1).

The pages for the women are more difficult to date. Nevertheless, for the Chang clan, p. 83 seems to be earlier than pp. 84-86; for the Chao clan, pp. 94-98 give definite signs of a progression in date; Li pages 67-70 also seem to progress, though there are additional entries of many generations at the end of page 70, continued by p. 71; similarly, the Kao pages 87-92 seem to progress, but with additional entries of various generations at the end of p. 92, continued by p. 93.

The dating of the pages (72-77), taken as of the Ai clan, which give for almost every entry a Hebrew-named daughter of a *chaf* כ Hebrew-named father (or of Adam), is almost impossible. It seems likely that these pages correspond to pp. 30-37 of the men, some of the entries being of very early generations. The attempt I have made to identify the Hebrew-named fathers in these pages (producing the doubtful "Ai marry Ai" cases) is perhaps unsound. For early generations, we may suppose identical Hebrew names for men of other clans whose records do not go back as far as those of the Ai clan.[1]

K. The Size of the Community

a. *Opinions*

Before we try to infer the number of living members of the com-

[1] We may note here that several whole pages are made up of *chaf* daughters; this argues against White's "adoption". So, incidentally does the fact that some sisters (nos. 424, 434) have *chaf* after each name rather than before the father's name. But I have no better interpretation ot *chaf* כ.

munity from the number of dead registered in our Memorial Book, let us examine the evidence and opinions of visitors to the community and of scholars, and also the figures given in the inscriptions.

The 1489 inscription writes of 70 clans (or surnames) as arriving in K'aifeng during the Sung dynasty. The 1679 inscription embellishes this to 73 clans and over 500 families, referring to the exact date of 1163. We can give little credence to this estimate; even the number of clans is doubtful, 70 perhaps to be replaced by 17 (see *Abr-Nahrain* V (1964-1965), pp. 2, 5, footnote 3).

The 1663a inscription writes that after the flood of 1642 which destroyed K'aifeng, those of the community who (escaped and) crossed to the north bank of the Yellow River hardly numbered more than 200-250 families (*Chia* 家). Presumably most of these families returned to K'aifeng after 1653.

Turning to the opinions expressed by visitors to the community, we have a variety of views, none of which can be taken as authoritative. Ricci, in 1605, talks of ten or twelve families (presumably surnames), but also of six or eight. In 1608, Ricci wrote that a Chinese brother sent to K'aifeng reported that the Jews were few but with a fine synagogue. Gozani wrote nothing of the size of the community, but Brotier (White I, p. 52), referring perhaps to c. 1723, wrote of their being reduced to seven families, comprising at the most 1000 persons. Diaz, quoting Longobardi and Fernandez for 1619 (see Löwenthal 1940, p. 145), mentions 10,000 Jews in Honan province. Kögler in 1779 wrote of 600 souls.

19th and 20th century reports are fairly convincing, though whether actual Jews or merely those who claim descent are included in the numbers is doubtful. In 1850, the Protestant delegates spoke of 200 persons, but in 1851 they reported that this figure was a decided underestimate and mention 300 at least (White I, p. 132). Martin in 1866 estimated three to four hundred people, Schereschevsky in 1867 two to three hundred families. Laufer (White III, p. 13), mentions 50 families, numbering about 250 souls, for 1901. White (see e.g. I, p. 153) writes of 200 families in 1921. Of the many estimates of later visitors, we may perhaps select Mikami, who writes of 100 Jews left in K'aifeng in 1940.[1]

[1] See Löwenthal's bibliographies for estimates by Mikami, Sogabe, Berthelot, and others. His table (1940, p. 119) is, however, inaccurate and full of misprints. The further estimate by Laufer for 1660 (White III, pp. 11-13) is based on his erroneous view of the Register and is worthless.

b. *The Number of Men*

Statistics of the Jews mentioned in the synagogue inscriptions are of no value for estimating the total size of the community, though they are of some use when estimating the relative influence (rather than actual size) of the seven clans. Here are the figures:

Table No. 10

The Men of the Inscriptions

Surname	1489 (+1512) Inscription	1663-1679 Inscriptions	1663-1679 not in Register	Total in all inscriptions
Ai	3	11	7?	14
Li	9	6	1?	15
Chang	2	1 (+ 1?)	— (+ 1?)	3 (+ 1?)
Kao	4	5	1?	9
Chao	2	14	9	16
Chin	5 (+ 2)	2	1	9
Shih	1	1	—?	2
Chou	1	—	—	1
Yen	2	—	—	2
Total	29 (+ 2)	40 (+ 1?)	19? (+ 1?)	71 (+ 1?)

The numbers in the 4th column are of course approximate, for others may have been registered with Hebrew names. They exclude those mentioned in the women's Register; in general these were still alive in 1663. The numbers for the Chao clan are slightly inflated as the 1679 inscription was mainly its concern.

In the previous section, we saw the possibility of arranging by generations a large proportion of those registered. The following statistics (based partly on our trees, partly on the generation characters) are necessarily approximate. The generations given for some of our trees (matched to the Ai clan tree) may be wrong; one or two of our generation characters (chart no. 5) may be wrong. Moreover, how many 10th generation men were still alive and not registered can hardly be determined.

We must also not forget those men of the Register who figure only as fathers, or only in the Register of women (as fathers or as husbands and sons).[1]

[1] In my Table No. 2 (*Abr-Nahrain* IV, 1963-1964, p. 30) I overestimated the number of fathers of the Register of men not actually registered. The last columns should read: Fathers, not in Register, Hebrew-named: 4, 9, 1, 4, 2, 7, 3, total

Table No. 11

Registered Men by Generations

Generation	Ai	Li	Chang	Kao	Chao	Chin	Shih	Total
2nd	4							4
3rd	2							2
4th	4	1						5
5th	9	1	1	1				12
6th	10	9	3	4				26
7th	20	12	3	6	2			43
8th	34	22	12	19	8	6	2	103
9th	42	26	18	32	13	17	6	154
10th	31	14	20	15	15	6	15	116
11th (+ 12th)	6	2	—	3	4 (+ 1)	—	4	19 (+ 1)
uncertain	2	42	16	15	30	10	9	124
Total	164	129	73	95	73	39	36	609

The above table allows us to estimate the size of the community. We can do nothing for the earlier generations, for clearly each clan kept separate records, some less accurate or complete than others. Even in the case of the Ai clan, we can hardly accept that R. Samuel was the only Ai man of the 14th Century. There were certainly Jews in K'aifeng, though perhaps without surnames, during the Yüan dynasty (1279-1368).

This table also makes clear that we cannot entirely rely on total numbers as reflecting the relative size of the clans. Not surprisingly, the total numbers correlate closely with the generation of the first entries. More reliable is the comparison between the 8th-10th generation numbers. It is reasonable to suppose that most dead members of all seven clans are registered for these generations. For the 10th generation, several men would have been still alive. Most of those of unknown generation are on pages suggesting that they were of the 8th-11th generations.

If we calculate the number of living as two adult generations and one of children, we obtain for the approximate total (around the 8th-9th generations, say in 1610, but perhaps based on survival after 1642) 250-300 men, with 200-250 wives and perhaps 300 children

30; Chinese-named: 3, 6, 0, 2, 3, 3, 0, total 17. Of these, approximately 20 (mostly Hebrew-named) were (first of the line) ancestors, of the 7th and earlier generations, who must surely have been dead. Most of the few others we may legitimately assume to be of the 9th or 10th generation and still alive.

(150 of each sex).[1] We shall see how these figures are confirmed by the Register of women.

c. *The Number of Women*

The total number of women registered (including sisters) is 387 odd. To divide these up by generation is far more difficult than for the men, for we are unable to reconstruct family trees for the women. However, in nearly 50% of cases (172 of 387), a father or husband or son can be identified with fair reliability in the men's Register and of a particular generation or date. The following approximate statistics are based on lists of dateable men in the women's Register.

Table No. 12

Generations in the Register of Women

Generation	6th	7th	8th	9th	10th	11th	12th	uncertain
Number of fathers	4	21	32	30	9	1	—	c. 60
Number of husbands	—	—	3	7	20	3	—	6
Number of sons	—	—	1	8	13	5	—	8
Number of grandsons	—	—	—	2	2	—	—	—
Number of Women	—	8	37	56	58	12	1	215

We can also subdivide these figures by clan of origin and by clan of marriage (see Part I, *Abr-Nahrain* 4, 1963-4, pp. 33-35, 38 for the clan pages).

Table No. 13

Generations of the Women by Clan of Origin

Generation	Ai	Li	Chang	Kao	Chao	Chin	Shih	uncertain (but Jewish)	Daughters of Adam	Total
7th	1	4	—	—	—	1	—	1	1	8
8th	7	10	3	4	1	5	—	—	7	37
9th	11	11	3	4	2	13	2	3	7	56
10th	13	7	4	6	3	2	5	5	13	58
11th (+ 12th)	4	1 (+1)	—	4	—	—	2	1	—	12 (+1)
Total dated	36	34	10	18	6	21	9	10	28	172
undated	17	32	13	15	11	10	4	28	85	215

[1] From our Ai clan tree, looking especially at the 6th and 7th generations, and remembering that only male children are given on the tree, it seems that 80% or more of those men registered must have been married. It is thus unlikely that male children (below 13 or 16 years old?) were registered. We must remember however, that bachelors, without progeny, are less likely to be remembered and recorded by later generations

Table No. 14

Generations of the Women by Clan of Marriage

Generation	Ai	Li	Chang	Kao	Chao	Chin	Shih	uncertian (mostly of Ai clan?)	Total
7th	4	1	1	—	2	—	—	—	8
8th	10	5	8	4	2	5	—	3	37
9th	6	14	11	12	5	5	2	1	56
10th	4	9	18	3	9	2	6	7	58
11th (+ 12th)	1	1	—	2	2	4	1	1 (+ 1)	12 (+ 1)
Total dated	25	30	38	21	20	16	9	13	172
undated	53	26	5	50	24	7	13	37	215

These tables are of course rough, for less than 50% of the women can be dated at all, and some of these attributions may be wrong. Nevertheless, some conclusions are legitimate. Dateable women are largely 8th to 10th generations, with a few matriarchs of the 7th generation. It seems unlikely that many women of early generations were included, except perhaps in the case of the Ai clan pages. So many of the "daughters of Adam" are undated that inferences about assimilation are unwarranted. The generation statistics of those dated do not seem to diverge from the statistics of the dated Jewesses. The three women of the Chou 周 and Tso 左 clans, labelled "daughters of Israel" are undated, but they seem to be of the 16th or 17th Century.

The correlation between these two sets of figures is quite good for the Li, Chang, Chao, and Shih clans: that is to say, for these clans the number of daughters who married Jews correlates with the number of men of the same clan. Similarly, we may compare the figures with the statistics of the men in our table no. 11. The correlation with the women by clan of origin is extraordinarily good for the Li clan, and excellent for the Chang, Chao, Chin and Shih clans. The correlation with the women by clan of marriage is good for the Chang, Kao, Chao and Shih, and fairish for the Ai, Li and Chin. The correlation of total figures by generation is quite good. Though the statistics obtained for the women are linked with those of the men, it is only in the case of husbands (not fathers or sons) that an invalid correlation is obtained.

The deteable women are less than 50% of the total registered. We can make a very rough guess for the generations of the remainder by extrapolation, or by assuming the women's pages (as those of the men) are arranged in accordance with the generations. Rough figures are:

Generation	7th (and earlier):	35
	8th	80
	9th	127
	10th	115
	11th	30
	total	387

This gives us 200 odd wives for the 8th and 9th generations, matching up well with the 250 odd for the men. We can feel confident that almost all the dead wives of the 8th to 10th generations were registered. How many daughters married out? None would have been registered, but we can still make a rough estimate.

From our family trees (especially that of the Ai clan), we see that perhaps 20-30% were without male progeny. This fits well with our smaller number of wives. Some of the men registered were bachelors. If we assume that the number of daughters was equal to that of the sons, that there was no infanticide, and that all who lived to maturity married, then we can suggest that at least 20% married non-Jews. When we add approximately 20-25% of the wives as being non-Jewish, we find that 30-40% or more of the Jewish daughters were not married to Jewish men. Going by the (less convincing) total numbers registered, over 50% of the Jewish women married out.

Laufer (White III, p. 12) claimed that "in the Jesuit relations it is asserted that the Jews, whilst they freely intermarried with Gentiles, did not allow their daughters to contract a marriage with one outside their religion". I have not found such Jesuit claims (cf. my Part II, *Abr-Nahrain* V, 1964-5, pp. 8-9). The above statistical argument suggests that marriage out of daughters was at least equally prevalent with the marriage in of non-Jewish wives. We may assume, I think, that the children of Jewesses who married out would no longer be considered as Jewish.

d. *The Rabbis*

Rabbis in the Register are usually labelled by *resh* ר. That this refers to rabbis is proved by the few cases of רבי (rabbi), for these sometimes refer to the same men (e.g. R. Mordecai, nos. 229, 230; R. Jeremiah, nos. 36, 187; R. Abishai, nos. 188, 189). Moreover, several are identifiable in the Hebrew-Persian colophons and there labelled רבי (rabbi).

Here is a table of all the rabbis mentioned in both Registers, together with the *Man-la*'s of the inscriptions;[1] and the rabbis of the colophons (fl. c. 1622-1626, most of whom are identifiable in the Register).

Table No. 15

The Rabbis

Surname	Rabbis in Men's Register	Rabbis with titles	Rabbis in Women's Register	Rabbis in Colophons	*Man-la's* in 1489 Inscription	*Man-la's* in 1663 Inscriptions (+ *Chang chiao*)
Li	20	7	2 (+3 or 4)	4	9	1 (+1)
Ai	22	1	2 or 3 (+2 or 3)	1	2	1
Kao	5	1		2		
Chao (+Yen)	5	1	(+1)		(1)	
Shih	3	1	1 (+1)			1
Chang	2				1	1
Chin	1		1			
(Chou)					(1)	
unknown			8 (distributed)	1		
Total	c.58	10	c.14	8	14	4 (+1)

[1] In my article "Some Notes on the Jewish Inscriptions of K'aifeng", *Journal of the American Oriental Society* 82 (1962), pp. 352-354, I queried the interpretation of *Man-la* 满剌 as *Mullah*, and also as referring to the rabbi. That *Man-la* was used by Moslems in China, presumably referring to the *Mullah*, is shown by the many examples in Tazaka Kōdō 田坂興道, 中國における回教の傳來とその弘通 (*Islam in China, its Introduction and Development*), Toyo Bunko, Tokyo, 1964, 2 vols., pp. 888, 900, 994-5, 997, 1003, 1079, 1115, 1151, 1233, 1255, 1345. I was probably also wrong in doubting its interpretation as rabbi. My table reinforces Löwenthal's view that the *Man-la*'s are the rabbis (or just possibly the rabbis with titles) in the Register.

Further to my footnote No. 4, in *Abr-Nahrain* V, 1964-65, p. 5: the name An (or Yen) Tu-la 俺都剌 does not appear ,I believe, in the above-mentioned book on the Moslems. Abd Allah (Abdullah) is invariably written as 阿都剌 A-tu-la. However it does appear several times in the Dynastic History of the Mongol Period (see 元史語彙集成, edited by Tamura Jitsuzō 田村實造, 1962, Kyoto, Vol. II, p. 1502).

Most of these rabbis can be placed fairly accurately on our family trees, or at least by generation.

Table No. 16

The Rabbis by Generations

Generation	Ai	Li	Others	Total
1st	1			1
2nd	3			3
3rd	1	1		2
4th	1	1		2
5th		2		2
6th	1	3		4
7th	2	2		4
8th	4	3	1	8
9th	4	3	3 (or 4)	10 (or 11)
10th	4		6 (or 5)	10 (or 9)
11th			1	1
unknown	1	5	5	11
Total	22	20	16	58

For the 8th to 10th generations, which clearly reflect the true situation most accurately, there were approximately 10 rabbis per generation out of a male population per generation of approximately 150). This is a large proportion. How were they appointed? We do not know whether any training or examination were required. The *Man-la*'s were designated, according to the 1489 inscription, because "they were well-versed in the Law and encouraged others to do good." Most rabbis of the Li and Ai clans were the sons of rabbis. I would suggest that only those with some further title (הספר, המלמד, השליח, הרפה) should be looked on as true rabbis. Here is a list of these. Many of them are among the "nine sires" of the Li Clan.

In the inscription of 1663, the *chang-chiao* Li Chen stands alone as Leader of the Religion. Gozani (White I, pp. 39, 41) calls the *chang-chiao* that he met in 1704 "Ruler of the Synagogue". His description leaves little doubt that this post is that of chief rabbi. I suspect that Li Chen was Rabbi Jeremiah, the scribe, the teacher, the envoy.

Brotier (White I, p. 54) writes of the "mullah" as assisting in the service "to prompt the monitor". This suggests that he was an honoured layman, or at most an assistant rabbi or minister. The only rabbis registered with Chinese names are Rabbi Chang Hao and Rabbi

List No. 10

Rabbis with Titles

Name	Clan	Title in Register	Title in Colophon	In Register, no.	In Colophon?	Generation
R. Moses	Li	The physician	—	192	no	3
R. Moses	Li	The physician	—	186	no	uncertain
R. Ezekiel	Li	The scribe	—	22	no	7
Rabbi Reuben	Li	The scribe	—	155	no	uncertain
Rabbi Elidad	Li	—	The scribe, the teacher, the envoy	190, 189	yes	6
Rabbi Abishai	Li	The teacher, the envoy	—	189, 188	yes	7
Rabbi Jacob	Li	The teacher, the envoy	(our Master)	188, 187	yes	8
Rabbi Shadai	Li	—	The envoy	187	yes	9
Rabbi Jeremiah	Li	The scribe, the teacher, the envoy	—	187, 36	no	9
Rabbi Akibah	Ai	—	(Shekhter?)	91, 12	yes	9
R. Ezra	Ai	The teacher	—	45, 46	no	2
Rabbi Mordecai	Kao	The scribe	(Leader of Prayer?)	230, 229	yes	9
Rabbi Jacob	Kao	—	(witness?)	226, 225	yes	9
R. Judah	Shih	The scribe	—	331	no	10
Rabbi Phinehas	unknown	—	The teacher	—	yes	uncertain

Chang K'un, both "sons of Israel". The former is possibly the *man-la* of the 1489 inscription. Identification of other *man-la's* in the 1489 inscription is highly speculative. Was Li Jung, fl. 1445-1465, (Li) R. Jehiah, fl. 1450-1500? Was Ai Ching, fl. 1461, (Ai) R. Samuel, fl. 1400-1500? Perhaps, but there is no evidence. There are only four *man-la*'s in the 1663 inscriptions, Li Ch'eng-hsien, Shih Tzu-chün, Chang Wen-jui, and Ai Ta-sheng. I suggest that Shih Tzu-chün is R. Judah, the scribe, (or possibly R. Joshua), with several brothers and cousins named Tzu-. Chang Wen-jui and (Li) Ch'eng-hsien both figure only in the Register of women, as sons.

Summary and Conclusions

Laufer's article on the Chinese-Hebrew manuscript utterly distorted its real nature. White corrected many of Laufer's errors, and also managed to relate the manuscript with the stone inscriptions and one of the Hebrew-Chinese Colophons. But, once we have realised that we are dealing with a book devoted entirely to the dead members of the community, many baffling features become clear, and we are in a position to advance a long way beyond White. My aim has been to give an accurate and detailed analysis of this Memorial Book of the dead, concentrating on reconstructing the family trees and producing significant and reliable statistics. The protracted analysis of relationships, within the clan and between the clans, enables us to establish approximate generation dates and to check the identification of individuals in the inscriptions, the Hebrew-Persian colophons, and the local gazetteers. It also strengthens the dates arrived at by means of these identifications. It also allows us to calculate the number of living members of the community from the number of dead.

Some points are still baffling (e.g. the significance of *chaf* כ daughters). I have not been able to avoid some mistakes and minor contradictions in the family trees and generations (notably for the Kao clan). The Hebrew names still need analysing (I have followed White unchanged); and so do the Hebrew prayers. A study of the actual manuscript in Cincinatti (rather than of a microfilm) may be helpful.

Some of the deductions and conclusions I have arrived at are not new. But it has been my primary aim to produce objective arguments, based on the extant manuscript and its statistics, for these independent arguments confirm, and occasionally discredit, the earlier descriptions (by eye witnesses in a few cases). Discussion becomes less speculative, in particular about the Jewish surnames, the rabbis, the size of the community, its isolation, and intermarriage (cf. in this last case the conflicting and often erroneous statements of the Jesuit descriptions of the community).

Errata to Parts I and II

Part I (*Abr-Nahrain* 4 (1963-4), pp. 19-49):

Several of the tables (and also charts and lists) need slight revision in the light of new discoveries and more accurate family trees. However, such revision is only of marginal importance.

P. 20, note 2: I hope to give later full details of the stone inscriptions. Descriptions, by Tobar and others, are confused. In spite of several opinions to the contrary, there seems little doubt that the extant stone with the 1489, 1512 inscriptions is identical to that seen by Gozani in 1704 and Gaubil in 1723. The 1663 inscriptions given by Tobar and by Ch'en Yüan are based on the rubbings of 1704 (or 1723?) held in the *Zi-ka-wei* library in Shanghai. It is doubtful if the 1663 stone was still extant in 1850.

P. 21 : For further details of Chao Ying-ch'eng and his biographies and many appearances in the Chinese local gazetteers and other sources, see Part III, Ie.

P. 21, note 6: There is a fourth gazetteer of Hsiang-fu of 1647 in Peking (not seen).

Pp. 27, 31 : For further details, see also Part III, Section H "Some Peculiarities of the Register".

P. 28 : The calligraphy and family trees both strengthen my view of pages 44-45 as being of the Li clan.

P. 28, note 13: The family trees reinforce the objections to duplicated Li, Chang families in the Register.

P. 29, note 14: For GMLYN GYM, see part III, section Ia.

P. 30 : For revised figures in the last column of Table No. 2, see Part III, footnote to p. 39.

P. 31, note 31: For the correct interpretation of *dz* דז, etc., see Part III, section H.

P. 32 : There were several other pairs of sisters (in Hebrew script); see Part III, section H.

P. 34 : I now think White's Shih? for p. 103 is better than my Chin?

P. 47 : For further examples of double wives and mothers, see Part III, section H.

Part II (*Abr-Nahrain* 5 (1964-5), pp. 1-27):

P. 2 : The term *Shaliaḥ* שליח is applied only to R. Shadai, R. Jeremiah (Li Chen?), their father R. Jacob (fl. 1622-1626), their grandfather R. Abishai, and great-grandfather R. Eldad. It seems most unlikely that "envoys" would be sent *from* the Chinese community. One would expect "envoys" from Persia, who would probably not be related. Brotier (White I, p. 62), quoting Domenge of 1722, writes: "It is more than a century since there came to them a Doctor from Hsi-yü, which is the west". The *Shaliaḥ* is far more likely to have been the "Leader of Prayer" or "Representative of the Community".

Pp. 13-15 : GMLYN GYM is Chao Liang-ching, the grandfather of Abram (Chao Kuang-yü). I suspect that he is also Ezekiel. See also Part III, section Ie.

Pp. 16-19 : Kao clan trees and generations are not reliable. I now put (Kao) Tung- as 9th generation, not 8th. (Kao) Zebulun may perhaps be the father of Kao Yin. A further tree is given in Part III, Section If.

A Select Bibliography

The two bibliographies by Löwenthal give several hundred works. Basic are:

1a. Ch'en Yüan 陳垣, "K'ai-feng Yi-tz'u-lo-yeh Chiao" 開封一賜樂業教 (Judaism in K'aifeng), *Tung-fang Tsa-chih* 東方雜誌 17 (1920), 5, pp. 117-122, 6, pp. 119-126, 7, pp. 103-107.

1b. Ch'en Yüan, *K'ai-feng Yi-tz'u-lo-yeh Chi-o K'ao* 開封一賜樂業教考 (A Study of Judaism in K'aifeng), in the Yüan-an Tsui-chin Ts'ung-k'o 圓菴最近叢刻.

1c. Ch'en Yüan, *K'ai-feng Yi-tz'u-lo-yeh Chiao K'ao* (as above) (A Study of Judaism in K'aifeng) (*Islamism in K'aifeng*) (sic), Tung-fang Wen-k'u 東方文庫 no. 72, Commercial Press, Shanghai, 1923, 69 pages.

This 1923 booklet replaces the 1920 article, and also the undated version in the *Ts'ung-shu*. It has slight, but significant differences from these earlier versions. It includes a punctuated text of the stone inscriptions (except that of 1679), and also of the Archway, horizontal and vertical inscriptions from the synagogue. Though he had not seen the Chinese-Hebrew Manuscript, this is a basic study.

It includes, as an appendix, pp. 65-69, an inferior article by Yeh Han 葉瀚, "Yi-tz'u-lo-yeh Chiao P'ei-pa" 一賜樂叢教碑跋 (Postscript to the Jewish Stone

Inscriptions), also originally published in the *Tung-fang Tsa-chih* 東方雜誌.
2. (Bishop) William Charles White, *Chinese Jews*, University of Toronto, 1942, in 3 parts.

Part I "Historical", xxi + 211 pages. Includes the reports of visitors to the community.

Part II "Inscriptional", xiii + 184 pages. Text and translation of all the inscriptions.

Part III "Genealogical", xiii + 226 pages. Includes a translation of the Chinese-Hebrew Memorial Book.

An indispensable work, but full of mistakes.

3. Jérôme Tobar, S. J., *Inscriptions juives de K'ai-fong-fou*, Variétés Sinologiques No. 17, Shanghai, 1900 (1912 unchanged), vi + 112 pages.

Text, plus good French translation, of all the inscriptions (except the 1679 one).

4a. Rudolf Löwenthal, "The Jews in China: An Annotated Bibliography", *The Chinese Social and Political Science Review* XXIV, no. 2 (1940), pp. 113-234. (Revised from *The Yenching Journal of Social Studies* I (1939), pp. 256-291).

4b. Rudolf Löwenthal, "The Early Jews in China: A Supplementary Bibliography", *Folklore Studies* V (1946), pp. 353-398.

These provide a storehouse of valuable information on Chinese Jews and research on them. However, they also include a lot of material of doubtful interest, and do not distinguish adequately the wheat from the chaff. They give Ricci's accounts of the Jew Ai, in Italian (1940, pp. 215-222), and in English (1946, pp. 393-398).

5. (Bishop) George Smith (edit.), *The Jews at K'ae-fung-foo: Being a Narrative of a Mission of Enquiry to the Jewish Synagogue at K'ae-fung-foo, on behalf of the London Society for promoting Christianity among the Jews*, London Missionary Society's Press, Shanghai, 1851, xii + 83 pages.

Largely reproduced by White I, pp. 97-133; and also in part by Wells Williams in the *Chinese Repository* XX (1851), pp. 436-462. There are four parts:

"Introduction" by George Smith (pp. iii-xii);
"Journal of K'hew T'heen-sang to K'hae-fung-foo" (pp. 1-36);
"Journal of Tseang Yung-che from Shanghae to Ts'hing-keang-p'hoo; With Notices of Antiquities met with on the way" (pp. 37-49);
"Tseang Yung-che's Account of the 挑筋教 T'heaou-kin-keaou, or the religion which enjoins the extracting of the sinew" (pp. 50-82).

The first Journal was written in English. The second Journal and Account were translated from the Chinese. Only the less important Journal of the original description in Chinese is held by Cambridge University Library. The fourth part of the text of Smith includes copies and translations of some of the short inscriptions from the synagogue; and also inferior texts, and translations (by J. Edkins?), of the 1489 and 1512 inscriptions. The two Chinese delegates visited K'aifeng again in 1851, and brought back several valuable documents. A description "The K'ae-Fung-Foo Manuscripts" was given in the *North-China Herald*, Shanghai, no. 55, of August 16, 1851; this is quoted in the *Chinese Repository* (loc. sit.), pp. 462-466.

6. Matteo Ricci, S. J., *Opere storiche del P. Matteo Ricci S.I.*, edit. Pietro Tacchi-Venturi, S. J., Macerata, 1911-1913, 2 vols. Vol. I, pp. 468-473, and Vol. II,

pp. 290-293, both describe the visit of the Jew Ai. The latter is a letter from Ricci to Rome, dated July 26, 1605.

The story of Father Ricci and the Jew Ai, first published in 1620, has been translated into many languages. White I, pp. 31-37, quotes A. C. Moule, *Christians in China before the Year 1550*, N.Y., 1930. I have used Löwenthal's English translation (*Folklore Studies* V, 1946, pp. 393-398), which gives both versions of the story. Cf. also *Fonti Ricciane*, edited by Pasquale M. D'Elia, Rome, 1942, vol. II, pp. 314-325.

7. Jean-Paul Gozani, S. J., "Lettre du Père J. P. Gozani au Père Joseph Suarez, traduite du Portugais", *Lettres édifiantes et curieuses*, Paris, (1st edition), vol. VII (1707), pp. 1-28.

Besides other editions of the *Lettres*, there are translations into other languages. Zi, pp. 17-24 (and cf. 25-28) translates most of the letter into Chinese. White I, pp. 39-46, gives the English translation by John Lockman, *Travels of the Jesuits*, London, 1762, vol. II, pp. 11-22. Dated 5 November 1704, this letter is the first record of a visit to the community.

8. Gabriel Brotier, "Mémoire sur les Juifs établis en Chine", *Lettres édifiantes et curieuses*, (1st edition), vol. XXXI (1774), pp. 296-372.

Zi, pp. 28-47, gives most of it in Chinese; and White I, pp. 49-68, most of it in English.

Based on the letters of Gozani, Domenge and Gaubil, who visited the synagogue in 1701 and 1704, 1722, and 1723, respectively, this was written about 1770. Equally valuable with Gozani's letter. It was the basic western source on the K'aifeng Jews until Tobar's translations of the inscriptions appeared.

9. Ignaz Koegler, S. J., "Notitiae SS Bibliorum Judaeorum in Imperio Sinensi" *Journal zur Kunstgeschichte und allgemeinen Litteratur* 7 (1779), pp. 240-252, 9 (1780), pp. 81-92.

Also found in a book edited by C. von Murr, 1805, Halle; and again in C. von Murr, *Versuch einer Geschichte der Juden in China*, 1806, Halle. (Not seen).

10. Hsü Tsung-tse 徐宗澤 (Joseph Zi, S.J.), *Chung-kuo T'ien-chu-chiao ch'uan chiao shih kai-lun* 中國天主教傳教史概論 (Outline of the History of Catholic Missions in China), Sheng-chiao tsa-chih she 聖教雜誌社 (Société de la Revue catholique), Shanghai, 1938. Chapter 1, pp. 1-63, is "K'ai-feng Yu-t'ai-chiao" 開封猶太教 (Judaism in K'aifeng).

Reproduces the inscriptions of 1489, 1512, and 1663; and also (pp. 17-47) an article by Shen Kung-pu 沈公布 from 1931-1932 which translates most of Gozani and Brotier into Chinese.

11. James Finn, *The Orphan Colony of Jews in China*, James Nisbet, London, 1872, iv + 124 pages.

Includes the translation by M. C. Morrison of the letter sent by the K'aifeng community to T. H. Layton in 1850. The letter itself was received by James Finn in 1870. White I, pp. 71-94, includes this translation.

James Finn's earlier work, *The Jews in China*, B. Wertheim, London, 1843, viii + 86 pages, gives a summary of early western knowledge of the K'aifeng Jews. Much of this book is reproduced in the *Chinese Repository* XIV, 1845, pp. 305-334, 388-395.

12. Paul Pelliot, "Le Juif Ngai, Informateur du P. Mathieu Ricci", *T'oung Pao* 20 (1920-21), pp. 32-39.

A Chinese translation by Feng Ch'eng-chün 馮承鈞 is in *T'u-shu Chi-k'an* 圖書季刊, n.s., vol. 7, no. 3/4 (1946), pp. 63-68. White gives much of it in English, III, pp. 16-19. One of the first attempts to identify a Chinese Jew in the local gazetteers.

13. Berthold Laufer, "A Chinese-Hebrew Manuscript, a New Source for the History of the Chinese Jews", *The American Journal of Semitic Languages and Literature* XLVI, no. 3 (1930), pp. 189-197; reprinted in *Folklore Studies* IV (1945), pp. 319-326; and also reproduced by White III, pp. 6-15.

A. C. Moule has reviewed this in *T'oung Pao* 28 (1931), pp. 125-128 (mostly in White III, pp. 20-21). Laufer's work is stimulating but not reliable.

14. Kaufmann Kohler and Henri Cordier, "China", *The Jewish Encyclopedia*, 1904 (1916), Vol. IV, pp. 33-38.

Sinologically inferior, but useful for the Jewish views.

15. A. Neubauer, "Jews in China", *The Jewish Quarterly Review* VIII (1895-6), pp. 123-139.

Discusses the Hebrew manuscripts brought from K'aifeng in 1851. The first to realise that the Register was used for the Memorial of the Dead.

16. Elkan N. Adler "The Persian Jews: Their Books and their Ritual", *The Jewish Quarterly Review* X, (1898), pp. 584-625.

Pp. 624-625 deal with the Hebrew manuscripts from K'aifeng.

17. R. Löwenthal, "The Nomenclature of Jews in China", *Monumenta Serica* 12 (1947), pp. 97-126.

18. D. Leslie, "Some Notes on the Jewish Inscriptions of K'aifeng", *Journal of the American Oriental Society* 82 (1962), pp. 346-361.

Underestimates the Moslem connections.

19. Ch'en Tseng-hui 陳增輝, "Kuan-yü Li Ma-tou chi-chung chih Yu-t'ai-jen Ai Shih" 關於利瑪竇集中之猶太人艾氏 ("On the Chinese Jew Ai in Matteo Ricci's *Opera Storiche*"), *Hsieh-ta Hsüeh-pao* 協大學報 1 (1949), pp. 171-180.

This gives the first proof of Pelliot's claim that the Jew Ai was Ai T'ien 艾田.

20. Ch'en Tseng-hui 陳增輝, *Yu-t'ai-jen hua-hua k'ao* 猶太人華化考 (The assimilation of the Chinese Jews), unpublished M.A. thesis, Yenching University, Peiping, 1946. (Not seen).

21. (Rev.) Fang Hao 方豪, *Fang Hao Wen Lu* 方豪文錄 (*Studies in the History of the Relations between China and the West*), 1948, 346 pages. No. 28, pp. 277-280, is entitled "Ch'ing ch'u Yi-yü Yün-nan chih Yu-t'ai-jen" 清初宦遊雲南之猶太人 ("A Jew serving as official in Yunnan at the beginning of the Ch'ing dynasty").

This was first published in 1939 in 益世報:宗教與文化 (*Yi-shih-pao*; Religion and Culture), n.s., no. 6. Then revised in Fang Hao's book *Chung-wai wen-hua chiao-t'ung shih lun-ts'ung* 中外文化交通史論叢 (Essays in the History of Cultural Relations between China and Foreign Countries), Chungking, 1944, pp. 113-119. And then again in 1948.

22. Fang Chaoying, "Notes on the Chinese Jews of Kaifeng", *Journal of the American Oriental Society* 85 (1965), pp. 126-129.

A brilliant identification of Chao Ch'eng 趙誠.

ASHURBANIPAL AND SHAMASH-SHUM-UKIN DURING ESARHADDON'S REIGN

BY

SAMI AHMED

It is known that Esarhaddon (680-669 B.C.), father of Shamash-shum-ukin (died in 648 B.C.) and Ashurbanipal (died about 630 B.C.), had experienced some difficulty ascending the throne after the murder of his father, Sennacherib (680 B.C.) and, had it not been for the support of the Assyrian people and of the army, as he claimed, he might well have failed.[1] Obviously Esarhaddon did not wish to see his heir have the same difficulty, for such conflicts might turn Assyria into a battleground or lead to outside intervention. Accordingly, he hoped to settle the matter by appointing as crown prince the son he had chosen to rule Assyria. There was, however, an obstacle to this course of action: a clause in his treaty with Ramataia, king of Urukazabarna, of 672 B.C. which reads: "(you swear) that if Esarhaddon king of Assyria died during the minority of his sons" clearly specifies that his sons were still under age.[2]

Furthermore, he may have suspected that several factions, given the opportunity, would dispute the right of his successor to the throne. The same treaty may offer some clue to the identity of these groups:

> (you swear) that should one of his brothers; his uncles, his cousins, his family (or) one of his father's descendants, (or) any descendants of the former royalty (or) one of the chiefs (or) one of the governors, (or) one of the citizens of Assyria, or any foreigner . . . [3]

The fact that "his brothers" and "his uncles" head the list could imply either that the Assyrian monarch had granted his brothers, whom he fought at the beginning of his reign, mercy, or that, even if they had not been pardoned and did not reside in Assyria, they or their sons were still in a position to instigate trouble. Descendants of a former royal family were another possible threat since the present royalty had acquired the throne through Sargon II's usurpation. Esarhaddon's destruction of Tiglath-pileser III's remains may indicate that members of the latter's family were still quite popular and in a position to dispute the right of his house to kingship.[4]

In order to solve all these problems, it seems that Esarhaddon appointed his eldest son, Sin-apla-iddina, to be the crown prince of Assyria. A prayer of Esarhaddon concerning such installation exists and may be taken as evidence for such appointment.[5] It has been suggested that Esarhaddon had then nominated Shamash-shum-ukin for the crown princehood of Babylonia and that when Sin-apla-iddina died, Esarhaddon replaced him by Ashurbanipal.[6] The succession was settled by nominating the younger son, Ashurbanipal, to the Assyrian throne and the eldest son, then living, to the kingship of Babylonia.

The seniority of Shamash-shum-ukin to Ashurbanipal is well attested. A letter sent by a certain Adad-shum-usur to Esarhaddon makes this seniority quite clear.[7] In a *kudurru*, Shamash-shum-ukin, referred to himself as *māru ašaridu ša Aššur-aḫu-iddina.*[8] A clause in the treaty with Ramataia states: "you will not oust him . . . by helping one of his brothers, older or younger, to seize the throne." The "older" here could refer to none other than Shamash-shum-ukin.[9]

The twelfth of Ayyāru, 672 B.C., was selected for the oath-taking ceremonies, and a great celebration was held in which foreign ambassadors of countries subject to Assyria were also present.[10] After his appointment, Ashurbanipal entered the administration house (*bît ridūti*), and assumed his responsibilities as crown prince of Assyria. He was then already married, and in all probability he had at least one son. A letter from Ashur-bani-pal's sister, Sherua-eterat, to his own consort, Ashur-sharrat, dated to the time of Ashur-bani-pal's crown princehood, offers proof that he was married during the lifetime of his father.[11] The treaty with Ramataia refers to the pregnancy of Ashur-bani-pal's wife at that time.[12] A letter sent to Ashur-bani-pal from Adad-shum-uṣur and Marduk-shakin-shum early in his reign includes the phrase, "in regard to the son of this king, our lord" implying that by the early part of his reign, Ashur-bani-pal had a son.[13] Another letter from Adad-shum-uṣur to Ashur-bani-pal dated also to the beginning of his reign records: "for the life of the king my lord and the sons of the king", which testifies that the Assyrian king by then had even more than one son.[14] A document dated ten years after the death of Ashurbanipal's father mentions a certain Luqu as the *rāb kiṣir* of the king's son.[15] In another document dated to the year 660 B.C. one of the witnesses bears the title *mukin apāti.*[16] These two documents as well as others indicate that by this time Ashur-banipal had a son who was old enough to have a *rāb kiṣir* who could be appointed as crown prince.[17]

The reasons which may have led Esarhaddon to appoint a younger son as crown prince of Assyria and an elder son for Babylonia warrant some discussion. As was to be expected, Ashurbanipal declared that his selection was made by the order of the gods:

> Esarhaddon, king of Assyria, the father who begot me, respected the word of Ashur and Belit-ilê, his divinities, when they gave the command that I should exercise sovereignty." [18]

He further affirms that the gods had confirmed a kingly destiny upon him while he was still in his mother's womb.[19] In these assertions he was merely following precedent, for almost every monarch of the ancient Near East claimed that he had been called to kingship by the gods of the land.

Ashurbanipal also claimed, perhaps justifiably, that Esarhaddon had favoured and admired him for his bravery and intelligence:

> "The father, my begetter, saw for himself the bravery which the great gods decreed as my (portion). At the command of the great gods, he conceived a great love for me among (lit., in the assembly of) my many(?) brothers." [20]

Here too, however, he again attributed what he claimed to be his father's feelings, to the benevolence of the gods.

There is, nevertheless, convincing evidence that Ashurbanipal was in truth a favorite, and officials surrounding Esarhaddon apparently noticed this partiality. In some of the letters sent to Esarhaddon prior to Ashurbanipal's appointment, the correspondents accord preference to Ashurbanipal, which is probably a mere reflection of their master's sentiment.[21] One text makes reference to a statue having been made of Ashurbanipal, the crown prince, but there is no indication that any such statue was made of Shamash-shum-ukin.[22] Yet Esarhaddon's apparent real affection for this particular son was scarcely a sufficient basis for bequeathing to him the throne of Assyria. The major reason may well have been the status or perhaps the place of origin of their respective mothers, his wives. Although the name of Ashurbanipal's mother is still unknown, it may be assumed that she was of Assyrian origin. It is certain, however, that Shamash-shum-ukin was the son of a non-Assyrian wife from Babylonia.[23] Esarhaddon no doubt realized that to name as his successor in Assyria one whose mother was from the very heart of Babylonia could have serious consequences. Ashurbanipal, as the next eldest candidate among the other sons, was therefore the most logical choice as king of Assyria. On the other hand, Shamash-shum-ukin's appointment to the throne of Babylon was no doubt a move to appease the Babylonians, and Esarhaddon must have believed that they would be quite content to have Shamash-shum-ukin as their own monarch. Viewed in this light, Esarhaddon no doubt foresaw a unified Mesopotamia in the respective appointments of Ashurbanipal and Shamash-shum-ukin.

From available evidence, much can be surmised about Esarhaddon's will in regard to the succession. The treaty with Ramatia states:

> Lines 237-41: If Esarhaddon, king of Assyria dies during the minority of his sons (and) either an officer or a courtier put Ashurbanipal the crown prince to death and take over the kingship of Assyria . . .
>
> Lines 246-48: you will seize him and put him to death and you will then cause a son of Ashurbanipal of the succession house to be established on the throne of Assyria . . .

It is noteworthy that the name of Shamash-shum-ukin, who supposedly was to be Ashurbanipal's partner-brother in Babylonia, does not occur. This surely signifies that the line of kingship for the entire Assyrian empire was to be preserved through Ashurbanipal's own descendants.

While the treaty specifies the help Ramataia should render to Shamash-sham-ukin as well as to Ashurbanipal, and to the latter's heir in case of Ashurbanipal's death, it says nothing about help to be given to an heir of Shamash-shum-ukin in the event of his death. This omission may perhaps be explained by a prayer of Shamash-shum-ukin to Shamash during his later war with Assyria: "to him who is not worthy, you gave a male heir." [24] This statement may permit us to conclude that, in accordance with Esarhaddon's desire, if Shamash-shum-ukin died without male children, Ashurbanipal was to have the right to choose the next ruler of Babylon. Also, since Ashurbanipal had named a son as crown prince of Assyria prior to Shamash-shum-ukin's revolt, it may have been willed that, in the event of Ashurbanipal's death during the lifetime of his brother, the latter would be required to give his oath of allegiance to Ashurbanipal's son and successor.

It was probably Esarhaddon's desire also that, in the event of his death, Shamash-shum-ukin would ascend the throne of Babylonia at the following New Year festival, at which time he would grasp the hands of Marduk at Ashur and then accompany the image to Babylon.

In the treaty with Ramataia, Esarhaddon ordered his vassal not to hold back any of the gifts that the heir to the Babylonian crown and his other brothers had received, which were presents of land, orchards, houses and cattle.[25] It is to be assumed that a similar clause with respect to Ashurbanipal appeared in the will of succession.

Clauses in the same treaty also make it clear that Esarhaddon intended Ashurbanipal to rule over all Assyria, and that Shamash-shum-ukin's unquestioned domain should include not only Babylon and its surroundings but the entire south.[26] There is, however, no clause to the effect that the vassals should interfere in case of rebellion on the part of Shamash-shum-ukin against his brother. The exclusion of such a clause may indicate Esarhaddon's belief that the king of Assyria would be able to crush such a revolt if it occurred. It may also suggest that he conceived of Shamash-shum-ukin as merely a vassal and, as such, any such "revolt" would be a purely internal affair.

It is likewise clear that Esarhaddon's will in dealing with the succession required the Assyrian officials and citizens to swear to a single oath: namely to recognise Ashurbanipal as king of the entire empire. The oath of allegiance, as set forth by Zakuti, Esarhaddon's mother, immediately after the death of her son, doubtless was in accordance with the same will. Since Shamash-shum-ukin had sworn by the oath, we may presume that the oath was in agreement with his father's wishes.

In a prayer to the god Shamash, Shamash-shum-ukin asserts that Ashurbanipal had agreed not to challenge his authority in the area assigned to him, or to interfere in his affairs.[27] This suggests that the will of succession specified that Ashurbanipal was to treat his partner-brother as an equal.

Ashurbanipal claimed to have been trained in the art of kingship and taught the rules of government. He boasted in his annals that he stood before the king, his father and gave commands to the nobles of the land, and no governor was appointed nor prefect was installed in his absence.[28] There is no evidence, however, to indicate that these boastful claims were not entirely false.

In a letter sent to Ashurbanipal while he was crown prince by one Ibašši-ilu, the sender complains of the behaviour of Ashur-nad-kili, the captain of the city of Adidni.[29] Another sent by Marduk-shakin-shum to Esarhaddon, tells us that certain magical ceremonies were to be performed first by the king, then by the crown prince, and thirdly by the populace; there is no reference to Shamash-shum-ukin or to any of his brothers.[30] Shapea, who was apparently a supervisor over work undertaken in the city of Tarbisu, wrote to the crown prince, Ashurbanipal complaining about the behaviour of the workers and their supervisors, and gave an account of the work; he then asked his master's permission to transfer to Calah.[31] Adad-shum-usur, who no doubt held an important position during this period, records in a letter to Ashurbanipal, then crown prince, that he had constantly appealed to him.[32] Such letters provide adequate proof that Ashurbanipal, who still was crown prince, enjoyed wide authority, and that the supervision over state building activities was in his charge. Thus, Ashurbanipal's claims, as recorded in his annals, were not mere boasts, although they may have been exaggerated. When we find him inquiring of the god Shamash regarding the Cimmerians etc., we may with justice conclude that the crown prince had been given responsibilities concerning some aspects of international aflairs.[33]

While Ashurbanipal was enjoying this supreme status as prince *par excellence*, Shamash-shum-ukin was scarcely mentioned. Even in the salutation formulas of letters to Esarhaddon, his name usually appears only after that of his "superior" younger brother. Only three letters have been preserved which were sent by Shamash-shum-ukin to his father, very likely during the period of his crown princehood over Babylonia. Two of them unfortunately, are so mutilated that they reveal nothing; the third deals with the receipt of a few insignificant items from a certain Nabu-binaḫe.[34] There is one letter preserved that had been sent to Esarhaddon by Ashurbanipal during the time of his crown princehood.[35] Other letters are preserved but this particular one seems to be the only example which could be attributed to this period. It is a letter from Ashurbanipal to his father in answer to an order given by the king to him to question a certain citizen. Another letter refers to the authority Esarhaddon had placed in the hands of Ashurbanipal.[36]

All this correspondence reveals something of the responsibilities Ashurbanipal bore while he was still crown prince. During this period he was still young and undergoing training; it was therefore to be expected that he would carry on a good deal of correspondence with his father, report information received concerning affairs of the empire and matters of administration, and seek his father's advice and consultation.

Perhaps it is only because of the lack of recovery that there is so little correspondence during this period between Ashurbanipal and Shamash-shum-ukin; since, however, there is also such a small amount from the time of their joint kingship, the absence of such correspondence may be significant. Shamash-shum-ukin may have been so acutely aware of his brother's attitudes that, during his father's lifetime, he had no desire to humilate himself by contacting the proud, arrogant younger brother who had been assigned a better position than himself.

In summary, there is no direct evidence concerning relationship existing between Ashurbanipal and Shamash-shum-ukin during the period following the designation to their respective positions. Speculation, however, may enable us to conclude that is was not as good as it should have been. Ashurbanipal, as we have seen, obviously considered himself the central figure of power and authority, and boasted of his father's favoritism which he "modestly" attributed to the bravery and intelligence which the gods had bestowed upon him. This is merely another way of saying that he was braver and more intelligent than his brothers, and may imply that jealousy and competition existed among them all and was especially strong between Ashurbanipal and Shamash-shum-ukin.

Adad-shum-uṣur, apparently aware of the strained atmosphere, was not in favor of Esarhaddon's decision about their future posts. However, he reports that he had constantly appealed to Ashurbanipal when he was crown prince, thus implying that he respected Ashurbanipal's judgment and was rather attached to him [37]. This could not be the mere flattery of a courtier, for Ashurbanipal would have known whether or not he had appealed to him before. But in a letter to Esarhaddon, Adad-shum-uṣur declares forthrightly:

> ... What the king my lord has done with the young kings is no kindness to the land of Assyria.[38]

This is surely indicative of the tension which had developed between the two brothers, which must have been apparent to many, among whom Adad-shum-uṣur was courageous enough to face his lord with the bitter fact. Evidently he foresaw that the growing friction between the younger princes would eventually lead to disaster. Such a frank declaration to the king would naturally reach, and certainly would displease Ashurbanipal, and therefore Adad-shum-uṣur apparently fell from his favor. The last assumption is drawn from a message from the courtier addressed to Ashurbanipal, doubtless after his accession to the throne, in which he complained of being disliked by the king who had not invited his son, Arad-Gula, to stand with the sons of other nobles who had been invited in the palace. In the same letter he makes it clear that he is not liked by the palace officials.[39] In another letter he writes to the king begging for an audience with his overlord.[40] Consequently, it seems apparent that Ashurbanipal had acquired knowledge of Adad-shum-uṣur's message to his father, and that the nobleman had become unpopular with the Assyrian king. The monarch's sentiments would certainly have been obvious to all other palace officials who usually followed their master's precedent in such matters.

Certain other texts which have been the subject of controversy among scholars doubtless fall into the late years of Esarhaddon's reign and the early years of Ashurbanipal's. Among these are several letters referring to the *šar pūḫi*, or "substitute king"; it has been argued that these texts refer to a single occasion prior to the naming of Ashurbanipal as crown prince.[41]

We find Adad-shum-uṣur(?) requesting Esarhaddon to allow the substitute king, *šar pūḫi ša šarri*, to complete his regular term of 100 days, because an occurrence of an eclipse of the sun is still to be expected.[42] Another letter, probably sent by Adad-shum-uṣur and Marduk-shakin-shum, refers to the *šar pūḫi* in a communication to the "cultivator." [43] Akkullanu tells Esarhaddon that the image of the substitute king was coming, probably from Babylon, but that it stayed in Akkad for about twenty days.[44] In another letter to the same king, referring to the "crown prince" and to Shamash-shum-ukin without any title, the sender reports that he caused Adad-shum-uṣur to swear in the city of Akkad by the great gods of the kings that during the term of 100 days he would report whatever he noticed. He stated in the letter also that the *šar pūḫi* went to his fate.[45]

The arrival of the *šar pūḫi* on the 14th. of the month was reported to Esarhaddon by Mar-ishtar, who adds that on the 15th, when an eclipse took place, he was already in the palace.[46] An ornamentation for an image which had been made for the *šar pūḫi* is subject matter of a letter sent to Esarhaddon by Adad-shum-usur.[47]

One detailed text which sheds more light on the problem is a letter to Ashurbanipal from Mar-ishtar, doubtless dated to the early years of the monarch. An unfavourable eclipse was approaching and the people of Akkad in particular were fearful. A certain Damqi was to be appointed as a *šar pūḫi*, presumably for Shamash-shum-ukin who was then the king of Babylon. A mausoleum had been prepared, the body had been wept over, and the lamentations were properly done; the letter also proves that Damqi and his consort died in all probability, by a natural death. The phrase used in the text referring to their death is *ana simti it-ta-lak*, which could mean either that they died a natural death or that they were put to death.[48]

Two of the letters refer to the making of an image which could be used as a substitute for the king; the phrase could hardly in these instances refer to an actual substitution of the king. Other letters, however, clearly suggest the practice of having such a substitute king late in the reign of Esarhaddon and in the early part of Ashurbanipal's rule. The association of the installation of a substitute with an eclipse, which could be interpreted as an ill omen for the king, is clear throughout, but the several occurrences cannot all refer to a single occasion.[49]

In 669 B.C. Esarhaddon died while on his way to Egypt and Ashurbanipal was immediately declared the king of Assyria. In the New Year festival of 668 he started his first year while his brother Shamash-shum-ukin took the hands of Marduk and was declared the king of Babylonia.

NOTES

[1] Campbell Thompson, *A Prism of Esarhaddon and Ashurbanipal* (London, 1931) I, Col. 1, 47-52, 80; 70-73.

[2] D. J. Wiseman, "The Vassal Treaties of Esarhaddon" Iraq, XX. (1958), part I, 1.237.

[3] *Ibid.* 1s. 318-322.

[4] A. S. Anspacher, *Tiglath-pileser* III, (New York, 1912), p. 9.

[5] Knudtzon, *Assyrische Gebete an den Sonnengott* (Leipzig, 1893), prayer No. 107.

[6] H. Lewy, "Nitokris-Naqia", JNES, XI, (1952), pp. 264-286.

[7] R. F. Harper, *Assyrian and Babylonian Letters belonging to the Kouyunjik Collection of the British Museum*, part I-XIV, (Chicago, 1892-1914)., no. 870, obv. 1. p. 10-11.

[8] L. W. King, *Babylonian Boundary Stones and Memorial Tablets in the British Museum*. (London, 1912), p. 70, obv. 1.9.

[9] D. Wiseman, *op. cit.* ls. 69-70. See also B. Meissner, "Šamaššumukin und Ashurbanipal", MVAG, IX, (Berlin, 1904), pp. 181-84. A. H. Godbey, "The Esarhaddon Succession", AJSL, 22, (1905), p. 65.

[10] D. D. Luckenbill, *Ancient Records of Assyria and Babylonia* (Chicago, 1926), II, 766; M. Streck, *Assurbanipal und die Letzten Assyrischen Könige bis zum Untergang Nineveh's* (Leipzig, 1916), 1, p. 2; Luckenbill, *op. cit*,. II, 987; Streck, *op. cit.*, pp. 258 ff.

[11] Harper, *op. cit.* no. 308.

[12] Wiseman, *op. cit.* ls. 249-250.

[13] Harper, *op. cit.* no. 14, obv. 1.6.

[14] *Ibid.*, 9, rev. ls. 6-7.

[15] J. H. Stevenson, *Assyrian and Babylonian Contracts with Aramaic Reference Notes*, (New York, 1901), no. 7, pp. 6-7.

[16]. C. H. W. Johns, *Assyrian Deeds and Documents*, (London, 1898-1923), III, nos. 444 & 445.

[17] *Ibid.* no. 440.

[18] Luckenbill, *op. cit.*, II, 766; Streck, *op. cit.* II, p. 2.

[19] Luckenbill, *op. cit.* II, 986; Streck, *op. cit.* II, p. 254.

[20] *Ibid.*

[21] Harper, *op. cit.* no. 453, R. H. Pfeiffer, *State Letters of Assyria*, American Oriental Series, 6 (Baltimore, 1935), no. 258.

[22] C. Bezold, *Historische Keilinschrifttexte aus Assur*, (Sitzungberichte der Heidelberger Akademie der Wissenschaften, Jahrgang 1915, 8 abhandlung) text no. 75.

[23] Streck, *op. cit.* 1, p. CCXXVI, no. 2. Lehman C. F. *Šamaššumukin König von Babylonien* 668-648 V. Chr. (Leipzig, 1892), Zweiter Teil, p. 6, ls. 4-6.

[24] D. Prince, "A New Shamash-shum-ukin Series", AJSL, (1914-15) pp. 256-70, no. 12, 1.12.

[25] Wiseman, *op. cit.* lns. 89-01; and 275-278.

[26] *Ibid.*, lns. 84-89.

[27] D. Myhrmann, *Babylonian Hymns and Prayers*, 1. No. 1, (Philadelphia, 1911), no. XVII; Prince, *op. cit.* no. XVII.

[28] Luckenbill, *op. cit.* II, 986; Streck, *op. cit.* II, p. 254.

[29] Harper, *op. cit.* no. 500; Pfeiffer, *op. cit.* no. 173.

[30] Harper, *op. cit.*, no. 18.

[31] *Ibid.*, no. 885; Pfeiffer, *op. cit.*, no. 179.

[32] Harper, *op. cit.* no. 10.

[33] E. G. Klauber, *Politische-Religiöse Texte aus der Sargonid* Zeit, (Leipzig, 1913), no. 44; Olmstead A. T., *History of Assyria*, (Chicago, 1923) Harper, *op. cit.*, nos. 65, 187, 189, 430, 445 etc.

[34] Harper, *op. cit.* no. 535 and 536.

[35] *Ibid.*, no. 1026.

[36] *Ibid.*, no. 434. Pfeiffer, *op. cit.*, no. 15.

[37] *Ibid.*, no. 10.

[38] *Ibid.*, no. 870; Pfeiffer, *op. cit.*, no. 151.

[39] *Ibid.*, no. 2 Pfeiffer, *op. cit.*, no. 160.

[40] *Ibid.*, no. 659.

[41] W. Von Soden, "Bemerkungen zu den von Ebeling in "Tod und Leben", Band 1, ZA, 43, (1936), pp. 256-276; R. Labat, RA, 40, (1945), pp. 127 ff.; Thureau-Dangin, *Ritual Accadiens*, (Paris, 1921), pp. 37 ff.

[42] Harper, *op. cit.* no. 359, Pfeiffer, *op. cit.* no. 313.

[43] Harper, *op. cit.*, no. 362.

[44] *Ibid.*, no. 46.

[45] *Ibid.*, no. 594, Pfeiffer, *op. cit.* no. 338.

[46] Harper, *op. cit.*, no. 629, Pfeiffer, *op. cit.*, no. 323.

[47] Harper, *op. cit.*, no. 653.

[48] *Ibid.*, no. 437. For Mar-Ishtar's time and activities cf. W. Von Soden, *Festschrift Viktor Christian* (Vienna, 1956) pp. 103-104 and B. Landsberger, *Brief des Bischofs von Esagila an König Esarhaddon* (The Netherlands, 1965) pp. 45-49.

[49] See A. Schott and J. Schaumberger, "Vier Briefe Mar-Ishtar an Esarhaddon uber Himmelserscheinungen der Jahr 670-668", ZA, XLVII, (1943), pp. 89-103. cf. E. Ebeling, *Leben und Tod nach den Vorstellungen der Babylonier* (Berlin, 1931), pp. 65 ff. Also R. Labat,"Le Sort des Substituts Royaux en Assyrie au Temps des Sargonids", RA, 41, (1945-46), pp. 123-42.

RAWSHANĪYYA MOVEMENT

BY

S. A. A. RIZVI

Rawshanīyya or Rawshānī movement which started as a pantheistic Sufic movement among the restless Afghān tribes, known as Pakhtūns in the modern political jargon and inhabiting the areas lying in between the political Durand Line and river Indus, subsequently took a militant form and assumed the role of a movement for the liberation of Afghān tribes against the rule of the Mughals even under its founder, Bāyazīd Rawshanā'ī. It gained adherents in the sixteenth and seventeenth centuries on account of religious as also for political reasons. Due to fulminations of the orthodox Sunnīs that thundered against them and the Mughal forces seeking to extend their control over the plains and passages through the mountains leading to Kābul, they were never able to lead a peaceful life but the trials and tribulations only sharpened their power of resistance. Bāyazīd united tribal sentiments in a surge of enthusiasm that carried all before it. Internal jealousies and mutual dissensions spelt failure and the movement came to a macabre end but a strange mingling of pride and lamentation always dominated the minds of the Afghāns. The author of *Dabistān-i-Mazāhib*, compiled in Shāh Jahān's reign (1628-1658), himself heard Pērī Sulṭān, who later on received the title of Zū'lfaqār Khān say: "When by order of Sa'īd Khān, I visited the family of 'Abdul Qādir (to obtain their surrender) I took with me large variety of victuals and drinks so that they might be seduced through their effect. One day an aged Afghān, after having tasted sweetmeats, rose on his legs and said, 'O 'Abdul Qādir! From the time of your honoured ancestors, never the foot of a Mughal reached this place; the gentleman who has now come intends to seduce you with garments red and yellow, and with victuals pleasing and sweet, which are coveted by those who are slaves of their belly, but which are abhorrent to the rule of *darvīshes*; the best measure therefore is to put him to death, as an example to terrify others from coming here'. But 'Abdul Qādir and his mother Bībi 'Alā'ī, the daughter of Miyān Jalāl-ud-Dīn, did not agree to it. On the day when 'Abdul Qādir entered the camp of Sa'īd Khān, his horse was frightened at the noise of kettle drums and horns, and dashed from amid the crowd to one side. An Afghān observed, 'The horse executes what the Lord Miyān Rawshan had ordered but you do not; be sure you shall suffer from the aftersickness of this desertion'. 'Abdul Qādir said, 'What has Miyān ordered?'. The Afghān replied, 'To keep at a distance and to beware of the Mughals'." [1] The editor of *Ḥāl Nāma*, an autobiography of Bāyazīd Rawshanā'ī, compiled in the early years of Aurangzēb's reign (1658-1707), summed up the panorama of the movement thus, "The four generations of Bayazīd ruled over Afghān tribes and remained on terms of war with the Mughals for about seventy years. Sometimes they came out victorious and sometimes they lost. Most of the Afghān tribes on the other hand struggled once or twice but submitted later on. None of the enemies could overpower the Rawshanā'īs. It was on account of their mutual dissentions that they deserted each other and joined the Mughals".[2]

Bāyazīd Rawshanā'ī

Bāyazīd Anṣārī, popularly known as Bāyazīd Rawshanā'ī, was the son of Qāẓī 'Abdullāh and the grandson of Qāzī Shaikh Muḥammad, the son of Shaikh Bāyazīd Parindā (a flyer or a bird).[3] The family descended from Shaikh Sirāj-ud-Dīn Anṣārī [4], a descendant of Abū Ayyūb Anṣārī, a devoted companion of Prophet Muḥammad, in whose house he stayed at Medina after his emigration. The family rose to heights of eminence amongst the Afghāns on account of the learning and piety of its members. They lived in Kānīgurām situated in the heart of Mahsūd Wazīristān, in the upper Baddar Valley at a height of about 7,000 feet. The father of 'Abdullāh, Shaikh Muḥammad was a successful businessman. Of the brothers of 'Abdullāh, Khudādād lived at Bhīrā while he himself resided in Kānīgurām. Bāyazīd was born of 'Abdullāh's second wife Aymana [5], the only daughter of a pious and rich man Ḥājī Abā Bakr who resided at Jallandhar in the Punjab. According to the editor of *Ḥāl Nāma*, the *jadd* (grandfathers) of Aymana and 'Abdullāh were real brothers. The father of 'Abdullāh, Shaikh Muḥammad once reached Jallandhar in connection with trade and stayed in the house of Ḥājī Abā Bakr. The manners of the host's family highly impressed the guest and he pressed him to marry his daughter to one of his twelve sons and went to the extent of agreeing to the condition of Aymana's parents that the bride need not be sent to the mountains. Shaikh Muḥammad's son who was also named Muḥammad married Ḥājī Abā Bakr's daughter at Jallandhar.[6] Two daughters were born to him but after some time Muḥammad died. Subsequently ʿAbdullāh reached Jallandhar and married his brother's widow Aymana. Bāyazīd was born at Jallandhar. It is probably on account of his birth there that he was known as a Hindustānī [7] (Indian).

Bāyazīd was barely forty days old when ʿAbdullāh left for his homeland leaving his wife and son at Jallandhar due to Aymana's refusal to accompany him in the mountainous regions. ʿAbdullāh had another wife Fāṭima in his homeland. A son and three daughters were born to him from his first wife. However, he used to send provisions and other necessities of life to Bāyazīd's mother in Jallandhar.[8]

During Bābur's invasion of Bhīra in February 1519, some of the Bhīra people were molested by the Mughal soldiers.[9] Bābur's efforts to restore confidence among the Afghāns seems to have made little headway and his hold over the territory was strongly resisted by them. Khudādād also appears to have suffered some loss during one of the Mughal raids and he left Bhīra for Jallandhar with his family in about 1525. Bāyazīd's mother extended a warm welcome to them. Khudādād had three daughters. He betrothed one of them to Bāyazīd who seems to have been born shortly before the emigration of Khudādād.[10] The Afghān rule of India came to an end after the defeat of Ibrahīm Lōdī at the battlefield of Pānīpat (20 April 1526). Their leaders shifted to the eastern part of India and Bihār became one of their strongholds under Sulṭān Maḥmūd Lōdī son of Sulṭān Sikandar Lōdī. Khudādād also left for Bihār. Bāyazīd's mother stayed at Jallandhar for some time but subsequently she had also to migrate to Bihār.[11] After some time ʿAbdullāh deputed one Maḥmūd to bring the mother of Bāyazīd and the family of Khudādād to Kānīgurām. When Maḥmūd reached Khudādād, he informed him that the Mughals had established their outposts at different places and it was not possible for them to reach Kānīgurām safely. They could later on accompany some caravan going to the mountainous region. Meanwhile the Afghāns were attacked by the Mughals. The Afghān families scattered to different directions to find refuge. A large number of them lost their life on account of hunger and thirst during their hazardous treking. The remaining ones wended their way towards Tirhut where a large number of them fell ill. A few of them met their death. These calamities engendered a desperate mood in the Afghāns and they resolved upon launching a united attack on the Mughals rather than to thin their own ranks under miserable conditions. About fourteen thousand Afghāns are said to have attacked a force of eighteen thousand Mughals. Dividing themselves into two forces, one wing of the Afghān archers and swordsmen forged ahead for a head-on collision with the Mughals while the other with match-locks lay in ambush. Under a planned strategy, the Afghān archers began to beat a slow retreat before the mighty onslaught of the Mughals till the latter came within the range of the Afghāns lying in ambush, who suddenly fired the volleys of matchlocks over the Mughals. The retreating Afghāns turned back and attacked the Mughals. About six thousand Mughals were killed and many of them were drowned in the river. The Afghāns reoccupied Bihār and the scattered families hastened back to their original homes. They attributed their victory to the blessings of Khudādād and offered considerable gifts to him, which relieved his family of privations and sufferings.[12] The effects of the victory were, however, very short-lived for the Afghāns were attacked again by the Mughals probably under Bābur and were routed. Bihār again passed into the occupation of the Mughals and the Afghān families took refuge in different directions.

Khudādād and the family of ʿAbdullāh accompanied a caravan leaving for the mountainous region but on reaching Qanauj, they were detained by Mahdī Khwājā, the brother-in-law of [13] Bābur. When he came to know of the fact that they were Afghāns, he ordered their general loot and annihilation. Khudādād with a large number of Afghāns escaped only after proving that they were Anṣārīs [14] and had nothing to do with the Afghāns. Later on the leaders of the caravan sent a *peshkash* (quit-rent) of seven lakh *tankās* to Bābur with an *arzdāsht* (petition). The Emperor allowed them to pass through his frontiers unmolested. Thus Shaikh Khudādād and the mother of Bāyazīd reached Kānīgurām after braving hazardous odds.[15]

ʿAbdullāh gave some portion of his belongings to Khudādād just to enable him to establish himself and betrothed his daughter to Ismāʿīl the son of Khudādād. To the great misfortune of Bāyazīd and his mother, the first wife of ʿAbdullāh, Fātima by name, and her son Yaʿqūb could not tolerate Bāyazīd and his mother's presence in Kanīgurām. ʿAbdullāh took the side of Fātima and Yaʿqūb. The life became hellish for Bāyazīd and his mother and they were compelled to leave Kanīgurām for Jallandhar. But the slender financial resources of Bāyazīd's mother forced her to dispatch Bāyazīd back to his father at Kānīgurām, only to be treated as an unwelcome member of the house. He was then merely a child of seven years, but he too was not spared all those indignities, which had been his mother's lot, at the hands of his step-mother and step-brother. Khudādād detested the treatment meted out to Bāyazīd. He therefore left for Betūr with the intention of calling Bāyazīd there with his family soon after settling down himself there. To the great misfortune of Bāyazīd, Khudādād was killed there by an enemy of his host who mistook him for the owner of the house. Khudādād's premature death deprived Bāyāzīd of the only source he could look to for some help and thus he was forced to pass his days in miserable circumstances.[16] ʿAbdullāh was also greatly moved but he could not help Bāyazīd in the face of the opposition of his wife and her son. He explained to Bāyazīd his inability to help him and advised him to win over his opponents to his cause by devoted service to them. Bāyazīd accordingly began to serve them with increasing humility. This softened down their hostility and ʿAbdullāh could send him to the school of his own pupil Mullā Pāyandā.[17]

Bāyazīd was earnestly devoted to his studies and religious exercises. When he had finished the study of the *Qur'ān* within a short period, his father, in keeping with the prevailing Afghān custom, was supposed to arrange for a feast to his classmates and presents for his teacher. But how could ʿAbdullāh see his way through with a hostile Fāṭima? It was a severe hurt to Bāyazīd's pride. Fāṭima could not brook the idea of allowing higher education to Bāyazīd. With a view to distracting him from his studies, she assigned him sundry jobs to do. Helpless in the teeth of opposition of his wife, ʿAbdullāh could do nothing but to advise Bāyazīd to have *Qur'ān* as his companion at every place so that he could study it in his leisure hours.

Bāyazīd was meditative and inquisitive from his very childhood. The torments of hell always kept him terrified. He, consequently, was inclined towards leading a pious life. Illegal food, lies and mischievous deeds were abhorrent to his nature. He served his father, teacher, *ʿulamā*, *faqīrs* and guests, who came to his house, with great devotion. All sorts of formal prayers and devotional exercises were performed by him with increasing sincerity. He was humane, tolerant and possessed great forbearance. If he went out to tend his own cattle, he did not mind looking after the cattle of others. Whenever sent to keep watch over fields, he gladly looked after the fields of others.[18] Presuming himself to be the greatest of the sinners, he boldly confessed his sins, and sought the Almighty's forgiveness. He regularly read *Qur'ān* and studied preliminary works of Islāmic law and theology with care.[19] Gradually he commenced giving vent to truth without mental reservation. To the question of a local saint, Khwāja Ismā'īl, which of the two he loved more—the faith or the world; he frankly admitted that he loved the world more since he devoted much of his time in mundane aflairs.[20] Music always put him into a state of mystical trance and he had an impassioned love for it so much so that even his father's strong disapproval and opposition could not withhold him from lending his ears to the sweet notes of music.[21] The domestic chores assigned to him by his step-mother left him with little time to devote to the acquisition of knowledge. He, therefore, left Kānīgu-rām, with a view to proceeding to Mecca. But four days later he was brought back by his father who insisted that he should study under him for he was regarded by the Afghāns as a teacher of repute.[22]

Later on 'Abdullāh took him to various places for trade which began to prosper and brought them good returns. By now Bāyazīd was sixteen and was grown up enough to manage things on his own.[23] The persistent hostility and rough treatment of his step-mother forced him to seek establishing himself separately and independently of his father. 'Abdullāh did not agree to his son's request for a division of property which, the latter claimed, was acquired by their joint efforts. It was, however, after great persuasions and intercessions of his relations and influential men like Ismā'īl who were favourably inclined towards the claim of Bāyazīd that 'Abdullāh reluctantly apportioned Bāyazīd's share; but even this step failed to bring differences and quarrel to an end.[24]

An utter sense of frustration goaded Bāyazīd on to resolving upon secretly putting an end to the life of Ya'qūb whom he considered to be the main source of all his troubles. Seeing Ya'qūb enjoying a sound sleep on a high mountain cliff, Bāyazīd decided to throw Ya'qūb into the lap of death by pushing him into the ditch, but the thought of retribution on the day of Judgment stayed his hands off the murderous assault. Besides, a sudden stroke of wisdom purged his heart of all evil intentions against Ya'qūb and he deemed it unprofitable to persist in his quarrel with 'Abdullāh and Ya'qūb for wordly goods.[25]

He was in those days studying *Qudūrī* and *Lubāb-ul-Akhbār* with 'Abdullāh. He visualised the risk of imbibing the habits of his teacher in him if he continued his tudies under him. He, therefore, took to trading independently. His honesty and fair dealings crowned him with considerable success. One of his uncles, Shaikh Ḥasan, married his daughter to him and the friends and relations of ʿAbdullāh began to visit Bāyazīd's house to the latter's great satisfaction. He tried to please ʿAbdullāh too but in vain.[26]

According to Ākhund Darwīza, it was during these sojourns that Bāyazīd came in contact with Indian Yōgīs at Jallandhar and was imbued with metempsychosis. One Mullā Sulaimān, by name, a *mulḥid*, presumably an Ismāʿīlī, is also said to have impressed upon him his own Ismāʿīlī ideology.[27] Though *Ḥāl Nāma* makes no mention of extraneous influences over him, his sojourns to different lands and his contacts with the people of diverse views and beliefs seem to have widened his mental outlook and he started concentrating more and more on the nature of Ultimate Reality.

He had studied elementary works on theology but avoided the study of advanced works on *fiqh* for he did not like to take up the career of a *qāẓī*. He was gradually convinced of the idea that a perfect religious guide was indispensable for the acquisition of the Divine Realities.[28] The mountainous region was inhabited by a number of religious guides who undertook the task of guiding the people on account of either knowledge of *sharīʿat* or owing to their have descended from some eminent *pīr* (religious guide). Some of them had acquired eminence due to the wealth and riches which they had amassed. They could afford him no spiritual satisfaction. He began to seriously ponder over the qualities which a *pīr* was required to possess. A conviction took root in his mind that none could attain the status of a *pīr* unless he had full acquaintance with the knowledge possessed by the prophets. He believed that a *pīr* enjoyed the same status in his tribe which a prophet possessed amongst his *ʿummat* (followers).[29]

Meanwhile, his cousin Shaikh Ismāʿīl, son of Khudādād saw a vision in which his father informed him that a certain book contained *Ism i-Aʿẓam* [30] and that its repetition in seclusion would bring great spiritual benefits to him. Shaikh Ismāʿīl accordingly performed many *chillās* [31] in seclusion in a dark cell, repeating the *Ism i-Aʿẓam*. Constant vigils, starvations and performance of *ẓikr* [32] worked up such a profound spiritual change in him that he laid claims to showing the Almighty to anyone who sought to undergo the rigorous and austere religious exercises as were practised by him. The simple-hearted and unsophisticated Afghāns looked askance at his claims. They believed that God could be seen by the blessed in paradise but seeing His vision in this world was unthinkable to them. The *ʿulamā* and *mashā'ikh* approached 'Abdullāh to prevail upon Ismā'īl, who was his nephew as well as his son-in-law, to give up his wild claims or else to allow them to kill him on account of his heresy. 'Abdullāh did not yield to their request. He asked them to leave him to his lot for he was bound to meet with divine wrath.

Three people are said to have performed ascetic exercises as prescribed by Shaikh Ismā'īl and gained insight into Divine Mysteries. He rode successfully over the tide of opposition of *'ulamā* and *mashā'ikh*, and achieved immense popularity. Obviously Shaikh Ismā'īl was the only man tallying with Bāyazīd's conception of a perfect guide and he became highly enamoured of him.[33]

He begged leave of his father to perform *tawba* [34] at Ismā'īl's hands and to become his disciple. 'Abdullāh did not relish the idea of his son becoming a disciple of his nephew when he was himself acknowledged as most learned of all the sons of Shaikh Muḥammad. He, therefore, advised him to become the disciple of a descendant of Shaikh Bahā-ud-Dīn Zakariya [35] who resided at Multān. Bāyazīd was in no mood to accept this advice.[36] Much distressed and mortified at his father's opposition, he took to wandering about in wilderness. While moving about in this predicament he received inspiration that as the Almighty heard everything, he should repeat the *kalima* [37] in his heart and indulge in *ẕikr-i-khafī*.[38] Meanwhile an invisible voice informed him that the *kalima* of *sharī'at*, (*Lā Ilāhā*) meant that there is no God but Allāh, that of *ṭarīqat* meant that nothing should be yearned except Allāh, whereas that of *ḥaqīqat* stipulated that there does exist nothing in both the worlds except Allāh. Bayāzīd devoted himself to the repetition of *kalima* in accordance with *pās-i-anfās* [39] for three or four years and was confirmed in his belief that nothing but Allāh existed, either in this world or in the world to come. Wherever he would caste his eyes, his spiritual eyes would catch the glimpse of the Almighty.[40]

He continued in this state of *ma'rifat* and *ḥaqīqat* for some time until one night when he was going to sleep he was accorded the position of *qurbat* (nearness) which enabled him to perceive and feel every voice as if it emanated from Allāh.[41] He felt himself to have been enjoined upon by the Almighty not to disclose the secret of his having attained the stage of *qurbat*. He returned thanks to the Almighty for having taken him out of the state of darkness (*tārīkī*) to that of light (*rawshan'ī*) and to have guided him on to the light of vision of Almighty from the darkness of blind ignorance, to the light of nearness from the gloom of separation, to the light of constant *ẕikr* and the knowledge of *Ẕāt* (Being) from the darkness of oblivion and ignorance.[42]

He devoted a few years to strenuous repetition of the silent *ẕikr*, until he realized as if he were being asked by a Divine Voice to explain as to what he meant by *m'arifat*. He observed, "O Almighty! To which ever direction I turn or what ever object I see, I perceive Thine existence in each with the eyes of heart. Whatever voice I hear, I find it as Thine own voice. Whatever in this world or in the world to come, I find, I take it to be existing through Thine *wujūd*." He again felt he had been asked to account for his own existence if he regarded everything existing through the *wujūd* of the Almighty. Bāyazīd replied, "O God! My existence is dependent on Thine *wujūd*, and has no separate entity". The Divine Voice then asked him to explain as to why he said that he saw Him or recognised Him when he did not discriminate between his own existence and that of the *wujūd* of the Almighty. That remark established the fact that there were two beings, one of the Almighty and the other that of his own. Bāyazīd could find no answer to this question. He scratched his head to strike at an answer to the problem and pondered over it. In his predicament he heard a Divine Voice enjoining upon him to declare, "O Bāyazīd! Say 'O God! I see Thee, through Thee and recognise Thee through Thee' ". This voice made Bāyazīd realise that the above stage was undoubtedly higher than that of the *qurbat* and the aforesaid realization was loftier than his earlier attainments. This led him to the stage of *waṣlat* from that of *qurbat*. In this state he realized his own existence submerged in that of the Almighty and found everything which existed as identical with the *wujūd* of God. He found himself hearing the voice of Almighty through Him. He experienced his own existence to have disappeared and realized that everything was done and moved by Him.[43]

This stage also did not set Bāyazīd's mind at rest and he constantly mixed with *darwīshes* and saints and served them with increasing devotion. He, however, never revealed his own attainments to anyone. After traversing all the stages from *sharī'at* to *waṣlat* in about eleven years,[44] he felt himself to have been directed to commence the repetition of *Ism-i-A'ẓam* to pave his way to the permanent acquisition of the stage of *tawḥīd*. After some time whichever voice he heard he found it pronouncing *Ism-i-'Aẓam*. In this stage he underwent the thrilling experience of having realized the secrets of the knowledge of the Divine Essence. These strange experiences enhanced his mental tension for he was conscious of his own shortcomings in regard to learning and righteousness, and knew that he did not possess such other qualities as warranted the bestowal of such a lofty grace on him. This conflict was again resolved on account of his constant meditation. He was commanded to merge his own existence into the Divine Essence and regard nothing but His Being as existent. He was also ordained to obliterate all the considerations of "I' and 'Thee' from his mind, and realise that he was one with God.

He devoted the Friday nights to the repetition of *Ism-i-ʿAẓam* in a cell in wilderness and remained absorbed in that state until the *ẓuhr* (mid-day) prayers with only short breaks.[45] Once, after similar devotional exercises, he reached a spring and wished to take a bath.[46] Just then he heard a Divine Voice telling him that the bath of *s͟harīʿat* implied keeping the body clean from phenomenal pollution; the bath of *ṭarīqat* was to get the heart rid of the temptations of carnal self and Satan and to shun the sins; the bath of *ḥaqīqat* consisted in weaning the heart away from everything but Almighty and in being constantly absorbed to the thought of God; the bath of *maʿrifat* sought to create a strong and firm belief in the existence of Almighty; the bath of *qurbat* enjoined upon the seeker to shut the ears to all the voices but that of God; and to comprehend the praise of the Almighty repeated by every object of the phenomenal world; the bath of *waṣlat* amounted to the realisation that nothing but the Being of Almighty existed in the phenomenal world; and the bath of *waḥdat* insisted on being imbued with the attributes of God. He was, therefore, ordained to select the bath of *waḥdat* for himself so that he might be endowed with the attributes possessed by Almighty. This brought him to the critical stage of the advisability of performing the formal prayers, for that amounted to the realization of a sort of duality between the Creator and the created. A Divine Inspiration prompted him to attach no particular importance to formal prayers of the believers and to perform the prayers of the prophets which implied that the devotee should regard himself one with the Almighty. He should do nothing either for his own self or for others. None else but God Almighty be regarded as a Reality. The editor of *Ḥāl Nāma* has supported Bāyazīd by extensively quoting from the aphorisms of S͟haik͟h ʿAbdul Qādir Jīlānī (d. 1166 A.D.) and from the *Masnawī* of Maulānā Rūm.[47] (d. 1273 A.D.), but the claims were too extravagant and wild for the orthodox theologians to tolerate. A system which sought to emphasise the meditation at the expense of formal prayers was nothing but heresy to them.

Bāyazīd had by this time completed the 40th year of his age. He retired to a cell for some time to perform vigil, reduced his diet and kept himself occupied in the repetition of *Ism-i-ʿAẕam*. *Namāẕ* in its formal form was also not given up. It was followed by the repetition of *ẕikr*.[48] Though he subsequently returned home due to the persuasions of two of his friends Ḥasan and ʿUs̤mān, he did not give up the routine that he had of late adopted. He claimed during this period to have had revealed all the secrets of God, and bestowed such knowledge as enabled him to discern the inner conditions of a living being. He noticed some pious men of repute, earlier regarded by him as perfect saints, steeped in *shirk*, some in *kufr* and some in hypocrisy.[49] This shook his faith in their claims. His outspokenness earned for him the hostility of *ʿulamā*, *ṣūfīs* and *darwīshes*.[50] At this stage he felt himself, in accordance with his own wishes, to have obtained the knowledge of the inner condition of hearts of different people. He came to believe that the first state related to carnal or inordinate desires and led the believers to the mundane affairs. The second was related to Satan and led the people to sins. The third was concerned with the heart itself and led the people to the obedience of Almighty and ensured paradise for them. The fourth was related to the (purified) soul and led the people to *maʿrifat* and vision of Almighty. Bāyazīd composed a *qaṣīda* (elegy) giving a detailed description of all the stages of the development of the heart of human beings.[51]

On account of being constantly absorbed in *ẕikr* and meditation, Bāyazīd neither mixed with people nor did he hold conversations with them. His wife Bībī Shamsū did not approve of his way of life and was uneasy due to the apprehension that Bāyazīd, left to himself, might become a *qalandar* and say good-bye to the worldly pursuits. She prevailed upon him to earn his livelihood. Bāyazīd was also tired of his life in Kānīgurām. He left his house with a caravan of merchants apparently to eke out his livelihood but in reality with the hope of coming in contact with some Perfect Spiritual Guide.[52]

He reached Qandāhār where he was informed of a *qalandar* who had neither come out of his cell for the past three years nor had indulged in conversation with anyone else. Bairam Khān [53] had posted his guards there to protect him against those who sought to disturb him in their own interest. Bāyazīd went to his cell only to return to his camp without obtaining an access to him. He considered him to be a fruitless tree incapable as such of benefiting anyone. The same day the *mutṣaddīs* [54] of Bairam Khān, dividing the belongings of the merchants into six parts, took off five portions as *zakāt* of *rāhdārī*[55] and left only one portion with the merchants. Of the goods of Bāyazīd they took only two-thirds, leaving one-third with him. The leaders of the caravan, together with Bāyazīd, approached Bairam Khān for the redress of their grievances but did not succeed. Meanwhile, Bāyazīd felt himself to have been divinely instructed to abandon worldly pursuits and go back to his native land to stay there for five years in his home in retirement with absolutely no desire to enter into worldly life.[56] He returned to Kānīgurām and wished to leave once more for Hindustān in quest of some Perfect Spiritual Guide but forsook the idea when reminded by his wife of the Divine Ordinance to stay at home for five years. He shifted to an underground cell prepared by him for meditation. While living in this state he received a Divine Inspiration that if some true devotee approached him he should ungrudgingly lead him to the correct path so that many lamps might be lighted from one lamp.[57] His wife Bībī Shamsū[58] was first to offer herself to be enrolled as a disciple and was admitted to the cell to live a life of austerity and meditation. ʿAlī Sher Barkī of Kānīgurām, an ironsmith and man of considerable piety, who already held Bāyazīd in great respect, volunteered to undergo arduous ascetic exercises as prescribed by him. He was also admitted to the same cell. ʿAlī Sher's presence in the cell prevented Bībī Shamsū from moving out freely during day time, but ultimately Bāyazīd allowed her to move about in the presence of ʿAlī Sher with veil on her face and was asked by Bāyazīd to treat him as a brother.[59] Bāyazīd did not discourage such promiscuous mixing among both the sexes of his disciples. Ākhund Darwīza in his own derisive style says, "Whenever he found anyone inclined towards his own self, he suffered him to mix in promiscuous assemblies; forgetting that sensuality is like a fire hidden in stone".[60] He ascribed Bāyazīd's success to the free rope said to have been given by him to his disciples for licentiousness.

In the first instance Bībī Shamsū, ʿAlī Sher and Shādī Khān and Nek Bakht two other disciples of Bāyazīd completed a *chilla*, which was followed by the distribution of sweets among friends and relatives; but ʿAbdullāh did not approve of his activities particularly the freedom which he had allowed to his wife, who was ʿAbdullāh's niece.[61] Ultimately he paid a visit to his son who is said to have informed him, "It should be a matter of great satisfaction for you to see your son elevated to such spiritual eminence. I implore you to warn me if you find me acting against the injunctions of the *Qurʾān* and *Ḥadīs̤*".[62] He also told ʿAbdullāh that his wife always appeared veiled before his disciples and that he enjoined *z̤ikr-i-khafī* upon them. ʿAbdullāh was astonished to see his son quote *Qur'ān* and *Ḥadis* in defence of his contentions for he had never taught him the works which Bāyazīd had mastered. He, however, tried in vain to persuade his son to practise only the formal rules of *sharīʿat*. The ranks of Bāyazīd's disciples began to swell, a circumstance which was sufficient to excite the feelings of jealousy and ill-will against him in the hearts of contemporary saints and religious guides who started a campaign of vilification against Bāyazīd and his followers, but their tactics failed in the initial stages. Bāyazīd ultimately ordered his disciples to keep their tenets strictly secret from their enemies and warned them of the risk of substituting in their hearts the light of *mʿarifat* with the darkness in the event of acting contrary to his instructions.[63] ʿUs̤mān, son of Mannā, one of the most inveterate enemies of Bāyazīd, sought to dissuade the people from joining the ranks of Bāyazīd's disciples by telling some that being ascetics and saints themselves they needed no Bāyazīd, while impressing upon others the futility of having a *pīr* being *ʿālims* themselves.[64] The affluent section of the society could not embrace the life of poverty and austerity. ʿUs̤mān's tactics seemed to have the desired effect, for Bāyazīd felt increasingly disheartened but his drooping spirits were cheered up allegedly by a Divine Voice which bade him call the people to Almighty and lead them to the right path.[65] He began to preach his mission of *tawḥīd* openly. He found none of his contemporaries on the right path. The rulers according to him, indulged in mutual quarrels and the Muslims were sacrificed at the altar of their selfish designs. The *pīrs* were interested in nothing but amassing wealth and riches in the name of guiding people. *Darwīshes* and *ʿālims* too had lost every regard for the spirit of religion and faith. He pondered over their inner condition and finally decided not to hesitate in declaring the truth, howsoever bitter it might be. He cautioned the Muslims that none of them were acting in accordance with the tenets of *Qur'ān* and *Ḥadīs̤*. This amounted to condemning all those as heretics who did not give ear to his teachings. His tirades irritated ʿUs̤mān and the other enemies of Bāyazīd; so they approached his father, who was also a Qāẓī and sought redress against the wild allegations which his son had been making. ʿAbdullāh sent his disciples to Bāyazīd to dissuade him from making his wild assertions but they were struck dumb with his subtle and effective arguments. They enrolled themselves as the disciples of Bāyazīd.[66]

He and his disciples are said to have received a Divine Call that Bāyazīd should be called as *Miyān Rawshan* or *Pīr-i-Rawshan*. This raised a great hue and cry among his opponents and they refused to give any weight to them for Bāyazīd himself was not formally initiated to *ṣufic* discipline by any recognised saint.[67] Bāyazīd informed the disciples of his father, some of whom were again deputed by him to verify the truth of his claims, that he initiated his disciples to the secrets of *tawḥīd* and added that it was very easy to call Him one but exceedingly difficult to understand Him as one. ʿAlī Sher also informed ʿAbdullāh about the four injunctions which he had received from Bāyazīd thus, "I am required to serve the cause of Islām and shun the sins. Secondly I have to avoid heedlessness and indulge in *ẕikr*. Thirdly I must avoid ignorance after being initiated into the subtleties of *tawḥīd*. Fourthly I am required to abstain from behaving ill-manneredly after having been directed to the path of right manners". [68] Due to his popularity, his cousin Muḥammad, brother of Shaikh Ismāʿīl who had a considerable following among the Dawr [69] tribe also became his disciple and came forward with the declaration that due to the *chilla* performed by him under the direction of Bāyazīd, he had acquired the stages of *qurbat*, *waṣlat* and *waḥdat* while under his own brother, Shaikh Ismāʿīl, he could acquire only the stage of *mʿarifat*.[70] He also tried to persuade ʿAbdullāh and his son Yaʿqūb to follow Bāyazīd but they did not yield to his persuasions.[71] All those who came in contact with Bāyazīd found themselves completely changed men after performing *chilla* under his guidance. Excessive religious exercises and deep meditation transported them to a different kind of spiritual world which they or their preceptor found difficult to define in theological terminology. After some time he appointed Muḥammad as his *khalīfā* and christening him as 'Muḥammad Kamāl'; passed over to him the right to initiate only those as disciples who were sincerely devoted to him. "If a disciple were to catch hold of your hand, tell him that he is holding the hand of *Pīr-i-Rawshan*. Don't call yourself a *pīr* but should assert that there is only one *Pīr* and I am initiating disciples for him and guiding them on behalf of the *Pīr*. I am his deputy. There cannot be more than one *quṭb* [72] in an age."

Muḥammad obtained considerable success in his mission as a *khalīfā* of Bāyazīd.[73] His other disciples too led a number of people to the stage of *mʿarifat* and to the knowledge of *tawḥīd*. Bāyazīd's sweeping generalization branding the believers and the contemporary *pīrs* as hypocrites brewed a storm of opposition against him. In retaliation a number of *ʿālims* and saints together with ʿAbdullāh declared Bāyazīd a lunatic and assembled at his house with a view to imprisoning him. Bāyazīd's adherents also collected together.[74] A debate was arranged. The eminent people of the town sat in the middle just to ward off any direct collision between the two factions.[75] To each of the questions put by his opponents regarding Islāmic faith and the laws of *sharīʿat*, Bāyazīd gave prompt replies supported with verses from *Qur'ān* and popular traditions on the subject. He gave a clear exposition of the conditions in which the performance of *namāz*, *rōza*, *zakāt* and *ḥaj* could be treated as legal and profitable. He also defined all the eight stages of spiritual development which he allegorically explained. But Bāyazīd's explanation did not afford satisfaction either to his adversaries or to his father ʿAbdullāh and his brother Yaʿqūb.[76] Yaʿqūb and others girt their loins to kill or imprison him, but the stubborn opposition of Bāyazīd's disciples foiled their attempts. However, his enemies continued to call him mad and a heretic. They accused him of possessing an inadequate and superficial knowledge of religious principles and *sharīʿat*; of making unjustifiable claims of being a guide though he was not formally appointed *khalīfā* by a *pīr*; of wrongly claiming to have received Divine Inspiration; of condemning the Muslims as hypocrites and of disobeying the behests of his parents and relatives.[77]

Bāyazīd persistently reiterated that a *hādī* was a guide and he, as one of them, sought to show the path of Prophet Muḥammad. Similarly he also guided the seekers on the right lines. He, like Prophet Muḥammad, called the people towards the Almighty hence the path of both was identical.[78] Once Malik Lōdī, Maulānā Zakariya and his son Aḥmad enquired the cause of his parents' dissatisfaction with him. He replied, "They want me to indulge in worldly pursuits and give up the path of faith. I claim that the act of my guidance is free from falsehood because I pull the people out from blindness, deafness, dumbness and *shirk* and lead them towards *tawḥīd*. God will protect everyone who shall follow me".[79] He also gave an explanation for the firm attitude adopted by him. He attributed his earlier restricted outspokenness to his being initiated into the preliminary stage of *maʿrifat*, but after being acquainted with *tawḥīd* he invited the people towards the correct path with conviction and courage as he found the living being engrossed in *shirk*.[80] Maulānā Zakariya claiming to have the knowledge of *ma'rifat* and *tawḥīd* wished to test him in these branches. Bāyazīd told him that Zakariya should first enquire about *sharī'at* and proceed step by step for no explanation of *ma'rifat* could be given without an adequate understanding of its initial stage, i.e. *sharī'at*.[81] To the son of Maulānā Zakariya his reply was that his *pīr* was Prophet Muḥammad. He likened himself to Uwais who obtained profound spiritual benefits from the Almighty due to Prophet Muḥammad's blessings, without coming into his contact. As the mission of different apostles of God was revealed to them through Gabriel, the successors of prophets also obtained Divine Inspiration from Him. He added, "*Ilhām* (Divine Inspiration) is not confined to the prophets alone, but it is a light which helps in seeing the reality of every phenomenal object. *Ilhām* is associated with *walīs* (saints) while *waḥy* (Divine Revelation) with prophets. Those who are incapable of seeing the Lord in the world with the eyes of heart, cannot see Him in the next world".[82]

After their complete discomfiture at arguments with Bāyazīd, Maulānā Zakariya decided to have recourse to arms and cow him down with violence, but the fear of Bāyazīd's followers restrained him from behaving rashly. They, due to the intercession of certain tribal leaders, offered to make compromise on the following conditions:

1. Bāyazīd should not accuse the believers of being engrossed in *shirk*;
2. He should not accuse them of being *munāfiqs* (hypocrites);
3. He should desist from claiming to have been visited by Gabriel.
4. He should not accuse people of being engrossed in darkness;
5. He should make no claims of being a *Mahdī*.

Maulānā Zakariya challenged Bāyazīd's claims of being acquainted with the secrets of heart and capable of divulging the same, by offering to become his disciple if he found his claim to be true. Bāyazīd, who perceived a sort of dynamic character in the science of heart, replied, "I am able to find out the secrets of hearts, but there is no heart in you. Had you possessed a heart, I could have informed you about its state of affairs". Maulānā Zakariya asserted, "I offer myself to be killed. If a heart comes forth of my body, Bāyazīd should be put to death so that the people may get rid of his vicious teachings, and if no heart comes out he can be spared and the believers may enter into his discipleship". Bāyazīd retorted, "The heart you speak of will come forth of a calf, or a kid if it is killed but that lump of flesh is not the heart. The *Ḥadīs̤* tells, 'The heart of the faithful is more elevated than the empyrean heaven; and more spacious than the extent of the ninth heaven'. And again, 'I could neither enter the earth nor the heaven but the heart of the believers'. And again, 'Hearts bear witness to hearts' ".[83] The tribal leaders said, "How can the truth of the respective claims be finally decided?" Bāyazīd replied, "There are seven towns in this *wilāyat* (territory). Let one man from one of these join me and practise devotional exercises for forty days and nights under me. Likewise, one man for a similar period of time should associate himself with other *'ālims*. After the expiry of the stipulated period both should be subjected to a severe test with a view to finding out as to who had acquired greater benefits". To those who took exceptions to his prescribing hard ascetic exercises, he replied that nothing could be achieved without undergoing hardships.[84] A person named Malik Mīrzā said, "O Bāyazīd! Don't accuse the believers of ignorance. One who obtains guidance from you cannot forsake you, but one who has no faith in you cannot tread on the path shown by you through violence". Bāyazīd replied, "I shall put an example before you. A number of persons are asleep in a house. Accidentally it catches fire. Just then one of them gets up. Now should he wake up the others or not?" His opponents said, "Those who are asleep should certainly be awakened". Bāyazīd instantly retorted, "I find everyone fallen into the slumber of forgetfulness. I want to shake them off this state of stupor to save them from being consumed by the fire of heedlessness".[85]

For about three years Bāyazīd resisted the onslaughts of arguments hurled at him but subsequently yielded in the face of mounting opposition to his claims. This submission brought considerable change in his attitude and behaviour. Formerly he did not even greet anyone for he considered everyone polluted with *s̲hirk*, but later on he began to greet the people. He declared:

"1. I don't claim that Gabriel comes to me but I do assert that I receive inspiration from Him;
2. I don't claim to be a Mahdī; I only claim to be a guide (*hādī*);
3. I don't say that all the people are *munāfiqs* and *kāfirs*; I simply maintain that all those who are made *munāfiqs* or *kāfirs* by Almighty would remain as such to the eyes of others." [86]

Adjustments and compromises of this type are frequently noticeable in the career of Bāyazīd but it appears that he never gave up the claims of assuming the status of a perfect guide, reaching well near the status of a *Mahdī*.[87] Nor were his opponents ever satisfied with his interpretations and expositions. He, however, highly impressed his contemporaries with his piety. He acted as an *Imām* and did not request for any remuneration, taught *Qur'ān* and other theological works without expecting anything in return for it. Free from worldly avarice he was contented with whatever Almighty bestowed upon him.[88]

After completing the period of five years' retirement he moved out of his residence. The occasion was celebrated by his followers with joyful festivities.[89] Later on he reached Sang Tāwī, a place lying at a distance of one day's journey from Kānīgurām, where a large number of followers of both sexes flocked to him. People enquired of Bāyazīd about the piety of Shaikh ʻUryā, a grandson of Ḥājī Wāṣil a celebrated and resourceful saint of the locality. Bāyazīd replied that none could become a *pīr* on account of simply being descended from a *pīr*. "A *pīr* is one who is acquainted with the knowledge possessed by the Prophet Muḥammad and can direct his disciples to the path of God".[90]

His outspokenness estranged him from Shaikh ʻUryā who became one of his strongest opponents. He did not make only the tribal leaders hostile to Bāyazīd, but also mobilised the opinion against him at Kānīgurām too. Bāyazīd, though running a high temperature, had therefore to leave Sang Tāwī for Kānīgurām in increasingly distressing circumstances.[91]

Shaikh ʻUryā's letter had already been received by the tribal leaders of Kānīgurām with the result that Bāyazīd had hardly stepped on to the soil of his homeland when he was faced with a number of plots against him. Bāyazīd had, meanwhile, softened down his attitude to some extent and had ceased to be harsh to his opponents. But this did not earn for him the desired respite from his adversaries—the *ʻālims* and other religious dignitaries.[92] Shaikh ʻUryā prevailed upon the tribal leaders of Kānīgurām to expel him from the town. Bāyazīd accordingly left the town with his wife, Bībī Shamsū, their son Shaikh ʻUmar, daughter Kamāl Khātūn and some other ladies and companions.[93] Some of the people of the town, however, later on succeeded in effecting a reconciliation between Bāyazīd and his father and persuaded him to live with his father and elder brother for some time. He was also made to pay a visit to Shaikh ʻUryā together with his brother Ya'qūb though against the wishes of his companions and followers. The opposition subsided a little. Bāyazīd evinced due consideration and respect to his father and Ya'qūb, but his own popularity indirectly fed their envious feelings towards him.[94] 'Abdullāh began to insist that Bāyazīd should perform *nafl* [95] prayers; Bāyazīd on the other hand, insisted on the performance of obligatory prayers and *zikr-i-khafī* which enabled him and his followers to meditate on the Almighty. They did not, however, leave any stone unturned in making their actions and behaviour conform to *sharī'at* so as to reconcile themselves with their adversaries.[96] The respite was temporary and Bāyazīd had ultimately to retire to a place in the vicinity of Bētūr where his khalīfā Muḥammad Kamāl lived. In the course of his sojourns, contrary to the prevailing Afghān customs, which did not find it objectionable on the part of the theologians to obtain food forcibly from those who were unable to resist, Bāyazīd's followers abstained from obtaining the articles of their needs from the inhabitants of the locality without their permission. Their modesty, forbearance and performance of obligatory prayers highly impressed the unassuming Afghāns. Bāyazīd built a dark cell like a temple near the mosque of the town and bade his followers sit there. They were required to perform the congregational prayers in the mosque and later on retire to the cell for *zikr* and meditation.[97] After some time he, at the invitation of the Dawrīs of the Tochī Valley in the northern Wazīristān, moved there. He exhibited a number of miracles in that territory.[98] After some trivial opposition in the initial stages a large number of Dawrīs accepted him as perfect guide and Pīr-i-Rawshan or Miyān Rawshan.[99] His mission seems to have received favourable response even outside the regions inhabited by the Afghāns. Khalīfā Maudūd and Mullā Arzānī reached from Hindustān and became his disciples. Khalīfā Maudūd compiled a treatise entitled *Maqṣūd uṭ-Ṭālibīn* and Mullā Arzānī [100] wrote *Mir'āt-ul-Muḥaqqiqīn* together with a *Dīwān* in *Pashtū*. Khalīfā Maudūd belonged to the Tarīn tribe of Afghāns and resided at Sarhind where he lies buried.[101]

He deputed one of his disciples Shaikh Bāyazīd brother of Shaikh Ni'mat Dawrī to *Tīrāh* [102] who converted many of the Orakzīs [103], Tīrāhīs and Āfrīdīs [104] to the tenets of the Master. From Tīrāh he moved to the land of Bangash on Kōhāt and Kurram. After considerable resistance a number of saints and theologians embraced Rawshanā'ī tenets. Bāyazīd later on moved to Tīrāh and despatched a detailed narrative of his activities to Bāyazīd Rawshanā'ī.[105] Meanwhile, a Mughal force from Pēshāwar suddenly attacked the Orakzīs and Bāyazīd was done to death by them. Bāyazīd Rawshanā'ī, however, on receipt of the letter of his *khalīfā*, decided to repair to Tīrāh and summoned his family from *Kanīgurām*.[106] Meanwhile, Mohmandzīs of Pēsshāwar and adjacent borders became enamoured of Bāyazīd's teachings and they invited him to visit their land.[107] He, therefore, set off for Tīrāh via Bangash where he was accorded a warm reception. At Tīrāh, Orakzīs, Āfrīdīs and other people of Tīrāh, who had embraced Rawshanā'ī tenets, welcomed him with great enthusiasm.[108] Thence he proceeded towards Sarban and reached Pēshāwar where he stayed with Malik Shānī, the leader of the Khalīl tribe. Most of the people of his tribe accepted Bāyazīd as their spiritual guide. Members of the Khalīl, Mohmand and Dāwūdzī tribes flocked to Bāyazīd in ones and two daily to become his disciples. He obtained converts to his ideas and beliefs among Mohmandzīs, Gagyānīs and Yūsufzīs, Tu'īs and Ṣāfīs.[109] The Rawshanā'ī movement appears to have obtained considerable popularity amongst the Mohmandzīs due to Mullā Dawlat Khān's conversion to the Rawshanā'ī tenets. Ākhund Darwīzā has severely condemned his baneful influence over the Afghāns of the locality which, according to him, became an ultimate cause of the decline of Islāmic orthodoxy there.[110] Malik Ḥabīb Bakhīl, a leader of the Khalīl tribe, however, turned into one of his inveterate adversaries there.[111] He approached Jānish Khān [112] *ṣubēdār* of Pēshāwar on behalf of Mīrzā Muḥammad Ḥakīm and strongly complained against Bāyazīd's heresies, portending him to be a potent danger to their rule. Jānish Khān deputed some scholars who were his companions to make investigations, but they are said to have returned convinced of the piety and religiosity of Bāyazīd. Ḥabīb Bakhīl collected twelve thousand rupees to bribe Jānish Khān, but he had already decided to join the services of Akbar. He, therefore, advised him to approach Mīrzā Muḥammad Ḥakīm [113], foster brother of Akbar and ruler of Kabul (1554-1583). Ḥabib Bakhīl saw the *wazīrs* and nobles of Mīrzā Muḥammad Ḥakīm and succeeded in getting Bāyazīd summoned to Kābul.

On his way to Kābul, Bāyazīd converted a sizable section of Tu'īs to his discipleship. Ḥabīb Bakhīl persuaded the nobles of Mīrzā Ḥakīm to prevail upon their ruler to allow Bāyazīd to be done to death without any investigation; but Mīrzā Ḥakīm did not yield. He summoned Bāyazīd to his presence and later sent him to Qāẓī Khān, the *qāzi* of Kābul, with a view to getting the allegations investigated.[114] Bāyazīd had a series of discussions with Qāzī Khān and explained to him, "I only claim to be a *hādī* (guide) and direct the people to the path of *tawḥīd* and save them from error, ignorance and *shirk*. Those who bear envy towards me accuse me of claiming myself as *Mahdī* instead of *hādī* and Prophet instead of a *walī*". Qāẓī Khān enquired of Bāyazīd if he claimed to be receiving *waḥys*. Bāyazīd replied in the negative, but affirmed that he received *ilhām* and heard Divine Calls. Qāẓī Khān further enquired as to how he differentiated between *waswasa* [115] and *ilhām*, between the Divine Call and the call of Satan. Bāyazīd replied that the verses from *Qur'ān*, *Hadis̤* and aphorisms of the saints were the sole criteria for the differentiation.[116] To the question if he claimed to have received *waḥy* and compiled a book entitled *Chihl Subyān*, Bāyazīd replied, "It is a baseless allegation for I claim that Almighty has inspired a book into my heart entitled *Khair-ul-Bayān* which comprises forty *bayāns* (chapters). It may be compared with *Ghawṣiyya* [117] compiled by Ghawṣ-ul-Aʿẓam on the basis of Divine Inspiration, but the people do not differentiate between *waḥy* and *ilhām*." [118]

Bāyazīd further added in reply to a query of Qāẓī Khān that he had acquired spiritual perfections through Prophet Muḥammad direct and was an *Uwaisī*.[119] No guide or teacher had taught him the knowledge which he propounded. Qāẓī Khān was convinced of the piety and righteousness of Bāyazīd so much so that he personally took him to Mīrzā Muḥammad Ḥakīm and spoke in highly appreciative terms of his eminence to Mīrzā. Ākhund Darwīza almost corroborating the event says, "He exhibited a profound veneration for the *sharīʿat*, practised its ordinances very strictly; strongly refuted his previous utterances so much so that everyone came to have a pity on him.[120] He heavily bribed some of the *wazīrs* of Mīrzā Muḥammad Ḥakīm and obtained his liberation." [121] It seems that bribes were used by both the factions. According to the editor of *Ḥāl Nāma*, which has hardly any iota of truth, Mīrzā Muḥammad Ḥakīm was so highly impressed of Bāyazīd that he decided to become his disciple. The *wazīrs* and nobles of Mīrzā Muḥammad Ḥakīm, however, explained to him, "Afghāns have been the subjects of the Mughals and have always been fighting against us. If you were to enrol yourself amongst the disciples of Bāyazīd, he would not allow us to realise *kharāj* (revenues) from the Afghāns and it would become impossible for us to rule over them. If you do not give up your intentions we would retire to India and serve Akbar." In view of their threats Mīrzā Muḥammad Ḥakīm dismissed Bāyazīd with honour. He returned to Pēshāwar [122]. Meanwhile, Jānish Khān had been replaced by Ma'ṣūm Khān. Bāyazīd settled down with the Mohmandzī tribe and gained considerable popularity with them. He contracted blood relationships with influential men of the tribe.[123] Of the two leaders of Mohmandzīs, Pāyandā Khān and Pahār Khān, Bāyazīd married his daughter Kamāl Khātūn to 'Alī Khān son of Pāyanda Khan, and his son 'Umar to the daughter of Pahār Khān. He married his son Jalāl-ud-Dīn nicknamed as Jalalā to the daughter of Māmā Khān, another prominent leader of the tribe. Datī, a lady wielding considerable influence among the tribe, Bāyazīd took as his own wife.[124] He sent Maudūd as his *khalīfā* or *dā'ī* to Qandāhār and to the people of the Kāsī tribe. Shinwārīs and Mohmandzīs swelled the ranks of his followers.[125]

He deputed many other men of pleasing eloquence and profound knowledge in music as his *khalīfās* to different Baloch tribes and to other places. A centre was established by them at Saiyidpūr near Ḥaydarabād Sindh. Bāyazīd himself moved to Kalla Dher in Hashtnagar and deputed his emissaries to all the rulers of the neighbouring countries.[126] He sent his *khalīfā* Daulat Khān with a book written by him named *Sirāt-uṭ-Tawḥīd* to Akbar who, in turn, is said to have received the messenger with due regard and dignified him with a robe of honour.[127] One, Yūsuf, was deputed as *khalīfā* with a treatise entitled *Khair-uṭ-Ṭālibīn* to the court of Mīrzā Sulaimān of Badakhshān. Mīrzā asked the *'ulamā* of his court to discuss with the messenger and critically study Bāyazīd's teachings. They are said to have returned with a fairly high estimate of Bāyazīd's teachings, so much so that Mīrzā Sulaimān sent a message to Bāyazīd that he regarded himself as one of his disciples.[128] Bāyazīd deputed some of his *khalīfās* to Balkh and Bokhārā too. One of them named Arzānī was deputed by him to Hindustān probably to the eastern part of India.[129] His teachings gained considerable popularity in the homeland of Afghāns and its vicinity, though the account of the impressions which the Rawshanā'īs are said to have made over Akbar and Mīrzā Sulaimān appears to be unfounded and exaggerated.

It appears that some of his followers interpreted his mystical and allegorical teachings very literally. Members of the Tu'ī tribe went to the extent of believing that the Day of Judgment had arrived. Under the inspiration of their leader 'Abdul Karīm they gave up their worldly pursuits, collected all their belongings, chattels and provisions at one place so that they should be able to devote themselves to meditation together, and should thus await the approach of the Day of Judgment. All the inhabitants of the village, men and women, retired to a mosque and started keeping themselves occupied in fasting, night vigils and *zikr-i-khafī*.[130] At this time a caravan of merchants from Hindustān happened to pass that way. They felt it repulsive to their mind to allow the members of the caravan to be engrossed in worldly pursuits and thus waste their energies especially when the Day of Judgment was so near. They attacked the caravan, the occupants of which thought that Bāyazīd had taken up arms against them. They fled towards Kābul. The tribesmen piled together the goods and chattels of the caravan and for some time made these the target of their arrows. Later on they got all the merchandise trampled under the hooves of their horses.[131] The merchants lodged a complaint against the tribe with Mīrzā Muḥammad Ḥakīm who deputed a force of five hundred horsemen to set the matter right. The tribesmen also took up arms against them. There were only fifteen horsemen among them. The dust raised by the galloping horses gave an illusion to the Mughals of there being a huge army to attack them. They took to their heels but they came to know of the reality very soon. They turned back, killed all of them, imprisoned their families and took them to Kābul.[132]

When Bāyazīd was informed of the incident, he wrote a letter of apology to Mīrzā Muḥammad Ḥakīm and explained to him that the Tu'īs had gone mad and that they had suffered the consequences of their lunacy. He requested Mīrzā Muḥammad Ḥakīm to release the innocent prisoners. *Wazīrs* and nobles of Mīrzā Muḥammad Hakīm were not convinced with the explanation, and they said to him, "We had previously warned you that Bāyazīd will not allow us to imprison the families of Afghāns." They convinced him that the Tu'īs had attacked the caravan at Bāyazīd's instigations and it was imperative on his part to nip the mischief in the bud. Mīrzā Muḥammad Ḥakīm issued a *farmān* to Ma'ṣūm Khān [133] to either imprison Bāyazīd or to kill him. When the orders were received by Ma'ṣūm Khān, Pāyandā Khān and Pahār Khān, the leaders of Mohmandzīs were present there. Pahār Khān immediately asked Pāyandā Khān to reach Bāyazīd post haste and inform him of the orders before the Mughal forces attacked him. Bāyazīd had to leave for the land of Yūsufzīs.[134] In the beginning Mohmandzīs also accompanied him but later on due to the persuasions of Pahār Khān, who was released by Maʿṣūm Khān on the condition that he would make the Afghāns return to their homeland, some of the Mohmandzīs left the company of Bāyazīd and repaired to their own land.[135] Maʿṣūm Khān attacked Bāyazīd with a force of Mughals and Afghān tribal leaders. Bāyazīd had only 313 followers with him but in a desperate action, the Mughals were defeated and fell back on Pēshāwar. Bāyazīd named the place as Āghāzpūr, to commemorate the beginning of the armed struggle against the Mughals. Those who took part in the battle were named as Āghāzpurīs by him.[136] The author of *Dabistān-i-Maẕāhib* says, "It is said that Bāyazīd received a Divine Command to take up arms against all those who were not acquainted with God but he did not comply with the Divine Command repeatedly for three times. Ultimately he was peremptorily ordered to start fighting. Unable to resist, he girt himself for the war against them in battlefields." [137]

He left for Tīrāh and Khaibar. The governor of Pēshāwar again invaded Tīrāh only to be defeated by Orakzīs, Āfrīdīs and Tīrāhīs. Shortly afterwards they discovered that the Mughal infiltrators entered Tīrāh on account of the connivance of the inhabitants of that territory. Rawshanā'īs tried to make short work of them. The plan leaked out and the Tīrāhīs took up arms against the Master. Bāyazīd feigned a conciliatry attitude; wrote to his former adherents, "You have grossly sinned by drawing your sword against your *pīr* and by imputing wrong motives to him. In order to show repentance you should present yourself to kiss my feet with your hands tied." [138] Three hundred and twenty Tīrāhīs on account of their folly came out of the fort and were executed in cold blood by Bāyazīd. Afterwards he spelt ruin and destruction to the entire Tīrāh. Some of the Tīrāhīs escaped to Ningrahār. Tīrāh became a stronghold of the Rawshanā'īs. Afterwards Bāyazīd proceeded to Ningrahār with a few thousand foot and horsemen and attacked the village Barwār. Muḥsin Khān Ghāzi led an expedition against him from Jalālābād with sixty horsemen and fell upon the Rawshanā'īs suddenly. Bāyazīd was finally defeated at Torragha; fled on foot and died of exhaustion at Kāla Pānī in the vicinity of Hasht Nagar. He breathed his last in 980H/1572-73 A.D., two and a half years after the commencement of the armed struggle against the Mughals.[139] Yūsufzīs and a number of other tribes, hostile to the Mughals, sincerely supported him and he was regarded as a leader of the liberation of Afghāns against the dominance of the Mughals. He seems to have gone to the extent of declaring that he sought to invade India and overthrow the empire of Akbar.

He acquired horses from merchants on loan promising to pay them after the conquest of India.

NOTES

[1] *Dabistān-i-Mazāhib* (Lucknow 1904) Pp. 310-311.

[2] ʿAlī Muḥammad bin Abā Bakr Qandāhārī: *Ḥāl Nāma* (Subḥānuʾllāh manuscripts, ʿAlīgath Muslim University Library) F. 465b.

[3] It is said that he used to offer prayers at Mecca very frequently, a legend ascribed to a number of saints, hence the title, Parindā. (*Ḥāl Nāmā* F. 2b).

[4] The following genealogy is given in *Ḥāl Nāma* (Ff. 2b-3a) Shaikh Bāyazīd, son of ʿAbdullāh Qāẓī, son of Shaikh Muḥammad, son of Shaikh Bāyazīd Parindā, son of Shaikh Muḥammad, son of Shaikh Sirāj ud-Dīn, son of Chirāgh ud-Din, son of Shaikh Maulānā Ibrāhīm Dānishmand, son of Shaikhzādā Ḥamza, son of Khwājā Maḥmūd, son of Shaikh Dāwūd, son of Shaikh Shams ud-Dīn, son of Shaikh Khalīl, son of Shaikh Luqmān, son Shaikh Khudādād, son of Shaikh Manṣūr, son of Shaikh Muḥammad, son of Khwājā Zāhid, son of Muḥammad Anṣārī, son of Shaikh Manṣūr Muḥammad, son of Shaikh Aḥmad, son of Shaikh-zāda, son of Khwājā Ayyub Anṣārī. According to *Dabistān-i-Māzāhib*, Shaikh Sirāj ud-Dīn Anṣārī was the seventh ancestor of Bāyazīd (P. 304).

[5] The author of *Dabistan-i-Mazāhib*, on the authority of *Ḥāl Nāma*, mentioned her name as Banīn (variants Nabīn or Tabīn) (*Dabistān-i-Mazāhib* P. 304).

[6] *Ḥāl Nāma*, Ff. 5a-5b.

[7] Nizām ud-Dīn Aḥmad, the author of *Ṭabaqāt-i-Akbarī* says, "In former times a Hindustānī came among a tribe of the Afghāns and promulgated a heretical and heterodox religion and made many of the fools of the country his disciples and gave to himself the name of Pīr-i-Rawshan. (Nizām-ud-Dīn Aḥmad: *Ṭabaqāt-i-Akbarī* Vol. II (Bib. Ind.) P. 398, Mullā ʿAbdul Qādir Badāūnī: "*Muntakhab-ut-Tawārīkh* Vol. II (Bib. Ind.) P. 349; Shaikh Farīd Bhakkarī: *Zakhirat-ul-Khawānīn*, (Ḥabībganj Collections, ʿAlīgarh Muslim University Library; Ms.) F. 84b.

[8] *Ḥāl Nāma* F. 6a.

[9] Babur himself says, "As it was represented to me that some of the soldiery were behaving without sense and were laying hands on Bhīra people, persons were sent who caused some of those senseless people to meet their death-dom, of others slit the noses and led them round the camp". A. S. Beveridge: *The Bābur Nāma in English* Vol. I (London 1922) P. 383.

[10] *Dabistān-i-Mazāhib* P. 304.

[11] *Ḥāl Nāma* F. 6b.

[12] *Ḥāl Nāma* Ff. 7b, 8a.

The author of *Ḥāl Nāma* appears to have given an exaggerated account of the battle as also the comparative strength of the Mughal and Afghan forces. But Sulṭān Maḥmūd, as a head of the Afghan confederacy, had undoubtedly established a firm hold over Bihār and had collected about 10,000 Afghāns. They had occupied the eastern regions as far as Lucknow, a contingency which compelled Bābur to march towards the East, early in 1529 and to reconquer the parts which had passed under the control of the Afghāns. (Bābur Nāma in English Vol. II PP. 639-689).

[13] *Ḥāl Nāma* has only *dāmād* (*Ḥāl Nāma* F. 8b). Mahdī Khwāja was assigned Etāwah by Bābur and apparently Qanauj too was under him. (*Bābur Nāma in English* Vol. II Pp. 644-686).

[14] This confirms Ākhund Darwīza's contention that Anṣarīs were not of the Afghān origin. (*Tazkirat-ul-Abrār Waʾl Ashrār* (Delhi 1892, P. 137).

[15] *Ḥāl Nāma* Ff. 8b-9a.

[16] *Ḥāl Nāma* F. 10a.

[17] *Ibid.* F. 11a; *Taẕkirat-ul-Abrār Waʾl Aṣhrār* P. 137.

[18] *Ḥāl Nāma* Ff. 13b-14a, *Dabistān-i-Maẕahib* P. 304.

[19] *Ḥāl Nāma* F. 14a.

[20] *Ḥāl Nāma* F. 14b.

[21] *Ḥāl Nāma* Ff. 15b-16b.

[22] *Ibid.* Ff. 17a-18b.

[23] *Ibid.* F. 18b, Bāyazīd: *Sirāṭ-uṭ-Ṭawḥīd* (Rāmpur, Raza Library Ms. Pp. 30-33).

[24] *Ḥāl Nāma* Ff. 21a-22a.

[25] *Ibid.* Ff. 26b-27b.

[26] *Ibid.* Ff. 29a-30a. According to Ākhund Darwīza, Bāyazīd married an Afghān lady named Shamsī in Jallandhar (*Taẕkirat-ul-Abrār Waʾl Aṣhrār* P. 137).

[27] *Taẕkirat-ul-Abrār Waʾl Aṣhrār* P. 137. *Makhzan-ul-Islām*, India Office, London, Ethé 2633, F. 101b, Ethé 2467, F. 102a; Bibliothèque Nationale, Paris, Supp. 1220, F. 136a; British Museum London, Or. 6724, F. 118a, Or. 4234, F. 130b.

[28] *Ḥāl Nāma* Ff. 32b-33a.

[29] *Ibid.* F. 33b.

[30] The mysterious name of God, which is not known to anyone.

[31] The forty days of lent, during which the ṣufīs had either to shut themselves up in their cells, or remain at home.

[32] *Zikr*: Literally "Remembering". The act of devotion, which is practised by the various religious orders. *Zikrs*, are of two kinds: *zikr-i-jalī*, that which is recited aloud and *zikr-i-khafī*, that which is performed either with a low voice or mentally. T. P. Hughes: *A Dictionary of Islam*, P. 703.

[33] *Ḥāl Nāma* F. 36b.

[34] A vow of repentance.

[35] He was a prominent saint of Suhrawardī order and wielded immense influence in Multān, its neighbourhood, Sindh, and parts of the Punjab. Sulṭān Shams ud-Dīn Iltutmish (1210-1235 A.D.) held him in great esteem and the Shaikh had amassed fabulous wealth due to the state patronage. He died on 7 Ṣafar 661 H/21 December, 1262 A.D.) (Jamālī: *Siyar-ul-ʿĀrifīn* (Delhi 1893, Pp. 103-106).

[36] *Ḥāl Nāma* F. 37a, *Sirāt-uṭ-Ṭawḥīd* Pp. 39-42; *Dabistān-i-Maẕāhib* P. 304.

[37] The Muslim confession of faith, i.e. "There is no God but God, and Muḥammad is apostle of God."

[38] *Ḥāl Nāma* F. 40b.

[39] Guarding or holding the inspirations and respirations. It generally amounts to a complete control of one's self.

[40] *Ḥāl Nāma* F. 46b.

[41] *Ibid.* F. 47a.

[42] *Ibid.* Ff. 46a-47b.

[43] *Ḥāl Nāma* F. 48a-49a.

[44] *Ḥāl Nāma* Ff. 60a-62b.

[45] *Sirāṭ-ut-Tawḥīd* F. 86a.

[46] *Ḥāl Nāma* F. 64a.

[47] *Ḥāl Nāma* F. 66b.

[48] *Ibid.* F. 68b.

[49] *Ibid.* F. 71b.

[50] *Ibid.* Ff. 72-74a.

[51] *Ibid.* Ff. 74b-75b.

[52] *Ḥāl Nāma* Ff. 78b-79a.

[53] Qandahar was assigned to Bairam Khān by Humāyūn in November 1545

which remained in his possession until December 1554 when he proceeded to India with Humāyūn for its conquest.

[54] Tax collectors.

[55] A kind of tax levied on merchants.

[56] *Ḥāl Nāma* Ff. 80b-81a.

[57] *Ḥāl Nāma* F. 83a.

[58] This has also been concocted to strike a similarity between Prophet Muḥammad and Bāyazīd for Khadīja, the wife of the Prophet also was first to accept Muḥammad as an apostle of God.

[59] *Ḥāl Nāma* Ff. 85a-85b.

[60] *Tazkirat ul-Abrār Wa'l Ashrār* P. 138.

[61] *Ḥāl Nāma* F. 86b.

[62] *Ibid*. F. 87a.

[63] *Ibid*. F. 91a.

[64] *Ibid*. F. 92b.

[65] *Ibid*. F. 95a.

[66] *Ibid*. F. 97b-99a.

[67] *Ḥāl Nāma* Ff. 100b-101a.

[68] *Ibid*. F. 104a.

[69] Tribes which now inhabit the Tōchī Valley and the Bannū plain.

[70] *Ḥāl Nāma* F. 104a.

[71] *Ibid*. Ff. 105a-110a.

[72] *Quṭb* occupies the highest place in *ṣufic* hierarchy. Hujwīrī says, "Of those who have power to loose and to bind and are the officers of the Divine court there are three hundred, called *Akhyār*, and forty, called *Abdāl* and seven, called *Abrār*, and four, called *Awtād* and three called *Nuqabā*, and one called *Quṭb* or Ghauṣ". (Nicholson R. A.: The *Kashf ul-Maḥjūb* (London 1936) P. 214.

[73] *Ḥāl Nāma* F. 121a.

[74] *Ibid*. F. 125a.

[75] *Ḥāl Nāma* F. 136a.

[76] *Ibid*. Ff. 140a-145b.

[77] *Ibid*. F. 151a.

[78] *Ibid*. Ff. 154a-155a.

[79] *Ibid*. Ff. 157a.

[80] *Ibid*. Ff. 157b-158a.

[81] *Ibid*. Ff. 158b.

[82] *Ḥāl Nāma* F. 159a.

[83] *Ḥāl Nāma* Ff. 166a-166b; *Dabistān i-Mazāhib* P. 306.

[84] *Ḥāl Nāma* Ff. 167b-168a.

[85] *Ibid*. Ff. 168b-169a.

[86] *Ḥāl Nāma* F. 171a.

[87] For a discussion on *Mahdī* and *Mahdawī* movement in India—see, Rizvi, S.A.A.: *Muslim Revivalist Movements in Northern India in the Sixteenth and Seventeenth Centuries*. (Agra 1965), Pp. 68-135.

[88] *Ḥāl Nāma* F. 171b.

[89] *Ibid*. F. 172a.

[90] *Ḥāl Nāma* F. 174a.

[91] *Ibid*. Ff. 179a-180a.

[92] *Ibid*. F. 185a.

[93] *Ibid*. F. 188b.

[94] *Ibid*. Ff. 193a-194b.

[95] A term applied to such acts of devotion as are not enjoined by the teaching of Prophet Muḥammad, or by his example, but are performed for spiritual benefits.

[96] *Ḥāl Nama* Ff. 197b-198b.

[97] *Ibid.* F. 211b.

[98] One of the many miracles attributed to him is as follows: 'One night Bāyazīd was reading a book. When the oil in the lamp had been consumed the flame died out. Bāyazīd asked his servant to pour oil into the lamp. The servant reported that there was no oil in the house. Bāyazīd asked him to pour water in place of oil into the lamp. The servant did as was asked to do. The lamp was again burning and Bāyazīd could read the book in the light without any difficulty. This, according to the editor of *Ḥāl Nāma* strengthened the belief of the people in his being Pīr-i-Rawshan. Aba Bakr has also quoted the following apocryphal tradition from *Tazkira i-Jahangīr Bādshāh*, not available in the *Tuzuk* or in other works written during the period. According to it when Pīr-i-Rawshan took out a book to read in the dark night, he kept it before his face. The light from his face enabled him to read the book easily. (Ff. 219b-220a).

[99] *Ḥāl Nāma* Ff. 215b-220a.

[100] Mullā Arzānī was a scholar of considerable eminence. He could express himself in Afghānī (Pashtū), Persian, Arabic and Hindawī. Ākhund Darwīza's tirades regarding his heretical views tend to show that he held liberal religious tendencies even long before coming in contact with Bāyazīd. He became a staunch follower of Bāyazīd but, according to Ākhund Darwīza, he preferred to desert Bāyazīd when the latter took to a career of pillage and plunder. He subsequently retired to India. (*Tazkirat ul-Abrār Wa'l Ashrār* P. 149).

[101] *Ḥāl Nāma* F. 220b.

[102] "Tīrāh is a hill country 32 *Kos* long (i.e. from East to West) and 12 broad. On the East is Peshawār, West Maidān, North Bārā, South the district of Qandāhār. It has defiles full of ups and downs and difficult of traverse." (Beveridge, H.: *The Akbar Nāma of Abūl Fazl*, P. 781). In the footnote, Beveridge writes, "Tirāh is S.S.W. of Pēshāwar. It was the seat of the campaign of 1897. There is a map of Tīrah in Yate's life of Col. J. Haughton, Murray, 1900".

[103] Karlanrī Pathāns inhabiting South Tīrāh.

[104] Karlanrī Pathāns inhabiting North Tīrāh, Bazār, Khaibar and Kōhāt Pass.

[105] *Ḥāl Nāma* Ff. 231b-233a.

[106] *Ibid.* F. 235a.

[107] *Ibid.* F. 238b.

[108] *Ibid.* F. 239b.

[109] *Ibid.* F. 262a.

[110] *Tazkirat ul-Abrār Wa'l Ashrār* P. 153.

[111] *Ḥāl Nāma* Ff. 263a-264b.

[112] *Jānish Bahādur*: He was at first in the service of Mīrza Muḥammad Ḥakīm of Kābul. After the death of his master, he came with his sons to India. Soon after, he served under Zain Khān Kōkā against the Yūsufzīs, and saved Zain's life in the Khibar catastrophe. In the 35th year of Akbar's reign he served under the Khān Khānān in Thathah, and returned with him in the 38th year to Court. Later on he served in the Dakhin. He died in the 46th year of Akbar's reign (1601-2 A.D.). (Blochmann, H; and Phillot, D. C.: *The Ā'īn-i-Akbarī by Abūl Fazl ʿAllāmī* Pp. 537-38).

[113] *Ḥāl Nāma* Ff. 263a-265a.

[114] *Ḥāl Nāma* F. 265b.

[115] An evil inspiration.

[116] *Ḥāl Nāma* F. 267a.

[117] A treatise on the principal teachings of Shaikh Abū Muḥammad Muhyialdīn Saiyid Abdul Qādir Jīlāni, entitled Ghauṣ-ul-ʿĀẓam (d. 1166 A.D.) the celebrated

founder of the Qādirī order. He also wrote another work on principles of *ṣūfism* entitled *Futūḥ al-Ghaib*.

118 *Ḥāl Nāma* F. 267b.

119 Uwais al-Qaranī lived in the time of Prophet Muḥammad but was prevented from seeing him, firstly by the ecstasy which overmastered him, and secondly by duty to his mother. The Prophet is said to have remarked to his companions: "There is a man at Qaran, called Uwais, who at the Resurrection will intercede for a multitude of my people, as many as the sheep of Rābi'ā and Mizār." Then turning to 'Umar and 'Alī, he said: "You will see him. He is a lowly man, of middle height, and hairy: on his left side there is a white spot, as large as a *dirhem*, which is not from leprosy (*pisti*), and he has a similar spot on the palm of his hand. When you see him, give him my greeting, and bid him pray for my people." A number of ascetic sayings and aphorisms are ascribed to him.
(Nicholson, R. A.: *The Kashf al-Mahjūb by Hujwīrī* (London 1936), Pp. 83-84. *Lūfīs* who do not belong to any particular order, and claim to have received direct inspiration from Prophet Muḥammad or some other eminent saint are known as Uwaisīs.

120 *Tazkirat-ul-Abrār Wa'l Ashrār* P. 153.

121 The author of *Dabistān-i-Mazāhib* has quoted the following account on the authority of Mīrzā Shāh Muḥammad entitled *Ghaznī Khān*. "It was in 949H/1542-43 A.D. that Miyān Rawshan gained strength and established his religion. My father Shāh Beg Khān Arghūn, surnamed Khān Daurān said that he had seen Miyān Bāyazīd before he took up arms against the Mughals. He was brought to the court of Mīrzā Muḥammad Ḥakīm and the (*'ulamā*) were confounded in the religious debates with him. He was inevitably given leave to depart." (*Dabistān-i-Mazāhib* P. 309).

122 *Ḥāl Nāma* F. 269.

123 *Ibid.* Ff. 271a-272b.

124 *Ibid.* F. 281b.

125 *Ibid.* Ff. 282a-288b. For his popularity see *Tazkirat ul-Abrār Wa'l Ashrār* Pp. 146-148.

126 Ākhund Darwīza: *Makhzan ul-Islām* (India Office, London, Ethe 2633) F. 104b *Tazkirat ul-Abrār Wa'l Ashrār* P. 153.

127 *Ḥāl Nāma* F. 291b.

128 *Ibid.* Ff. 292a-293a.

129 *Ibid.* F. 293b.

130 *Ibid.* F. 294b.

131 *Ibid.* F. 296a.

132 *Ibid.* F. 296b.

133 Apparently Ma'ṣūm Khān Kābulī, a foster brother (Kōkā) of Mīrzā Muḥammad Ḥakīm. Having been involved in quarrels with Khwājā Ḥasan Naqshbandī who had married the widow of Mīr Shāh Abūl Ma'āli, Ma'ṣūm Khān in the 20th year (1575-76 A.D.) went to Akbar and was made a commander of five hundred (Blochmann and Phillot: *The Ā'īn-i-Akbarī* P. 476, note no. 1.)

134 *Ḥāl Nāma* F. 298.

135 *Ḥāl Nāma* F. 299a.

136 *Ḥāl Nāma* F. 300b.

137 *Dabistān-i-Mazāhib* P. 309.

138 *Tazkirat-ul-Abrār Wa'l Ashrār* Pp. 154-155.

139 *Ḥāl Nāma* F. 301b.

REVIEW

Michael C. Astour, *Hellenosemitica.* An Ethnic and Cultural Study in West Semitic Impact on Mycenaean Greece, with a Foreword by Cyrus H. Gordon. 415 pp., two folding maps. Leiden, E. J. Brill, 1965.

Christian Europe's heritage from the Greek and Semitic worlds has always been a powerful element in the forming of its civilization. In the scholarly world, opinion on the relationship between these two has swung, pendulum like, between the poles of togetherness and apartheid. In recent years, a determined effort has been made in some quarters to push the pendulum over towards togetherness. And it seems clear that, whether as a result of this effort or in spite of it, the swing of the pendulum is at present towards that togetherness. As archaeological and historical research throws more and more light upon the past of pre-classical Greece, upon Anatolia and the lands lying to her East, it is becoming a commonplace to say that the East had a profound influence upon what was to become the Greek civilization.

Unfortunately, these assertions have usually been left cautiously vague and general. Even more unfortunately, some attempts to parade an impressive array of specific points of contact have had rather the opposite eflect, claiming too much and proving too little, making a positive assertion where a tentative proposal might have been in order.

Hellenosemitica by M. C. Astour is not a book that will be lightly read, but it is one that will, I think, add momentum to the movement of the pendulum.

One of the immediate merits of *Hellenosemitica* is that it has abandoned the haphazard approach to comparative mythology, the pairing of a motif here and a name there, and instead the comparisons are sought for elements within certain families of Greek myths. The book falls into four major sections: the first deals with the identification of Danaans and Danunians, and with the myths surrounding Danaus; the second is concerned with the myths about Cadmus, legendary Phoenician founder of Thebes; the third treats the symbolism and mythology of healing gods in Greece and in the East; and finally, in the fourth section, the evidence and also the silence of archaeology is discussed.

Astour begins with the thorny problem of the relationship of Danaans and Danunians. The Amarna letter of Abimilki, EA 151, leads him to conclude that the Danunians occupied eastern Cilicia as early as the fourteenth century B.C. On the other hand, the inscriptions of Rameses III concerning the Sea Peoples class the Danaans emphatically as islanders. Astour, accepting the identification of Danaans with Danunians, concludes that there must have been two tribes of Danunians, one in the East where Eastern Cilicia touches North Syria, and one in the West, in the Aegean basin.

Which came first? That some of the Western Danunians settled in the East during the movements of the Sea Peoples in the twelfth century would be quite possible, were it not for the Amarna letter of Abimilki. A complete absence of Mycenaean pottery in Anatolia before the fourteenth century, coupled with an equally complete absence of Greek place names, precludes the hypothesis of an earlier colonizing movement from the West. Therefore, if there were any link, it must have been from East to West.

Astour considers the Phoenician text of the Karatepe bilingual to be the original and the pantheon and epithets of the gods to be Canaanite. The people of the Hieroglyphic Hittite inscription were a ruling class, and the native majority of the Cilician Danunians were West Semites. The place names of East Cilicia, names that are Hurrian, Akkadian, and West Semitic, are mustered to confirm this conclusion. The population of East Cilicia was the same as that of North Syria in the middle and late second millennium, a mixture of West Semitic and Hurrian elements "living in close symbiosis and ethnic harmony and sharing the same civilization" (p. 44). Astour seeks to reconcile these conclusions with the exigencies of Hittite geography and the location by many scholars of Kizzuwatna precisely in Eastern Cilicia.

If then one may say that the Danaans of the Aegean are descended from the Danunians of Cilicia, what evidence can be found to confirm this in the myths associated with these Western Danaans? If they came from the Semitic East, and the myth of Danaus sprang up among them, it should have close analogies to the West Semitic myths told of the hero whose name the Cilician Danunians bore. Astour looks for this to the epic cycle of Danel at Ugarit. Danaus and the Danaides brought fertility to the Argive plain, finding springs, watering the country, and were perhaps pictured with pitchers on their shoulders.

Danel of the Ugaritic myth is an "agrarian-chthonic" figure responsible for the fertility of his land; his daughter's standard epithet is "who shoulders water, spreads the dew on the barley, knows the course of the stars".

Io, progenitrix of Danaus, priestess of Hera, was loved by Zeus, turned into a cow and driven by Hera from country to country, until in Egypt she recovers her human shape and gives birth to a child. For Astour, this is a tale "with immemorially ancient roots in the religious ritual and symbols of the West Asian cultural complex" (p. 83).

The arrival of the Danunians in Argos is placed after the Hyksos period in Egypt, in which it is suggested they may have taken part, and before the Mycenaean ascendency in Greece, i.e. c. 1550-1450 B.C. The route taken is said to be along the south coast of Asia Minor, through Rhodes. It may be noted that Astour hopes to write a sequel to the present work consecrated to an analysis of the Rhodian stories on the Phoenicians which derive from West Semitic myths.

Astour's treatment of the myths connected with Cadmus begins with a careful preparation of the ground. Herodotus reports that "there were in the island now called Thera, but then Calliste, descendants of Membliaros the son of Poikiles, a Phoenician; for Cadmos son of Agenor, in his search for Europe, had put in at the place now called Thera; . . ." (IV: 147). Semitic etymologies or connections, not always convincing, are found for Thera, also the island of Anaphe, for Membliaros, Poikiles, and Europa.

Our attention is then turned to Cadmus, founder of Thebes, who is claimed by the foundation myth to be a Phoenician. (It is interesting to note that, according to M. P. Nilsson, Thebes is the only Greek town to have such a foundation myth — cf. *The Mycenaean Origin of Greek Mythology*, p. 120-127). Astour sets out to substantiate the Phoenician origin of Cadmus by showing that there was a Cadmus in the East with the necessary attributes and functions. He finds his man in a Ugaritic text (BH I, 7-8) where *qdm* is used in parallelism to *šḥr*; so Cadmus becomes a Ugaritic god, the Morning Star, in eternal pursuit of Europa, the Evening Star in the West.(How this fits the context needs explanation.)

The figures linked with Cadmus in the myths get a thorough going-over to discern whatever traces of Semitic origin they may conceal. There is Harmonia, Teiresias, Actaion (presumed not only a parallel to but etymologically linked with Aqhat of the Ugaritic myth), Semele, Pentheus, Dionysus and Zagreus. There is also the triplet Palaimon-Melicertes-Learchos, derived from Baʿal-hāmôn and Melqart; an assortment of Boeotian names with possible Semitic etymologies; and finally the indebtedness of Hesiod's *Theogony* to the myth of Kumarbi.

Astour concludes: "Each of these rapprochements may seem unimportant and fortuitous by itself, but taken together, added to the great Cadmid cycle, this agglomeration of Semitic elements in one relatively small area cannot fail to make a certain impression" (p. 217).

The third section is somewhat more difficult. Here we leave the cycles of myths to concentrate on individuals linked by their functions as healers and by the symbols connected with them in mythology. First of all Bellerophon is explained as the Semitic Lord of Healing, and parallels are sought in the Sumerian Ninazu and Ningišzida, Sumerian Muš and Ugaritic Mṡ, in Rpu Baʿal and the Rephaim and other Semitic figures.

Astour then discusses the symbols associated with healing deities, especially snakes and birds, and these play a considerable role in the search for Semitisms in the islands of Cos and Anaphe, in the name of Merops, king of Cos, of Chalciope, daughter of Eurypylus who ruled Cos after the Meropids. Turning from Cos to the genealogy of Bellerophon, Astour finds Semitic etymologies for Sisyphus, his two brothers Cretheus and Salmoneus, his wife Merope, and his son Glaucus. There are Semitic analogies for Bellerophon's dealings with Anteia, and for the Chimaera and Pegasus. Three more mythical fliers, Icarus, Marpessa, and Abaris, get Semitic etymologies, as do Jason and his peers, and Cheiron and Asclepius. Frequently the reader will feel that his credulity is being severely strained, yet almost as often some detail will turn up which makes it difficult to brush everything aside as pure coincidence.

The final fifty odd pages of *Hellenosemitica* are devoted to a consideration of archaeology's contribution to the problem under discussion. Astour is mainly concerned with the negative aspect: does archaeology contradict Semitic penetration into the Aegean?

What we now know of the Mycenaeans and the Phoenicians leaves us in no doubt of their capabilities to mount far-ranging expeditions by sea, so that from this point of view there is no problem. Astour may regret the absence of pottery finds to confirm his thesis, but he points out that some Canaanite jars have been found in Mycenaean cities, and he stresses that the Amorite invasion of Assyria, Babylonia, and Upper Mesopotamia became known to us "exclusively through onomastic data" (p. 333). This is perfectly correct; no pottery does not necessarily mean no people, though it would be comforting to have some tangible, material evidence for their presence.

The Linear B tablets are also pressed into service. A dozen borrowed words and some eighty names which have analogies from Syria are adduced to show that at least some Syrians "came to the Aegean not only as sailors and merchants, but as permanent settlers as well" (p. 344).

Astour is going too far when, in his insistence on the active role of the Ugaritic merchants in any interchange, he denies the existence of a Mycenaean enclave at Ugarit, on the grounds that no ethnic or geographical names of the Greco-Aegean world can be found in the Ugaritic texts. This absence is puzzling, but the mute evidence of cult figurines, ritual vessels, and abundant pottery surely calls for more than a fleeting presence. Astour cannot have his cake and eat it; if he accepts names without pottery, he should be ready to accept pottery without names.

The previous pages give but the barest outline of the main themes of *Hellenosemitica*; there is a great deal which it is impossible to mention. Much of it may seem irrelevant or improbable; one feels that there has been a certain compulsion at work to include almost every possibility. This is understandable, since every shred of evidence builds up the case, but it is also regrettable since it makes the book very heavy going, and with a series of doubtful identifications it is often the doubt which accumulates in the reader's mind rather than the positive evidence.

Another feature which gives rise to doubts is the tendency to draw on linguistic data from any of the West Semitic languages indiscriminately, the comparison of late with early myths and so on. Much of this may be unavoidable, but it should be strictly and explicitly controlled.

The method used in footnote references is a drawback, since it makes unnecessary demands on the reader. Works are cited by Roman numerals which refer to the bibliography of more than 550 entries; one must either ignore the majority of the footnotes or waste a lot of time looking up the bibliography simply to know what author or which of his works is being referred to. The system is not at all satisfactory.

An aspect of Astour's presentation which is most interesting arises from his treatment of Danaans and Danunians and of the Cadmus myths. The implications are considerable because this involves tribal groups and their movements and the founding of a major Greek city, which is a far cry from cultural transmission through occasional contact in trade etc. A thorough evaluation of Astour's work here requires competence in the fields of Hittite geography and comparative semitic and classical philology. Even the experts often disagree in these fields, and it may well be some time before a consensus is reached.

Considering the consensus that seems to have been reached already about Eastern influence on Greece, it is a pity that Astour's tone is at times unnecessarily aggressive. His cause would be better served had he harped less on the disagreements of the past and were he to adopt a more eirenic approach.

The value of Astour's work lies in his treatment of specific blocks of myth, which are tied to particular regions and must have been transmitted at a determined time. In this way, we pass from general propositions to specific instances that can be tested, verified, accepted or rejected; we move from interesting speculation towards a contribution to the writing of history. *Hellenosemitica*, even if many of its suggestions may be discarded, will certainly help to throw more light on the relationship between Mycenaean Greece and the Levant, and cannot be disregarded by anyone interested in this field.

A. F. Campbell

MYER FOUNDATION GRANTS-IN-AID FOR SHORT-TERM STUDY LEAVE ABROAD IN THE HUMANITIES 1967-68

The Australian Humanities Research Council, in association with the Myer Foundation, is offering five (5) grants-in-aid for short-term study leave abroad during 1967-68 to scholars who are working in the field of the Humanities and who are resident in Australia.

The grants are designed to assist scholars engaged in full-time teaching or other full-time employment throughout the year. They are available to full-time members of the teaching staffs of Australian universities and to distinguished scholars outside the universities.

The grants will normally be made to applicants who have already begun research work of a kind for which a short visit overseas is essential for its further advancement or completion, and who have already published work in a similar or related field. The grants will consist of $ 800 which will be paid as a contribution to the cost of the return air fare between the applicant's place of work in Australia and his centre of research abroad.

The Council will not award grants as a contribution to periods of study leave abroad taken by university staff members as a part of their study leave entitlements after three years or six years service. The Council expects that the typical university applicant will be asking for aid towards study abroad during the long vacation.

An applicant for a grant-in-aid will be asked to:

1) Provide evidence that he has obtained the consent of the Head of his Department and Vice-Chancellor, or of equivalent authorities, to his application;

2) State the nature of the work in hand and the university, institute or library, etc. abroad at which attendance is essential for its advancement;

3) List work already published especially in the field related to the work at present in hand;

4) Provide the names of two referees;

5) State any other grant applied for or received for a similar purpose;

6) State the date of departure from and return to the applicant's normal professional duties.

Application forms are available from:

The Secretary,
Australian Humanities Research Council,
c/-Australian National University,
P.O. Box 4, CANBERRA. A.C.T.

Applications for grants for 1967 must reach the Council's Canberra office before 30 June 1967.

AK